Royal Zoological Society of Ireland

The Irish Naturalist

Royal Zoological Society of Ireland
The Irish Naturalist
ISBN/EAN: 9783744732185
Printed in Europe, USA, Canada, Australia, Japan
Cover: Foto ©ninafisch / pixelio.de

More available books at **www.hansebooks.com**

A Monthly Journal

OF

GENERAL IRISH NATURAL HISTORY,

THE OFFICIAL ORGAN OF

The Royal Zoological Society of Ireland; The Dublin Microscopical Club;
The Belfast Natural History and Philosophical Society;
The Belfast Naturalists' Field Club; The Dublin Naturalists' Field Club;
The Armagh Natural History and Philosophical Society;
The Cork Naturalists' Field Club; The Limerick Naturalists' Field Club.

EDITED BY

GEORGE H. CARPENTER, B.Sc., Lond.

AND

R. LLOYD PRAEGER, B.A., B.E., M.R.I.A.

Printed by Alex. Thom & Co. (Limited), 87, 88, & 89, Abbey-street, Dublin.

CONTRIBUTORS
TO THE PRESENT VOLUME.

ANNA N. ABBOTT, Cork.
MARY K. ANDREWS, Belfast.
G. E. H. BARRETT-HAMILTON, Kilmannock, New Ross.
E. C. BARRINGTON, 17, Earlsfort-terrace, Dublin.
W. B. BARRINGTON, 58, South Mall, Cork.
H. M. BARTON, 4, Foster-place, Dublin.
ERNEST H. BENNIS, Limerick.
REV. S. A. BRENAN, B.A., Knocknacary, Antrim.
D. C. CAMPBELL, Ballynagard, Londonderry.
A. S. G. CANNING, Rostrevor, Down.
G. H. CARPENTER, B.SC., Science and Art Museum, Dublin.
THOMAS CHANDLEE, Athy, King's Co.
PROF. GRENVILLE A. J. COLE, F.G.S., Royal College of Science, Dublin.
R. LANGTON COLE, London.
NATHANIEL COLGAN, 1, Belgrave-road, Rathmines, Dublin.
W. E. COLLINGE, Mason College, Birmingham.
ARTHUR J. COLLINS, Belfast.
C. P. CRANE, M.D., Waterford.
R. N. CREIGHTON, M.D., Ballyshannon.
PROF. R. O. CUNNINGHAM, M.D., F.L.S., F.Z.S., Queen's College, Belfast.
H. K. GORE CUTHBERT, Recess, Blackrock, Dublin.
REV. ALEXANDER DELAP, M.A., Valencia, Kerry.
REV. A. H. DELAP, M.A., Letterkenny, Donegal.
G. E. DONOVAN, Timoleague, Cork.
J. J. DOWLING, Stillorgan, Co. Dublin.
J. E. DUERDEN, A.R.C.SC., Royal College of Science, Dublin.
THOMAS FARRINGTON, M.A., F.C.S., F.I.C., Cork.
MAURICE FITZGIBBON, Howth, Dublin.
REV. HILDERIC FRIEND, F.L.S., Cockermouth, Cumberland.
L. S. GLASCOTT, New Ross, Wexford.
H. and J. GROVES, F.L.S., Jeffreys-road, Clapham, London.
J. ERNEST GRUBB, Carrick-on-Suir.
PROF. A. C. HADDON, M.A., F.Z.S., Royal College of Science, Dublin.
J. N. HALBERT, Science and Art Museum, Dublin.
W. A. HAMILTON, J.P., Ballyshannon.
PROF. G. V. HART, LL.D., Q.C., Howth, Co. Dublin.
H. C. HART, B.A., F.L.S., Carrablagh, Portsalon, Co. Donegal.
N. S. HIND, Ferns, Co. Wexford.
H. LYSTER JAMESON, Killencoole, Co. Louth.
PROF. T. JOHNSON, D.SC., F.L.S., Royal College of Science, Dublin.
REV. W. F. JOHNSON, M A., F.E.S., Armagh.
JAMES JOHNSTON, Bray, Co. Wicklow.
W. F. DE VISMES KANE, M.A, F.E.S., Drumreaske, Monaghan.
WILLIAM KENNEDY, Londonderry.
G. H. KINAHAN, M.R.I.A., Fairview, Dublin.
MARY J. LEEBODY, Londonderry.
REV. H. W. LETT, M.A., Loughbrickland, Co. Down.
GEORGE E. LOW, Dundrum, Dublin.

Contributors.

DAVID M'ARDLE, Royal Botanic Gardens, Glasnevin.
E. J. M'WEENEY, M.A., M.D., 15, Ely-place, Dublin.
C. B. MOFFAT, Ballyhyland, Co. Wexford.
A. G. MORE, F.R.S.E, F.L S , 74, Leinster-road, Rathmines, Dublin.
GEORGE A. MUSGRAVE, F.R.G.S., F.Z S., Bournemouth.
FRANCIS NEALE, 35, Catherine-street, Limerick.
A. R. NICHOLS, B.A., M.R.I.A., Science and Art Museum, Dublin.
JOHN H. O'CONNELL, Kilkenny.
ROBERT PATTERSON, M.B.O.U., Belfast.
R. A. PHILLIPS, Ashburton, Cork.
GREENWOOD PIM, M.A., F.L.S., Monkstown, Dublin.
R. I. POCOCK, British Museum (Nat. Hist.), S. Kensington.
JAMES PORTER, B.E., Cork.
R. LLOYD PRAEGER, B.E., M.R.I.A., National Library, Dublin.
WILLIAM E. PRAEGER, Keokuk, Iowa, U.S.A.
J. G. ROBERTSON, Dublin.
R. F. SCHARFF, PH.D., B.SC., Science and Art Museum, Dublin.
W. E. SHARP, Ledsham, Chester.
J. R. SHERIDAN, Achill Island.
OWEN SMITH, Nobber, Co. Meath.
PROFESSOR W. J. SOLLAS, LL.D., F.R.S., Trinity College, Dublin.
WILLIAM STARKEY, Jun., Rathmines, Dublin.
WILLIAM SWANSTON, F.G.S., Belfast.
J. H. H. SWINEY, C.E., Belfast.
JAMES TANK, Dublin.
J. TAYLOR, Mullingar.
R. J. USSHER, J.P., Cappagh, Co. Waterford.
REV. C. H. WADDELL, B.D., Saintfield, Co. Down.
AMY WARREN, Ballina.
ROBERT WARREN, Ballina.
S. WESTROPP, Cork.
E. WILLIAMS, Dublin.

ERRATA.

Page 26, line 6, *for* "Carval" *read* "Caracal."
 ,,   16 and 17 from bottom, for "as Monstroma does from *Ulva*," read "as *Ulva* does from *Monostroma*."
 ,, 173, ,, 27, for "*Ammophila sabulosa*," read "*Pompilius fuscus*."
 ,, 227, last line but one, for "Scharff" read "Schaeff."
 ,, 229, line 33, for "Cotton" read "Collon."
 ,, 229. The note on *Azolla* should be transferred to special heading "Vascular Cryptogams."
 ,, 243, foot-note, line 2, for "formed" read "former."
 ,, 279, last line, for "fourth, fifth, sixth, and seventh" read "third, fourth, fifth, and sixth."
 ,, 280, line 2, for "seventh" read "sixth."
 ,, 302, line 41, for "extractor" read "retractor."

INDEX.

Abbott, A. N.—Plants Flowering in December, 83; White Centaury, 23.
Acherontia atropos, 252.
Acrospermum graminum, 195.
Ajuga, white, 23.
Algæ, Marine, 313.
Allium scorodoprasum, 23.
American Bird-Visitors to Ireland, 29, 87, 203, 293.
Ampelis garrulus, 85, 114, 114, 114.
Anatomy of *Arion flagellus*, 316.
Anchorella uncinata, 81.
Andrews, M. K.— Denudation at Cultra, 16, 47.
Andromeda polifolia, 254.
Anthelia juratzskana, 116.
Aphanomyces sp., 117.
Aran Islands Ethnography, 303; flora, 75, 106.
Argyroneta aquatica, 99, 147.
Arion flagellus, 302, 316.
Armagh flora, 11, 27, 34, 59, 91, 127, 155, 182, 212, 228, 250; Lepidoptera, 24; Nat. Hist. and Philosophical Society, 28, 116, 145, 225, 299, 320.
Auk, Little, 324.
Autumnal Blossoming of Spring Flowers, 299, 321, 321; Autumnal Disappearance of Woodcock, 85.
Azolla caroliniana, 229, 318; *filiculoides*, 318.

Bacterium rubescens, 26.
Badger, 25.
Ballyrudder Gravels, 27.
Barrett-Hamilton, G. E. H.— Hoopoe in Wexford, 177; Black Redstart in Wexford, 177; Western Variety of the Red-breasted Snipe in Ireland, 323.
Barrington, E. C.—Hairy-armed Bat in Dublin, 277; Quails in Wicklow, 230.
Barrington, W. B.—Early arrivals of Migrants in Cork, 177; Osprey and Quail in Cork, 201.
Barton, H. M.—Arrested Development of Frog's Tadpole, 149.
Bat, Hairy-armed, 277; Reddish-grey, 230.
Bee-eater, 25.
Beggiatoa roseopersicina, 117.
Belfast Nat. Hist. and Philosophical Society, 27, 51, 82, 116, 172, 254, 319.

Belfast Nat. Field Club, 27, 51, 82, 116, 145, 173, 196, 225, 226, 254, 297, 319.
Ben Bulben flora, 22.
Bennis, E. H.—Earliness of the Season, 199.
Birds: American, in Ireland, 29, 87, 203, 293, 302; of Midland Lakes and Bogs, 231, 261; of Lough Swilly, 25; of Strangford Lough, 67.
Bittern, 86, 114.
Botaurus stellaris, 86, 114.
Bourgainvillia n. sp., 196.
Boyne Mouth, Plants of, 299.
Brama raii, 230, 253.
Bream, Ray's, 230, 253.
Brenan, S. A. — *Sirex gigas* and *Acherontia atropos* in Antrim, 252; a Correction, 277; Wasps in Antrim, 252.
Bubo maximus, 113.
Bugle, white, 24.
Building Stones, Irish, 168, 179.
Burkitt, R. J., obituary, 224.
Bustard, Little, 256.
Buzzard, Honey, 25.

Campbell, D. C.—Iceland Gull at Londonderry, 178; Macrolepidoptera of Londonderry District, 19, 43, 72, 147; Reappearance of Quails near Londonderry, 202; Spring Migrants at Londonderry, 201; Waxwing near Londonderry, 85, 114.
Carex rhynchophysa, 83, 184.
Carpenter, G. H. — A deceptive Caterpillar, 279; Irish Wasps, 199.
Casual Plants, 300.
Caterpillar, A deceptive, 279.
Centaury, white, 23.
Centipedes, 309.
Cephalozia catenulata, 319.
Ceryle alcyon, 293.
Chandlee, T.—*Euphorbia cyparissias* in King's County, 250.
Characeæ, 163; of Armagh, 214.
Chionis alba, 56, 82, 151, 202.
Chirolepus aureus, 297.
Chlorocystis sarcophyci, 318.
Ciliata, 117.
Cionus thapsus, 51.
Circus cinereus, 253.
Clare Plants, 251.

Coal in Ireland, 56.
Coccyzus americanus, 203 ; erythrophthalmus, 205.
Cole, G. A. J.—Animal Footprints in Old Red Sandstone, 115 ; Beauty and Use of Irish Building Stones, 168, 179.
Cole, R. L.—Coal in Ireland, 56.
Coleoptera : of Ardara, 53 ; of Beauparc, 299 ; of Dublin, 139, 160, 229 ; of Dundalk and Carlingford, 227 ; of Wexford, 301.
Coleopterist in Ireland, 139, 160.
Colgan, N.—Inconstancy of Colour in Flowers, 111 ; Lough Neagh Petrifactions, 178 ; Notes on the Flora of the Aran Islands, 75, 106 ; Notes on the Flora of Co. Dublin, 283 ; *Ricciocarpus natans* in Dublin, 250 ; The Shamrock, a further attempt to fix its Species, 207 ; The Shamrock, a Postscript, 250.
Colias edusa, 301.
Collinge, W. E.—Some Notes on the Irish Slugs, 148 ; Anatomical Characters of *Arion flagellus*, Cllge., 316.
Collins, A. J.—Arrival of Spring Migrants, 201 ; Bittern in Ireland, 114 ; Supposed Hybrid Harerabbit, 25.
Colour of Wild Flowers, 111, 174, 229.
Columba œnas, 202, 253.
Conopteryx rhamni, 252.
Cordyceps entomorrhiza, 146, 195 ; *militaris* var. *sphærocephala*, 26.
Cork Mollusca, 200 ; Plants, 23, 23 ; Nat. Field Club, 28, 51, 116, 173, 197.
Corrib, L., Crustacea, 24.
Coturnix communis, 201, 201, 202, 230.
Crane, C. P.—Ray's Bream in Waterford, 230.
Creighton, R. N.—Crustacea from L. Erne and L. Corrib, 24 ; *Spongilla lacustris* at Ballyshannon, 322.
Crisia ramosa, 146.
Crossbill, 25, 150.
Crustacea of Loughs Erne and Corrib, 24.
Cuckoo, Black-billed, 205 ; Yellow-billed, 203.
Cultra, Denudation at, 16, 47.
Cunningham, R. O.—*Chionis alba*, 202.
Curlew, white, 86.
Cuthbert, G. H. K.—A Correction, 277 ; Coleoptera from Courtown, 301.

Cygnus bewickii, 114.
Cynoglossum officinale, 173.
Delap, Alex.—Tree Mallow in Ireland, 112.
Delap, A. H.—Additional Localities for Land and Fresh-water Mollusca, 84.
Denudation at Cultra, 16, 47.
Didymoprium grevillei, 117.
Dolomite of Cork, 117, 135, 221.
Donegal Coleoptera, 53 ; Lepidoptera. 147 ; Land and Fresh-water Mollusca, 230.
Donovan, G. E.—Goosander in Cork, 86.
Dowling, J. J.—Quails in Dublin, 201.
Dublin Coleoptera, 139, 160, 173, 197 ; Flora, 283 ; Hymenoptera, 197 ; Lepidoptera, 322 ; Microscopical Club, 26, 50, 81, 115, 172, 195, 278, 297, 318 ; Nat. Field Club, 27, 51, 82, 145, 196, 226, 254, 298, 320.
Duck, Feruginous. 114 ; King, 177.
Duerden, J. E.—Some North of Ireland Polyzoa, 165.

Earthworms of Ireland, 6, 39, 89, 121, 188, 216, 238, 272, 288.
Egg-collecting and Egg-destruction, 57.
Eleocharis acicularis, 276.
Entomology, Irish, 32.
Epicoccum purpurascens, 115.
Erica mediterranea flowering in October, 321.
Erne, L., Crustacea of, 24.
Erosion, Marine, 16, 47.
Erythræa centaureum, white, 23.
Ethnography of Aran Islands, 303.
Euphorbia cyparrissias. 250.
Eurite containing Riebeckite, 172.
Farrington, T.—Magnesian Limestone of the Cork District, 135.

Festuca sylvatica, 84.
Fitzgibbon, M.—Lepidoptera at Woodenbridge, 175.
Flora of Aran Islands, 75, 106 ; of Armagh, 11, 27, 34, 59, 91, 127, 155, 182, 212, 228, 250 ; of Donegal, 84 ; of Dublin, 283 ; of Kildare, 321 ; of North-east of Ireland, 51 ; of Queen's County, 321 ; of Rathlin Island, 53.
Flowers ; Autumn Blossoming of, 299, 321, 321 ; early Flowers, 199 ; Inconstancy of Colour of, 111, 174, 229.

Footprints in Old Red Sandstone, 115.
Foraminifera, 27.
Fratercula arctica, 202.
Friend, H.—The Earthworms of Ireland, 6, 39, 89, 121, 188, 216, 238, 272, 288; *Trichia chrysosperma*, 83.
Frog; A native of Ireland, 1, 85, 95, 177; Arrested Development of Tadpole, 149, 176.
Fungi: of Beauparc, 298; of Dublin district, 245, 257; of South-west, 227; of Wicklow, 146, 227, 245, 257, 320.

Gallinago cœlestis, 83; *cœlestis* var. *sabinii*, 302, 324; *major*, 302.
Galway Algæ, 313; Ethnography, 303.
Garden Warbler, 185.
Geologists' Association, 253.
Glacial deposits, 27.
Glascott, L. S.—A Plea for the Rotifera, 191.
Glencree Royal Forest, 199.
Goosander, 86.
Grebe, Great Crested, 25.
Groves, H. and J.—Notes on Irish Characeæ, 163.
Grubb, J. E.—Arrival of Spring Migrants, 201.
Gull, Iceland, 178, 202.
Gyrodon rubellus, n. sp., 320.

Haddon, A. C.—The Aran Islands, a Study in Irish Ethnography, 303; Review of Jordan's Report on Mollusca from South-west, 80.
Hæmonia appendiculata, 146, 148.
Halbert, J. N.—Coleoptera in Dublin, 229; *Hæmonia appendiculata* in Dublin, 148; *Lema erichsoni* at Santry, 252.
Hamilton, W. A.—Buff-coloured Snipe, 86.
Harpa-lejeunea ovata, 278.
Harrier, Montagu's, 253.
Hart, G. V.—Lepidoptera at Howth and Castlebellingham, 322; Lepidoptera of Londonderry District, 275.
Hart, H. C.—Autumn Blossoming of Spring Flowers, 321; Flora of Donegal, a Correction, 84; Sabine's Snipe, a Correction, 324; *Spirula*, *Ianthina*, and *Velella* at L. Swilly, 55.
Hawkweeds, new Irish, 53.
Helianthemum vulgare, 228.
Helix arbustorum, 302; *fusca*, 302; *pisana*, 300; *rufescens*, 277, 301.

Hemiptera of Dundalk and Carlingford, 227.
Hepatics; of Ben Bulben, 22; of Howth, 197; of Leixlip, 111.
Hieracia, new Irish, 53.
Hippuraria egertoni, 50.
Hoopoe, 177.
Hybrid Hare-rabbit, supposed, 25.

Ianthina rotundata, 277.
Irish Entomology, 32.

Jameson, H. L.—*Argyroneta aquatica* in Captivity, 147; Bewick's Swan in Armagh, 114; *Macroglossa stellatarum* in Sligo, 323; Reddish-grey Bat in Louth, 230; *Siser ngas* and *Macroglossa stellatarum* in Louth, 229; *Timarcha tenebricosa* in Waterford, 199; Yellow-billed Sheathbill on the Irish coast, 151.
Johnson, W. F.—Coleoptera at Ardara, 53; Early Spring Butterflies, 176; Lepidoptera at Ardara, 147; Lepidoptera at Armagh, 21; Obituary Notice of Rev. George Robinson, 296; *Polypodium calcareum* at Carlingford, 22; Spring Migrants at Armagh, 177; Water-spiders in Captivity, 99.
Johnson, T.—A Visit to Roundstone, Co. Galway, 313.
Johnston, J.—Autumnal Disappearance of Woodcock, 85.
Jubula hutchinsiæ var. *integrifolia*, 196.

Killala mollusca, 55.
Kane, W. F. de V.—Eagle Owl and Magpie in Ireland, 113; Irish Entomology, 32; Is the Frog a Native of Ireland, 95; Puffin in the Irish Midlands, 202.
Kennedy, W.—*Ianthina rotundata* at Portrush, 277.
Kinahan, G. H.—The Scalp, 231.
Kingfisher, Belted, 293.

Larus leucopterus, 178, 202.
Lavatera arborea, 112.
Leebody, M. J.—Colour-variation of Wild Flowers, 229; *Spiranthes romanzoviana* in Londonderry, 228.
Lejeunia diversiloba, 82.
Lema erichsoni, 252.
Lepidoptera, 28, 147, 254; ditto, early, 176; of Armagh, 24, 176, 320; of Donegal, 147; of Howth, 322; of Londonderry, 19, 43, 72, 147, 175; of Louth, 322.
Lett, H. W.—*Malva moschata*, 228; *Sphagnum austini* in Ireland, 22.
Lichens, 28.

Limerick Nat. Field Club, 15, 28, 83, 118, 321.
Limosella aquatica, 300.
Linota linaria, 114.
Liverworts, 22, 111, 147.
Londonderry Lepidoptera, 19, 43, 72, 147, 175.
Lophyrus pini, 55.
Louth Lepidoptera, 322.
Low, G. E.—*Thera firmata* in Dublin, 277.
Loxia curvirostra, 25, 150.
Lumbricidæ, 6, 39, 89, 121, 188, 216, 238, 272, 288.
Lutra vulgaris, 56.
Lycopodium clavatum, 250.

Macroglossa stellatarum, 229, 277, 323.
Macrolepidoptera of Londonderry, 19, 43, 72, 147, 175.
Macrorhamphus griseus, 302; var. *scolopaceus*, 323.
Magnesian Limestone of Cork, 117, 135, 221.
Magpie, former Scarcity of, 113.
Mallow, Tree, 112.
Malva moschata, 228.
Marten, 202.
Martin, Purple, 87.
M'Ardle, D.— Rare *Hepaticæ* at Leixlip, 111; *Selaginella selaginoides* in Dublin, 174.
M'Weeney, E. J.—Fungi from Altadore, 227; Fungi from the South-west, 227; Fungi from Woodenbridge, 146; Notes on the Fungi of the Dublin District, 245, 257; Plants Flowering in mid-November, 23.
Megaptera boops, 119.
Meles taxus, 25.
Melitia aurinia, var. *hibernica*, 118.
Mergulus alle, 324.
Mergus merganser, 86.
Merops apiaster, 25.
Migrants, Arrival of, 150, 177, 177, 201, 201.
Mitrula paludosa, 173.
Moffat, C. B.—Review of Mivart's Birds, 79; White Bugle, 84; White Centaury, 23.
Mollusca, Land and Freshwater, 84, 148, 316; of Cork, 200; of Donegal, 230; of Sligo, 301; of Wicklow, 149.
Mollusca, Marine: of Killala Bay, 55; of Lough Swilly, 55; of the South-west, 80.
More, A. G.— *Erica mediterranea* flowering in October, 322.
Mosses of Ben Bulben, 22.

Motacilla alba, 200.
Motella cimbria, 176.
Musgrave, G. A.—The Selborne Society, 123.
Mustela martes, 202.
Myriopoda, 309.

Neale, F.—*Conopteryx rhamni* and *Nonagria arundinis* near Limerick, 252.
Neagh, Lough: Silicified Wood of, 83, 102, 178.
Nichols, A. R.—*Pleurophyllidia loveni* in Ireland, 176.
Night-Heron, 324.
Nonagria arundinis, 252.
Numenius arquatus, 86.
Nyctea scandiaca, 25.
Nyctocorax griseus, 324.
Nyroca ferruginea, 114.

Obione portulacoides, 229.
Obituary—R. J. Burkitt, 224; G. Robinson, 296.
O'Connell, J. H.—Breeding of Squirrel and Otter, 56.
Odontopera bidentata, 280.
Odostomia delicata, 252.
Old Red Sandstone, Footprints in, 115.
Oligochæta, 117.
Orobanche minor in Cork, 23.
Osprey, 201.
Otis tetrax, 56.
Otter, 56.
Owl, Eagle, 113; Snowy, 25.

Pandion haliætus, 201.
Patterson, R.—Among the Birds on Strangford Lough, 67; Frog in Ireland, 85; Little Auk in Belfast, 324; Night-Heron near Belfast, 324.
Pelomyza palustris, 117.
Pernis apivorus, 25.
Peronospora pygmæa, 278.
Phalarope, Grey, 25.
Phalaropus fulicarius, 25.
Phillips, R. A.—Additions to the Shell-fauna of Cork, 200; *Allium scorodoprasum* in Cork, 23; *Orobanche minor* in Cork, 23; The Shamrock, 251; *Valvata cristata* in Cork, 112.
Phytoptus geranii, 301.
Pica rustica, 113.
Pieris daplidice, 322.
Pim, G.—*Azolla caroliniana* in fruit, 229; Notes on the Fungi of the Dublin District, 245, 257.

Plæsocœrus alpinus, 278.
Planorbis crista, var. *nautileus*, 149; *riparius*, 55, 149.
Plants: Aliens at Greenisland, 300; flowering in December, 83; flowering in mid-November, 23; of Armagh, 11, 27, 34, 59, 91, 127, 155, 182, 212, 228; of Beauparc and the Boyne, 298; of Boyne mouth, 299; blossoming in Autumn, 299, 321; of Clare, 251; of Dundalk and Carlingford, 226; of Kildare, 321; of North-east of Ireland, 51; of Queen's County, 321.
Platyarthrus hoffmanseggii, 26, 320.
Pleurophyllidia loveni, 176.
Pocock, R. I.:—Notes upon some Irish *Myriopoda*, 309.
Podicipes cristatus, 25.
Polypodium calcareum, 22.
Polyzoa, 198; of N.E. Ireland, 165.
Porter, J.—Magnesian Limestone in the Neighbourhood of Cork, 221.
Praeger, R. Ll.—Alien Plants at Greenisland, 300; Autumnal blossoming of Spring Flowers, 299; Colour-variation of Wild Flowers, 174; *Eleocharis acicularis*, 276; Flora of Co. Armagh, 11, 27, 34, 59, 91, 127, 155, 182, 212, 228; Flora of Donegal, a Correction, 84; Flora of Rathlin Island, 53; *Helix arbustorum* in Leitrim, 302; *Lycopodium clavatum* in Armagh, 250; *Obione portulacoides* at Dundalk, 229; Pine Sawfly in North of Ireland, 55; Plants of Boyne mouth, 299; Queen's County Plants, 321; *Sirex gigas* in North of Ireland, 113; Strawberries in November, 321.
Praeger, W. E.—American Bird-visitors to Ireland at Home, 29, 87, 203, 293.
Progne subis, 87.
Protective coloration, 279.
Puffin in the Midlands, 202.
Pycnogonida, 198.

Quail, 201, 201, 202, 230.
Quedius cruentis, 51.

Rabbit, 277.
Ranunculus petiolaris, 252.
Rathlin Island flora, 53.
Redpoll, Mealy, 113.
Redstart, Black, 177.

Reviews: Guy's South of Ireland Pictorial Guide, 224; Jordan's Report on some Species of *Buccinum*, &c., dredged off S.W. Ireland, 80; Mivart's Birds, the Elements of Ornithology, 79; Red, White, and Blue, 144; Saunders' *Hemiptera Heteroptera* of the British Islands, 80; Theobald's British Flies, 144.
Ricciocarpus natans, 250.
Robinson, Rev. G., Obituary, 296.
Robertson, J. G.—Royal Forest of Glencree, 199.
Robin, American, 29.
Rocks, igneous, of Carlingford, 198.
Rotifera, 117, 181.
Royal Dublin Society, 52, 118, 198.
Royal Irish Academy, 51, 118, 197.
Royal Zoological Society, 26, 50, 81, 115, 145, 172, 195, 225, 254, 278, 297, 318.
Ruticilla titys, 177.

Sawfly, Pine, 55; Great, 113, 229, 252, 277.
Scalp, 241.
Scharff, R. F.—A new Irish Species of *Arion*, 302; Arrested Development of Frog's Tadpole, 176; *Helix fusca* in Dublin, 302; *Helix rufescens* in Belfast, 277; Is the Frog a Native of Ireland, 1; Mealy Redpolls on Achill Island, 113; Molluscs from Woodenbridge, 149; *Motella cimbria*, L., a Fish new to Ireland, 176; *Planorbis riparius*, 55; *Planorbis riparius*, a Correction, 149; the Rabbit on the Irish Islands, 277; Rare Shells from Sligo, 301; *Spongilla fluviatilis* in the Barrow, 277; *Testacella scutulum*, 200.
Sciurus vulgaris, 56, 324.
Scolopax rusticus, 85.
Sea-weed Tracks in Sand, 255.
Selache maxima, 25, 200.
Selaginella selaginoides, 174.
Selborne Society, 113, 198.
Serin, 114.
Serinus hortulanus, 114.
Shamrock, 207, 250, 251.
Shark, Basking, 25, 200.
Sharp, W. E.—The Coleopterist in Ireland. 139, 160.
Sheathbill, Antarctic, 56, 82, 151, 202.
Sheridan, J. R.—King Duck in Achill Island, 177.
Silicified Wood, 63, 102, 178.

Sirex gigas, 113, 229, 252, 277.
Sligo Mollusca, 301; Plants, 23.
Slugs, 148, 316.
Smith, O.—Squirrels in Ireland, 324.
Snipe, Buff-coloured, 86; Great, 302; Red-breasted, 302, 323; Sabine's, 302, 324.
Sollas, W. J.—Seaweed Tracks in Sand, 255.
Somateria spectabilis, 177.
Sphagnum austini, 22.
Spiders, Water, 99.
Spiranthes romanzoviana, 159, 228.
Spongilla fluviatilis, 277; *lacustris*, 322.
Sporodinia aspergillus, 318.
Squirrel, 56, 324.
Starkey, W.—Early Spring Butterflies, 176.
Strawberries in November, 321.
Sterna leucoptera, 253.
Stock-doves, 202, 253.
Strangford Lough Birds, 67.
Swallow, albino, 145.
Swan, Bewick's, 114.
Swans in Mayo, 150.
Swanston, W.—Silicified Wood of Lough Neagh, 63, 102; Some North of Ireland Polyzoa, 165.
Swilly, Lough; Birds of, 25; Mollusca, 55.
Swiney, J. H. H.—Birds of Lough Swilly, 25.
Sylvia hortensis, 185.

Tank, J.—Little Bustard in Kerry, 56.
Taylor, J.—Crossbill and Grey Phalarope near Mullingar, 25.
Tern, White-winged Black, 253.
Testacella scutulum, 200, 253.
Thera firmata, 277.
Thiamis suturalis, 51.
Timarcha tenebricosa, 199.
Tracks in Sand, 255.
Trichia chrysosperma, 83.
Triticellæ, 50.
Trochus duminyi, 252.
Tubiclava cornucopiæ, 319.
Turbellaria, 117.
Turdus migratorius, 89.

Upupa epops, 177.
Urocystis anemones, 278.

Ussher, R. J.—Breeding of Garden Warbler in the Shannon Valley, 185; Birds of the Midland Lakes and Bogs, 231, 261; Crossbills breeding in Armagh, 150; Early Arrivals, 150; Frog Remains in Ballynamintra Cave, 177; Obituary Notice of Dr. Burkitt, 224.
Ustilago receptaculorum, 278.

Valvata cristata, 112.
Venturia sp., 116.
Vespa arborea, 199.
Vespertilio nattereri, 230.
Vesperugo leisleri, 277.
Visit to Roundstone, Co. Galway, 313.

Waddell, C. H.—Mosses and Hepatics of Ben Bulben District, 22.
Wagtail, White, 200.
Warren, A.—*Helix rufescens* in North of Ireland, 301; *Trochus duminyi* and *Odostomia delicata* on the Irish Coast, 252.
Warren, R.—Basking Shark on the Sligo Coast, 200; Hump-backed Whale on the Irish Coast. 119; Supposed Iceland Gull at Londonderry, 202; White Wagtail in Mayo, 200.
Wasps, 199, 252.
Waxwing, 85, 114, 114, 114.
Westropp, S.—*Colias edusa* at Cork, 301.
Wexford Coleoptera, 301.
Whale, Hump-backed, 119.
Wicklow Lepidoptera, 175; Mollusca, 149.
Wildmannia miniata f. amplissima, 26, 50, 195.
Williams, E.—Bee-eater in Wicklow, 25; Great Snipe and Sabine's Snipe in Ireland, 302; Montagu's Harrier in Ireland, 253; Redbreasted Snipe in Ireland, 302; White-winged Black Tern in Ireland, 253.
Woodcock, Autumnal Disappearance of, 85.
Worms, Earth, 6, 39, 89, 121, 188, 216, 238, 272, 288.
Wrightia arenosa, 26.

Xylaria rhopaloides, 297.

The Irish Naturalist

VOL. II.   JANUARY, 1893.   No. 1.

IS THE FROG A NATIVE OF IRELAND?
BY R. F. SCHARFF, PH.D., B.SC.

THE following paper does not profess to answer this question decidedly in the affirmative, but I venture to think that I shall be able to show that the belief generally held that the Frog has been introduced by man, is not supported by sufficient evidence.

In an inquiry into the origin of any Irish animal we naturally consult first Thompson's standard work on the Natural History of Ireland,[1] and in the case of the Frog we find that the author had no doubt that it had been artificially introduced into this country, and that it was therefore no true native. His belief appears to be principally founded on a passage referring to Ireland by St. Donatus,[2] who died in the year 840, of which the following lines are a translation:—

> "No savage bear with lawless fury roves,
> No raging lion through her sacred groves,
> No poison there infects, no scaly snake
> Creeps through the grass, no croaking frog annoys the lake."

Thompson also refers to an introduction of the Frog, which does certainly seem to have taken place some time about the year 1699, when Dr. Guithers, one of the Fellows of Trinity College, Dublin, placed spawn from England in a ditch in the University Park, whence the species is supposed to have spread all over Ireland.

But Thompson, without comment, also quotes this passage from Stuart's History of Armagh: "The first Frog that was ever seen in this country made its appearance in a pasture

---

[1] W. Thompson, "The Natural History of Ireland," vol. iv., 1856.
[2] Camden's "Britannia," vol. vi., p. 234, Gough's edition.

A

field, near Waterford, about the year 1630, and is noticed by Colgan in a work printed in 1647." It appears, therefore, that before the introduction of the Frog into Dublin, it already existed in Waterford.

Before further consideration of this evidence, a few remarks on the Frog and its geographical range may not be out of place. The Frog is certainly a most useful animal to man, living as it does largely on slugs and insects destructive to crops, but as it is often believed to be a fruit-eater it is generally killed when found in strawberry-beds, which it frequents in order to eat the small black slug, *Arion hortensis*, which commits such ravages among the ripe fruit.

All frogs which have been hitherto discovered in Ireland are of the species known as the Common Frog (*Rana temporaria*, L.), but in England the Edible Frog (*Rana esculenta*, L.),occurs also. One of the most characteristic features by means of which these two species may be distinguished, is the dark triangular patch behind the eye in the Common Frog. This latter varies very considerably in colour, between grey, yellowish, and light brown, and, as a rule, the male is darker than the female.

The Edible Frog has a limited distribution in the British Isles, occurring only in some of the eastern counties of England. The Common Frog, on the other hand, is found all over England, Scotland, and Wales. Both species have a very wide general distribution—the Edible Frog ranging into Northern Africa, and from Eastern Europe, across Palestine and Persia, into China and Japan. The more northern of the two is certainly the Common Frog, and while it ascends the Alps to a height of 9,000 feet,[3] the Edible Frog is seldom found higher than 3,000. This seems to indicate that the former is able to resist greater extremes of temperature than the other, but it may mean also that it is the more ancient species of the two.

It is generally acknowledged that many of the quick-breeding mammals, and also some fishes, are easily introduced artificially into districts which they have not previously inhabited, provided that they find similar conditions to those to which they are accustomed. But even in the case of vertebrate animals, many resist artificial introduction, although the

[3] J. von Bedriaga, "Die Lurchfauna Europa's" (part I.), 1891.

general surroundings and climate may be perfectly suited to their requirements.

In invertebrate animals artificial introduction almost invariably fails. The Journals of Natural History Societies abound in records of the details of such attempts, and surprise is often expressed at the fact that not a single specimen has survived after a year or two, out of the dozens which were set at liberty.

Now anyone would suppose that it must be a very easy thing to introduce the Edible Frog into such a country as England, for its range all over Continental Europe proves that it must be indifferent as to whether the climate is wet or dry. Yet although about 2,000 living specimens, and a great quantity of spawn were brought by Mr. Berney[4] from France (he not being aware that the Italian variety of the Edible Frog already existed in the country), and deposited in the ponds and ditches of Norfolk, between the years 1837 and 1842, very few remain in the neighbourhood at the present day, after fifty years, to tell the tale. They have not spread, either, to any of the surrounding counties, for, curiously enough, although the Edible Frog is common in some of the eastern counties of England, Mr. Boulenger[4] points out that all the specimens, the capture of which has hitherto been recorded, are not the descendants of those introduced by Mr. Berney, but are of Italian type and origin. The suggestion that the Italian type of the Edible Frog has been introduced at a much earlier date than the French type, by monks from Italy, appears to Mr. Boulenger[5] to be the most plausible explanation, but how the poor monks in the good old days could have carried live frogs or even spawn from Italy, with the primitive means of conveyance then at their disposal, he leaves us to imagine!

Mr. Berney's ignorance of the pre-existence of the Edible Frog in the very neighbourhood in which he sought, with so much trouble and expense, to establish it, is worth noting in connection with this attempt at introduction. It shows how oblivious of the lower forms of animal life even those much interested in them may be.

To return to the subject of the Frog in Ireland, Dr. Joyce

---

[4] G. A. Boulenger, "Note on the Edible Frog in England," *Proc. Zool. Soc.*, 1884.
[5] G. A. Boulenger, "On the Origin of the Edible Frog in England," *Zoologist*, 3rd series, vol. viii., 1884.

has very kindly drawn my attention to the historical works of Giraldus Cambrensis, a whole chapter in which is devoted to the story of a Frog, which had then been found in Ireland. Giraldus acted as secretary to Prince John, who was sent on a visit to Ireland by his father, King Henry II. The portion of these works on the "Topography of Ireland" was written in 1187. As this seems to be the first record of an Irish Frog, I hope I may be excused for quoting some of his statements in full from a faithful translation.[6]

"There are neither snakes nor adders, toads nor frogs, tortoises nor scorpions nor dragons in Ireland. It produces however, spiders, leeches and lizards, but they are quite harmless. It does appear very wonderful that, where anything venomous is brought there from other lands, it never could exist in Ireland. I have also heard it said by merchants, that on some occasions, having unloaded their ships in an Irish port, they found toads in the bottom of the hold; having thrown them on shore in a living state, they immediately turned on their backs and bursting their bellies died, to the astonishment of many who witnessed it. Nevertheless, a frog was found, within my time, in the grassy meadows near Waterford and brought to Court alive before Robert Poer, who was at the time Warden there, and many others, both English and Irish. And when numbers of both nations, and particularly the Irish, had beheld it with great astonishment, at last Duvenold, King of Ossory, a man of sense among his people and faithful, who happened to be present, beating his head, and having deep grief at heart, spoke thus:—'That reptile is the bearer of doleful news to Ireland.'

"No man, however, will venture to suppose that this reptile was ever born in Ireland, for the mud there does not, as in other countries, contain the germs from which green Frogs are bred. If that had been the case, they would have been found more frequently, and in greater numbers, both before and after the time mentioned. It may have happened that some particle of the germ, hid in the moist soil, had been exhaled into the clouds by the heat of the atmosphere, and wafted hither by the force of the winds, or perhaps, that the embryo reptile had been swept into the hollow of a descending cloud, and being by chance deposited here, was lodged in an unhospitable and ungenial soil. But the better opinion is that the Frog was brought from some neighbouring port, and being cast on shore, succeeded in subsisting and maintaining life for a time, as it is not a venomous animal."

There seems therefore to be no doubt that a Frog was actually found near Waterford, about the year 1187; and that, in those earlier times, no one thought of introducing frogs into Ireland, may be assumed, as he would have fared very badly on account

---

[6] Giraldus Cambrensis, "The Topography of Ireland; its Miracles and Wonders."—Bohn's Antiquarian Library, 1881.

of the general prejudice againt them and kindred animals. The history of Giraldus contains frequent allusions to the supposed sacred quality of the soil and air of Ireland, which was believed not only to render the existence of poisonous animals impossible, but even caused all poisons brought here to become innocuous. We may certainly believe the people to have done their utmost to support this belief so agreeable to their pride of country, and which helped to bring pilgrims (the tourists of that time!) to the "Isle of Saints."

Giraldus, in the passage quoted, states that the Frog is not venomous, but the scene described by him, and his remarks elsewhere, tend to the belief that frogs, as well as toads, were generally held to be poisonous by the Irish.

It may indeed be that most people were really ignorant of their existence in the country. I venture to think that many people would deny at the present day that toads live in Ireland, and yet they are plentiful about Dingle Bay. Waterfowl also were then much more plentiful, as the country was more thinly inhabited, and these birds, in pools and marshes which they now do not frequent, would keep down frogs.

Authorities differ as to whether there is an Irish name for the Frog, Dr. Hyde informing me that there is none, and that the word for "frog" used in the Irish translation of the Bible, which was made about the year 1620-50, is "losgan," a Scotch Gaelic word, not in use in any part of Ireland now, while Dr. Joyce says that the word now used is "cnadan" which is not a very ancient one. This might be explained by the supposition that frogs and other of the lower animals, not being hunted or useful for food, were, in ancient times, spoken of collectively under a name uniting them all, such as "worms," just as many people now-a-days speak of snails and kindred invertebrates as "insects." Dr. Frazer kindly pointed out to me that there is a frog sculptured on the Drumcliffe cross in Co. Sligo, which dates from about the 11th century. There is a drawing of this interesting cross in his wonderful collection of sketches, made principally by himself, of Irish antiquities. However, I attach no special importance to this figure in aiding the present enquiry into the origin of the Frog in Ireland, and we must search for something more tangible to prove its presence there in ancient times.

One of the most convincing proofs of an animal's existence

in a country in former times is the finding of its remains in a fossil condition, and the bones of the Frog have been found associated with those of the bear and other extinct animals in the caves of Ballynamintra, in the County Wexford. But of as much importance is a knowledge of its present distribution. For if, as we are told, the Frog was introduced into Ireland from Trinity College Park, Dublin, it ought to be most common in the suburbs of the city and get rarer as we proceed westwards, as all the lower animals spread with extreme slowness, and radiate outwards from the point where they first obtained a footing. However, as it happens, the Frog is much more common on the west than it is on the east coast. In Kerry it flourishes in great numbers up to certainly 2000 feet on the mountains; from the mountainous regions of Donegal, I have seen many specimens collected by Mr. Patterson; and in Connemara I have found it common, though it is absent from the Aran Islands.

There are undoubtedly few places in Ireland whence the Frog would have less chance of spreading than the College Park, lying as it does almost at sea-level, the current and floods of rivers being generally held to be the principal factors in animal distribution. Besides, we know that frogs and their spawn are killed by sea-water—how then did they reach Achil Island, where we are told by Thompson that they exist.

I have now stated as much as I have been able to ascertain about the supposed introduction of the Frog into Ireland, and the reasons for my belief that it is a true native, and I hope that any of the readers of the *Irish Naturalist* who possess further information on the subject may be induced to send it to the Editors for publication.

THE EARTHWORMS OF IRELAND.

BY REV. HILDERIC FRIEND F.L.S.

THROUGH the courtesy of Dr. Scharff of Dublin, and other naturalists resident in Ireland, I have been able during the past few months to make some notes on this hitherto greatly neglected branch of natural history, and as the subject is new, and any information respecting the classification, identification, and distribution of Irish earthworms will prove of service to future investigators, I venture to lay before the reader an account of those species which have thus far been identified.

The indigenous earthworms of Great Britain are, as far as at present known, without exception, members of one family—the *Lumbricidæ*. This family is composed of some half a dozen genera, four at least of which are represented in our fauna. These genera bear the following names, *Lumbricus*, *Allolobophora*, *Dendrobæna*, and *Allurus*. One or two others, (as *Crodrilus*, and *Tetragonurus*) are at the present time either unknown within our borders, or their affinities are doubtful. Further research will alone enable us to decide some points which sadly need elucidation, and our readers will render good service to science by doing all in their power to aid in the solution of these difficulties. Meanwhile I shall be content to treat only of such genera and species as I have been able personally to examine and determine. As indicative of the present state of knowledge on this subject it may be remarked that my paper communicated to the British Association last year, contained an account of a score of indigenous species, whereas ten years ago it was assumed that we had only eight or nine native worms in Great Britain. Since that paper was written the number has been raised to twenty-four or twenty-five. There are five species of *Lumbricus*, and as many of *Allurus*, while all the rest belong to the two remaining genera, whose boundaries have yet to be accurately defined.

In this first part of my paper I confine my attention to the oldest genus, and describe only those species of *Lumbricus* which are known to-day as Irish. These are five in number, but there is every reason to believe that one other species might be found in the Island. We may take them in the order in which they were made known to the public.

Lumbricus terrestris, Linn.—COMMON EARTHWORM. At last, after the lapse of nearly a century and a half, since Linnæus first named this animal, we are able to give an accurate account of the same. Confusion has been worse confounded again and again by the mixing up of half a dozen different species under the old name, and even so recently as the last decade systematists had not discovered the difference between the long worm (*Allolobophora longa*, Ude), and the earthworm, though they belonged to separate genera. To distinguish these two genera attention must be paid to the formation of the head, and the method by which the front lobe is inserted into the first ring. If the first ring is cut entirely in two by the backward prolongation of the front lobe or prostomium, when viewed from above (fig. 1) we conclude that the worm is a species of *Lumbricus*; if it is only partially cut (fig 2) we are examining a representative of the genus *Allolobophora*. There are exceptions which will be noted later. The earthworm is usually about five inches long, of a dark brown colour, iridescent, with a flattened tail and cylindrical body. When adult the girdle is prominent, and always extends from the 30th to the 37th segment. Under four girdle segments we find a band (fig. 3) on either side, and on segment 15 a pair of swollen protuberances, or papillæ, carrying the male pores. The setæ are in four couples, the individuals of which are nearly close together (fig. 4).

DISTRIBUTION IN IRELAND. *Lumbricus terrestris* has reached me from Valentia Island, Kerry (Miss M. J. Delap); Newcastle, Co. Down (Mr. Praeger); Clondalkin and Leeson-park, Dublin (Dr. Scharff); Letterkenny, Co. Donegal (Mr. H. C. Hart); Malahide, Co. Dublin (Mr. J. Trumbull), and Loughbrickland, Co. Down (Rev. H. W. Lett).

Lumbricus rubellus, Hoffmeister—RED WORM. This worm has been known for about half a century, and its distribution is very wide. It is usually about three inches in length, and has all the characters of the typical *Lumbricus*. It can be readily distinguished from the foregoing, however, by the utter absence of papillæ on the 15th and other segments, and by the position of the girdle, which occupies segments 27 to 32. As usual in this genus, a band known as the puberty band (or *tubercula pubertatis*) runs along the four innermost segments of the girdle. The worm is very active, and abounds in most parts of the British Isles, in all kinds of soil and every conceivable locality.

DISTRIBUTION IN IRELAND. *Lumbricus rubellus* has been sent from half-a-dozen localities. Mr. Praeger has supplied it from Newcastle, and Dr. Scharff from Leeson-park, Dublin; in the latter case they were all immature. It has also reached me from Letterkenny (Mr. Hart); Malahide (Mr. J. Trumbull); Glasnevin (Mr. J. R. Redding); Loughbrickland (Rev. H. W. Lett), and Powerscourt, Co. Wicklow (Dr. Scharff).

Lumbricus purpureus, Eisen—PURPLE WORM. This is the smallest of the worms in this genus. It averages about two inches in length, and is readily identified as a genuine *Lumbricus* by its colour, iridescence, 'mortise and tenon' shaped head, close setæ, and girdle of six segments extending from the 28th to the 33rd. It is exceedingly active, and can run backwards almost as rapidly as forwards. Savigny undoubtedly knew the species long before Eisen described it, for he gives its characters very accurately—so far as they were observed in those early times—in connection with a species which he named *Enterion castaneum*.

DISTRIBUTION IN IRELAND. *Lumbricus purpureus* is widely distributed. I have specimens from Valentia Island, Kerry, sent by Miss Delap; Newcastle (Mr. Praeger); Leeson-park and Clondalkin, Dublin, and Powerscourt (Dr. Scharff); Malahide (Mr. Trumbull), and Letterkenny (Mr. Hart).

Lumbricus rubescens, Friend—RUDDY WORM. This interesting worm has recently been sent me from Ireland. It comes midway between the common earthworm and the red worm, is from three to four inches in length, and has the girdle on segments 34 to 39, with the band on the four innermost segments. Like the common earthworm it has papillæ on the under surface of the 15th segment, upon which the male pores are placed. In colour and shape it exactly corresponds with the other species of the genus. It was first described by me in 1891 from specimens found in Yorkshire, and has since been discovered in many parts of the United Kingdom, though no continental investigator seems to have found it hitherto. It may have been known to Dugès, and early writers of this century, but the old diagnosis is too meagre to satisfy the demands of modern science.

DISTRIBUTION IN IRELAND. Five beautiful specimens of *Lumbricus rubescens* reached me in good form during the month of October from J. R. Redding, Esq., Glasnevin. One specimen at least carried on its under surface those remarkable sacs known as spermatophores. I have thus far failed to find these appendages on any other species of *Lumbricus*. Dr. Scharff has also found this worm at Powerscourt. In Yorkshire I have discovered this species hybridizing with the red worm.

Lumbricus papillosus, Friend—PAPILLOSE WORM.—This species is new to science, and is at present known to occur only in Ireland, where it is limited to the County of Dublin. Further study will no doubt reveal its existence elsewhere. A full description has been sent to the Royal Irish Academy, with drawings to illustrate its specific peculiarities. The type will be placed in the Dublin Museum of Science and Art, as one of the series of British Earthworms which I am supplying to that institution. The girdle occupies only five segments (33-37) on two of which (the 34th and 36th) we find a pair of remarkable papillæ. Hence the specific name which I have suggested. On the Continent we similarly find another species of *Lumbricus* which has only five girdle segments (*L. melibœus*, Rosa), but their situation differs from that of *L. papillosus*. Our new species closely resembles the Common Earthworm and the Ruddy Worm, being four inches long, and possessed of papillæ on the fifteenth segment. There is also a peculiar ridge connecting the girdle with the male pores.

DISTRIBUTION IN IRELAND.—*Lumbricus papillosus* first reached me on 16th June, 1892, in a consignment of worms from Dublin, collected by Dr. Scharff in his garden at Leeson Park. I was uncertain about its specific relationships till November, when I again obtained it, from Glasnevin, where it was found by Mr. Redding on a bare pathway in Botanic-road.

It may be helpful if I add a table setting forth the main external features of these species.

Lumbricus.	Segments Occupied by:				Average.	
	Girdle.	Band.	1st Dorsal Pore.	Papillæ.	Length, inches.	No. of Segments.
terrestris, Linn. ...	32-37	33-36	8/9	15, 26	5	150-200
papillosus, Fr. ...	33-37	34-37	9/10	15,34,36	4	—
rubescens, Fr. ...	34-39	35-38	6/7	15, 28	4	120-150
rubellus, Hoffm. ...	27-32	28-31	7/8	0	3	110-140
purpureus, Eis. ...	28-33	29-32	5/6	10	2	90-120

For the encouragement of collectors I may add that I have received from Dr. Scharff at least one species of worm (*Allolobophora hibernica,* Friend) which has not been recorded for any other of the British Isles (an account of which is published in the *Proceedings of the Royal Irish Academy*); while another new species (*Allurus macrurus,* Friend) has come from Mr. Trumbull, L.R.C.S., of Malahide. I have in addition a further specimen which is new to Britain, but the relationships and position of which cannot be determined till a maturer specimen has been examined.

After what we have learned of late respecting the distribution of plants and animals, and the Continental affinities of various Hibernian forms, we may not unnaturally look for some further interesting illustrations from the Emerald Isle. I shall esteem it a favour if correspondents will furnish me with supplies from all parts of the country packed in soft moss. They should be sent alive in tin boxes, the moss being intended to keep them in health. My address is Idle, Bradford, Yorkshire. I may add that it is best to send such packages by Parcels' Post, marked "NATURAL HISTORY SPECIMENS ONLY," as the authorities seem to eye them carefully, and more than one valuable consignment has been lost *en route*.

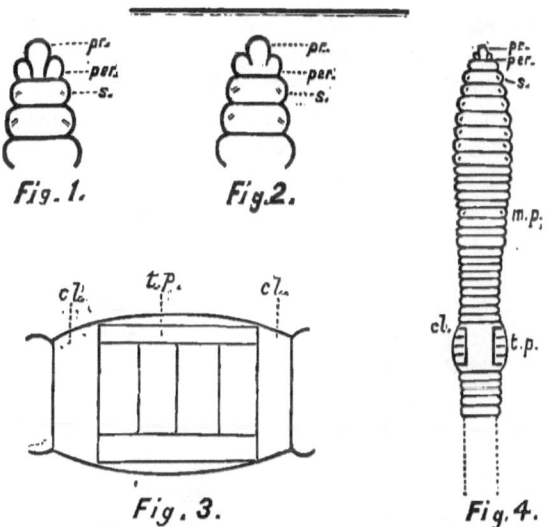

Fig. 1. Diagram of head of *Lumbricus*.
    pr. prostomium, or lip.
    per. peristomium, or first segment, without setæ.
    s. setæ.
Fig. 2. Diagram of head of *Allolobophora*.
Fig. 3. Girdle or clitellum of *Lumbricus*.
    cl. clitellum extending over six segments.
    t. p. tubercula pubertalis in the form of a band over four innermost segments.
Fig. 4. Diagram of *L. rubellus*, Hoff.
    m. p. male pores. Other letters as in fig. 1, 3.

(TO BE CONTINUED.)

THE FLORA OF COUNTY ARMAGH.
BY R. LLOYD PRAEGER, B.E., M.R.I.A.

DISTRICT 10 of "Cybele Hibernica," including as it does the counties of Tyrone, Fermanagh, Armagh, Monaghan, and Cavan, may be termed the north-central botanical district of Ireland. The north-eastern maritime district of Down, Antrim, and Derry (No. 12) lies between it and the North Channel, and the north-western maritime district of Donegal (No. 11) cuts it off from the Atlantic; district 10, the largest of the twelve Irish botanical regions, having a surface of over 3,700 square miles, is entirely an inland area, touching estuarine waters only for a few miles at Newry in the south-eastern extremity, and near Strabane in the north-west. This large tract presents a considerable diversity of character, both geological and physical; extensive bogs and lakes are somewhat numerous, and yield a fairly representative flora; several mountain ridges rise to over 2,000 feet, but they are remarkably poor in alpine and montane species; the poverty of the maritime and mountain floras will probably keep the total flora of district 10 below that of districts 11 or 12, even when it has been thoroughly worked out.

The tenth botanical district has not claimed by any means a great amount of attention from Irish botanists, and a glance at "Cybele Hibernica" shows a very large number of blanks in the "district 10" column of the table of distribution, many of even the most widely-spread species being unrecorded. Since the publication of "Cybele," however, Messrs. S. A. Stewart,[1] R. M. Barrington,[2] H. C. Hart,[3] and others, have wiped out many of these blanks, and have added a number of interesting plants to the flora of the district. Their observations having been made chiefly in the western portions of the region under consideration, it appeared to me that further examination of the eastern part might be desirable, not the less so since a number of old records of rare plants existed, the confirmation of which would alone be of some importance

---

[1] Report on the Botany of the mountainous portion of Fermanagh and Cavan.—*Proc. R. I. A.*, 1882.
[2] Report on the Flora on the shores of Lough Erne.—*Proc. R. I. A.*, 1883.
[3] Notes on the Plants of some of the mountain ranges of Ireland.—*Proc. R. I. A.*, 1883. Rare Plants from Co. Tyrone, *Jour. of Bot.*, 1887.

With this end in view, I found time during the past season to spend some three weeks botanising in Co. Armagh, the most easterly county of district 10, and the results of my investigation I now lay before the readers of *The Irish Naturalist.*

The County of Armagh has an area of 512 square miles. Its surface presents a considerable variety of petrological characters, which influence the flora to a greater or less degree, as I shall endeavour to show. The whole northern boundary of the county is formed by Lough Neagh, in itself an interesting botanical region. Stretching along its margin is a broad belt of low, flattish land, characterised by extensive peat bogs which overlie lacustrine clays supposed to be of Pliocene age. In the north-east, a tongue of the basalts of Antrim penetrates into the county as far as Richhill, where it is met by a corresponding tongue of Carboniferous Limestone, the north-eastern extremity of the great limestone area of the Central Plain. North of the city of Armagh, a triangular patch of New Red Sandstone intervenes between the Pliocene and the Carboniferous. South of the basalt and limestone, the Lower Silurians cover the whole centre and south-west of the county, as they do a great portion of the adjoining counties of Down, Monaghan, and Cavan. In the south-east, a mass of ancient granites and basalts, the continuation of the Carlingford mountains, extends and rises in a series of rugged isolated hills, culminating in Slieve Gullion (1,893 feet). These are the only important highlands in the county, the rest of the surface being low, undulating, and (with the exception of the northern bogs) well-tilled; north of Newtownhamilton the Silurians rise in broad ridges to a height of 1,200 feet, but are cultivated almost to their summit. To the south of Keady, and also orth-west of Crossmaglen, groups of lakelets occupy deep hollows in the Silurian rocks; other small lakes are scattered through the county, so that with the addition of Lough Gullion and Lough Neagh on the north, the waters of the Blackwater on the west, and the Bann and Newry canal on the east, the conditions for aquatic plant life are favourable. In the extreme south-east the estuary of the Newry river affords for a few miles a habitat for the characteristic flora of the salt-marsh.

Probably the earliest records of Armagh plants are those in Sir Charles Coote's "Statistical Survey of the County of

Armagh" (Dublin, 1804), in which a few of the more striking species are quoted, not always with accuracy. Dr. Mackay's "Flora Hibernica" (1836) supplies some better authenticated notes, which are, however, very few in number. In the "Irish Flora" (1846) Co. Armagh is almost entirely overlooked. The first contribution of importance to the flora of the county is contained in Mr. More's paper "Localities for some Plants observed in Ireland," read before the Dublin University Zoological and Botanical Association, in May, 1860, and published in the *Natural History Review* for that year. The first part of this paper enumerates the rarer plants "noticed in the County of Armagh during April and May, 1854," and is the result of observations made by the author during a stay at Loughgall, in the northern portion of the county; a number of the characteristic plants of Lough Neagh and the northern bog district are here recorded for the first time. Dr. Dickie's "Flora of Ulster" (1864) gives some interesting notes of Mr. John Templeton's, dating about the beginning of the century, and also some good finds made in the county by Rev. George Robinson, and by Messrs. G. C. Hyndman, William Thompson, and the author himself. More's notes are here republished, but with the addition of an unfortunate mistake. Mr. More, writing from Loughgall during his visit there, sent to Dr. Dickie a "London Catalogue" with all the plants observed by him in Co. Armagh checked off. The author of "Flora of Ulster" assumed that the plants named had all been found *at Loughgall*, and published as growing there, for instance, such rarities as *Calamagrostis stricta* and *Lathyrus palustris*, which Mr. More had seen on an islet in Lough Neagh, and as subsequently transpired, not in Armagh at all, but in the adjoining county of Tyrone. In "Cybele Hibernica" (1866) these errors are for the most part rectified, and the proper stations given; some further records by Rev. Mr. Robinson appear, and some valuable notes by Dr. D. Moore. One or two additional notes are gleaned from Mr More's "Recent Additions to the Flora of Ireland," published in the *Journal of Botany* for 1873. Stewart and Corry's "Flora of the North-east of Ireland" (1888) though dealing with an adjoining district, contains references to one or two rare Armagh plants. From the *Proceedings of the Belfast Naturalists' Field Club*, 1863-92, are gathered a number of records of plants obtained by members in the county during the excursions of that society; an appendix to the *Report* of 1885-6, "The Ferns of Ulster" by Mr. W. H. Phillips and the writer supplies a number of stations for the rarer Filices. So far as I am aware, this completes the enumeration of the published records of Armagh plants.

Of unpublished material, a considerable amount has been forthcoming, and I am deeply indebted to several good friends for their hearty co-operation and willing assistance. Mr. A. G. More and Mr. S. A. Stewart have, with their usual kindness, helped me considerably with notes and advice. To Rev. H. W. Lett, M.A., and Rev. W. F. Johnson, M.A., my best thanks are due for kindly placing at my disposal their herbaria of Armagh plants. The former collection was made principally about Ardmore Point, on Lough Neagh, between 1865 to 1885, the latter in the neighbourhood of Armagh during 1880; from both collections a large number of valuable records were obtained. Mr. Lett also assisted me by forwarding a bundle of fresh *Rubi*, collected in the parish of Ballymore or Tanderagee, and Mr. Johnson by sending up several gatherings of *Carices*. Rev. Geo. Robinson kindly supplied me with some additional notes; the herbarium of the Belfast Natural History and Philosophical Society yielded one or two Armagh stations, and my own note-book from 1881 to 1892 added a few notes of plants observed in various parts of the county during that period. To the above material, which would in itself have formed a very respectable local list, I have been able to add largely by my recent observations.

The flora of Co. Armagh, leaving out of account such plants as have no claim to be considered native, and those which, though recorded from the county, do not appear to now exist in their former habitats, numbers 615 species and 20 varieties. The total species enumerated in the present paper is 665, made up as follows:—indigenous plants, 593; possibly introduced, 12: probably introduced, 10; certainly introduced, 40; recorded from the county, but not now to be found, 10; total, 665. There is a poverty of maritime and of mountain plants. The former is to be expected. As regards the latter, although Slieve Gullion overtops any of the Antrim hills, the hard and sterile nature of the primary basalt of which it is composed, so different from the rich friable basalts of Antrim, and the absence of projecting rocks and cliffs, sufficiently account for their absence. I did not find a single Hawkweed (excepting, of course, the ubiquitous *H. pilosella*) on the Armagh mountains, while at least fifteen different forms flourish on the adjoining granite hills of Down. Comparing the Armagh flora with that of the counties comprising district 12, we find that the flora of Down numbers about 710 species, Antrim, 750, Derry, 670. The flora of Donegal, I am informed by Mr. H. C. Hart, comprises about 720 species. All these counties possess a fair share of mountain plants, and have a wide extent of both rocky and sandy seashore, inhabited by many species which affect such situations. The area of each of the north-eastern counties is from one and a-half times to twice the area of Armagh, and Donegal is nearly four times as large, so that when the small size of the county is taken into consideration, the flora of Armagh is decidedly a rich one. The adjoining western counties cannot enter into this comparison, their floras being so little known, except perhaps, Fermanagh, to which the combined lists of Stewart,[1] Barrington,[2] and the writer[3] assign a flora of some 450 species; here mountain plants are rare, and maritime species absent.

Of Mr. Watson's Atlantic type, Co. Armagh possesses only five out of forty-one Irish species—*Sedum anglicum, Cotyledon umbilicus, Pinguicula lusitanica, Lastrea æmula, Hymenophyllum tunbridgense*. Out of eighteen Irish Germanic plants, one only, *Orchis pyramidalis*, grows in the county. Equally poor is the alpine flora, only four of the forty-seven Irish plants of Highland type occurring—*Galium boreale, Vaccinium vitis-idæa, Selaginella spinosa*, and *Isoetes lacustris*, and none of these are confined to alpine situations in the county, *Galium* growing on the shores of Lough Neagh (50 feet elevation), *Vaccinium* being recorded from the northern bogs (under 100 feet), *Isoetes* ranging from 286 to 444 feet, and *Selaginella* growing from 700 feet upwards.

(TO BE CONTINUED.)

Another Irish Field Club. "The cry is still they come." Limerick has followed the excellent example of Cork, and we congratulate our friends most heartily on the successful formation of a Naturalists' Field Club in that city. Limerick is the centre of a highly interesting district, which can still bear with advantage much careful investigation, and we have no doubt that the new Club will soon make its influence felt in Irish scientific circles.

---

[1] *Op. cit.*   [2] *Op. cit.*   [3] *Irish Naturalist*, 1892, p. 113.

DENUDATION AT CULTRA, CO. DOWN.

BY MARY K. ANDREWS.

(Read before the Belfast Naturalists' Field Club, December 20th, 1892).

TRADITION, history, and geological evidence all bear testimony to the continued interchange, within certain limits, of land and water. Although the deep depressions of the ocean and the main trends of the land seem, from the very earliest geological periods, to have preserved their same general positions on the globe,[1] yet a careful comparison of the upheaved stratified formations, with the layers of gravel, shells, sand, and mud deposited in the comparatively shallow seas around our coasts, leaves little doubt that very large portions of our land areas, were, at one period or another, laid down upon the floor of the sea. Subject to the action of internal forces they have experienced many oscillations of level, insular conditions at one period predominating, continental at another; crustal movements, modified by denudation and deposition, governing the relative levels of land and sea.

It was a fundamental proposition of the Huttonian Theory, "That in all the strata we discover proofs of the materials having existed as elements of bodies, which must have been destroyed before the formation of those of which these materials now actually make a part."[2] One portion of the earth's surface is slowly and constantly wasted, denuded, and transported to the sea, whilst another portion, formed from similar materials of pre-existing land, is as constantly consolidated and raised to take its place. In this sequence of events, protracted through an indefinite period of time, Hutton recognized one general constant order in nature, the ruins of an older world always forming the foundations of a newer. In the decay of

---

[1] "Geographers must, for the present, be content to take the world as they find it. What we do know is that our lands are distributed over the surface of a great continental plateau of irregular form, the bounding slopes of which plunge down more or less steeply into a vast oceanic depression. So far as geological research has gone, there is reason to believe that these elevated and depressed areas are of primeval antiquity—that they antedate the very oldest of the sedimentary formations."—*Address to the Geographical Section of the British Association*, 1892, by Professor James Geikie, LL.D., etc.

[2] Playfair's "Illustrations of the Huttonian Theory," p. 23.

the solid rocks, and the transportation of their material, he also saw the source of our beautiful systems of mountains and valleys, of hills and fertile plains. He thus opened up the border land between geology and physical geography, and gave an impetus to the fascinating study of those epigene or surface agents, which in the present, as in the past, are altering and moulding the scenery of our globe. Their work is constant; denudation and erosion are always in progress. Each mountain rill, each wave that beats against our coast, each shower of rain, leaves a mark upon the surface of the earth.

The effects may be too faint for our observation, or for the observation of generations, but the geologist sees the accumulated results in the deep fissures of the mountain, in the indented shore with sea-worn cave and isolated stack, in the pinnacles and hillocks that lend such varied form and beauty to the undercliff. And further still, along great lines of coast, far above the highest tide-level, caves, escarpments, and successive gravel-capped terraces bear testimony not only to the erosion of former periods, but also to vast movements of elevation, interrupted by long periods of rest, probably also by periods of temporary subsidence.

From the raised beaches of our own coasts to the great terraces of Patagonia, rising like mighty steps one behind the other, we see the effects of the same co-operating actions—erosion, deposition and upheaval. So also in the present, we know that some regions of the earth are relatively rising, others are gradually sinking; the sea is making encroachments on certain coasts, it is receding on others. As a general rule, where the rocks are hard, erosion is slow, where they are soft and more easily disintegrated, it is rapid.

Striking illustrations of marine erosion might be drawn from the tunnelled caves and imposing sea-stacks of our Irish coast, but the encroachment of the sea at Cultra Bay, on the southern side of Belfast Lough, to which I wish to draw attention in the present paper, has left no such impressive features.

Much land has been washed away, of which no trace would have remained, had it not been for one insignificant land-mark, and before it too disappears, I have made a few notes of the encroachment of the sea to which it testifies, which I hope may not be devoid of interest.

The landmark to which I refer is a shaft of crown Memel pine, about twenty-three feet high, standing on the beach opposite Cultra Point, a mile north-east of Holywood, It formed part of a windmill pump, which was erected, I am informed by Mr. John Lennox, in 1824 or 1825, to remove the water from an old quarry. The upright standard above the much decayed suction-pipe of the pump still remains, with a loose iron rod attached to a small handle at the top. Although fifty feet distant from present high water-mark, and surrounded by the sea to a depth of three feet at high tide, this old pump (Plate 1) marks the centre of a sandstone quarry, opened in what was formerly known as the Point Field.

An inhabitant of Holywood, Mr. William Nimick, who remembers the locality since 1829, informs me that the sea was at that time fifty feet distant from the centre of the quarry, and that the fields, through which a broad carriage drive passed to Cultra Quay, and in which he saw numerous tents pitched, and large crowds of spectators assembled, to watch one of the celebrated regattas[1] of the Northern Yacht Club, have now completely disappeared. He estimates that about five acres of land have since been washed away between Cultra Point and Cultra Pier.[2]

Disintegrated by the action of rain, frost, and other sub-aerial agents, portion after portion of the low cliffs have slipped down, an easy prey to the warfare of wave and current; the destruction of the land being still further aided by the removal of sand and gravel from the beach below. And now, at ebb tide, instead of the vanished fields, we see low denuded reefs that carry us back through vistas of time immeasurably vast.

Here in this one small bay we find represented each great division of the geological record. Shales that carry us back to the Palæozoic era, and recall the gradual submergence of the Devonian continent, beneath the waters of the Carboniferous ocean; sandstones that bring us to the Mesozoic era, and restore for us the vast Triassic lakes; dykes that link us with the great basaltic sheets of Tertiary time, and covering the low surrounding cliffs, drift deposits that bring us to Post-Tertiary periods and gradually forward to the time we are considering. (TO BE CONCLUDED.)

---

[1] The Belfast Regatta of 1829 lasted for nine days—See "The Belfast Newsletter," June 19th, 1829, and following Nos.

[2] The extremities of Cultra Bay, scarcely a quarter of a mile distant from each other.

THE
MACRO-LEPIDOPTERA OF THE LONDONDERRY DISTRICT.

BY D. C. CAMPBELL.

THE district surrounding the old historic city of Derry is most interesting to the student of nature. Of course every district, be it never so barren and seemingly unfruitful to the casual observer, is full of interest to the naturalist. I think, however, we can claim a special interest for Derry, lying as it does with Lough Foyle and Lough Swilly almost at its doors, and having all the varied beauties of river and wave-washed shore, and of woodland, mountain, and moorland, within reach. Such a land, of course, provides a wide field for the entomologist.

The localities I include in the district are almost all within some ten to fifteen miles of Derry city. One or two favourite spots such as Magilligan, at the mouth of Lough Foyle, and Ballycastle, on the Antrim coast, are farther removed.

The entomological work, of which the following list shows the results, was done by my brothers, Messrs. W. Howard Campbell, M.A., and Thomas V. Campbell, M.B. (both now of Cuddupah, Madras), and myself. We were ably assisted by our friend, Mr. James N. Milne, of Culmore. Our collecting days extended from 1875 to 1884, and during these years we explored and hunted almost every accessible locality in our neighbourhood. The list may not be very large, yet it contains many species of some rarity, and some of extreme interest, as new to Ireland. In 1878 we captured *Heliothis scutosa*, a moth so rare in the British Isles, that Newman omitted it altogether in his work on British moths. This specimen was, of course, the prize of our collection. We also took the very interesting species *Nyssia zonaria* on the Antrim coast. The fact that the female is wingless, and that the species had previously only been taken on the coast of Cheshire, adds additional interest to the discovery. I am confident that a careful entomological investigation of Donegal would bring to light many rare, and as far as Ireland is concerned, new species. I have to acknowledge our indebtedness to the late Mr. Birchall for his kindness in identifying specimens for us, also to Mr. W. F. de V. Kane. The advice we received from him from time to time greatly helped us; the interest he took in our captures, and his unfailing kindness in identifying specimens stimulated our ardour for further investigation.

RHOPALOCERA.

The butterflies we found form a small company. The number of species is only about half of that in Mr. Birchall's list of 1868. Many of the absent species *should* occur here, and probably on further investigation will be found. The beautifully-situated, warm, sheltered woodland about Rathmullan, on the Lough Swilly shore, must harbour many butterflies, and should yield some interesting kinds.

Pieris brassicæ, Linn.
P. rapae, Linn. } All very common.
P. napi, Linn,
Euchloe cardamines, Linn.—Fairly common.
Colias edusa, Fab.—This beautful butterfly appeared here in some numbers in 1876. We had never seen the species before, and I have never noticed it in this district since; I find the dates of capture in our note-book, 27th June, 15th July, and 9th September, 1876.
Argynnis paphia, Linn.—Not very common, but to be met with in almost all wooded localities. In 1879, I noticed it in some profusion in the glades of the beautiful woods of Ards, near Dunfanaghy.
A. aglaia, Linn.—Common on the coast.
Vanessa urticæ, Linn.—Common everywhere.
V. Io, Linn.—We never found this richly-marked species, but Mr. Wm. Hart took it in Innishowen, and Mr. John Cowie reports its occurrence near Derry many years ago.
V. atalanta, Linn.—Not abundant, but in every district.
V. cardui, Linn.—We took a few specimens only of this pretty, cosmopolitan insect every season. In 1880 and 1884, however, it was *very* abundant.
Pararge egeria, Linn. } Very common.
P. megæra, Linn.
Satyrus semele, Linn.—Common on the coast. Mr. Milne reports having seen this butterfly *swarming* at Castlerock, between 4 and 5 a.m., on an August morning, although throughout the day only a small number, comparatively speaking, were seen.
Epinephile janira, Linn.—Very common.
E. hyperanthes, Linn.—Rare and local in this district. We found it abundant at Ballymoney, Co. Antrim.
Cœnonympha pamphilus, Linn.—Common.
C. typhon, Rott.—I met this species for the first time, on 22nd July, 1892, on the moors between Gartan and Glenveagh, Co. Donegal, and again at L. Salt, on 23rd July. The specimen I secured is similar to the English variety of the insect (*rothliebii*).
Polyommatus phlæas, Linn.—Common.
Lycæna icarus, Rott.—Found everywhere, but especially abundant upon the coast.

SPHINGES.

Acherontia atropos, Linn.—Several specimens of the "Death's Head" have been found here, but we have never been so fortunate as to take one. Mr. Milne secured a fine one at Ballycastle, Co. Antrim.

Smerinthus populi, Linn.—Very abundant. We have met with some very beautiful varieties.

Macroglossa stellatarum, Linn.—Occurs in most localities, more abundant on the coast. We took the larvæ, feeding on *Galium*, on Magilligan sandhills.

Zygæna filipendulæ, Linn.—Very common on the shores of Lough Swilly. We took a strange variety, having six spots on one wing, and only five on the other.

We never saw any *Sesiidæ* in the Londonderry district.

BOMBYCES.

Nola confusalis, Herr-Schäff.—One specimen.
Nudaria mundana, Linn.—Common.
Euchelia Jacobææ, Linn.—Common.
Nemeophila plantaginis, Linn.—Generally distributed, but not common.
Arctia caia, Linn.—Common.
Spilosoma fuliginosa, Linn.—Common. We found the larvæ swarming on the Magilligan sandhills.
S. lubricipeda, Esp. }
S. menthastri, Esp. } Very common.
Hepialus hectus, Linn.—Common in the wooded localities.
H. velleda, Hüb.—Common, but seemed to be abundant only in alternate years, during some seasons, hardly a specimen appeared.
H. humuli, Linn.—Very common.
Orgyia antiqua, Linn.—Fairly common.
Eriogaster lanestris, Linn.—Larvæ very abundant on the stunted blackthorn on Magilligan sandhills. We found much difficulty in rearing the larvæ, and only succeeded in bringing out a few imagines. Probably they missed the fresh sea-air of their original home. I believe *E. lanestris* sometimes remains as long as six or seven years in the pupal state, although three years was the longest period with us.
Pœcilocampa populi, Linn.—Two specimens. Mr. Milne has taken the larvæ.
Bombyx rubi, Linn.—Common
B. quercus, var. **callunæ,** Palmer.—Common. We found the larvæ in thousands on the Innishowen moorlands. Unfortunately a large proportion of them were attacked by ichneumons.
Odonestis potatoria, Linn.—Common.
Saturnia pavonia, Linn.—Common.
Drepana lacertinaria, Linn.—Pretty common at Buncrana. We found the larvæ in some numbers in the young birch woods.
Dicranura vinula, Linn.—Common.
D. bifida, Hüb.—One specimen.
D. furcula, Linn.—Rare.

Phalera bucephala, Linn.—Very common.
Pygæra pigra, Hufn.—Common on the shores of Lough Swilly. We took the larvæ plentifully on dwarf sallow at Rathmullan.
Lophopteryx camelina, Linn.—Common.
L. dictæa, Linn.—Common.
L. dictaeoides, Esp.—We took two larvæ on birch at Rathmullan.
L. ziczac, Linn.—Common.
L. dromedarius, Linn.—Common.
Thyatira derasa, Linn.—Common.
T. batis, Linn.—Common.
Cymatophora or, Fab.—We took a few larvæ on birch on Lough Swilly shore.

We never found any of the *Lithosiidæ* near Londonderry. It seems strange that they did not turn up at Magilligan, as lichens grow very abundantly upon the dwarf blackthorns on the sandhills.

(TO BE CONTINUED.)

NOTES.

BOTANY.

MUSCI.

Mosses and Hepatics of the Ben Bulben District. Since I sent the note of Ben Bulben Mosses (*Irish Naturalist*, vol. i., p. 194), I came upon a packet which had been overlooked, containing the following species, which I would like to add to the other list :—
At Bundoran, *Hypnum lutescens,* Hudson, with old fruit, and *H. intermedium,* Lindb.; in ravine on Scafin Mountain, *Orthothecium intricatum,* Hartm., growing with *O. rufescens;* in Slish Wood, *H. borreri,* Spruce, *Georgia pellucida,* L., and *Lepidozia reptans,* L.—C. H. WADDELL, Saintfield, Co. Down.

Sphagnum austini (Sull.) in Ireland. While collecting mosses in 1889, on a mountain about two miles south of Glenariff, in the County Antrim, I found a large tussock of *Sphagnum austini,* Sull. I am not aware that it had previously been collected in Ireland, and in September, 1892, while moss-hunting on a part of the Bog of Allen, in the parish of Geashill, King's County, in company with the Rev. Canon C. D. Russell, I discovered a very large clump of this same rare moss. In this last case the whole of the bog for hundreds of yards round had, some months previously, been burned over, and every scrap of heather, bog plants, and moss, cleared off by fire, except this big colony of *Sphagnum austini,* showing how much water it must have contained when the surface of the bog had been blazing. And since then Canon Russell has sent me another specimen of the same moss, which he found in another bog not far from Geashill railway station.—H. W. LETT, Aghaderg, Co. Down.

FERNS.

Polypodium calcareum, at Carlingford, not indigenous. The editorial note in the December number of the *Irish Naturalist* (vol. i. p. 195), on Professor Hart's note concerning *Vanessa io* at Howth, reminds me of my own transgressions. In 1878, my brother and I planted a quantity of *Polypodium calcareum* on Carlingford Mountain. I had forgotten all about it, when, in 1889, the Rev. G. Robinson asked me, as I was thinking of going down to Omeath, if I would look on Carlingford Mountain for *P. calcareum*, as it had been found there by some gentlemen from Rostrevor, and he could not understand its presence there. I was, of course, able to explain the matter, and I write this note to let it be known, through the medium of the *Irish Naturalist*, that *P. calcareum*, if found on Carlingford Mountain, is not indigenous.—W. F. JOHNSON, Armagh.

PHANEROGAMS.

Plants Still Flowering in Mid-November.—On November 13th, Dr. Scharff and I went for a ramble along the Upper Dodder, between Tallaght and Fort Bridge, through the Ballinascorney Gap, and across Mount Seskin to "Embankment." We found quite a surprising number of species still in flower at that very advanced time of year, long after the end of the ordinary flowering-period. The following is the list:—*Ranunculus bulbosus, R. flammula, Reseda lutcola, Barbarea vulgaris, Nasturtium officinale, Capsella bursa-pastoris, Sisymbrium officinale, Brassica nigra, Cardamine hirsuta, Polygala vulgaris* (purple flowers), *Arenaria serpyllifolia, Cerastium semidecandrum, Rubus fruticosus, Potentilla reptans, Alchemilla vulgaris, Ulex europæus, Trifolium procumbens, T. minus, T. pratense, Pimpinella saxifraga, Daucus carota, Geranium robertianum, Sherardia arvensis, Carduus lanceolatus, C. palustris, Matricaria inodora, Hieracium sp., Achillea millefolium, Bellis perennis, Senecio jacobæa, S. vulgaris, Centaurea nigra, Erigeron acre* (extremely abundant), *Lapsana communis, Sonchus oleraceus, Jasione montana, Chlora perfoliata, Origanum vulgare, Lamium album, Teucrium scorodonia, Veronica chamædrys, V. montana, Erica cinerea, Anagallis arvensis, Myosotis versicolor*. The continuance in flower of such a strikingly large number of species is really a fact of much interest, and a striking commentary on the character of our climate.—E. J. M'WEENEY, Dublin.

Allium scorodoprasum, L. in Co. Cork.—As this is one of the rarest of Irish plants, and hitherto recorded only from Killarney and Foaty ("Cybele Hibernica"), it may be worth noting that in the summer of 1890 I found it plentiful in the woods at Castlefreke, Rosscarbery, and again this year whilst botanising with the Cork Naturalists' Field Club on 1st August, it formed the "find" of the day, growing in great profusion in the woods near Bantry.—R. A. PHILLIPS, Ashburton, Cork.

Orobanche minor, L. in Co. Cork.—This plant is recorded in "Cybele Hibernica" as an introduced plant in two stations rather close together, *i.e.*, Aghada and Trabolgan. From observations made during the last few years, I am inclined to think that, though it may not be entitled to rank as a native plant, it certainly deserves a place among the established species. It occurs in many widely-separated districts in this county, plentiful in some, and scarce in others. In the district around Clonakilty it seems to be most abundant, occurring not alone in recently-cultivated clover fields, but almost as plentifully in pastures which have not been ploughed for many years. It also occurs in old pastures near Eastferry, Midleton, and at Youghal. Last year it was most luxuriant in a newly-planted field of *Trifolium pratense* near Cork, but although the clover had not been disturbed, the *Orobanche* did not appear this year.—R. A. PHILLIPS.

White Centaury (Erythræa centaurium). As noticed in the *Irish Naturalist* (vol. i., p. 168), this is rather an uncommon plant, but numerous specimens may be found on the headland of Currabenny, Cork Harbour, along with that beautiful little plant the Milkwort (*Polygala vulgaris*), which grows here in great abundance in July and August.—A. N. ABBOTT, Cork.

I believe white Centaury is local rather than rare. There is a small mill-stream at Ballyhyland, along the lower part of whose banks all the Centaury is white, while that which grows in the field above is of the usual pink. Not far away are some dry, stony fields, in which both pink and white Centaury flourish abundantly. The latter ground is also productive of great variation in the colouring of *Prunella vulgaris* (Self-heal), of which, besides specimens of the ordinary purple hue, large quantities of white, marjoram-pink, and faint lavender-tinted blossoms, may be gathered every year.—C. B. MOFFAT, Ballyhyland, Co. Wexford.

White Bugle (Ajuga reptans). This summer I counted fourteen plants of *Ajuga reptans*, all bearing white flowers, under one tree, in a wood at Ballyhyland. Within this circumscribed space I saw no spike whose flowers were of the normal colour. The ground, though shaded, was not perceptibly more so than throughout the rest of the wood, where the *Ajuga* is uniformly blue.—C. B. MOFFAT.

ZOOLOGY.

CRUSTACEA.

Crustacea from Upper Lough Erne and Lough Corrib. The following list of species captured by me in Upper Lough Erne, in the years 1886-88 may be of interest. Several of them were identified by Professor G. S. Brady:—The Phyllopods comprised—*Daphnia pulex* common near the shores; *D. galeata*, on two occasions at surface in centre of lake, when the sun was shining; *Sida crystallina*, common in the bays, especially amongst the weeds, often adhering to lower surface of leaves of water-lilies, etc.; *Leptodora hyalina*, common; *Bythotrephis sp.* taken in large numbers at the surface in centre of lake, on a hot afternoon in August, 1886: it was then so plentiful that a tumbler dipped in the lake would bring up three or four specimens. I have since obtained it on other occasions, but never in such profusion; *Bosmina coregoni*. The Copepods were—*Cyclops coronatus, Diaptomus castor, Tenura velox,* and *Argulus foliaceus*, the last very common, both free-swimming and on perch, etc. *Pontoporeia affinis* represents the Amphipods; two specimens only were found amongst weeds in a sheltered bay; the importance of this form (together with *Gammarus neglectus* and *Mysis oculata*, var. *relicta*) lies in their being looked upon as relics of an old marine fauna. I have heard that *Mysis* occurs in Lough Neagh. If any reader of the *Irish Naturalist* comes across it, I should be extremely obliged for specimens.

From the "Proceedings of the Dublin Microscopic Club," reported in *Quarterly Journal of Microscopic Science*, vol. xii., we learn that Mr. Arthur Andrews found the following species in Lough Corrib:—*Pholyphemus pediculus*, on one occasion whilst fishing in Lough Corrib with a small muslin net, hundreds were taken at a single dip in a sheltered sunny creek, while further search along the same shore failed in procuring a single specimen; *Lynceus elongatus, Sida crystallina, Daphnia mucronata,* and *Acantholebris curvirostris,* Lilly, (*acanthoccocus,* Schöll.), plentiful in most small bog pools. *Lynceus elongatus* and *Bosmina longirostris* are reported from Clonhugh lake, near Mullingar.—R. N. CREIGHTON, Ballyshannon, Co. Donegal.

INSECTS.

Lepidoptera at Armagh.—Last year I picked up a larva of *Lophopteryx camelina* on oak, and a fine specimen emerged last May. From Mr. Halbert's note, *Irish Naturalist*, vol. i., p. 195, I see that it has hitherto only been recorded from the south. It may interest him to know that I took *Zanclognatha grisealis* here in 1889, *vide Ent. Monthly Mag.* (2) vol. i. p. 140. In August *Melanthia ocellata* flew into my house, and on September 23rd, I saw a specimen of *Vanessa atalanta* flying up the road. It was remarkable that this butterfly and *V. cardui* should appear here this year, for it has been about as bad a year as possible for Lepidoptera. I took a specimen of *Stigmanota regiana* in June sitting on the wall of the Cathedral. *Peroneæ* were very scarce. I got only one *P. perplexana*, and a couple of *P. variegana*. Besides these, the only captures worth mentioning are *An-*

chocelis pestacina and *Himera pennaria*. Sugar was a total failure, producing nothing but disappointment, and a dissipated specimen of *Xylophasia monoglypha*.—W. F. JOHNSON, Armagh.

FISHES.

Sharks in Irish Waters.—Mr. W. F. de V. Kane contributes to the *Field* of 10th December, 1892, an interesting article on this subject, giving accounts of the capture of the Great Basking-Shark (*Selache maxima*) off the west coast, and discussing the economic value of the fishery.

BIRDS.

The Birds of Lough Swilly.—Having an intimate acquaintance with Co. Donegal generally, and those parts south and west of Lough Swilly more particularly, I was greatly interested in Professor Leebody's paper on the "Birds of Lough Swilly," but must take exception to his statement (*Irish Naturalist*, vol. i., p. 175), as to Wigeon flying to inland waters at dusk, and to sea or saltwater at dawn. They may do so at Inch, but they do exactly the opposite on the western side of the lough, where often in flight-shooting I have brought down Wild Duck, Teal, and Wigeon, at night on their way *from* Lough Fern to Lough Swilly, and in the morning have frequently seen them return. Within the last few years Cormorants have come in great numbers from Lough Swilly to Lough Fern in the evening. Formerly they did not do so, although there were always a few about the lough, both by day and night. Lough Fern is a sheet of fresh water about one and a-half miles long by one mile broad, some four miles as the crow flies, west of Lough Swilly.—J. H. H. SWINEY, Belfast.

Crossbill (Loxia curvirostra) and Grey Phalarope (Ph. fulicarius) near Mullingar. It may interest readers of the *Irish Naturalist* to know that I shot these birds in November, the latter on Lough Eunell.—J. TAYLOR, Belvidere, Mullingar.

Nesting of the Great Crested Grebe (Podicipes cristatus, L.). To the *Zoologist* for December Rev. Allan Ellison contributes an interesting note on the nesting of this bird at Hillsborough, Co. Down, where several pairs bred last season.

Honey Buzzard (Pernis apivorus, L.) in Co. Wexford. Mr. E. Williams records in the *Zoologist* for December a male Honey Buzzard, shot in the middle of October, in a wood near the town of Gorey.

Bee-eater (Merops apiaster L.) in Co. Wicklow. A female Bee-eater in first year's plumage was shot by Mr. John Graydon on a bog near Delgany. It was one of a flock of six.—E. WILLIAMS (in the *Zoologist* for December).

Snowy Owl (Nyctea scandiaca, Linn.), on Achill Island. In the "Irish Times" of December 14th, Mr. R. Harvey states that he shot a specimen of this rare owl on Achill Island.

MAMMALS.

The supposed Hybrid Hare and Rabbit an English Hare. In the October number of the *Irish Naturalist* (vol. i. p. 147) I described a supposed hybrid between hare and rabbit, which I had received. Mr. Eagle Clarke, of the Edinburgh Museum, has given this specimen careful examination, and finds that it is only *Lepus timidus*—the English Hare, which has been introduced at a few places in Ireland.—ARTHUR J. COLLINS, Belfast.

The Badger (Meles taxus), in Ireland. Various correspondents to the *Field*, in November, 1892, agree in stating that this animal is fairly common in Ireland, though it is unfrequently seen on account of its nocturnal habits.

PROCEEDINGS OF IRISH SOCIETIES.

ROYAL ZOOLOGICAL SOCIETY.

Recent donations to the Gardens comprise a Mongoose from Captain Guiness; Pheasants from F. Norman, Esq., and Mr. Hunt; three Guinea Pigs from J. A. Higgins, Esq., and a Peregrine Falcon from W. Corbett, Esq. Two Seals, a Mongoose, a Racoon, a Carval, and a Porcupine have been acquired by purchase.

4,500 persons visited the Gardens in November.

DUBLIN MICROSCOPICAL CLUB.

NOVEMBER 25th.—The Club met at PROF. E. P. WRIGHT'S.

Wrightia (*Atractylis*) *arenosa*, Wr., was exhibited by PROF. A. C. HADDON. This is a gymnoblastic hydroid, new to Ireland, recently discovered on the west coast.

Nemastoma bacilliferum, Sim., and *Sabacon paradoxus* Sim., were shown by MR. G. H. CARPENTER. These are two curious phalangids collected in the Pyrenees by Dr. Scharff.

Platyarthrus Hoffmanseggii was shown by DR. R. F. SCHARFF, who procured it at Leixlip, Co. Kildare. This crustacean belongs to the woodlouse family (*Oniscidae*), and is an inhabitant of ants' nests. It had not been previously taken in Ireland, but it has occurred in the south of England, France, and Spain. Besides being perfectly white, it is easily distinguished from the other Irish species of woodlice by its club-shaped and flattened antennae.

Cordyceps militaris (var. *sphaerocephala*) was shown by MR. GREENWOOD PIM. It has been sent by Rev. Canon Russell, who received it from Wales. This interesting variety, according to Dr. Cooke's work on Entomogenous Fungi just published, is only recorded from Saxony. Hence this seems to be the first time it has occurred in Britain. It differs from the normal form in having the capitulum more or less spherical instead of clavate, and the conceptacles containing the filiform, asci and spores project considerably, and, being deep red in colour, make this an exceedingly beautiful object with condensed light.

Bacterium rubescens, Lank., was shown by MR. F. W. MOORE, who had observed it in some *Sphagnum* from the Dublin mountains. Its presence in quantity imparts a highly red colour to the *Sphagnum*, even the cell walls being stained. The minute cells of the *Bacterium* are seen to be arranged in various ways under a high power, presenting very beautiful combinations.

Wildmania amplissimum Kjell., was shown by PROF. T. JOHNSON. This seaweed differs from *Porphyra* in being two-layered, as *Monstroma* does from *Ulva*. The plant was collected by the late Dr. D. Moore on the coast of Antrim in 1838. A specimen, in the Trinity College Herbarium, collected in the Orkneys by Pollexfen, was exhibited by Dr. E. P. Wright's permission. Attention was called to another specimen in the Herbarium of Science and Art Museum, and collected by Miss A. Ball at Clontarf. The only record of the plant in Ireland hitherto is by Holmes and Watters, who have seen a specimen from the south-east coast of Ireland. Kjellman founded the genus on plants growing in the Arctic sea. The distribution is thus interesting.

Longitudinal Sections of the Stems of Robinia pseudacacia and Wisteria sinensis were shown by MR. H. H. DIXON. These sections showed the peculiar form of the "slime" masses contained in the sievetubes. Usually near the middle of the tube there is a spindle or barrelshaped body which is suspended in that position by a filament running to each end of the tube. The central body and the filament give the same reactions as the so-called "protoplasmic slime" of typical sievetubes. In some sieve-tubes the "slime" mass lies against one of the plates, while the filament running to the other plate is greatly elongated.

BELFAST NATURAL HISTORY AND PHILOSOPHICAL SOCIETY.

DECEMBER 6th.—The President (PROF. FITZGERALD) in the chair. MR. A. TATE, C.E., submitted his report, as delegate from the Society, to the 1892 Meeting of the British Association. MR. R. LLOYD PRAEGER, M.R.I.A., gave a lecture, entitled "Botanical Rambles in Co. Armagh." A full account of the results of the lecturer's rambles is now appearing in the pages of the *Irish Naturalist*. MR. R. M. YOUNG, M.R.I.A., read a paper, entitled "Antiquarian Notes on Bushfoot and Ballymagarry."

BELFAST NATURALISTS' FIELD CLUB.

NOVEMBER 22nd.—The President (MR. JOHN VINYCOMB), delivered his Opening Address on the subject of "The Origin and Significance of our National Emblems." The Senior Secretary (MR. R. LLOYD PRAEGER) submitted the report of the sub-committee appointed to investigate the glacial gravels of Ballyrudder, near Larne, Co. Antrim. The report gave a detailed account of the interesting bed in question, and lists of the fossils found in the different zones; the following are the conclusions of the sub-committee :—

"The deposits at Ballyrudder consist of a bed of stratified gravels underlying a thick layer of unstratified Boulder Clay. There is no clear line of demarcation between the two beds, the one merging gradually into the other. The fauna of the gravels shows that they were deposited during a period of intensely arctic conditions. The gravels represent a former shore-line, which a subsequent submergence has covered with marine Boulder Clay. The clay, and all the zones of the gravels yield flints derived from the Chalk. These are frequently broken, and flakes and core-like objects are the result. The flakes are usually quite shapeless, and only one was found by the committee bearing a bulb of percussion. None of the flints found bore any character which might lead the sub-committee to suppose that they were formed by human hands."

MR. WM. GRAY, M.R.I.A., then presented his report as a delegate from the Club to the 1892 Meeting of the British Association, dealing particularly with the destruction of native plants and birds' eggs, and the work of the ethnographical and geological photographs committees.

MR. JOSEPH WRIGHT, F.G.S., then made some remarks on rare local foraminifera recently found, of which he exhibited diagrams. He said that on the dredging cruise which the Club had some years ago in the steam-tug "Protector," one of the hauls was taken in deep water, a hundred fathoms, about midway between Belfast and Portpatrick. This material, which has only recently been examined microscopically, has yielded a large number of foraminifera, several of them being rare and interesting species; the most noteworty are *Technitella legumen*, *Hyperammina arborescens*, *H. elongata*, very large in size, *Webbina clavata*, and *W. hemispherica*. The last of these is a very simple organism, of great rarity, and hitherto only known from three specimens—one fossil from the Sutton Crag, the other two from dredgings taken by Messrs. Norman and Robertson, off the Durham coast. In a dredging recently taken by a member, Mr. Hamilton M'Cleary, in Strangford Lough, no fewer than eighty-five different species of foraminifera were obtained, two of them, *Ammodiscus shoneanus* and *Discorbina parisiensis*, being very rare forms.

DUBLIN NATURALISTS' FIELD CLUB.

NOVEMBER 15th.—DR. E. J. M'WEENEY, President, in the chair. PROF. A. C. HADDON, M.A., gave an account, illustrated by lantern views, of his visit to the Aran Islands with Dr. C. R. Browne, for the purpose of ethnological research. The physical characters, dress, occupations, and habits of the people of the island were described with much interesting detail. Rev. M. H. Close, Dr. C. R. Browne, Mr. J. Shackleton, and Mr. H. Wigham, took part in the discussion.

Mr. T. Chandlee exhibited models, made by himself, of a cromlech at Glanworth, Co. Cork, and of a stone cross at Moone Abbey, Co. Kildare.

Armagh Natural History and Philosophical Society.

November 21st.—Rev. W. F. Johnson, President, in the chair. The President gave his Annual Address on "The History of the Society," in which he traced the course of the Society from its first origin in October, 1839, to the present day.

December 5th.—The President in the chair. After the ordinary business had been concluded, the President exhibited a case of British Butterflies. Among these was a North American species, *Danais archippus*, which Mr. Johnson informed the meeting was endeavouring to establish itself in the south of England, after spreading from Canada to the Amazons, and across the Pacific Islands to New Zealand, Tasmania, and Norfolk Island.

Cork Naturalists' Field Club.

November 2nd.—The President, Prof. M. M. Hartog, D.Sc., in the chair. The Secretary gave an account of negociations carried on with various committees with the object of obtaining for the club space in the Crawford Municipal Buildings in which to form a museum. The matter had not been finally arranged, and further meetings were to take place.

Prof. Hartog then gave his Inaugural Address, entitled the "Life of a Cell," dealing with the formation and gradual development of the cell in vegetable and animal tissues, illustrating by numerous diagrams, and by the manipulation of pieces of dough, the various shapes assumed, the manner of absorbing food, and the curious process of cell-division.

November 16th.—The President in the chair. The Secretary stated that the use of a large corridor in the Crawford Municipal Buildings had been granted to the club for museum purposes.

Mr. G. Foster read a paper entitled, "Scale Wings," in which he treated the subject of our butterflies and moths very fully, giving details of each group, the likely food-plants on which to find the larvæ, and the best modes of catching and rearing them. He illustrated the paper with a large number of specimens collected by himself, including *Bupalus piniaria* from Co. Wicklow, believed to be the second recorded capture in Ireland, also *Mamestra persicariæ* from Co. Down, a very rare moth in Ireland.

Mr. Copeman (Hon. Sec.), also exhibited a box of insects collected du ing the club excursions.

December 7th.—Mr. D. J. O'Mahony, in the chair. Mr. J. Sullivan gave a paper on "Rare Irish Lichens." Having dealt very carefully with the structure, classification, and means of identification of these interesting plants, he exhibited and described a large number of specimens, being a selection from 159 new species added to the flora of Cork since the publication of Dr. Power's work on that subject in 1844. Many of the specimens shown are quite new to Ireland. Mr. Sullivan also showed a list of the new species which he is preparing for publication in the *Irish Naturalist*. At the close of the paper a discussion took place, and many questions were asked relative to the collecting, preserving, and identifying of these lowly, though, in many cases, beautiful and interesting plants, all of which were fully answered by Mr. Sullivan.

Limerick Naturalists' Field Club.

December 13th.—This Club was organised at a meeting held at the rooms of the Protestant Young Men's Association, when twenty-five members were enrolled, and the following officers were elected:—President, Mr. Murray; Vice-President, Dr. Fogerty; Hon. Trecasurer, Mr. Stewart; Hon. Secretary, Mr. F. Neale.

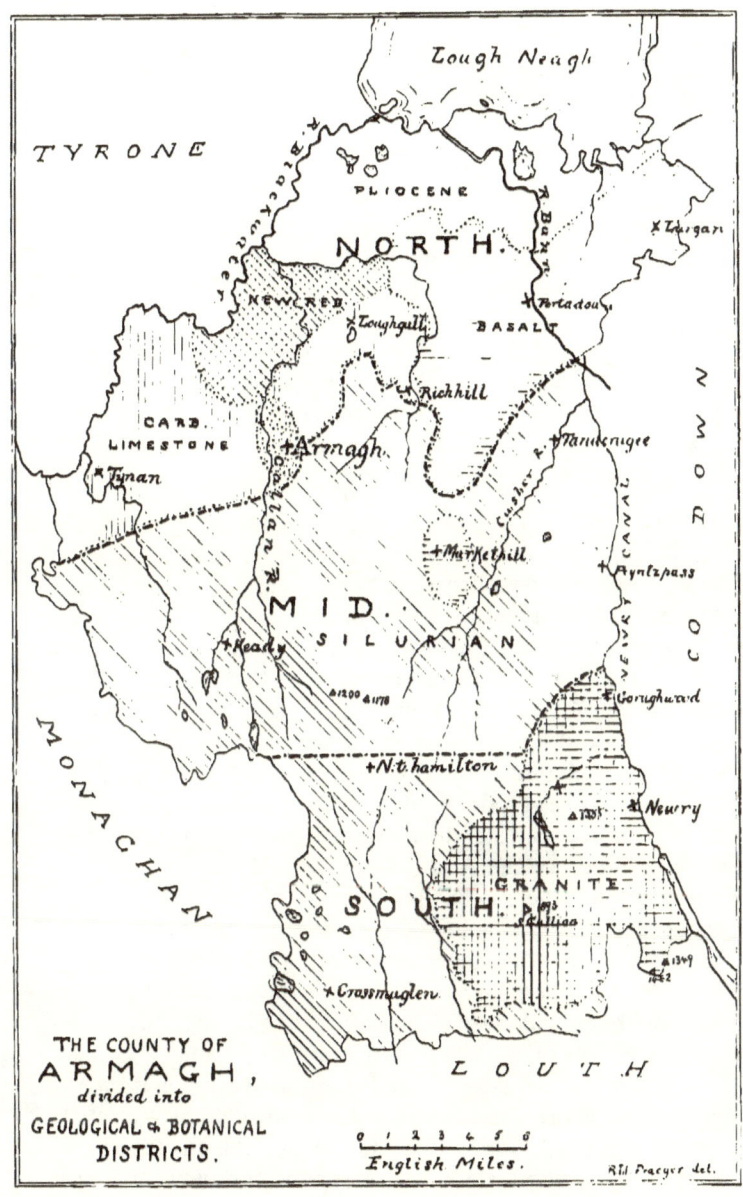

The Irish Naturalist.

VOL. II.　　　　FEBRUARY, 1893.　　　　NO. 2.

AMERICAN BIRD-VISITORS TO IRELAND AT HOME.

BY W. E. PRAEGER, OF KEOKUK, IOWA.
(Associate Member American Ornithologists' Union).

I. THE AMERICAN ROBIN (*Turdus migratorius*).

THE capture of an American Robin in County Dublin was recorded in the *Irish Naturalist*, April, 1892 (vol. 1 page 4). There is some probability that the example in question may have escaped from confinement, but as no evidence is forthcoming on the point, the bird is entitled to the benefit of the doubt. While the Robin is one of those that would be likely kept as a cage-bird, being nearly omnivorous, and of attractive appearance, and exceptional vocal powers; yet, on the other hand, it is so abundant on the American continent, performs such extensive migrations, and is at the same time able to endure such extremes of temperature, that if American land-birds ever do cross the Atlantic—and some undoubtedly do— the Robin would be one of those most likely to accomplish the journey.

The Robin is the most abundant, conspicuous, widely distributed, and best known of the North American thrushes. It is distributed all over the continent, but migrates out of the more northern portions in winter. It has no very near allies on the eastern side of the Rocky mountains, but on the Pacific coast there are several species not distantly related; none of these are likely ever to reach Ireland in a wild state, though individuals have crossed the continent and been obtained on the East coast.

In the locality in which I am situated, the Robin is a abundant migrant and summer resident, and an occasional winter resident; indeed Robins have been known to remain much farther north, and to endure even the rigours of a Dakota winter without apparently suffering; but such cases are rare. If the weather be mild, a few Robins are likely to be seen with us during February. However, it is not till the middle of March that they really arrive; the first warm south wind after the 10th of that month is sure to bring them. Where there were no birds the day before, now from every grove of trees can be heard the Robin's cheerful notes, and on every lawn from which the snow has hardly melted, they are busy in the pursuit of the early worm.

In his exquisite description of an American spring, the author of the "Biglow Papers" says:—

> "Then gray hossches'nuts leetle hands unfold
> Softer'n a baby's be at three days' old;
> That's Robin-redbreast's almanick; he knows
> That arter this ther's only blossom-snows;
> So, choosin' out a handy crotch an' spouse,
> He goes to plast'rin' his adobë house."

For the benefit of Irish readers it should be explained that "adobë," is the dried earth of which houses in Mexico and some of the south-western States (where there is a partly Mexican population) are built. Mud, indeed, enters largely into the composition of the Robin's nest. The nest is that of a typical thrush, consisting of the three layers seen in the Blackbird's or Missel-thrush's nest, and it is somewhat between the nest of those two in structure; there are more sticks than in a Blackbird's, and less moss and wool than is usually found in a Missel-thrush's. In building, the rough outer framework is put up first, then the layer of mud is put in, and then the finer lining of roots and grass, much as in the two Irish species already mentioned. The nest is placed in the fork of a tree, or on a horizontal bough, usually at between ten and twenty feet from the ground; it is better concealed than a Missel-thrush's, being among the thinner branches where there are more leaves. The trees with which the streets of our American cities are lined are favourite breeding-places for these birds, and it is thus common in our streets through the summer. On a July evening, after the first brood of young had left their nests, I once counted twenty-seven Robins on a single tennis-court which was quite surrounded by houses.

The eggs of the Robin are four or five in number, and of a very beautiful pure greenish-blue, unspotted, their average size being about the same as Blackbirds' eggs.

The Robin's food consists chiefly of insects and worms; especially in the spring and summer months, when the young are still in the nest, the numbers of grubs destroyed by these birds is enormous, and the benefit to agriculture almost incalculable. It is doubtful if a young Robin ever indulges in any vegetable diet. When in the nest, the birds seem actually to require more than their own weight of food daily to keep them in good health; a nestling Robin has been known to eat as many earthworms in twelve hours as laid end to end, would measure fourteen feet. But grubs, caterpillars, grasshoppers, and beetles, probably form a greater part of their diet than earthworms, as in the hot summer the ground is mostly too hard and dry to obtain the latter. In the autumn, berries and fruits form a considerable part of the bird's food.

A curious part of the Robin's life-history, only recently noticed by naturalists, is its habit of forming large "roosts" in the late summer and autumn. These "roosts" are often frequented by thousands, or even tens of thousands of birds which come from all the surrounding country to spend the night together. The reason of this habit is not fully understood yet, if it ever will be; but it seems to be formed, at a time when the females are busy with their second broods, by the males and young of the first brood, which thus meet every night in some convenient and safe thicket for mutual protection.

The song of the Robin consists of but few notes, but these are strong, pure, and singularly buoyant and cheerful, and are the most welcome to me of all the voices of the American spring; the bird also utters a "cluck-cluck" as it flies from the lawn to take refuge in the nearest tree; both in flight and on the ground, the movements and attitudes of the bird are noticeably like those of the Irish Blackbird.

That the Robin not only looks a bold and powerful bird, but can take good care of himself and nest, was proved by a fight between one and a marauding Blue-jay, witnessed by a friend of mine, in which the Jay was left a corpse in the field, or rather tree of battle, and the skin of the vanquished afterwards added to my own collection.

The Robin bears no resemblance to any British bird, further than the Thrush family-likeness. The red breast, black head, white throat, grey back, with darker wings and tail, are very distinctive. The female differs but little from the male, but the young, when they first leave the nest, are more brown, with the breast spotted.

IRISH ENTOMOLOGY.

BY W. F. DE V. KANE, M.A., F.E.S.

UNTIL quite recently we have been almost wholly indebted for any published information on the subject of Irish Entomology to English naturalists. For although Haliday made some collections of Diptera and Coleoptera, chiefly in Ulster ; and Tardy, Greene, and Bristow, of Lepidoptera in Wicklow, and Mrs. Battersby in Westmeath, and Mr. Fetherston-H, in Mayo, yet their captures were not at all comparable to the results of the labours of Birchall, Bouchard, Wollaston, Barrett, and numerous occasional collectors, who from time to time crossed the Channel to test the capabilities of this country for supplying English museums and private collections.

Of late years, however, a recrudescence of zeal in this branch of natural history has been displayed by Irish naturalists, and a host of contributions have swelled the lists in the pages of entomological serials. But our knowledge is still scanty in nearly all the groups, and unfortunately it cannot be said to rest upon reliable data, for the earlier collections, notably those of Tardy and Birchall, have disappeared, or been merged with British ones, so that in most cases it is now impossible to refer to their original specimens. It is also undeniable that a large amount of error has crept into the lists published from time to time, owing to the acceptance of unreliable statements without enquiry. One of the latest of these lists of Irish captures appeared in the *British Naturalist* of December, 1889, on the authority of Mr. Gregson of Liverpool, whose name should be a sufficient voucher for scientific accuracy. This list purports to be a record of Mr. Curzon's captures in Ireland during the preceding season. It so happens, however, that I have letters and data of Mr. Curzon, which throw some doubt on the authenticity of the list. I think Mr. Gregson must have fallen into the error of taking for granted that all the insects in Mr. Curzon's boxes were Irish. It is very probable that English larvæ and pupæ may have accounted for some of the specimens, as was the case with Mr. Curzon's collections both in 1890 and 1891. I should much like to know did Mr. Curzon correct and authenticate the list which Mr. Gregson compiled before publication? The capture of *Hecatera chrysozona*, *Anchocelis rufina*, *A. litura*, *Hadena protea*, *Ephyra linearia* and *Ennychia cingulata* would be interesting if Mr. Curzon would state the localities and number of specimens of these species he took.

However, as I have a disclaimer written by Mr. Curzon of the capture of another of the species noted, it shows the necessity of greater caution in accepting second-hand evidence.

I may mention that the *Dianthœciæ* taken by him were not exclusively from Howth, as stated by Mr. Gregson, but partly from Galway. In addition I would call attention to what I believe to be an erroneous record of *Epunda lutulenta* in Co. Antrim, contained in a later paper by Mr. Gregson in the same journal of May, 1890. The larvæ sent from that locality were of *E. nigra*, as Mr. Gregson at first rightly suspected, and I saw imagines bred from them; but the ova of *E. lutulenta* sent him subsequently in September were from a wholly different locality, namely Sligo. His description of the larvæ of the latter rare moth is, therefore, valuable, and if he can supplement it, which I hope is the case, with a record of the ultimate results, and what varieties of the imago he obtained, it would be of much interest. Mr. Curzon told me that, in his experience, the greater proportion of his *E. nigra* larvæ never completed their metamorphosis, dying in numbers from some inexplicable cause when almost full-fed. In the case of a large number he took again in 1891, none came to perfection. Was this the case with Mr. Gregson's larvæ of *E. lutulenta*? In writing the above criticisms, my chief object is to appeal to Irish naturalists to assist in the work of verifying our lepidopterological data, by making collections *with localities marked on their labels*. The condition and setting are of minor importance. If these were from time to time sent to the Science and Art Museum in Dublin, or to myself for identification, it would secure accuracy. The researches of Mr. J. F. X. King, of Glasgow, into our Neuroptera have much advanced the study of this group, and I am glad to find increasing interest developed in that of our Lepidoptera. Unfortunately the more prolific fauna of Great Britain tempts our entomologists to neglect that of their own country, and the want of respectable quarters in our out-of-the-way districts hinders systematic exploration. Nevertheless it is extremely probable that very valuable results still await the more careful examination of our marshes, coasts, and woodlands. From time to time I hear reports of insects having been seen or taken, but not preserved, which warrant the belief that most interesting additions still await us. Meanwhile let us have no more doubtful or careless items foisted upon our record to puzzle and confound our speculations as to the origin and development of our indigenous fauna. Although extremely interesting from a scientific point of view, Ireland is not rich enough to tempt the regular visits of the professional collector. A few occasionally drop down upon Howth to secure a few *Dianthœcia barretii*, but Mr. Meek's unprofitable venture some years ago in the Co. Kerry is not forgotten. We are thus left to our unaided resources, a matter not wholly without its advantages, and Ireland still offers virgin tracts for exploration, and it is to be hoped that her sons and daughters will increasingly add to our store of knowledge in this branch of natural science.

THE FLORA OF COUNTY ARMAGH.

BY R. LLOYD PRAEGER, B.A., M.R.I.A.

(*Continued from page* 15.)

DURING the course of my observations, I endeavoured to trace variations in the flora corresponding with differences of petrological conditions, hoping that I would find on the Tertiary basaltic area, plants characteristic of Antrim and Derry; on the Carboniferous Limestone, species of the limestone plain; on the Silurians, a repetition of the Co. Down flora; and on the granite hills, a similarity to the flora of the Mourne mountains. Some of my expectations were fulfilled, others were not; but Armagh may certainly be divided into several botanical regions, defined by physical or geological conditions, and characterised by the presence or absence of certain plants. (See Map, Plate 2.)

1. LOUGH NEAGH AND RIVERS.—Includes shores of Lough Neagh, and the banks of the Bann, Newry canal, Blackwater, and Ulster canal. *Cicuta, Œnanthe fistulosa, Butomus*, and *Sagittaria* are abundant throughout these waters, all of which are in direct connection with Lough Neagh, and with the exception of a single station for *Cicuta*, none of the species mentioned are found in any other lakes or rivers in the county. A group of much rarer plants occurs at and about Lough Neagh only—*Ranunculus cincinatus, Typha angustifolia, Potamogeton filiformis, Calamagrostis hookeri.*

2. NORTHERN BOGS.—Embraces the extensive bogs that cover the district, chiefly Pliocene, lying south of Lough Neagh, from Maghery to Ardmore Point. Confined to this district, and occurring in some abundance therein, are *Drosera anglica, D. intermedia, Vaccinium oxycoccos, Rhynchospora alba, Osmunda regalis.* These bogs have an elevation of fifty to a hundred feet; among their rarer plants are *Andromeda polifolia, Vaccinium vitis-idæa, Spiranthes romanzoviana, Listera cordata. Ulex gallii* is conspicuously absent.

3. LIMESTONE REGION.—Includes the area of Carboniferous Limestone that stretches from Richhill and Castlerow westward through the city of Armagh to Benburb and Middletown, and also the patch of New Red Sandstone which adjoins to the northward, and which yields a similar flora. Surface low and undulating. *Carduus acanthoides, Veronica anagallis, Lamium album, Orchis pyramidalis, Juncus glaucus, Briza media*, are characteristic of this district, most of them being abundant here, and all very rare in, or absent from the rest of the county.

4. SILURIAN REGION.—The lower Silurian grits extend over the whole of the central portion of the county. Surface well tilled, undulating, and hillocky, rising to 1,200 feet near Newtownhamilton (the Fews mountains), cultivation being carried nearly to the summit. Its flora is uninteresting generally, but it was in this region that *Carex rhynchophysa* was obtained. *Lepidium smithii*, unknown further north, is common on this area. *Linaria vulgaris* becomes much more frequent; *Ulex gallii* haunts the neighbourhood of the higher grounds; *Veronica anagallis* and poppies are conspicuously absent.

5. HILL REGION.—Includes the granite and basalt hills of the south-east, and the adjoining portion of the Silurians in the south-west. The hills are somewhat isolated, with flat stretches of poor land between. There is, as before remarked, a poverty of mountain plants, *Selaginella spinosa* being the only species confined to the higher grounds. Compared with the northern bog district, we find *Ulex europæus* replaced by *U. gallii*, and *Myosotis palustris* by *M. repens*. The higher cultivated ground is full of *Raphanus raphanistrum*, *Lotus major*, *Chrysanthemum segetum*, which are not abundant north of the Silurian area. *Viola tricolor*, *Teucrium scorodonia*, *Jasione montana*, *Lepidium smithii*, are also characteristic plants. The fine mountain mass of Slieve Gullion is disappointingly poor in highland species. The following is a list of the plants observed on the summit (1,893 feet):—*Potentilla tormentilla*, *Galium saxatile*, *Vaccinium myrtillus*, *V. vitis-idæa*, *Calluna*, *Erica cinerea*, *Empetrum*, *Luzula erecta*, *L. maxima*, *Juncus squarrosus*, *Eriophorum vaginatum*, *Scirpus cæspitosus*, *Carex pilulifera*, *C. binervis*, *Aira flexuosa*, *Agrostis canina*, *Festuca ovina*, *Nardus*, *Lastrea dilatata*.

The Tertiary basalts of the north-east appear to effect no change in the flora. This is accounted for by the fact that the characteristic plants of the Antrim and Derry basalts are all, or almost all, hill plants, flourishing on the steep escarpments which fringe the plateau. The low fertile surface of the basalt in Armagh furnishes no habitat for these.

The shores of the estuary of the Newry River yield, of course, a group of maritime species not found elsewhere in the county. Of these *Beta maritima*, *Obione portulacoides*, and *Lepturus filiformis*, are the only plants worthy of note.

While the lists which follow have no claim to be considered exhaustive, for it is not possible to examine five hundred square miles of ground in three weeks, I believe they convey, nevertheless, a pretty accurate idea of the nature and extent of the flora of Co. Armagh; and while there can be no doubt that additional stations will in time be found for a number of the rarer plants, I do not anticipate that more than thirty or thirty-five species will ultimately be added to the flora of the county. I am well aware that the brambles, roses, willows, and pondweeds require further study, and in the sedges there are yet still some blanks to be filled. Among the plants which are still unrecorded from the county, a few of the most likely are *Arabis hirsuta, Hypericum elodes, Geranium lucidum, Gentiana campestris, Salix repens, Habenaria bifolia, Hymenophyllum wilsoni;* the first four of these may be expected in the limestone district.

A few rare species recorded from the county I failed to re-find. Of these, several have (or had) their habitat on the shores of Lough Neagh. There can be little doubt that the drainage works, completed about 1855, which reduced the mean level of the lake by some three feet, and the winter floods to a greater extent, are the cause of the disappearance of some of these previous inhabitants. To this change is probably due the apparent absence now of *Subularia aquatica, Elatine hydropiper,* and *Pilularia globulifera,* and I am inclined to set down to the same cause the disappearance of *Lathyrus palustris, Cladium mariscus, Carex elongata,* and *C. filiformis,* on the adjoining Antrim shores of the lough, and possibly also of *Carex buxbaumii,* and of *Calamagrostis hookeri* in some of its stations.

Of the plants enumerated in the lists which follow, 104 are additions to the flora of District 10 of "Cybele Hibernica":—

Ranunculus peltatus.
R. circinatus.
Papaver argemone.
P. dubium.
Fumaria pallidiflora.
F. densiflora.
F. muralis.
Sisymbrium thalianum.
Cochlearia officinalis.
C. danica.
Diplotaxis muralis.
Silene noctiflora.
Sagina maritima.
Arenaria serpyllifolia.
A. leptoclados.
Cerastium tetrandrum.
Spergularia rubra.
S. media.
Scleranthus annuus.
Hypericum dubium.
Radiola linoides.
*Trifolium hybridum.
Rubus plicatus (var).
R. rhamnifolius.

R. nemoralis (var.)
R. villicaulis.
R. lindleianus.
R. macrophyllus (var.)
R. salteri.
R. pyramidalis.
R. leucostachys.
R. mucronatus.
R. anglosaxonicus.
R. borreri.
R. drejeri.
R. radula.
R. scaber.
R. rosaceus.
R. coryllifolius.
†Rosa rubiginosa.
Myriophyllum spicatum.
Sedum anglicum.
*S. rupestre.
Apium graveolans.
Daucus carota.
Torilis nodosa.
Chærophyllum temulum.
Galium mollugo.

Aster tripolium.
Anthemis nobilis.
‡Matricaria chamomilla
Arctium majus.
*Crepis nicæensis.
Jasione montana.
Myosotis repens.
Linaria vulgaris.
L. repens.
‡Mentha piperata.
Lamium amplexicaule.
L. intermedium.
Stachys arvensis.
Glaux maritima.
Statice bahusiensis.
Armeria maritima.
Plantago coronopus.
P. maritima.
Sueda maritima.
Beta maritima.
Salicornia herbacea.
Atriplex erecta.
A. deltoidea.
A. hastata.
A. babingtonii.
Obione portulacoides.
Polygonum lapathifolium.
*Humulus lupulus.

Euphorbia exigua.
Callitriche autumnalis.
Salix alba.
S. smithiana.
Spiranthes romanzoviana
Triglochin maritimum.
Juncus maritimus.
J. gerardi.
Typha angustifolia.
Sparganium natans.
Eleocharis multicaulis.
Scirpus maritimus.
S. tabernæmontani.
S. fluitans.
S. savii.
Carex dioica.
C. vulpina.
C. rhynchophysa.
Schlerochloa maritima.
S. distans.
S. rigida.
Hordeum pratense.
Lepturus filiformis.
Chara polyacantha.
C. hispida.
C. vulgaris.
C. contraria.
Nitella translucens.

Of the above, three were first gathered in the county by Mr. Lett; eight more go to the credit of Mr. Johnson; one is added by Rev. G. Robinson; and the remainder are the result of my own collecting.

Among the more interesting plants which I found in the county are *Carex rhyncophysa*, which is an addition to the British flora; *Spiranthes romanzoviana*, whose only other European station is in Co. Cork; *Calamagrostis hookeri*, which in Britain is found only around the Lough Neagh shores, where it is now extremely rare; *Rubus nemoralis, R. lindeianus, R. anglosaxonicus, R. borreri, R. drejeri, R. scaber*, and **Crepis nicæensis*, are additions to the Irish list; while *Fumaria densiflora*, ‡*Diplotaxis muralis*, *Silene noctiflora*, *Lepigonum rubrum*, *Galium mollugo*, *Chaerophyllum temulum*, *Linaria repens*, *Typha angustifolia*, and *Potamogeton filiformis*, have in Ireland a very limited number of stations.

(TO BE CONTINUED.)

THE EARTHWORMS OF IRELAND.
BY REV. HILDERIC FRIEND, F.L.S.
(Continued from page 10.)

THE genus *Allolobophora* is represented in Great Britain by some fifteen species. I shall, however, treat half-a-dozen of them under the more expressive and accurate designation of *Dendrobæna*, or tree-worms, thus leaving about half-a-score for discussion under this head. So large a group is certain to present a considerable variety of forms, and by a systematic study of each species it is possible to separate the genus into two or three well-marked groups, thus enabling the student the more readily to identify the various forms. Before we proceed to this subdivision, however, it will be desirable to obtain a clear idea of the genus as a whole.

It was exactly twenty years ago that Eisen, after a very exhaustive study of the worms of Scandinavia, decided to split up the old genus *Lumbricus* into three. He retained the earlier name for the genus discussed in the first part of my paper; and adopted two new names for the genera he had separated therefrom. These names, if they lack meaning at first sight, and when studied independently of their history, are found to be very expressive when their origin is recalled. As I have already pointed out, the genus *Lumbricus* is readily recognised by the complete mortise and tenon arrangement of the head. Some worms, however, were seen to have the lip but partially dovetailed into the first segment or prostomium, and they were at once set apart as "the worms with a different head," or in scientific language, *Allolobophora*. One or two worms again, had not only a different head from that which characterised *Lumbricus*, they had further a differently shaped tail and differently placed male pores from both *Lumbricus* and *Allolobophora*, and so merited the name of "the worms with a different tail" or *Allurus*. The genus *Dendrobæna* was an afterthought, and the name was invented to express the fact that the worms so named inhabited decayed trees and timber.

Thus, while the genus *Allolobophora* agrees with *Allurus* in the manner in which the lip is inserted or imbedded in the first ring, it differs from that genus in the shape of the tail and the position of the male pores. Again, while some of the species belonging to the genus *Allolobophora* closely resemble the true *Lumbrici*, they may always be distinguished by the shape of the hinder part of the lip, or its mode of insertion.

It may be well to give an outline of the leading characters of the genus. In *Allolobophora* the lip or prostomium only partially bisects, or is dovetailed into the first ring or peristomium (see page 10, fig. 2). The setæ are arranged in four pairs on each segment except the first, the individuals of each couple being either close together or somewhat widely separated. The girdle or clitellum is composed of a variable number of segments—as few as four, and as many as eight or ten in the British species (even more in some Continental forms), commencing on the 26th or some more posterior segment. The clitellar papillæ (*tubercula pubertatis*) are variable, being sometimes on alternate, and at others on contiguous segments. They may appear either as pores, as in the Green Worm (*A. chlorotica*, Savigny), as a distinct band, or as prominent but continuous protuberances. One species (*A. profuga*, Rosa), forms a connecting link between this genus and the last, for it has the head of an *Allolobophora*, with the typical girdle and band of a *Lumbricus* as already figured (page 10, fig. 3). The male pores are on segment 15 as in *Lumbricus*, and are, I think, without exception accompanied by papillæ. The colour-range is very much greater than in the other genus; we have green, steel-blue, clay, flesh, rose-red, red-brown, sienna-brown, and brindled forms, to mention no others. As a rule there is little if any iridescence. The first dorsal pore is either between segments 3-4 or posterior to this. Spermathecæ are absent, or variable in number. Some of the species, notably the Green Worm (*A. chlorotica*, Savigny) carry spermatophores. This general outline will suffice for present purposes, a full tabular statement being reserved for a later stage.

Our next business is to ascertain how the different species included in the genus are related, and what characters are best suited for separating the whole into a few natural groups. The work would be comparatively easy if we had to include the European species with those which are indigenous to Great Britain (all of which have now also been sent to me from Ireland). As it is, we have one or two instances in which well-defined groups are represented in these islands by only a solitary species, and thus the sections may be made almost as numerous as the species. This, however, in the present state of things cannot be avoided.

The characters by which groups may be formed are very various. Habitat doubtless affects species very largely, and I shall have to deal somewhat fully in another paper with this topic. At the same time there is a certain amount of constancy in the disposition of the setæ, the position of the first dorsal pore and the girdle, the arrangement of the papillæ, the colour, the presence or absence of turbid fluid, the shape of the body and other external features, to merit attention. Rosa has pointed out also that there is ground for improving our system of classification by observing the way in which the *receptacula seminis* open from within outwards. In fact, so long ago as 1884, in his valuable little work on the Earthworms of Piedmont, he divided this genus, including *Dendrobæna*, into four groups, solely on the strength of this important character. Since then our knowledge has increased, and new worms have been added to our lists, so that the analysis of the genus which Rosa adopted only partially answers our purpose. So far as it goes, however, it does not at all clash with that which I shall follow in the present instance.

So far as we are able at present to tabulate our indigenous worms, the genus *Allolobophora* falls naturally into four well marked groups. Two of these groups have hitherto been represented in Great Britain by a solitary species in each instance. A third has only one representative in England, though two species belong to Ireland, while the fourth boasts five British species. In the following arrangement I shall simply extend that which I first submitted to the public in the *Essex Naturalist*, July, 1892.

GROUP I. **Lumbricoidea.**

The worms of this group are large, and closely resemble *Lumbricus*, so closely, in fact, as to have misled even Eisen himself, though he had been the pioneer of systematic helminthology. They are usually dark in colour, but may become lighter under the influence of their environment; the setæ are in four couples, the individuals of which are nearly close together. The body is cylindrical in front and flattened behind, showing that the worm is wont to lie exposed from its burrow just as the Common Earthworm does. The first dorsal pore is usually well back, while the male pores are on papillæ. They exude a slimy mucus when irritated, but no watery or turbid fluid, no coloured or pungent liquid. Usually found in rich soil, either arable or pasture, and not averse to manure; they reach their greatest dimensions in fat garden soil.

When found in lawns and meadows they are addicted to burrowing and making large worm-casts on the surface of the soil. The solitary British species is widely distributed.

GROUP II. Disjuncta.

In this group the most striking feature is to be found in the disposition of the setæ. As in the genus *Dendrobœna*, they form eight more or less equi-distant rows. The British worms resemble *Lumbricus* in the arrangement of the band (*tubercula pubertatis*) on the ventral sides of the girdle, but differ from that genus in the shape of the lip-insertion. The body is cylindrical in front, and somewhat octangular behind, owing to the arrangement of the setæ. The male pores are on papillæ on the fifteenth segment, and Rosa remarks that "I *receptacula seminis* sono in direzione della 3a setola."[1] A small quantity of yellow fluid is exuded from the posterior or anal extremity when the worm is irritated, and the smell of garlic or some similar vegetable seems to pertain to the animals, as is the case with some of our univalves. They are not averse to poor, heavy soil in England, being most frequently found in ploughed land which is rough, uncultivated, and cold.

GROUP III. Mucida.

Worms of medium size, exactly halfway between the true earth-worms and the tree-worms (*Lumbricus* and *Dendrobœna*), form the third natural group. They do not resemble either genus, however, in any other particular. The colour is very variable, and ranges from a delicate fleshy tint, through dull clay colour, to dirty green or yellow. The setæ are in close couples, and the worms are cylindrical throughout. The first dorsal pore is usually about the four-fifth or five-sixth inter-segment. All exude mucus, which in some cases is thick, leaving a granular sediment, and disagreeable. They are not favourites with the angler and do not as a rule frequent rich soil. They are found under stones, in woods, or on the margins of ponds and ditches, and sometimes in arable or pasture land, especially in localities which are too poor for the more epicurean *Lumbricus*. As they are not usually found lying half exposed from their burrows, the hinder part is not flattened, this being a device for gripping the burrow. These form Rosa's second group.

GROUP IV. Virgata.

Under this heading I include the species which constitute the first group in Rosa's classification. My own system is intended to show the connecting links between the genus *Lumbricus* on the one hand and the genus *Dendrobœna* on the other; and this is done in more ways than one. There is a beautiful gradation to be observed in size, colour, shape, arrangement, and disposition of parts, habits, and habitats, and the like, between the two extreme points, when studied systematically, as here presented. In the present group we find worms of which the principal types are banded. They exude coloured fluid, their setæ are wider apart than in the foregoing, and "I *receptacula seminis* si aprono lantano delle

---

[1] "The spermathecæ open in the direction of the 3rd row of setæ" (counting from below upwards).

setole presso alle linea mediana dorsale."[1] The species affect rich, decaying manure and vegetable matter, and even haunt decaying trees like the true *Dendrobænæ*.

It is but right to state that each of these groups more or less overlaps the other, so that no hard and fast line can be drawn between them; but the characters given are such as to make their identification very simple and easy. Every system breaks down if pressed too closely, and even among earthworms we find that Nature takes no freaksome leaps, but progresses on regular and well-marked lines.

I purpose in my next paper taking the four groups of worms here specified in the order in which they stand, beginning with that which has the nearest affinities to the old mothergenus. This is the more desirable as up till the present time the lumbricoid species of *Allolobophora* have been persistently confused with the true earthworm (*Lumbricus*), resulting in the greatest possible chaos in the nomenclature and diagnoses of our terrestrial annelids.

(TO BE CONTINUED.)

THE
MACRO-LEPIDOPTERA OF THE LONDONDERRY DISTRICT.
BY D. C. CAMPBELL.

(*Continued from page* 22).

NOCTUÆ.

Demas coryll, Linn.—Common in the woods on the shores of Lough Swilly.

Acronycta psi, Linn.—Common.

A. rumicis, Linn.—Common. We reared many of the beautiful larvæ of this moth. We noticed a strange habit of the larva. Having partially formed its cocoon on the side or in the corner of a box, it descended to the mould below and attached its threads to many small particles of earth, it then ascended again, and, ensconsing itself in the cocoon, drew up the little particles around it by means of the threads. I have watched the process from beginning to end.

Diloba cæruleocephala, Linn.—Larvæ very abundant on the stunted blackthorn on Magilligan sandhills. We never found it in any other locality.

Leucania littoralis, Curt.—Not uncommon at Magilligan; a few specimens inland.

L. impura, Hüb. } Common.
L. pallens, Linn. }

[1] "The spermathecæ open near the setæ in the region of the median dorsal line" (almost on the centre of the back).

Tapinostola fulva, Hüb.—Common. We took some beautiful varieties of a bright brick-red colour. We took the larvæ in the root-stems of the Cotton-grass and succeeded in rearing many specimens. We published full description of the larvæ in the *Entomologist*, November, 1883.

Hydrœcia nictitans, Bork.—Rather rare.

H. micacea, Esp.—Common.

Axylia putris, Linn.—Common.

Xylophasia rurea, Fab. ⎫
X. lithoxylea, Fab.   ⎬ Common.

X. monoglypha, Hufn.—Very common; the black variety occurs but not commonly.

Charæas graminis, Linn.—Common. Mr. Milne carefully observed this species and noticed that the males fly in large numbers in the early morning while scarcely a female is to be seen, and that on the other hand the females abound at night when hardly a male is to be seen. I suppose the females, after spending the night upon the wing, rest upon the herbage in the morning when the males are flying.

Cerigo matura, Hufn. One specimen taken at Giant's Causeway.

Luperina testacea, Hüb.—A few specimens.

Mamestra albicolon, Hüb.—One specimen at Magilligan.

M. furva, Hüb.—A few specimens at Ballynagard.

M. brassicæ, Linn.—Common.

Apamea basilinea, Fab. ⎫
A. gemina, Hüb.   ⎬ Common.

A. leucostigma, Hüb.—We always found this species at Ragwort flowers. We found it abundant only in certain seasons, usually alternate years. We took many beautiful varieties.

A. didyma, Esp.—Very common. We took some abnormal varieties which Mr. Birchall identified for us.

Miana strigilis, Clerck ⎫
M. fasciuncula, Haw.   ⎬ Common.
M. literosa, Haw.   ⎭

M. bicoloria, Vill.—Rather rare.

M. arcuosa, Haw.—This species was not included in Mr. Birchall's list. We took a few specimens at the Giant's Causeway, also a few here at Ballynagard. Mr. Milne has also taken it here.

Celæna haworthii, Curt.—Common in the bogs. We took the larvæ in the root-stems of the Cotton-grass, and published description in *Entomologist*, November, 1883.

Stilbia anomala, Haw.—Common on the coast: Giant's Causeway, Magilligan, and Buncrana.

Caradrina alsines, Brahm—Rather rare.

C. quadripunctata, Fab.—Very common.

C. morpheus, Hufn.—One specimen at Magilligan.

Agrotis vestigialis, Hufn.—Common on the Derry and Antrim coasts.

A. suffusa, Hüb.   ⎫
A. saucia, Hüb.   ⎬ Common.
A segetum, Schiff.   ⎟
A. exclamationis, Linn. ⎭

A. corticea, Hüb.—One specimen.
A. nigricans, Linn.—Occurs, but not commonly.
A. tritrici, Linn. ⎫
A. cursoria, Bork. ⎬ Very abundant at Magilligan.
A. præcox, Linn. ⎭
A. aquilina, Hüb. ⎫ Both species at Magilligan.
A. obelisca, Hüb. ⎭
A. agathina, Dup.—Not common; we succeeded in rearing some beautiful specimens by keeping the larvæ in a large flower pot, covered with gauze, in the open air.
A. strigula, Thunb.—Common.
Noctua glareosa, Esp.—Fairly common.
N. augur, Fab. ⎫
N. plecta, Linn. ⎬ Common.
N. c-nigrum, Linn. ⎨
N. brunnea, Fab. ⎭
N. triangulum, Hufn.—One specimen reared from larvæ.
N. festiva, Hüb.—Fairly common.
N. dahlii, Hüb.—Common at Magilligan and on Lough Swilly shores.
N. umbrosa, Hüb. ⎫
N. baia, Fab. ⎬ Common.
N. xanthographa, Fab. ⎭
Triphæna ianthina, Esp. ⎫
T. fimbria, Linn. ⎬ Common.
T. comes, Hüb. ⎨
T. pronuba, Linn. ⎭
Mania typica, Linn.—Rare. We reared one specimen from a larva. Mr. Milne has taken it once or twice.
M. maura, Linn.—A few specimens.
Pachnobia rubricosa, Fab.—Rare.
Tæniocampa gothica, Linn.—Common.
T. incerta, Hufn. ⎫ Common.
T. stabilis, View. ⎭
T. populeti, Fab.—One specimen from pupa.
Orthosia iota, Clerck—Rather rare.
O. macilenta, Hüb. ⎫ Common.
Anchocelis pistacina, Fab. ⎭
Cerastis vaccinii, Linn.—Common.
Scopelosoma satellitia, Linn.—Common.
Xanthia fulvago, Linn.—Common.
X. flavago, Fab.—Common. Mr. Milne took a beautiful variety, with the forewings of a uniform brick-red colour.
X. circellaris, Hufn.—Common.
Calymnia trapezina, Linn.—Not common.
Dianthœcia capsophila, Dup.—Very common on Lough Swilly shores, and on coasts wherever *Silene maritima* grows.
D. capsincola, Hüb.—A few specimens from larvæ at Lough Swilly.

Dianthœcia cucuball, Fues.—A few larvæ on *Silene inflata,* at Inch, Lough Swilly.

D. nana, Rott.—Common on Antrim coast at Portrush and Ballycastle, also at Magilligan.
We found *D. capsophila* very abundant on the Lough Swilly shores, and *D. nana* rare, whereas we found the latter abundant on Antrim coast, and *D. capsophila* rare.

Polia chi, Linn.—Common.

Epunda lutulenta, Bork.—One or two specimens.

Misella oxyacanthæ, Linn.—Common.

Agriopis aprilina, Linn.—Two specimens from pupæ.

Phlogophora meticulosa, Linn.—Common at ivy-bloom. We only once took a specimen of the June brood.

Euplexialucipara, Linn.—Common.

Aplecta occulta, Linn.—One specimen.

Hadena adusta, Esp.—Fairly common.

H. glauca, Hüb.—Rare. In 1879, we sent Mr. Birchall a very light-coloured variety. This species was not in Mr. Birchall's list. Mr. Kane reports it from Co. Westmeath.

H. dentina, Esp.—One specimen at Magilligan.

H. dissimilis, Knoch. ⎫
H. oleracea, Linn. ⎬ Common.
H. thalassina, Rott. ⎭

H. pisi, Linn.—Rather rare.

Xylocampa areola, Esp.—Common.

Calocampa vetusta, Hüb. ⎫ Common.
C. exoleta, Linn. ⎭

Cucullia umbratica, Linn.—Common.

Gonoptera libatrix, Linn.—Common.

Habrostola tripartita, Hufn.—Rather rare.

H. triplasia, Linn.—Common.

Plusia chrysitis, Linn. ⎫
P. festucæ, Linn.
P. iota, Linn. ⎬ Common.
P. pulchrina, Haw.
P. gamma, Linn. ⎭

P. interrogationis, Linn.—Local. We took both larvæ and imagines abundantly at Kilderry, some six miles from Derry.

Euclidia mi, Clerck—Very common on Magilligan sandhills.

Heliothis scutosa, Schiff.—My brother took a single specimen, flying in the sun, about 4 p.m., 19th August, 1878, near Buncrana, Lough Swilly. Mr. Birchall identified the insect, and wrote to us on 19th September 1878:—" Yours is, so far as I know, the first authentic British specimen; at least, all the previous ones have been doubted." The food plant, *Artemisia campestris,* grows on the shores not far from the spot where the specimen was caught. If any brother naturalist wishes to try for this very rare species, I shall be happy to direct him to the exact locality.

Anarta myrtilli, Linn.—Common.

(TO BE CONCLUDED.)

DENUDATION AT CULTRA, CO. DOWN.

BY MARY K. ANDREWS.

(*Concluded from page* 18.)

(Read before the Belfast Naturalists' Field Club, December 20th, 1892.)

ENCROACHMENTS of the sea, similar to those described, have taken place on the adjacent coast. Although no landmark survives, it is estimated that within living memory the sea has advanced more than 150 feet at Cooper's Bay, near Holywood; and Cooper's Green, once a favourite resort for rural games, has now, with part of an inner adjoining field, completely disappeared.

In confirmation of the foregoing notes it is interesting to trace the changes recorded on successive maps of the Ordnance Survey. On the six-inch map, surveyed and engraved in 1834, we find both the quarry at Cultra Point and the road leading to Cultra Quay, while on the same map, revised in 1858 and engraved in 1860, Cultra Point has a more smoothed and rounded appearance, the quarry is no longer marked, and all traces of the road are gone.

A comparison of successive Admiralty charts gives indications of somewhat similar interesting changes in Belfast Lough. In the chart for 1883, corrected up to 1891, the three-fathom line (close to the end of the new cut recently opened in continuation of the Victoria Channel) is more than 800 feet nearer to Belfast than in the chart for 1841, corrected up to 1856. Within the same period the three-fathom line has also approached more closely to Holywood and to Carrickfergus.[1]

As geological structure has an important bearing on the rate of erosion, it is necessary now to consider more closely the nature of the strata near Cultra. The first rocks that crop out on the beach a little north of Holywood belong to the upper mottled sandstone of the Bunter formation; further east, near the low cliff in the illustration, we find reddish-

---

[1] Mr. Moore (Harbour Office, Belfast) kindly drew my attention to the changes on the Ordnance maps, and to the approach of the three-fathom line towards Belfast, indicated on successive Admiralty charts. This latter observation has been confirmed by Mr. S. A. Stewart, F.B.S.E., who further observed the general advance of the sea towards Holywood and Carrickfergus.

brown, grey, and yellow sandstones, passing up into thinly bedded micaceous, rippled sandstones, and sandy marls referred to the Lower Keuper series of the midland counties of England.[1] The strata near Cultra Point are traversed by trap dykes, striking out to sea, which have greatly indurated the sandstone.

The Triassic rocks, overlain by Post-Tertiary gravels, extend round the curve of the bay till, about 200 yards south-west of Cultra Pier, a fault brings up the Lower Carboniferous shales.[2] A little east of the pier interesting beds of magnesian limestone are visible near to low water-mark. These were first described by Dr. Bryce, F.G.S., in 1835,[3] and from the evidence of the fossils they contain, were referred both by him[4] and by Professor King[5] to the Permian system.

All these strata are traversed by trap dykes, mostly small; a considerable one, however, occurs near Cultra Pier, where it has greatly indurated the shale, and converted it into flinty slate and hornstone rock.[6]

Here then, at the points where the strata are most hardened and altered, the resistance has been the greatest, while along the intervening curve of the bay where the cliff is softer, it has fallen an easier prey to denuding forces. But the difference, as we have seen, is only one of degree; the whole area has receded rapidly before the wasting influences to which it has been exposed.

The sandstones and shales could offer but feeble resistance to the action of the sea, and small landslips have hastened the destructive work. Winds and currents have aided, more especially under certain conditions. A strong southerly wind increases largely the rise of tide in Belfast Lough, and often blows at night accompanied with rain. If the wind then veer round to east or north-east a strong ground-swell sets in and undermines portions of the cliff, already loosened by rain and other sub-aerial agents. The material thus dislodged is

---

[1] Geol. Survey Memoir to sheet 29, p. 19.
[2] Ibid.
[3] *Jour. of the Geological Society of Dublin*, vol. i., part 3.
[4] Report of the British Association for 1852.
[5] Ibid.
[6] I have to thank Mr. S. A. Stewart, F.B.S.E. for his kindness in examining specimens of the altered shale.

drawn away in large quantities as the tide ebbs, with the sand and gravel of the bay.¹

As very complete sections of Triassic strata are laid open in Cheshire, it may be interesting before concluding to give an example of the denudation to which they have been subjected.

Mr. Woodcock informs me that at Hilbre Island, off the north-west side of Cheshire, the formation exposed belongs to the pebble beds of the Bunter series. Although at low water easily approached from the mainland, Hilbre Island is at high tide exposed to the full sweep of the waves. The result of the action of the sea, aided by subaerial agents, such as sand-charged wind, rain, spray, frost, and heat, has been to wear down and wear back the land area, so that what was originally a tongue of land stretching out into the sea is now three islets. The process of denudation which has separated them is at present distinctly operating upon the larger one, so that at its south-east end a small portion has become totally detached and this at high water forms another islet smaller than the rest.

I have only to add that much of the low cliff around Cultra Bay is now concealed behind a strong sea wall, which, for years to come, may offer effectual resistance to the inroads of the waves. We may regret the picturesqueness it has marred, the interesting spots now covered over, but we cannot close our eyes to the necessity of preserving the land, nor to the important bearing which the alteration of a coast-line may have on the maintenance of a harbour.

We have glanced at the apparent destruction of a small land surface, we have seen its materials loosened, disintegrated, falling a prey to the energy of waves and currents, but the destruction is not ultimate. The sea not only grinds down, it sorts and arranges the fragments and lays them down to form new strata on its floor. Consolidation and ultimate upheaval will surely follow, but the processes by which these stages in the earth's architecture are effected remain obscure. We await further light, satisfied if we have illustrated one small link in that marvellous cycle of order and change traceable throughout the whole Geological Record.

---

¹ I am indebted to Mr. James Shannon, boatman, Holywood, for the above information. He has further observed that the water in Cultra Bay has, within his own memory, become decidedly deeper.

PROCEEDINGS OF IRISH SOCIETIES.

ROYAL ZOOLOGICAL SOCIETY.

Recent donations include a Badger from W. A. Robinson, Esq.; four Rabbits from Master Moloney; a Squirrel from W. Despard, Esq.; a Goat from W. Dick, Esq.; and a Syrian Rat from H. Napier, Esq. Two Black Swans have been acquired by exchange.

DUBLIN MICROSCOPICAL CLUB.

DECEMBER 15th.—The Club met at DR. E. J. M'WEENEY'S, who showed—

Sections of the Swimming Bladder of Barbels affected with disease due to the presence of parasitic Protozoa. The wall of the bladder contains numerous small cyst-like cavities, stuffed with peculiar boat-shaped bodies, psorosperms of parasitic Protozoa belonging to the class Myxosporidia. These arise in the interior of the shapeless masses of amoeboid protoplasm which constitute the fully-developed parasite. The nuclei of the sarcode-mass arrange themselves in groups of three; each of these groups becomes surrounded by a wall, and forms a psorosperm. Two of the nuclei are symmetrically placed at one end of the psorosperm and give rise to the so called pole-capsules; the other occupies a mesial position towards the other end. When the psorosperm germinates, this latter nucleus creeps out, with a little protoplasm, in an amoeboid form and coalesces with others to form the huge, shapeless, perfect condition of the parasite. The specimens exhibited had been kindly sent by Dr. L. P. Peiffer of Weimar, the greatest European authority on parasitic Protozoa. Special attention is being at present directed to them as the probable producers of cancer.

Sections of Carinopora hindei, a polyzoan from the Devonian rocks of Ontario, lent by Dr. G. J. Hinde, F.G.S., were shown by PROF. COLE. This genus resembles a *Fenestella* with greatly developed keels along the ribs, indicating how *Hemitrypa* may have arisen by an extreme extension of this structure, intermediate genera being now known.

Triticella bœckii, G. O Sars, a species of Polyzoa new to Britain, was exhibited by MR. J. E. DUERDEN. The species was founded by G. O. Sars, who obtained specimens from Christiana Sound growing on the carapace and appendages of *Geryonis tridentis*, and this is the only locality from which it has been recorded up to the present. In his description of *Triticella korenii*, Sars, in the "British Marine Polyzoa," p. 546, Hincks mentions that it is possible *T. bœckii* may occur on our coasts, and he therefore gives one of Sars woodcuts of its shape. On examining the crustaceans obtained from Berehaven by the Royal Irish Academy Survey in 1885 a specimen of *Portunus depurator* was found with its eye-stalks and front carapace almost entirely covered with *Triticella*. On examining these under the microscope it was at once seen that they were different from *T. korenii*, which has been found very abundantly on the west coast of Ireland. They agreed fully with the figure and characters of *T. bœckii* given by Hincks, and with the more detailed description given by Sars himself in the *Forhandlinger Videnskabs-Selskabet, Christ.* for 1873. The west coast of Ireland has proved itself very rich in forms belonging to the rare and peculiar polyzoan family *Triticellidæ*, being the only place in Britain from which *Triticella bœckii*, Sars, has been recorded. *Hippuraria egertoni*, Busk, is only known to science from one locality—namely Berehaven. *Triticella korenii*, Sars, has been found by him abundantly, and more rarely *T. pedicellata*, Alder. Both these latter species have only previously been recorded from one British locality each.

Prof. Johnson's exhibit at the November meeting (*Irish Nat.* vol. ii, p. 26) should have been described as follows:—*Wildmania miniata*, f. *amplissima* Fosl. (*Diploderma amplissimum*, Kjell). This sea-weed differs from *Porphyra* in being two-layered, as *Ulva* does from *Monostroma*.

Proceedings of Irish Societies.

BELFAST NATURAL HISTORY AND PHILOSOPHICAL SOCIETY.

JANUARY 3rd.—The President (PROF. FITZGERALD) in the chair. MR. WM. GRAY, M.R.I.A, gave a lecture on "The Tracings of Primitive Man in the North of Ireland." MR. S. F. MILLIGAN, M.R.I.A., exhibited some Irish and Mexican antiquities.

BELFAST NATURALISTS' FIELD CLUB.

DECEMBER 20th.—The President in the chair. MR. EDWARD MCCONNELL communicated a paper entitled, "Notes on New Zealand Geology." MISS M. K. ANDREWS communicated a paper on "Denudation at Cultra, Co. Down," which appears in full in the *Irish Naturalist* for this and last month. MR. R. LLOYD PRAEGER, contributed "Local Botanical Notes, 1891 and 1892," exhibiting specimens of each plant mentioned. Among the recent additions to the flora of district 12 which were shown were *Ranunculus circinatus*, *Barbarea praecox*, *Poterium sanguisorba*, *Rubus chamaemorus*, *Hieracium hibernicum* (new species), *H. friesii* var. *stewartii* (new variety), *H. rubicundum*, *H. euprepes* (not previously recorded from Ireland), and *Carex aquatilis*. New stations in district 12 were mentioned for *Papaver hybridum*, *Hypericum dubium*, *Agrimonia odorata*, *Ligusticum scoticum*, *Myosotis collina*, *Typha angustifolia*, *Carex limosa*, and *Chara contraria*.

DUBLIN NATURALISTS' FIELD CLUB.

DECEMBER 13th.—PROF. HADDON in the chair. PROF. W. J. SOLLAS, F.R.S., exhibited a fine series of Volcanic Rocks from Co. Waterford, and gave an account of them illustrated by views and sections shown in the optical lantern (a paper on the subject will shortly appear in the *Irish Naturalist*). Rev. M. H. Close, Prof. Cole, and Mr. W. W. Watts took part in the discussion which followed. PROF. COLE showed a series of rhyolites from Hungary for comparison with the Waterford specimens.

MR. G. H. CARPENTER showed a live water-spider (*Argyroneta aquatica*), which he had received from Mr. Milne, of Londonderry.

MR. J. M. BROWNE showed beetles from the Aran Islands, including *Thiamis suturalis* (new to Ireland), and *Calathus melanocephalus* var. *nubigena* (a northern and alpine form).

MR. J. J. DOWLING showed, in the lantern, photographs of the junction of the granite with the Ordovician schist at Killiney bay.

MR. H. L. JAMESON showed a weevil, *Cionus thapsus*, and a rove-beetle, *Quedius cruentis*, from Loughgilly, Co. Armagh, both new to Ireland.

MR. J. N. HALBERT showed *Malachius bipustulatus* from Lucan (see *Irish Naturalist*, vol. i., p. 125).

MR. W. F. DE V. KANE showed *Testacella scutulum* from Kingstown, a new locality for this slug. He also exhibited a most remarkable melanic variety of *Spilosoma lubricipeda* from Yorkshire.

JANUARY 10th.—DR. E. J. M'WEENEY, President in the chair. This was the Annual General Meeting, and the report and statement of accounts were submitted and adopted. The following officers were elected for 1893:—President, Dr. M'Weeney; Vice-President, Dr. R. F. Scharff; Hon. Secretary, J. M. Browne, B.A.; Hon. Treasurer, Prof. T. Johnson, D. Sc.

CORK NATURALISTS' FIELD CLUB.

JANUARY 18th.—The President, PROF. M. HARTOG, in the chair. An interesting account of the Faroe Islands was given by the Hon. Secretary, MR. W. BENNETT BARRINGTON.

ROYAL IRISH ACADEMY.

NOVEMBER 14th.—A paper by MR. A. BELL was communicated, entitled "Notes on the Correlation of the Later and Postpliocene Tertiaries on either side of the Irish Sea, with a reference to St. Erth Valley, Cornwall." This paper contains a valuable comparison of the shells from the Wexford gravels and other Irish deposits with those from beds of approximately the same age in England.

A paper by REV. H. FRIEND, describing a new species of earthworm, *Allolobophora hibernica*, was communicated. This worm will be noticed in Mr. Friend's papers on the "Earthworms of Ireland" in the *Irish Naturalist*.

DECEMBER 12th.—PROF. HADDON and DR. C. R. BROWNE, gave a paper on the "Ethnography of the Aran Islands," and PROF. HADDON a paper entitled "Studies in Irish Craniology—the Aran Islands." He will lay some of his results before the readers of the *Irish Naturalist* in an article shortly.

A paper by REV. H. FRIEND described another new worm (*Lumbricus papillosus*) from Ireland. It was noticed in the *Irish Naturalist* for January.

ROYAL DUBLIN SOCIETY.

NOVEMBER 16th.—PROF. T. JOHNSON read a paper describing a new Irish alga, *Pogotrichum hibernicum* (see *Irish Naturalist*, vol. i., pp., 5 and 6). He considers it possible that this plant may however prove identical with *Litosiphon alliariæ*.

MR. G. H. CARPENTER read a supplementary report on Pycnogonida from Torres Straits, collected by Prof. Haddon.

DECEMBER 20th.—PROF. W. J. SOLLAS read a paper "On Pitchstone and Andesite from Tertiary Dykes in Donegal." He considers these dykes of Tertiary age, as they are similar to those of Arran. The pitchstone consists of a glass containing crystals of augite (which become smaller towards the edge of the dyke) and crystallites of an unknown mineral. The augite-andesite is crowded with glass.

The same author also gave a paper on the "Variolite and Associated Igneous Rocks of Roundwood, Co. Wicklow." This is a new locality for the interesting rock variolite. It has undergone great fissuring, believed to be due to the diminution of volume caused by the formation of epidote. The alteration of augite into chlorite in volcanic rocks is discussed; this change leads to expansion and the liberation of quartz, and this gives rise to the association of chlorite with quartz so often observed in veins.

MR. H. H. DIXON read a paper "On the Germination of Seedlings in the absence of Bacteria." Seeds whose outer coats had been sterilized did not decay after growth had ceased, but remained apparently unchanged for more than twenty months.

PROF. HADDON and MISS SHACKLETON contributed "Descriptions of new species of Actiniæ from Torres Straits."

NOTES.

BOTANY.

PHANEROGAMS.

Ranunculus petiolaris in Ireland.—In the *Journal of Botany* for December, Rev. E. S. Marshall writes that a specimen of buttercup in the British Museum, collected on the shore of Lough Bofin, Drumod, Co. Leitrim, on 30th May, 1871, by Mr. Dyer, appears to belong to this new species, though it approaches *R. flammula* somewhat closely. Irish botanists will do well to be on the look-out for this plant, which very possibly occurs in Ireland.

New Hawkweeds from Ireland. In the *Journal of Botany* for September, Mr. F. J. Hanbury, F.L.S., describes as a new species—*Hieracium hibernicum*, Hanb.—an interesting plant found by Mr. H. C. Hart, first in the Mourne mountains, and subsequently in Donegal, and, at the time, referred to a form of *H. argentum*. *H. eriniihiforme*, Backh., var. *hartii*, Hanb., is a new variety found by the same energetic botanist on Slieve League, Co. Donegal, and published in *Journal of Botany* for June, 1892. In the December number of the same journal, Mr. Hanbury describes as a new variety—*H. friesii*, Htn., var. *stewartii*, Hanb.,—a plant obtained by Messrs. Stewart and Praeger at Tollymore Park, and Hilltown, Co. Down; this form is enumerated in their paper on the Botany of the Mourne mountains, recently read before the Royal Irish Academy, as *H. friesii*, var. *latifolium*, to which it was at first referred by Mr. Hanbury.

The Flora of Rathlin Island.—In 1884 Mr. S. A. Stewart submitted to the Royal Irish Academy a report on the botany of this island, which lies several miles off the coast of Co. Antrim, and is an outlier of the basaltic plateau of the north-east of Ireland. Previous lists of the Rathlin flora had been published by Dr. Marshall (*Trans. R.I.A.*, 1837) and Miss Gage (*Nat. Hist. Review*, 1870), both being more or less incomplete. Perhaps the most important point in Mr. Stewart's report, which included 318 flowering plants and higher crytogams, was a negative result—the contradiction of Miss Gage's record of *Eriocaulon septangulare*. In 1889 I added a few plants to Mr. Stewart's list as the result of a three-days' visit to the island in the spring of that year (*Proc. B.N.F.C.*, 1889-90). They were *Brassica campestris*, *Raphanus raphanistrum*, *Drosera rotundifolia Honkeneja peploides*, *Cerastium tetrandrum*, *Alchemilla arvensis*, *Rubus idaeus*, *Scandix pectenveneris*, *Aster tripolium*, *Veronica scrpyllifolia*, *Populus tremula*, *Luzula maxima*, *Scirpus caespitosus*, *Carex praecox*, *Equisetum arvense*, *E. maximum*, *Lastrea dilatata*, *Botrychium lunaria*, as well as eight others which had certainly been intentionally or accidently introduced. Three other plants—*Veronica scutellata*, *Beta maritima*, and *Scilla verna*—which were noted in Miss Gage's list, but not observed by Mr. Stewart, I refound on the island. Last spring a second visit to Rathlin resulted in a few further additions to its flora—*Torilis nodosa*, *Veronica buxbaumii*, *V. hederifolia*, *Scirpus lacustris*, and *Carex disticha*. My friend Mr. Stewart has long been of opinion that the Tree Mallow, *Lavatera arborea*, is an original native of our maritime rocks, and on my second visit to Rathlin I obtained important confirmation of this point. The western and north-western portion of the island is fringed with huge cliffs topped by uncultivated and uninhabited heaths. Several isolated sea-stacks rise out of the water at a distance of some hundreds of feet from the shore. On one of these, a lofty rock called Stackaniskan, about a hundred feet in height, our guide—Paddy Morrison, the professional cliff-climber of Rathlin—pointed out to me a large clump of a tall plant growing in an inaccessible situation near the summit, which, he said, had "a wee pink flower, grew nowhere else on the island, and produced a seed on which the sea-birds fed"—the last statement being promptly contradicted by his brother-in-law, who accompanied us. With the aid of a glass, I made out the mysterious plant to be undoubtedly *Lavatera*, and I had no doubt in my own mind that it was perfectly indigenous there, as I do not see how it can have possibly been introduced to such a station—unless the sea-birds carried it! It grows sparingly also on the cliffs of the island, but I did not observe it in any cottage gardens in Rathlin.—R. LLOYD PRAEGER.

ZOOLOGY.

INSECTS.

Coleoptera at Ardara, Co. Donegal.—I was at Ardara from July 6th till August 12th. I found it a fairly-good locality for Coleoptera. There is great diversity of surface; mountain, lowland, estuary-shore, and coast-sandhills. The last-named locality proved about the best, but as it entailed a ten-mile walk, I could not visit it as often as I could have wished. The following are my captures:—*Carabus clathratus*, a pair on mountain among cut turf; *C. catenulatus*, common on mountain; *C. granulatus*, a handsome green form; *Nebria gyllenhalii*, *N. brevicollis*, *Notiophilus biguttatus*, *N. substriatus*, *N. palustris*, *N. aquaticus*, *Elaphrus cupreus*, *E. riparius*. These *Elaphri* I got on the estuary-shore and on the sandhills, but they were not plentiful, and none appeared on the edges of the lakes, which is their usual locality here. *Harpalus latus*, *H. œneus*, *Pterostichus madidus*, *Pt. versicolor*, *Pt. minor*, *Pt. gracilis*, *Pt. strenuus*, *Pt. vulgaris*, *Pt. nigrita*, *Pt. striola*, *Pt. vitreus*. The last-mentioned occurred freely on the mountain, under stones and bits of turf. *Amara plebeia*, under stones on the estuary-shore and on mountain; *A. aulica*, *A. communis*, *Anchomenus albipes*, *A. parumpunctatus*, *A. gracilipes*, I only obtained one specimen of this rare *Anchomenus* under stones on the estuary-shore. *Bembidium atrocœruleum*, *B. mannerheimi*, *B. bipunctatum*, *B. pallidipenne*, of this I took a few on the sandhills when looking for *Bledii*. On the mountain I took a single specimen of a *Bembidium*, which appeared to me most to resemble *B. schuppeli*; but Canon Fowler, to whom I referred it, considers that it is not that, though near it. *Trechus minutus*, *T. rubens*, a single specimen on the estuary-shore; *Loricera pilicornis*, *Olisthopus rotundatus*, *Clivina fossor*. I had hoped to get some *Dyschirii* on the sandhills with the *Bledii*, but found them very scarce, and only succeeded in obtaining a few *D. politus*. *Calathus cisteloides*, *C. micropterus*, *C. fuscus;* the latter two on the sandhills at roots of *Ammophila*. The *Halipli* were represented only by the two common species *H. ruficollis*, and *H. lineatocollis*. Pools and lakes on the mountains produced a good many *Hydradephaga*, but I was unable to find *Dytiscus lapponicus*, which was taken in Donegal many years ago by Mr. Somerville. The following are those I took:—*Hydroporus lepidus*, *H. lituratus*, *H. pubescens*, *H. morio*, *H. nigrita*, *H. obscurus*, *H. erythrocephalus*, *H. gyllenhalii*, *H. palustris*, *Agabus bipustulatus*, *A. sturmi*, *Rhantus exoletus*, *Dytiscus marginalis*, *Acilius sulcatus*, *Gyrinus natator*, *G. minutus*. This last was common on the mountain lakes. *Sphaeridium scarabæoides*, *Hydrobius fuscipes*. *Anacæna limbata*, *A. globula*, *Helophorus œneipennis*, *Laccobius sinuatus*, *Philhydrus melanocephalus*, I got a number of this species in a little pool choked up with *Sphagnum* on the mountain. *Cyclonotum orbiculare*, *Cercyon flavipes*, *C. lateralis*, *C. unipunctatus*, *C. melanocephalus*, *C. hæmorrhoidalis*, *Megasternum boletophagum*, *Aleochara fuscipes*, *A. lanuginosa*, *Homalota vestita*, *H. analis*, *H. longicornis*, *H. atramentaria*, *H. aterrima*, *Tachinus rufipes*, *T. marginellus*, *T. luticollis*, *Tachyporus nitidicollis*, *T. hypnorum*, *Quedius cinctus*, *Q. tristis*, *Philonthus succicola*, *Ph. politus*, *Ph. varians*, *Ph. agilis*, *Ph. quisquiliarius*, *Ph. puella*, *Ocypus cupreus*, *O. morio*, *Stenus juno*, *S. tarsalis*, *S. latifrons*, *Bledius arenarius*, *B. pallipes;* these were burrowing in the sandhills; the latter was much the most numerous. *Platystethus arenarius*, *Oxytelus laqueatus*, *O. tetracarinatus*, *Homalium rivulare*, *Necrophorus ruspator*, *N. mortuorum*, in a dead crow on the mountain; *Silpha rugosa*, *S. subrotundata*, *Anisotoma calcarata*, *Cercus rufilabris*, *Brachypterus pubescens*, *Meligethes viduatus*, *M. œneus*, *Cytilus varius;* *Coccinella vii-punctata*, *C. xi-punctata.*; both plentiful on the sandhills. *Geotrupes stercorarius;* I was much disappointed at meeting with no other exponent of this family, for I fully expected to get *G. vernalis* on the sandhills. *Aphodius rufipes*, *A. fimetarius*, *A. depressus*, with red elytra; *A. fœtidus*, *A. ater*, *A. rufescens*, common and varying a good deal in colour *A. lapponum*, with red elytra; dead specimens of *Anomala frischii* were frequent on the sandhills, but I did not meet with it alive. *Serica brunnea* was of course abundant on the sandhills. *Athous hæmorrhoidalis*, *A. niger*, a single specimen in the Rectory grounds. *Agriotes obscurus*, *Cryptohypnus riparius*, *C. dermestoides*, on estuary-shore, under stones. *Corymbites cupreus*, *Adrastus limbatus*, *Telephorus bicolor*, *Rhagonycha fulva*, *Anobium domesticum*, *Donacia sericea*, *D. discolor*, Panz. (comari, Suffr.), at Killystewart Lough, which is about 300 feet above sea-level. *Chrysomela staphylea*, *Phædon tumidulum*, *Crepidodera transversa*, *Longitarsus luridus*, *L. jacobææ*, Wat.; *L. suturalis*, *L. lævis*, *Cyphon variabilis*, *Helodes minuta*, *Apion bohemanni*, *A. apri-*

cans, A. viciæ, A. flavimanum, A. loti, A. cruentatum, A. violaceum ; Otiorhynchus sulcatus, A. atroapterus ; Philopedon cinratus, a large and very white form ; *Sitones tibialis, S. regensteinensis ; Nanophyes lythri*, plentiful on the Purple Loosestrife ; *Hypera polygoni, H. plantaginis, H. nigrirostris, Mecinus pyraster, Poophagus sisymbrii, Rhinoncus pericarpius.*

I took altogether 166 species, but this cannot be regarded as more than a sample of the species there, for I was there at a bad time for Coleoptera, viz., July and August, and of course had to discover the localities that were suitable, not always an easy task in a strange place.—W. F. JOHNSON, Armagh.

The Pine Saw-Fly (Lophyrus pini) in the North of Ireland. In September, 1891, Mr. W. H. Patterson and I observed a colony of larvæ about an inch in length, and of a pale green colour, with a row of ten to twelve black spots on each side, and glossy brown heads, busily engaged in devouring the leaves of an Austrian Pine (*Pinus austriaca*) at Sydenham, two miles from Belfast. Specimens were submitted to Mr. Edward Saunders, who identified them as the larvæ of the Pine Saw-fly, *Lophyrus pini.* Mr. W. F. de V. Kane having informed me that Co. Wicklow was the only Irish record for this species that he had previously known of, I wrote to the local press with the hope of obtaining further information as to its existence in the north of Ireland. As a result, Mr. William Hanna, of Antrim-road, Belfast, wrote me that about three years before, a great swarm of caterpillars attacked a pine in his garden, devouring almost every leaf on the tree. He kept some of them till they reached the pupa stage, and one of the cases he enclosed in his letter; this pupa-case, my friend Mr. G. H. Carpenter tells me, is certainly that of *Lophyrus pini.* Neither at Antrim-road, nor at Sydenham, has the species re-appeared. In September last, in the plantations of the Cave Glen, at Craigavad, near Holywood, I found a small colony of larvæ on an Austrian pine which were certainly identical with those found at Sydenham. We have thus three recent occurrences of this destructive, but happily rare insect, near Belfast: possibly this note may elicit information as to its appearance in other localities in Ireland.—R. LLOYD PRAEGER.

MOLLUSCA.

Spirula, Ianthina, and Velella at Lough Swilly.—In the *Irish Naturalist*, vol. i., p. 195, it is stated that I wrote to the *Zoologist* that these mollusca were washed up at *Portsalon*, Lough Swilly. It was at *Carrablagh* they were washed up, in the bay below my house. Portsalon is the name of the Post Office, a mile up the lough—a rocky coast where such a circumstance could not occur.—H. C. HART, Carrablagh, Co. Donegal.

Our New Planorbis, P. riparius, West.—In reference to Mr. Milne's note in the *Irish Naturalist*, vol. i., 1892, I may mention that the leading characters of the shell of *Planorbis riparius*, West. are as follows:—Shell very much flattened, finely striated, three to three and a-half whorls, the last very wide, with blunt keel, umbilicus large, all whorls being visible; breadth, 3-3½ mm. Its very wide umbilicus distinguishes it at once from *Pl. fontanus* and *Pl. nitidus.* In general appearance, indeed, it is more like a large *Pl. crista*, L., but there is no trace of the ridges on the whorls which are so characteristic of that species.—R. F. SCHARFF, Dublin.

Marine Mollusca of Killala Bay.—In the current number of the *Journal of Conchology*, Miss Amy Warren contributes a highly interesting article on the marine shells found on the shores of the bay of Killala, on the borders of Mayo and Sligo. Though the list is the result of shore-gathering only, it includes 183 species, some of them of great rarity; and as no list of the Mollusca of the district has been previously published, the record of even the commoner species add to our knowledge of their distribution. Annotations on the habitats effected by the littoral species shows a commendable amount of minute observation on the part of the authoress, and we are pleased to observe the name of Mr. J. T. Marshall standing as sponsor for the determination of the more critical forms; where rare or critical forms are concerned, reference to a recognised authority is highly desirable, and adds greatly to the confidence with which the announcement of discoveries is received. Among the rarest species which Miss Warren records from Killala Bay are *Lepton clarkiæ, Montacuta ferruginosa* (perfect), *M. dawsoni, Trochus duminyi, Rissoa proxima, Homalogyra rota, Odostomia warreni, O. nitidissima, Utriculus expansus, Philine angulata, P. nitida*. We trust that this able lady-conchologist will continue her labours, and that we shall learn more from her pen of the interesting marine fauna of the west coast.

BIRDS.

The Antarctic Sheathbill (Chionis alba) in Ireland.—In the *Zoologist* for January, Mr. R. M. Barrington records a specimen of this bird, shot at the entrance to Carlingford Lough on 2nd December. This species is an inhabitant of the islands lying off the southern portion of South America, and has not previously occurred in Europe. To what extent its long journey of 7,000 miles may have been aided by man's intervention is a point not easily determined.

Occurrence of the Little Bustard (Otis tetrax, L.) in Kerry. I have received from Mr. N. N. Darcy a fine specimen of the Little Bustard, which was shot on the 30th of December last, near Ballyduff, Co. Kerry, and is, I believe, the fifth example of this rare bird which has been obtained in Ireland.—JAMES TANK, Dublin.

MAMMALS.

Breeding of the Squirrel (Sciurus Vulgaris), and Otter (Lutra Vulgaris).—Mr. Barrett-Hamilton (*Irish Nat.* vol. i. p. 127), enquired about the breeding of the Squirrel and the Otter. With regard to the Squirrel. I can only say that I have met with the young in June. The Otter has come more under my scope of observation. Last May I received a present of a dead Otter to get mounted. I dissected it, and found it in young—it was an adult female—and there were three or four embryos fairly developed. Judging by their size and formation, I should say they could only be two or three weeks old. I have also heard references made to young Otters being found in July and August.—JOHN H. O'CONNELL, Kilkenny.

GEOLOGY.

Coal in Ireland.—Few passages in the evidence given last year before the Railway Rates Commission struck me so much as those in which the difficulties of Irish railways were described by their representatives. The serious disadvantages at which they are placed by the absence of any native coal supply were strongly brought out, and it was stated that a long period of stormy weather, by delaying their supplies, occasionally caused serious inconvenience. My own knowledge of Irish geology is too slight to enable me to give any opinion on the possibility of coal being worked in Ireland, but I understand that the prospect is by no means hopeless. If some of the subscribers to the *Irish Naturalist* could bring forward evidence on the subject, I think it would be of interest, not only to our readers, but to all who are concerned for the prosperity of the country. It is obvious that the development of manufactures in England and Scotland has been very greatly promoted by abundant supplies of coal, and it seems to me to be worth while to inquire (if it has not been done already), whether a similar course of events could not occur in the sister isle.—R. LANGTON COLE, 2 Shorter's-court, Throgmorton street, London.

NEST OF TERN, MEW ISLAND, BELFAST LOUGH.
From a Photograph by Mr. R. Welch, June, 1892.

The Irish Naturalist.

Vol. II.   MARCH, 1893.   No. 3.

EGG-COLLECTING AND EGG-DESTRUCTION.

THE last two issues of our contemporary *The Annals of Scottish Natural History* contain articles upon this subject by Rev. E. P. Knubley, M.A., and Lieut-Colonel Duthie, R.A., which we would commend to the serious attention of our readers, especially since the nesting season is again at hand. The rapid disappearance of many of our rarer birds, owing to the systematic and ruthless plundering of their breeding-stations, has of late been prominently before a number of our leading naturalists and scientific societies, and the pressing importance of the question is shown by the resolution passed at the meeting of Delegates at the last meeting of the British Association :—

"The Conference of Delegates having heard of the threatened extermination of certain birds, as British breeding species, through the destruction of their eggs, deprecates the encouragement given to dealers by collectors through their demands for British-taken eggs, and trusts that the Corresponding Societies will do all that lies in their power to interest and influence naturalists, landowners, and others, in the preservation of such birds and their eggs."

It is quite possible that in the near future legislative protection will be extended to the eggs of our rarer birds, as it is at present, during the breeding season, to the birds themselves, but meanwhile the danger impends. As Mr. Knubley says :—

"The eggs of every kind of wild bird, whether common or uncommon, useful or otherwise, are liable to be destroyed through thoughtless carelessness, wanton mischief, or sordid greed. At present there is nothing to prevent whole areas from being systematically plundered of every egg of every bird—and it is done. . . . It requires no prophet to foretell what will be the result of this system of pillage, if it is allowed to proceed unchecked."

In Ireland, fortunately, there has not been, so far at least, the wholesale plundering that has so devastated some of the English and Scotch bird-nurseries, but it is well that we should understand the condition of affairs, and be prepared to discountenance and prevent, by every means in our power, the unnecessary destruction of birds' eggs.

Not that we would have the egg-collector abolished, or driven an exile from our shores. Oology is an interesting and instructive study, and claims our sympathy as much as the many branches of natural science which require the sacrifice of animal life. But the collector forfeits our regard who allows his greed for large series, and craze for clutches of eggs, to master the feelings of fair play and humanity which every naturalist should possess. Mr. Knubley writes :—

"Fancy fifteen clutches of the eggs of the Peregrine Falcon in the same collection, and twenty of the Chough ; and what can we say of one collector whose boast it is to possess over one hundred Scottish-taken eggs of the Golden Eagle ? Would he take kindly to the suggestion of one of the members of the British Association, that he should have the feathers of the birds presented to him, with the addition of a little tar?"

Colonel Duthie tersely describes the various types of egg-collecting offenders. He says :—

"There are three kinds of collectors who require to be specially dealt with, viz: the Aimless, the Greedy, and the Mercenary Collector.

"The Aimless Collector should be *discouraged*. He is generally a person who knows little or nothing about birds or their habits. His collection is an accumulation of unauthenticated specimens stored away in ill-arranged boxes, totally regardless of order, species, or locality, and is useless to himself and of no interest to science.

"The Greedy Collector should be *restrained*. He should be satisfied, as a rule, with one clutch of eggs of each bird, with an occasional addition of an abnormal clutch or egg for comparison.

"The Mercenary Collector should be *abolished*. He it is who is mainly responsible for the extermination of species and waste of eggs. His collection is the result of gold, changed into silver and copper as it filters through the hands of dealers, gamekeepers, shepherds, herd-boys, and others, who, often in direct disobedience of orders from their employers, have robbed many an important eyrie, and with indiscriminating ignorance have swept some of our bird-nurseries bare. The size and value of this collector's store depends upon the length of his purse, and while proud to tell the market value of a particular egg, he may be unable to describe the bird that laid it, or the nest in which it was found.

"The True Collector should be a Naturalist, acquainting himself with birds, their habits, flight, migration, language, and breeding haunts; his egg-collecting being only one of the means of acquiring this knowledge. He should collect for himself, and should never receive an egg into his cabinet unless authenticated by an individual in whom he can implicitly trust. To him, therefore, no dealer need apply, and under these conditions egg-collecting has all the excitement of sport, and the final acquisition of a rare egg, after perhaps years of waiting and watching, is a triumph, and the egg is itself a trophy of which the possessor is justly proud. . . . When once the eggs of a particular bird have been obtained, they are rarely required again; but the breeding haunt being known, the return of the birds may be looked for in each succeeding year, and their habits watched and noted during the whole period of incubation."

We would also draw attention to the value of photography to the ornithologist, in affording a permanent record of the appearance of nest and eggs amid their natural surroundings. (see PLATE 3). By photographing a nest and taking careful notes, instead of plundering it, the naturalist will avoid useless sacrifice of life and happiness to the birds, and make a far more valuable contribution to science than by accumulating multitudes of empty shells displayed on cotton-wool.

Let us, then, so far as lies in our power, watch over and protect our rarer breeding birds, and discourage all unnecessary destruction of their eggs, lest, harried and persecuted, they be gradually exterminated, or be driven from our inhospitable shores to seek a securer home in far distant lands.

THE FLORA OF COUNTY ARMAGH.
BY R. LLOYD PRAEGER, B.E., M.R.I.A.

(*Continued from page* 38).

THE following plants I found in more or less abundance in every part of the county, and they require mention only for statistical purposes, and in order to make my enumeration of the flora complete.

Anemone nemorosa.
Ranunculus peltatus.
R. hederaceus.
R. sceleratus.
R. flammula.
R. ficaria.
R. auricomus.

R. repens.
R. acris.
R. bulbosus.
Caltha palustris.
Nymphæa alba.
Nuphar luteum.
Fumaria officinalis.

Nasturtium officinale.
Barbarea vulgaris.
Cardamine flexuosa.
C. hirsuta.
C. pratensis.
Sisymbrium officinale.
Brassica campestris.

Sinapis arvensis.
Capsella bursa-pastoris.
Raphanus raphanistrum.
Reseda luteola.
Viola palustris.
V. sylvatica.
V. tricolor.
V. tricolor var. arvensis.
Drosera rotundifolia.
Polygala vulgaris.
P. vulgaris var. serpyllacea.
Silene inflata.
Lychnis flos-cuculi.
L. githago.
Sagina procumbens.
S. apetala.
Stellaria media.
S. holostea.
S. graminea.
S. uliginosa.
Cerastium glomeratum.
C. triviale.
Spergula arvensis.
Scleranthus annuus.
Malva sylvestris.
Hypericum androsaemum.
H. tetrapterum.
H. perforatum.
H. pulchrum.
Geranium molle.
G. dissectum.
G. robertianum.
Oxalis acetosella.
Linum catharticum.
Euonymus europaeus.
Ulex europaeus.
Sarothamnus scoparius.
Medicago lupulina.
Trifolium pratense.
T. repens.
T. procumbens.
T. minus.
Lotus corniculatus.
L. pilosus
Vicia hirsuta
V. cracca.
V. sepium.
* V. sativa.
V. angustifolia.
Lathyrus pratensis.
L. macrorrhizus.
Prunus communis.
† P. communis var. insititia.
P. avium.
Spiraea ulmaria.
Agrimonia eupatoria.
Alchemilla vulgaris.
A. arvensis.
Potentilla anserina.

P. reptans.
P. tormentilla.
P. tormentilla var. procumbens.
P. fragariastrum.
Comarum palustre.
Fragaria vesca.
Rubus idaeus.
Geum urbanum.
Rosa tomentosa.
R. canina.
Crataegus oxyacantha.
Pyrus malus.
P. aucuparia.
Lythrum salicaria.
Epilobium hirsutum.
E. parriflorum.
E. montanum.
E. obscurum.
E. palustre.
Circaea lutetiana.
Myriophyllum alterniflorum.
Hippuris vulgaris.
Montia fontana.
M. fontana var. rivularis.
* Sempervivum tectorum.
Cotyledon umbilicus.
Chrysosplenium oppositifolium.
Hydrocotyle vulgaris.
Sanicula europaea.
Apium nodiflorum.
A. inundatum.
‡ Aegopodium podagraria.
Bunium flexuosum.
Pimpinella saxifraga.
Oenanthe crocata.
Œ. phellandrium.
Aethusa cynapium.
Angelica sylvestris.
Heracleum sphondylium.
Daucus carota.
Torilis anthriscus.
Scandix pecten-veneris.
Chaerophyllum sylvestre.
* Myrrhis odorata.
Conium maculatum.
Hedera helix.
Sambucus nigra.
Viburnum opulus.
Lonicera periclymenum.
Sherardia arvensis.
Asperula odorata.
Galium aparine
G. verum.
G. saxatile.
G. palustre.
Valeriana officinalis.
Valerianella olitoria.
Scabiosa succisa.

S. arvensis.
Petasites vulgaris.
Tussilago farfara.
Bellis perennis.
Pulicaria dysenterica.
Gnaphalium uliginosum.
Achillea millefolium.
A. ptarmica.
Matricaria inodora.
Chrysanthemum leucanthemum.
C. segetum.
Artemisia vulgaris.
Senecio vulgaris.
S. jacobaea.
S. aquaticus.
Centaurea nigra.
C. cyanus.
Carduus lanceolatus.
C. arvensis.
C. palustris.
Lapsana communis.
Hypochaeris radicata.
Leontodon taraxacum.
L. autumnale.
Sonchus oleraceus.
S. asper.
S. arvensis.
Crepis virens.
Hieracium pilosella.
Calluna erica.
Erica tetralix.
E. cinerea.
Vaccinium myrtillus.
Ilex aquifolium.
Fraxinus excelsior.
Erythraea centaurium.
Menyanthes trifoliata.
Convolvulus sepium.
Symphytum officinale.
Myosotis palustris.
M. caespitosa.
M. arvensis.
M. versicolor.
Digitalis purpurea.
* Linaria cymbalaria.
L. vulgaris.
Scrophularia nodosa.
Pedicularis palustris.
P. sylvatica.
Rhinanthus crista-galli.
Bartsia odontites.
Euphrasia officinalis.
Veronica scutellata.
V. anagallis.
V. beccabunga.
V. chamaedrys.
V. officinalis.
V. serpyllifolia.
V. arvensis.
V. polita.

The Flora of County Armagh.

V. hederifolia.
Mentha aquatica.
M. sativa.
M. arvensis.
Lycopus europæus.
Prunella vulgaris.
Nepeta glechoma.
Lamium purpureum.
Galeopsis tetrahit.
Stachys sylvatica.
S. palustris.
Teucrium scorodonia.
Ajuga reptans.
Pinguicula vulgaris.
Utricularia minor.
Primula vulgaris.
Lysimachia vulgaris.
L. nemorum.
Anagallis arvensis.
A. tenella.
Plantago lanceolata.
P. major.
Littorella lacustris.
Chenopodium album.
Atriplex angustifolia.
A. hastata.
Rumex conglomeratus.
R. sanguineus var. viridis.
R. obtusifolius.
R. crispus.
R. acetosa.
R. acetosella.
Polygonum amphibium.
P. persicaria.
P. hydropiper.
P. aviculare.
P. convolvulus.
Empetrum nigrum.
Euphorbia helescopia.
E. peplus.
E. exigua.
Callitriche verna.
C. stagnalis.
C. hamulata.
Urtica uren.
U. dioica.
Salix pentandra.
S. alba.
S. purpurea.
S. viminalis.
S. smithiana.
S. cinerea.
S. aurita.
S. caprea.
Myrica gale.
Betula glutinosa.
Alnus glutinosa.

Quercus robur.
Corylus avellana.
*Elodea canadensis.
Orchis mascula.
O. maculata.
O. incarnata.
Habenaria chlorantha.
Listera ovata.
Iris pseudacorus.
Alisma plantago.
A. ranunculoides.
Triglochin palustre.
Allium ursinum.
Endymion nutans.
Narthecium ossafragum.
Juncus effusus.
J. conglomeratus.
J. acutiflorus.
J. lamprocarpus.
J. supinus.
J. squarrosus.
J. bufonius.
Luzula maxima.
L. vernalis.
L. campestris.
L. erecta.
Typha latifolia.
Sparganium ramosum.
S. simplex.
Arum maculatum.
Lemna trisulca.
L. minor.
Potamogeton natans.
P. polygonifolius.
P. perfoliatus.
P. crispus.
P. pusillus.
Schœnus nigricans.
Eleocharis palustris.
Scirpus lacustris.
S. cæspitosus.
S. setaceus.
Eriophorum vaginatum.
E. polystachyon.
Carex pulicaris.
C. remota.
C. echinata.
C. leporina.
C. goodenovii.
C. panicea.
C. præcox.
C. pilulifera.
C. glauca.
C. flava.
C. binervis.
C. sylvatica.
C. hirta.
C. rostrata.

C. vesicaria.
Phalaris arundinacea.
Anthoxanthum odoratum.
Phleum pratense.
Alopecurus pratensis.
A. geniculatus.
Nardus stricta.
Phragmites communis.
Agrostis canina.
A. vulgaris.
A. alba.
Holcus lanatus.
H. mollis.
Aira cæspitosa.
A. caryophyllea.
A. præcox.
Arrhenatherum elatius.
Triodia decumbens.
Melica uniflora.
Molinia cærulea.
Poa annua.
P. trivialis.
P. pratensis.
Glyceria fluitans.
Cynosurus cristatus.
Dactylus glomerata.
Festuca sciuroides.
F. ovina.
F. rubra.
F. gigantea.
F. gigantea var. triflora.
F. arundinacea.
F. pratensis.
Bromus asper.
B. mollis.
Brachypodium sylvaticum.
Triticum repens.
Lolium perenne.
Equisetum arvense.
E. maximum.
E. sylvaticum.
E. limosum.
E. limosum var. fluviatile.
E. palustre.
Polypodium vulgare.
Lastrea filix-mas.
L. dilatata.
Polystichum angulare.
Athyrium filix-fœmina.
Asplenium adiantum-nigrum.
A. trichomanes.
A. ruta-muraria.
Scolopendrium vulgare.
Blechnum spicant.
Pteris aquilina.

In the annotated list of rarer plants which follows, the distribution of species in the county is shown by reference to three vice-counties—North, Mid., and South (N., M., and S.). North Armagh here means the district lying north of a line drawn through Middletown and Richhill, and includes the Pliocene, New Red, Basaltic, and Limestone areas. Mid. Armagh comprises the Silurian area as far south as a line joining Newtownhamilton and Goraghwood: and South Armagh comprises the Granite mountain district of the south-east, and the southern portion of the Silurians. These vice-counties, as well as the areas occupied by the various geological formations, are shown on the sketch-map of the county (PLATE 2). The signs used to denote the claims of species to rank as natives are those usually employed—†, possibly introduced; ‡ probably introduced; *, certainly introduced. Square brackets are used for species which have occurred merely as casuals or waifs, and not in any way established; round brackets for plants which have been recorded, but whose presence in the county is doubtful. The sign ! means that I have seen the plant in question growing in the locality described by the observer whose name is given; the abbreviation "spec.!" signifies that I have examined a specimen from the station mentioned. The following contractions are used for authorities:—

    Coote's Armagh—Sir C. Coote's "Statistical Survey of the County of Armagh," 1804.
    Flor. Hib.—Mackay's "Flora Hibernica," 1836.
    More N.H.R.—A. G. More, "Localities for some plants observed in Ireland," *Nat. Hist. Review*, 1860.
    Flor. Ulst.—Dickie's "Flora of Ulster," 1864.
    Cyb. Hib.—Moore and More's "Cybele Hibernica," 1866.
    B.N.F.C.—Annual Reports and Proceedings of the Belfast Naturalists' Field Club, 1863-92.
    Herb. N. H. P. S.—Herbarium of the Belfast Natural History and Philosophical Society.
    G. R.—Rev. George Robinson, M.A., Armagh.
    W. F. J.—Rev. W. F. Johnston, M.A., Armagh.
    H. W. L.—Rev. H. W. Lett, M.A., Loughbrickland, Co. Down.
    S. A. S.—Samuel A. Stewart, F.B.S.E., Belfast.
    R. Ll. P.—R. Lloyd Praeger.

My best thanks are due to Mr. James Groves, F.L.S., for examining and naming my series of *Characeæ*; to Rev. W. Moyle Rogers, F.L.S., who did the same with the *Rubi*; to Mr. Arthur Bennett, F.L.S., who went through my pondweeds and Bactrachian *Ranunculi*, as well as a number of other critical plants; and to the several local gentlemen mentioned above, to whom I am indebted for valuable and willing assistance.

(TO BE CONTINUED.)

THE SILICIFIED WOOD OF LOUGH NEAGH.

BY WILLIAM SWANSTON, F.G.S.

"Lough Neagh hones! Lough Neagh hones!
You put them in sticks, and you take them out stones."
Old Pedlar's Cry.

IRELAND is rich in legendary lore, there being scarce a river or lake throughout its green expanse which has not associated with it some wierd tale; many of these relate to their origin, while others refer, perhaps, to the virtues of their sparkling waters. It is no wonder, then, that Lough Neagh—the largest sheet of fresh water in the country—should have its strange stories. We have all heard how the mythical giant scooped the hollow which now holds the waters of the lough, and dropping the material in the Irish Sea, formed the Isle of Man. The legend which Moore has embalmed in verse points to a different source, indicative of inundation or subsidence of the area, evidence of which the strolling fisherman is credited with seeing :

"The round towers of other days
In the waves beneath him shining."

The virtue attributed to the waters of Lough Neagh of turning wood into stone, dates from an early period, and it seems strange that, while those legends referring to the lake's origin are abandoned in this age of progress, there are still many who would hesitate to pronounce the petrifying virtue of its waters a myth. Looking into the question of the origin of the Lough Neagh petrified wood, it is astonishing how many references have incidentally been made to it; in most cases the subject being touched cautiously, writers evidently not wishing to commit themselves to a decided opinion regarding it. It has been thought that a brief resumé of these, bringing the subject in a measure up to date, would not be inappropriate to the pages of *The Irish Naturalist*.

First, however, we must briefly glance at the geological features of the district. Stretching along the southern and south-western shores of the lake, attaining an area of 180 square miles, and a thickness of several hundred feet, is a series of greyish and whitish clays, resembling pipe-clays. Boulder clay and soil are spread over their surface. To the westward these clays overlie rocks of Secondary and Primary age; to the eastward they are said to repose on Tertiary basalts. These last extend over the adjoining counties of Antrim and Londonderry in vast level sheets, attaining a total thickness of some 1,200 feet, and containing between their successive lava-flows, deposits of earthy iron-ore with plant-remains, and occasional thin bands of lignite. The petrified or silicified wood has been found over the whole of the area occupied by these whitish clays which we have described, and fragments of it occur in boulder-drifts and other local Pleistocene deposits over a much larger area; but along the south-eastern margins of Lough Neagh especially have these trunks and branches of wood, turned into hard flinty rock, been found.

Let us now see what writers on Ireland and Irish geology have to say about the silicified wood. As early as the ninth century a writer states as follows:—

"There is another lough that hardens wood into stone. Men cleave the wood and when they have fashioned it they cast it into the lough, where it lies to the beginning of the year, and at the beginning of the year it is found to be stone, and the lough is called Lough Echach" (an early name for Lough Neagh).

In a famous but somewhat rare book "Ireland's Natural History," by Arnold Boate, dated about 1650, there is a section of a chapter devoted to this subject. In section 7, chapter 9, he writes:—

"Before we make an end of this chapter we must say something of the wonderful property which generally is ascribed to Lough Neaugh, of turning wood into stone; whereunto some do add, to double the wonder, that the wood is turned not only into stone but into iron; and that a branch or pole being stuck into the ground, somewhere by the side where it is not too deep, after a certain space of time one shall find that peece of the stick which stuck in the ground turned into iron, and the middle, so far as it was in the water, into stone, the upper end which remained above the water keeping its former nature. But this part of the history I believe to be a fable."

Harris, in his description of the Co. Down, 1744, goes very fully into this matter. After treating of the healing qualities of its waters, he writes:—

"The second property ascribed to this Lake—viz., of petrifying and converting Wood into Stone, challenges some Attention; and the more so, as Antiquity and universal Consent have conspired to give it this Quality. But Fable has been fruitful in adding a remarkable Particular to this Property ascribed to the Lough—viz., That the Wood is turned partly into Stone and partly into Iron."

Harris does not seem to have been convinced of this virtue said to be possessed by the water or soil of the lough, and in an ingenious manner tries to set it aside. After enumerating the arguments given in support of the belief, he thus reviews them:—

"To the First We Answer, 'It is now a determined point among Naturalists, *that Stones Vegetate as well as Plants*; it seems not impossible that these may be peculiar Stones, which though in the manner of their Growth they may resemble Wood, and especially Holly, yet are not from that Resemblance necessarily to be admitted such, any more than those Representations of the Shells of Cockles, Oysters, and Escalops, some forming and some formed, frequently observed in Lime-stone in the Peak of Derbyshire, are to be supposed ever to have been real Shells, or those exact Representations of Branches, of a Lion couchant, of a human Corps laid out; nay of several artificial Things, as Chairs, a Set of Organs, and innumerable other Sportings of Nature in the vegetating Lime-stone, are to be imagined to have ever been the real things they resemble."

Many other such quaint quotations might be given, but no solid ground of investigation is touched till the publication, in 1751, of Dr. Barton's famous lecture to the Royal Society on "The Petrifications, Gems, Crystals, and Sanative Qualities of Lough Neagh." The learned, but very wordy Doctor quotes all that had been previously written on the subject; but his strong point is original research, and the collection of an extraordinary series of specimens which he describes in his work most minutely. The reader will kindly excuse my inflicting upon him a few of the Doctor's paragraphs.

Turning to his third lecture on metamorphoses, he describes a specimen upon which he had a Latin inscription cut:—

"This wonderful saxo-ligneous mass is extremely hard on the outside, emitting fire, on collision with steel, in great plenty. Yet has it wood, which is very soft, internally. . . . The weight of the specimen, before a small fragment was separated, was seven hundred pounds, being weighed at the public crane in a market town.

"Specimen No. 2—A mass of wood and stone continuous is as much as two able men can lift in a frame whose joints are strengthened with iron. . . . It being the reverse of the former specimen—wood on the outside and stone within—it was necessary to frame it, that it might be fixed in so steady a manner as not to loose by friction the tender part of its substance which lay on the outside. Specimen No. 7—This stone is nearly twenty inches long and five broad; one side is ground to a flat surface, is a firm black stone, and gives a knife a good edge; the other side is wood and may be cut by that knife in several places without spoiling the edge. N.B.—There was a great quantity of wood which was broken off in the polishing."

And so on I might quote from his descriptions of two hundred and seventy-one specimens. The point I wish specially to note in those I have quoted is, that they are part wood and part stone. Dr. Barton then describes minutely the locality—Ahaness, half a mile south of the mouth of the Glenavy river—where he found the petrifactions in the greatest abundance, remarking quaintly that:—

"This place seeming to be the forge where these materials receive part of their form deserves a particular and accurate description; because future reasoning concerning these productions must in a great measure depend upon it."

After a description of the surroundings, he says that :—

"Upon digging a pit in this place (of which there are several made), the upper stratum of matter is red clay, three feet deep; the second stratum is stiff blue clay, four feet deep; the third stratum is a black wood lying in flakes, four feet deep; the next stratum is clay, etc."

In 1837, Dr. Scouler, of Dublin, was commissioned to examine these deposits of clay and lignite, and did so most systematically, engaging men to bore and otherwise excavate for examples. The results of this survey is given in the *Journal of the Geological Society of Ireland*, and the beds were in his opinion stated to be of Tertiary age,[1] and he further adds that "to Barton therefore is due the merit of being first to ascertain the relation of the Silicified Wood to the Lignites."

Griffith wrote fully on these clays and lignites, and pointed out the probability of silicified wood found in the drift as having been derived from these beds.[2]

Portlock, in 1843, states—"In respect to the connection of the Basalts and Silicified Wood more evidence is necessary."[3]

Two early members of the Belfast Naturalists' Field Club, in 1869, read a valuable joint paper before the Geological Society of London, on the "Iron Ores associated with the Basalts of the North-east of Ireland." The iron nodules with plant-remains, found on the lough shores, are referred to, and considered identical in age with the then only known leaf-beds of Ballypallady, and all are grouped as of Miocene age.

(TO BE CONCLUDED.)

---

[1] *Dublin Geological Journal*, vol. i., part 3.
[2] Griffith—Second Report of Railway Commission, p. 22.
[3] Report of the Geology of Londonderry, 1843, page 76.

AMONG THE BIRDS ON STRANGFORD LOUGH.
BY ROBERT PATTERSON.

STRANGFORD LOUGH anciently Lough Cuan, is an arm of the sea some twenty-five miles in length by four in breadth, situated in Co. Down. It is generally shallow, and scattered over its surface are a large number of small islands—366, so say the country-folk; one for every day of the year and two for Easter Sunday. According to the "Annals of the Four Masters," Lough Cuan was formed in the year of the world 2546 (1654 B.C.) when there occurred "an inundation of the sea over the land at Brena, which was the seventh lake-eruption that occurred in the time of Parthalon, and this is named Loch Cuan;" but the geologist sees in the low rounded hills of polished and ice-ground rocks that fringe the lough-shores, and in other local evidences of intense glaciation, a different origin of this shallow, island-studded inland sea.

Strangford Lough is a capital place for the naturalist in summer, as it is for the sportsman in winter. In the summer of 1890 I spent two days there with my cousin, Mr R. Lloyd Praeger, and our friend Mr. A. J. Collins, and the present sketch is compiled from our note books; our chief object was to investigate the breeding birds of the Lough.

We started on June 21st in an early train to Newtownards, armed with provisions for two days, extra rugs, to enable us to sleep on the islands if weather was suitable, boxes, vasculums, field glasses, etc. We breakfasted at Newtownards, and drove to Cunningburn, a small village about three miles down the lough, where we found our boatman, William Armour, waiting for us, and were on the water by 11 o'clock. Just as we started a Sheldrake (*Tadorna cornuta*) flew past at some little distance. On asking the boatman if Sheldrakes bred there, he replied that he believed they did, but lower down the lough. He stated that a pair or two were always to be seen in summer, and that he could get me one at any time, which statement was amply proved about a week later by the arrival in Belfast of a fine male Sheldrake in breeding plumage, and quite uninjured. The weather looked unsettled, and rain began to fall as we sailed down to Long Island and Boretree Island. As we approached, clouds of Terns rose from the islands and circled round us, keeping up a continual shrieking that was almost deafening. On landing, we found great quantities of Terns' eggs, spotted with dark brown and black, lying in twos and threes in slightly-formed hollows in the grass, seaweed, or pebbles (PLATE 3.). The seaweed fringe which marked last spring tides seemed an especially favoured place. From among the hundreds of eggs of both Arctic and Common Terns (*S. macrura* and *S. fluviatilis*) which lay scattered over the ground, we selected a few for our cabinets, and then beat the tall groves of Alexanders *(Smyrnium)* with which the islands were covered, drenched with recent showers, in the hope of getting Mergansers', but without result. A tremendous shower now came on, which no waterproofs could keep out, and which left us and our food pretty well soaked. But we searched through it all, and found two clutches of Ringed Plovers' *(Ægialitis hiaticula)*. The nest and eggs of the Ringed Plover, or "Dotterel" as it is called in the north of Ireland, are as pretty as the birds themselves. The nest consists simply of a neatly formed hollow in the dry shingle, often containing a few bright yellow shells *(Littorina obtusata)*, laid there perhaps to draw attention away from the eggs. These latter are buff-coloured, speckled with black, and as they lie in the nest with the four pointed ends neatly set together, the general effect is very pleasing.

Salt Island was searched in vain, and we sailed on to Gabbock Island, near which we had a very narrow escape from being upset. During a momentary lull in the westerly wind which prevailed all day, a most extraordinary little puff came from the eastward, without the slightest warning, causing the boat to suddenly heel over, and one of our party found himself unexpectedly sitting in the sea; but the good management of our boatman saved us from a capsize, and after a hearty laugh at the expense of the wet and unfortunate third, we safely reached Gabbock. Here we camped and had lunch; the stony shores of the island yielded more nests of Terns and Ringed Plovers. We sailed on to Long and Little Sheelah, which are in close proximity. And here the Terns' eggs were a sight! We had to pick our way among them most carefully, or we would frequently have tramped on them. They lay scattered in the utmost profusion over shingle, grass, and the flotsam and jetsam that fringed high-water mark, as if they had been sown broadcast over the islet. As the cloud of Terns, with much screaming and fluttering, settled down on the island after we had left it, we could not help wondering whether each bird was able to identify its own eggs among the hundreds that lay around, or whether each simply annexed the first clutch it came upon.

On Little Sheelah we found our first Oystercatcher's nest *(Hæmatopus ostralegus)*. Like the Ringed Plover's, the nest was a slight hollow scraped in the shingle; the eggs are of a duller hue than the Ringed Plover's, are spotted and streaked all over with dark brown and black, and are much larger. The parent birds, whose brilliant black and white plumage, and scarlet legs and beak render the Oystercatcher one of the most showy birds of the seashore, were flying uneasily around. Then away south to Bird Island, which however belied its name, as the only eggs that we saw on the island were a clutch of Ringed Plover.

It was now getting late, and repeated heavy showers had made us very wet, so we stood away for the point of Mahee Island, on the western side of the Lough, and landed on a second Bird Island close by. When we drew near, one Red-breasted Merganser (*M. serrator*), nine Oystercatchers, and five Redshanks (*Totanus calidris*) rose off the island, but we only came upon some broken Merganser's eggs in a clump of brambles—evidently last year's eggs—and a broken Oystercatcher's egg. Cold and hungry, we made for Mahee, and claimed hospitality for the night at Stewart's farm, where we were kindly received. We got our wet things out of the boat and soon had them drying at a huge fire in the kitchen. With the help of our obliging hostess, we got out our provisions and had a great tea—Mrs. Stewart being evidently much impressed by the extent of our appetites. Three collie dogs, each answering to the name of "Sheelah," that had been rather suspicious of us at first, we pacified with huge lumps of tinned meat. After a chat with our host, and writing our notes, we three turned into one small bed—the only one available—and tried to sleep, but as one of us had put over him a rug which he found in a corner of the room, and which we discovered in the morning belonged to the *dogs*, the result was not quite as satisfactory as could have been desired. But those who did sleep dreamt of islands where the ground was paved with eggs, and the air filled with the musical din of a thousand feathery things that dashed around like snowflakes in the eddy of a winter's gale. Our boatman, fearing a shift of wind, stayed out in the boat all night, and slept soundly, with the hard boards for a bed and the sail for a blanket.

The following morning we were up at half-past six, and after a snack of bread and a glass of warm new milk, forced a few shillings on our unwilling host, and were on the water by seven. The weather was still gloomy, but looking rather better. We ran southward and landed on Calf Island, which was barren. Then on to Sketrick Island, where we examined the ruins of the old castle, on the top of which we stood at eight o'clock, seriously disturbing the peace of a colony of Jackdaws established in the ruins. Though a large portion of the landward wall has fallen outwards, the massive square keep still stands, frowning in picturesque decay over the causeway which connects the island with the shore. How much more peaceful was the scene on which we gazed from its mossy rampart that summer's morning, than that which the O'Neill saw four hundred years ago, when having marched with his army into Clannaboy to assist his fellow chief McQuillan, he took and plundered the castle of Sgath Deirg (Sketrick), and handed it over to the keeping of his ally.

We next visited Trasnagh Island, Craigaveagh Rock, Roe Island, and Partan Island. On the latter we had good fortune, finding an Oystercatcher's, some Terns' among the seaweed, and a Merganser's with seven eggs, built among long grass and nettles at the foot of the wall of a ruined cottage. We saw the beaten track among the grass, and soon came upon a mass of down and bents; upon parting the down the beautiful drab-coloured eggs were found underneath. We could not help admiring the clever way they were concealed; the female was seen in the sea a short distance off. Then on to Darragh Island, where we landed about eleven, and had our breakfast. From this we tried Drummond Island, which was barren, as was also Great Minnis Island. Next visited Dunsey Rock, and another Long Sheelah, which yielded a few Terns', Oyster-catchers', and Ringed Plovers' nests, and then stood away to Black Rock, off Ringdufferin, where we found another Oyster-catcher's. On several of these islands we found numerous nests of Terns and Plovers, but the eggs had been taken.

Now we turned northward again and sailed before a gentle breeze up Ringhaddy Sound, and landed under the trees below the ruined church, which crowns the hill above. Here dinner engaged our attention for some time, and when we were ready to start it was half-past six. The wind now completely died away, and a steady rain came on. There was nothing for it but to make our belongings as weather-proof as possible, and pull all the way back; so we set out on our long row of nine miles through the mist and rain, and against the tide, and slowly came up through the islands, past the point of Mahee, where we could see our hospitable farmhouse, across the lough, and reached Cunningburn as darkness was setting in, at half-past nine. It was dead low water, and as we could not have been much wetter, we just waded ashore as we were, carrying our belongings on our backs. We left all we could in our boatman's cottage, and taking our bags and our precious eggs, set off at ten, and tramped back into Newtownards, where, towards midnight, we made night hideous with frantic efforts to awaken the people of the Ulster Hotel. A man in a state of hilarious inebriation, who happily turned up, advised us to try the Londonderry Arms instead, where after a lengthened solo on the knocker, we effected an entrance, and lost no time in getting to bed. The following morning we returned to Belfast by an early train.

During our two days on the water, which, in spite of unsettled weather, were most interesting and enjoyable, we saw many Cormorants, Herons, Curlews, Green Plover and Black-headed Gulls, but I have no notes of any importance. The only eggs we found in addition to those already mentioned were one Rock Pipit's and one Land-rail's. The Rock Pipit's egg was lying among bare gravel, without a trace of nest; the Land-rail's was in a grove of *Smyrnium*, also without nest; the Ringed-plover's and Oystercatcher's, were, as before stated, among gravel, in a slight hollow, in which a few bright shells had been laid—some of the former were overhung by grass.

We observed that all the Oystercatchers' eggs were laid at a *point* on the islands; never in the middle of a straight stretch of shore. The Lesser Tern *(S. minuta)*, we did not see at all, although a close watch was kept; later on in the summer, however, I saw specimens which were procured on Strangford Lough. We made enquiries also about the Roseate Tern *(S. dougalli)*, but without result.

By the kindness of my friend Mr. R. Welch, I am enabled to give the illustration (PLATE 3) which accompanies this paper. It is a photograph of the nest and eggs of a Tern (Arctic or Common) on Mew Island, at the entrance of Belfast Lough; here the birds usually lay in slight hollows which they form in the short turf which covers the rocky surface of the island.

THE MACRO-LEPIDOPTERA OF THE LONDONDERRY DISTRICT.

BY D. C. CAMPBELL.

(*Concluded from page* 46.)

GEOMETRÆ.

Uropteryx sambucaria, Linn,—Rare. Mr. Milne has noticed that the conspicuous swallow-tail often falls a victim to bats, probably owing to its large size and pale yellow wings. This beautiful species was one of the prizes of our early collecting days.

Epione apiciaria, Schiff.—Common at Ballynagard; we took it on Ragwort.

Rumia luteolata, Linn.—Very common.

Metrocampa margaritaria, Linn.—Common.

Ellopia prosapiaria, Linn.—Local. Very common at Kilderry among Scotch firs. We found it very easily attracted by light.

Selenia bilunaria, Esp.—Common.

Odontoptera bidentata, Clerck } Common.
Crocallis elinguaria, Linn.

Eugonia quercinaria, Hufn.—One or two specimens at Ballynagard.

Himera pennaria, Linn.—A few specimens.

Phigalia pedaria, Fab.—Fairly common.

Nyssia zonaria, Schiff.—In June, 1883, we discovered this interesting species near Ballycastle, Co. Antrim. Mr. Milne found the first larvæ on the short grass on the wind-swept shore. We found the larvæ very abundant and succeeded in rearing a large number. Their favourite food was *Lotus corniculatus*.

Amphidasys betularia, Linn.—Common.

Cleora lichenaria, Hufn.—We took one perfect specimen and four or five larvæ at Rathmullen.

Boarmia repandata, Linn.—Common.

Gnophos obscuraria, Hüb.—One specimen at the Giant's Causeway.

Geometra vernaria, Hüb.—Rather rare.

Iodis lactearia, Linn.—Common at Buncrana.

Venusia cambrica, Curt.—One or two specimens at Innishowen.

The Macro-Lepidoptera of the Londonderry District. 73

Acidalia dimidiata, Hufn. ⎫
A. bisetata, Hufn. ⎬ Common.
A. trigeminata, Haw. ⎪
A. aversata, Linn. ⎭
Cabera pusaria, Linn. ⎫ Very common.
C. exanthemata, Scop. ⎭
Halia vauaria, Linn.—Rare.
Numeria pulveraria, Linn.—Buncrana.
Scodiona belgiaria, Linn.—Rare.
Ematurga atomaria, Linn.—Common.
Abraxas grossulariata, Linn.—Common.
Lomaspilis marginata, Linn.—We have only found it in one locality—Kilderry, six miles from Derry.
Hyberniarupicapraria, Hüb. ⎫ Common.
H. marginaria, Bork. ⎭
H. defoliaria, Clerck—Fairly common.
Cheimatobia brumata Linn.—Very common.
Oporabia dilutata, Bork.—Common.
O. filigrammaria, Herr.-Schäff.—We reared one specimen from larvae. This species was not included in Mr. Birchall's list.
Larentia didymata, Linn.—Very common.
L. multistrigaria, Linn.—Distributed, but not abundant.
L. cæsiata, Lang—Common.
L. salicata, Hüb.—Not common.
L. viridaria, Fab.—Common.
L. olivata, Bork.—Two specimens at Buncrana.
Emmelesia alchemillata, Linn. ⎫ Common.
E. albulata, Schiff. ⎭
E. unifasciata, Haw.—One or two specimens.
Eupithecia venosata, Fab.—Common on coast near Magilligan.
E. pulchellata, Steph. ⎫
E. oblongata, Thunb. ⎬ Common.
E. castigata, Hüb. ⎪
E. vulgata, Haw. ⎭
E. rectangulata, Linn. ⎫ Not common.
E. virgaureata, Dbl. ⎭
Lobophora sexalisata, Hüb.—A few specimens.
L. carpinata, Bork.—Two specimens.
Thera variata, Schiff.—Very common.
Hypsipetes trifasciata, Bork. ⎫ Common.
H. sordidata, Fab. ⎭
Melanthia bicolorata, Hufn. ⎫
M. ocellata, Linn. ⎬ Common.
M. albicillata, Linn. ⎭
Melanippe hastata, Linn.—One specimen.
M. sociata, Bork. ⎫ Common.
M. montanata, Bork. ⎭
M. galiata, Hüb.—Magilligan, rather rare.

Melanippe fluctuata, Linn.—Common.
Anticlea badiata, Hüb.—Not common.
Coremia munitata, Hüb.—Common, but local.
C. ferrugata, Clerck } Common.
C. unidentaria, Haw.
Camptogramma bilineata, Linn.—Common.
C. fluviata, Hüb.--One male specimen at Cushendall, on Antrim coast.
Phibalapteryx vittata, Bork.—Rare.
Triphosa dubitata, Linn.—Two specimens.
Cidaria siterata, Hufn.—One specimen at ivy.
C. miata, Linn.—Not common.
C. corylata, Thunb.—A few were taken by a friend in Co. Derry.
C. truncata, Hufn.
C. immanata, Haw. } Common.
C. suffumata, Haw.
C. silaceata, Hüb.—Strabane.
C. prunata, Linn. } Common.
C. testata, Linn.
C. populata, Linn.—Abundant on Innishowen mountains.
C. fulvata, Forst.—Common.
C. dotata, Linn.—Common at Magilligan.
Pelurga comitata, Linn.—Common.
Eubolia limitata, Scop.—Common.
E. plumbaria, Fab.—Two or three specimens.
Anaitis plagiata, Linn.—Common.
Chesias spartiata, Fues.—Common.
Tanagra atrata, Linn.—One specimen. Mr. Milne has seen it in numbers in Co. Tyrone.

CORRIGENDA.

Chœrocampa elpenor, L. should be added to the Sphinges (p. 21). We took a few specimens near Derry.

Mr. Kane has pointed out to me that *Hadena dissimilis* was inserted by error among the Noctuæ (p. 46). This species should have therefore been omitted. Mr. Leebody draws my attention to the fact that *Artemisia campestris* (mentioned as the food-plant of *Heliothis scutosa*) does not grow at Buncrana; it is *A. vulgaris* which occurs there.

Our list contains but 261 species and is, of course, very incomplete. If any of our Irish naturalists will investigate the Lepidoptera of the district about Lough Swilly and Lough Foyle, I feel sure he will be amply rewarded. The great stretch of sandhills which runs almost across the mouth of Lough Foyle, at Magilligan, provides a splendid field for the naturalist, be he entomologist, botanist, or conchologist. If one wants a day of pure pleasure, let him choose a fine warm day in June or July, and stroll through the Magilligan valleys, where the exquisite grass of Parnassus carpets the ground, and the pearly white wild rose blooms close beside the beach where the Atlantic waves break unceasingly.

NOTES ON THE FLORA OF THE ARAN ISLANDS.

BY NATHANIEL COLGAN.

SMALL insular areas have always had a peculiar attraction for students of Natural History, perhaps for this reason, among other and weightier ones, that they present to the investigator a field of inquiry clearly defined by unmistakable natural boundaries, and not so extended as to discourage minute and thoroughgoing examination. Just such an area is to be found in Galway Bay, in the group of three limestone islands known as the South Isles of Aran, a group which amongst botanists, at least, has made its attractions felt from an early period. The first investigator to visit the islands was Dr. Edward Lhwyd, that intrepid explorer of the Irish flora, who in his account of his plant-hunting "On the Mountains of Keri," in the year 1700, tells us how his scientific curiosity was "frustrated by the Tories."[1] To Lhwyd we owe the earliest record of the Maiden-Hair Fern in the Arans. A century later (1805), we find Dr. Mackay, author of the "Flora Hibernica," visiting the group and discovering there the *Helianthemum canum*; and after him, at more or less lengthy intervals, comes a succession of botanists down to Mr. H. C. Hart, who made a careful survey of the islands in the summer of 1869. Mr. Hart's results were published in 1875 in the form of a detailed flora carrying up the number of species for the Arans from 159, recorded by Dr. E. P. Wright in 1866, to a total of 372. Finally, in 1890, two English botanists, Messrs. J. E. Nowers and James G. Wells, visiting the islands at a season two months earlier than Mr. Hart, succeeded in adding no less than 42 species to his total.

It will thus be seen that no great extension of the number of Aran species was to be looked for from further examination of the group; and it was with no such expectation I visited the islands towards the end of last May (1892). My object was merely to make acquaintance with the peculiar Aran species, to re-discover, if possible, the long derelict *Ajuga pyramidalis*, one of the rarest of Irish plants, first found in Aranmore by

---

[1] *Phil. Trans.*, vol. xxvii., 1712. It need hardly be said that the Tories here referred to professed no definite political principles, but were mere footpads who found in the fastnesses of the Kerry Highlands a favourable field for brigandage.

Mr. David Moore in 1854, and to search for *Neotinea intacta*, which had just been discovered in a new station on the neighbouring limestone of the Co. Clare, and in the opinion of my friend, Mr. A. G. More, was extremely likely to re-appear on the similar formation of the Arans.

It was mid-day on the 25th May when I landed at Kilronan, in Aranmore, after a passage of three hours and a half by steamer from Galway; and about mid-day on the following Monday I returned to the mainland, taking advantage of a favourable wind to cross by hooker from Inisheer, or South Island, to the nearest point of the Iar-Connaught coast at Inverin. This stay of five days was insufficient for anything more than a hasty survey of the islands; for short as the distances are—Aranmore, the largest of the group, being only nine miles long with an average breadth of a mile-and-a-half —progression, off the highways, is made extremely slow and extremely trying to the temper and the muscles by the extraordinary wealth of dry stone walls which chequer the surface of the country. Each of these walls is a triumph of equilibration, and except in parts of the South Island, where passages wide enough for a man but too narrow for a sheep are occasionally left, no breach can be found in these crazy ramparts. You can only pass from one field to another, to dignify by the name of field the areas of naked and crevassed limestone covering almost three-fourths of the surface, by climbing what is almost impossible to climb without imminent risk of bruised shins or heels. My first day's work amongst these stone dikes was so tedious and so disheartening that on the following days I engaged a stout native boy who proved very useful, rather as a dilapidator than as a guide and porter. He carried my camera and vasculum, and cheerfully threw down with a push of his shoulder any uncommonly difficult or dangerous wall that happened to lie in our path. I should have hesitated to do this for myself; but the young islander, with an adroit touch of flattery, gave me to understand that though the natives would be loath to take such a short method with the walls for their own convenience, they would never dream of objecting to its use on behalf of a distinguished stranger. By this means I was enabled to examine a large part of the surface of the islands in my short stay.

During the first day's ramble in Aranmore the prevalence of

markedly limestone species such as *Rubia peregrina*, *Asperula cynanchica*, *Galium sylvestre*, *Poterium sanguisorba*, *Asplenium trichomanes*, and *A. ruta-muraria* made itself apparent. At the same time I was struck with the rarity of another apparently lime-loving species, *Ceterach officinarum* so abundant on the limestone to the east of Galway. In Inisheer, or South Island, this fern seems quite as rare as on Aranmore, though on Inishmaan, or Middle Island, Mr. Hart found it in great profusion and luxuriance. Of species with a less strongly-marked preference for limestone, *Geranium lucidum*, *Rubus saxatilis*, and *Saxifraga tridactylites* were very abundant, the last-named frequently reaching to a height of more than six inches, while among ferns it would be hard to say whether the commonest species in Aranmore is *Scolopendrium vulgare* or *Pteris aquilina*. Both are extremely abundant, but whereas the Hart's Tongue, which seems to have a rather well-marked predilection for limestone, grows most vigorously in the rock-clefts, the Bracken is everywhere very stunted. Even more stunted in growth, as observed by Mr. Hart, was *Eupatorium cannabinum*, plentiful in the maze of rock-fissures below the grand old cyclopean stone fort of Dun Ængus, where it contended for shade and moisture with the Maiden-Hair, only now beginning to send up its tender young fronds amongst the withered foliage of last year.

At this season the most striking of all species, both in mass and brilliancy of flower, appeared to be *Lotus corniculatus* and *Geranium sanguineum*; while, perhaps, even more abundant, if less obtrusive, were *Cerastium arvense* and the form of hypnoid saxifrage, *Saxifraga sternbergii* (Willdenow), usually regarded as peculiar in the British Isles to Ireland. Having compared this Aran saxifrage with other hypnoid forms which I have gathered on Seafin, in the Ben Bulben district of Sligo, and at a height of 3,000 feet on Brandon in Kerry, I find that while the Aran plant is decidedly distinct from the typical *Saxifraga hypnoides* of Sligo, with bristle-pointed leaves and bulbiferous axils, it is hardly distinguishable by any important character from the Brandon specimens. The Brandon plant is evidently the same as that described by Mackay and Babington under *S. hirta* (Smith), but the dense hairiness and greater laxity of growth of this mountain form is all that separates it from the *S. sternbergii*, which grows so profusely down to sea-level in the Arans. And the Aran form, when growing in moist situations, frequently approaches in laxity of growth to the Brandon *S. hirta*, so that the sole remaining distinction left between the two forms is to be found in the more profuse hairiness of the alpine plant. Under change of conditions all the forms of this bewildering group are probably highly flexible. A very weak straggling form which I gathered last July on Crookaline mountain, north-east of Lough Currane, Co. Kerry, at a height of 1,800 feet, where it grows profusely in mossy rills, entangled with luxuriant *Chrysosplenium*, has developed, when grown in an open situation in my garden, into a cushion of dense even-headed rosettes. A serious attempt to reduce to order the Irish hypnoid saxifrages by a study of a full series of authentic dried specimens, and of plants under cultivation from Aran, Kerry, Ben Bulben, and Antrim, might, perhaps, give some positive results.

The second day in Aranmore was given up chiefly to an examination of the sandy tracts around Killeany, towards the south-east of the island, and the most notable result was the discovery of a quantity of the elegant little *Astragalus hypoglottis*, nowhere native in Ireland outside the Aran Islands. Lough Atalia, a brackish pool near the shore of Killeany bay, was carefully searched, and, though I failed to discover *Menyanthes*, recorded from this station by Mr. Hart, I found here the only horsetail of the islands, noted but not determined by him in August, 1869. It turns out to be *Equisetum arvense*. Close by the same pool a few plants of *Lysimachia nemorum* turned up, a species apparently not recorded from these islands since the visit of Dr. Wright in 1866. The stately *Allium babingtonii* was abundant, both in sandy places near the shore, and in deep clefts of the rock. This species, the "Inyon feechaun,"[1] or wild onion of the islanders, was formerly grown in small quantities in the garden plots of the Arans for use as an anthelmintic; but I could discover no certain tradition that it had ever been grown for culinary purposes. *Allium ursinum*, the "Gaurlyoge" or Garlic of the natives, is thoroughly well-established in rock-terraces close by Lough Atalia at a distance from ruins or dwellings.

(TO BE CONCLUDED.)

---

[1] Throughout these notes I have endeavoured to represent phonetically the Irish plant names.

REVIEWS.

Birds: The Elements of Ornithology. By St. George Mivart, F.R.S. London: R. H. Porter, 1892.

Mr. Mivart's book may briefly be described as about the most comprehensive science-primer which the student of ornithology is likely to have met with. Its opening pages, indeed, scarcely prepare one to expect this characteristic. Nearly the first half of the volume consists of a copiously illustrated introduction, in which, beginning with the Common Fowl, our author passes in rapid review more than 200 species of birds, 140 of the kind referred to being also figured from original drawings. Though this chapter has in truth little apparent connection with the rest of the treatise, and is professedly written with a view to enabling the student to obtain a mental grasp of the outlines of Cuvier's arrangement of birds, it is not easy to regret the adoption of a course which has certainly embellished the volume, and contributed one popular chapter to a strictly scientific work. Still the reader who has gone to Mr. Mivart in due ignorance of Cuvier's classification will be somewhat perplexed at finding himself required to learn, and retain in memory, for convenience' sake, to the end of the book, a system, against which he is at the same time gravely cautioned is not only superficial but obsolete. Here and there, in the course of this chapter, one drops on amusing instances of the modern tendency to speculation. Thus, in explanation of the remarkable habit acquired by the Kea Parrot (*Nestor notabilis*) of New Zealand, which, since the introduction of sheep into that colony, has taken to carnivorous practices, alighting on the helpless animal's back, and eating down into its kidneys, Mr. Mivart tenders the curious suggestion (due, it appears, to the ingenuity of Dr. H. Woodward, F.R.S.), that this parrot, in pre-colonial days, was used to prey in similar fashion on the now extinct Dinornis!

The remaining chapters deal respectively with the external structure, internal skeleton, development, geographical distribution, and classification of birds. In the last-named department, Mr. Mivart seems to have been fortunate in securing the important assistance of Dr. R. Bowdler Sharpe, whom, indeed, we are asked to regard as responsible for the entire arrangement of the 53 families of Passeres. The arrangement of the orders is as follows:—(1) Passeriformes, (2) Coraciiformes, (3) Piciformes, (4) Coccyges, (5) Columbiformes, (6) Psittaci, (7) Raptores, (8) Steganopodes, (9) Herodiones, (10) Alectorides, (11) Galliformes, (12) Limicoliformes, (13) Tubinares, (14) Pygopodiformes, (15) Lamellirostres, (16) Impennes, (17) Crypturi, (18) Struthiones. The position of priority in the whole class is assigned to the Rook, dimly recognizable as *Trypanocorax frugilegus*. A little carelessness is noticeable in that part of the work dealing with geographical distribution. For example, Mr. Mivart makes (on pp. 117, 244, and 248) three statements respecting the range of the Pycnonotidae, each of which contradicts both the others. But such occasional symptoms of hasty writing will not seriously detract from the value of this interesting and welcome publication.

C. B. M.

The Hemiptera Heteroptera of the British Islands. By
EDWARD SAUNDERS, F.L.S. London: L. Reeve & Co., 1892. 14s.
(with coloured plates, 48s.).

This is an excellent work on the British species of a comparatively neglected group of insects, and should lead many entomologists to take up its study. Mr. Saunders, who is a well-known authority on the Hemiptera, gives us an introduction on the anatomy of the order, with hints on collecting (we are glad to see that he insists on recording the locality of captures), and clear synopses, with full descriptions of the families, genera, and species found in the British Islands. The arrangement of the families is that of Puton, and the nomenclature has been brought well up to date. The cheap edition is without illustrations, except one good structural plate; but the descriptions are so excellent that the careful student should not fail to correctly identify his captures.

A list of known British localities is appended to each species. Records from Ireland are not very numerous. Our esteemed contributor, Rev. W. F. Johnson, is responsible for most of them. We notice that in the last issue of the *Ent. Monthly Mag.* (Feb., 1892) he enumerates 89 species of Heteroptera, and 13 of Homoptera, from the north of Ireland. We hope that other entomologists in the country will take up the study of these interesting insects, and so increase our knowledge of animal distribution in the British Isles.

Report on Some Species of the Genera Buccinum, Buccinopsis and Fusus Dredged off the South-west of Ireland.
By HENRY K. JORDAN. *Proc. Royal Irish Acad.* (3) vol. ii., pp. 391-396.

This communication has a certain amount of value to the systematist but scarcely any from a faunistic point of view. Of the twenty-eight records of species, the only locality whence they were obtained is that contained in the title of the paper; "Jars A-F," and "Boxes 1-7," are not edifying localities! Incidentally we learn that Box 4 was marked "Station 3, 1885," and Box 7, "Exp. 1886, log. 44, 108 fms.," but no further reference is vouchsafed. This is slovenly work. The species recorded are *Buccinum undatum*, Linn.; *B. humphreysianum*, Ben., and its var. *ventricosum*, Kien. Mr. Jordan states that "the specimen under notice clearly connects the two species" (*B. humphreysianum* and *B. ventricosum*, Kiener). *Buccinopsis dalei*, J. Sow.; *Fusus antiquus*, Linn., "intermediate in form between *antiquus* and *despectus* of Linn." *F. despectus*, Linn.; *F. islandicus*, Chem.; *F. gracilis*, Da Costa; *F. propinquus*, Ald., "and at least two new varieties,"—var. *intermedia*, Jordan (connecting *F. propinquus* and *F. jeffreysianus*), var. *nana*, Jordan, and possibly a third, var. *incrassata*; *F. jeffreysianus*, Fisch.; *F. berniciensis*, King (first Irish specimens); *F. fenestratus*, Turt. "*B. ventricosum* of Kiener—a Lusitanian and Mediterranean form—is new to the British fauna, and its connection with *B. humphreysianum* is established. Again, it is in company with *F. islandicus*—a boreal and Arctic species." It is not quite clear what Mr. Jordan means by "in company," as the ormer was in "Jar C," and the atter in "Jar A," and we are kept in the dark where either came from.

A. C. H.

PROCEEDINGS OF IRISH SOCIETIES.

ROYAL ZOOLOGICAL SOCIETY.

Recent donations comprise a Peregrine Falcon from Miss Dennis; a Badger from E. Winter, Esq.; and a pair of Dormice from Dr. Kenny. An opossum, a Ring-tailed Coati, two Spider-Monkeys, and four marmosets have been purchased. 3,420 persons visited the Gardens in January.

DUBLIN MICROSCOPICAL CLUB.

JANUARY 19th.—The Club met at Dr. FRAZER'S.

Epithelial carcinoma, from the human subject, was exhibited by Dr. E. J. M'WEENEY, showing the peculiar globular bodies which have been described by Sjöbring, Podwyswzki and Sawbschenko, Foà, Ruffer and Walker, and Metschnikoff, as occurring imbedded in cancer cells, sometimes in the nucleus and sometimes in the protoplasm, and which are looked on by these authors and others as parasitic Protozoa allied to the Gregarinida. Owing to assumed symbiosis between these intracellular parasites and the epithelial cells, the latter are supposed to receive a peculiar stimulus causing them to multiply to a degree prejudicial to the interests of the organism at large, and thus form a tumour. The sections had been cut in paraffin, arranged in series on the slide, and stained with Biondi's reagent. Dr. M'Weeney also exhibited a series of slides illustrative of the various kinds of intracellular infection that exist among the lower animals. The psorosperms of the liver and intestine of rabbits; the sarcosporidia that inhabit the muscular fibres of pigs and sheep, and the myxosporidia that live in the swim-bladder and urinary bladder of fishes were clearly demonstrated in this series of beautifully stained sections, for which the exhibitor was indebted to his esteemed correspondent, Dr. L. Pfeiffer, of Weimar, whose researches have thrown much light on the obscure field of comparative pathology. These minute organisms have one feature in common—their plant-like tendency to break up completely into spores, and this process of spore formation has lately been described as occurring in the supposed parasite of human cancer cells. He also exhibited a series of micro-photographs also lent by Dr. Pfeiffer, showing cancer parasites in man, and the various kinds of parasitic Protozoa in insects, mollusca, and vertebrates, at different stages of development.

Dr. J. A. SCOTT also showed some of the coccidia-bodies recently described as a possible cause for cancer. The sections were taken from a case of Paget's disease and an epithelioma of the tongue. He also exhibited two photographs, by Mr. Pringle of London, of a cancer. In all the specimens and photographs similar small spherical bodies could be seen in the cells of the new growth, but their exact import must still remain an open question.

Anchorella uncinata, a parasitic Copepod (male) was exhibited by MR. W. F. DE V. KANE, who said this species was not uncommon on Codfish in Dublin Bay. He showed that this sex, which continues as a free organism all its life, retains the two pairs of maxillipeds, situated in juxtaposition and provided with talons, and lives as a parasite on the female. The latter, however, in its fixed adult stage has both pairs diversely modified and altered in their relative positions, the inner pair being retained as minute buccal appendages, while the outer pair are separated from them by the whole length of the cylindrical cephalic process, and are placed at its basal extremity, where they are soldered together and form a button-shaped tenaculum, which is immovably fastened into the skin of the host. He further remarked that in the present species, and in those of the genus *Chondracanthus*, the microscopically minute male seemed only to be found on the genital ring of the female, whereas, in other *Lernæo-*

podidæ whose male is easily discernible by the aid of an ordinary lens, they are found clinging to other portions of the female. The female of the present species was also shown, and measures about five lines in length from the mouth to the extremity of the ovaries.

Lejeunea diversiloba, Spruce, was exhibited by MR. MCARDLE. This liverwort is one of the Microlejuneæ, and is remarkable for the irregularity of the lobule. This is often equal to the leaf in size, more frequently half as large, sometimes reduced to a mere rim, and on some of the branches the lobule is altogether obsolete. The plant is very rare, and has only been found at Killarney, from which locality the specimen exhibited came. He also showed a drawing of the plant with the peculiar parts magnified, as well as the folioles, perianth, and cells.

Pollen Grains of Encephalartus villosus were exhibited by MR. HENRY H. DIXON, in the first stages of germination. The ripe pollen-grain is oval in longitudinal section, reniform in transverse. It has three nuclei, two of which are lenticular, and are applied to the portion of the inner coat of the pollen-grain, opposite the point where the pollen-tube will be protruded. The remaining nucleus moves into the pollen-tube as soon as the latter is formed; neither of the lenticular nuclei, up to the sixth day of germination, when the pollen-tube was about twice as long as the diameter of the grain, had moved into the tube.

BELFAST NATURAL HISTORY AND PHILOSOPHICAL SOCIETY.

JANUARY 27th.—The President (PROF. FITZGERALD) in the chair. MR. J. MURPHY read a paper on "The Division of Angles and Arcs by Mechanical Methods."

FEBRUARY 7th.—The President (PROF. FITZGERALD) in the chair. MR. F. FRANKFORT MOORE read a paper entitled "An Artificial Age."

BELFAST NATURALISTS' FIELD CLUB.

JANUARY 17th.—The President (MR. J. VINYCOMB) in the chair. PROF. A. C. HADDON gave a lecture on "The Aran Islands: a Study in Irish Ethnography." There was a very large attendance. The subject-matter of this lecture will be shortly laid before our readers in a paper by Prof. Haddon.

JANUARY 18th.—MR. W. H. PATTERSON in the chair. Adjourned meeting. PROF. HADDON described the steps now being taken by a committee of the British Association to carry out an ethnographical survey of the British Islands. A local committee was appointed to carry on the work in Ulster.

FEBRUARY 9th.—Microscopical Section. The Chairman (MR. ALEX. TATE, C.E.), presided. MR. H. MCCLEERY read a paper on "The Honey Bee," which was illustrated with the lantern microscope by Mr. John Brown. MR. JOHN DONALDSON gave an exposition of Photo-micrography, with illustrations.

DUBLIN NATURALISTS' FIELD CLUB.

FEBRUARY 14th.—The President (DR. M'WEENEY) in the chair. MR. GREENWOOD PIM read a paper by himself and DR. M'WEENEY on "Some Recent Additions to the Fungal Flora of the Counties of Dublin and Wicklow," which will be published in *The Irish Naturalist* during the present year.

MR. J. J. DOWLING read some notes on the use of a hand-camera in the study of natural history, exhibited a home-made hand-camera, and showed in the optical lantern photographs taken with it.

MR. R. M. BARRINGTON showed an Antarctic Yellow-billed Sheathbill (*Chionis alba*), from Carlingford Lough (see *I. Nat.* ii., p. 56).

Mr. W. F. De Vismes Kane showed some female specimens of *Parnassius*, with reference to Scudder's late investigation as to the formation of the abdominal pouch in females of this genus.

Mr. Greenwood Pim showed an old Topographical Map of Counties Dublin and Wicklow.

LIMERICK NATURALISTS' FIELD CLUB.

January 17th.—Dean Bunbury in the chair. Dr. W. A. Fogarty delivered an address, illustrated by diagrams and living microscopic examples, on "Some Low Forms of Animal Life."

Mr. J. Stewart showed male and female specimens of the Emperor Moth (*Saturnia pavonia*), also entire cocoons of the species, exhibiting their formation and the position of the contained pupæ.

Mr. F. Neale showed specimens of the Silver-Washed Fritillary (*Argynnis paphia*), from Cratloe, Co. Clare, one of them having the left wings marked as in males of the type, whilst the right wings showed as in the typical females.

February 15th.—Dr. W. A. Fogarty, Vice-President, in the chair. Miss Bennis read a paper on "Plants, the Structure and Functions of their Organs," illustrating the subject by diagrams and specimens. Mr. Belshaw, Mr. Taylor, Mr. Moroney and others took part in the discussion which followed.

Dr. Fogarty exhibited a piece of osier, showing "*fasciation*" to a remarkable extent.

Mr. Belshaw showed the large fins or "wings" of a flying fish.

Mr. F. Neale showed specimens of the Reed Mace (*Typha latifolia*) in the stems of which, when gathered last August, he found some pupæ, the identity of these latter not being as yet established.

NOTES.

BOTANY.

FUNGI.

Trichia chrysosperma, DC.—Some moss which reached me from Valencia, Kerry, as packing for earthworms, was covered with very beautiful specimens of this fungus. This may be of interest as a record of distribution.—Hilderic Friend, Idle, Bradford.

PHANEROGAMS.

Plants still flowering in latter end of December.—On December 27th I went for a ramble in the Ballyhooley suburbs of Cork City, N.E., and found the following species:—*Capsella bursa-pastoris, Arabis hirsuta, Bellis perennis, Stellaria media, Trifolium pratense, Euphorbia peplus, Petasites vulgaris, Senecio vulgaris, Veronica chamædrys, Lamium purpureum, Ulex europæus*, the six last mentioned very abundant. In a garden in the same district I gathered *Primula vulgaris, P. veris, P. elatior, Fragaria*. These all testify to the extreme mildness of our southern climate up to the above date.—Anna N. Abbott, Cork.

A Sedge new to Britain.—In the *Journal of Botany* for February, Mr. R. Lloyd Praeger announces the discovery in Co. Armagh, of the fine sedge *Carex rhynchophysa*, C. A. Meyer, a native of Russia and Scandinavia, and not previously known to occur in the British Isles. An excellent figure and description of the plant by Mr. Arthur Bennett, F.L.S., accompanies the paper.

Festuca sylvatica in Co. Cork.—Mr. R. W. Scully writes to the *Journal of Botany* that he has added this handsome grass to the flora of Co. Cork, having found it in 1891 growing in a rocky wood overhanging the Glanmire estuary.

The Flora of Donegal—A Correction.—Mr. H. C. Hart, F.L.S., writes us, as follows:—"Kindly correct an error on page 15 of your last [January] issue.—'The flora of Donegal, I am informed by Mr. H. C. Hart, comprises about 720 species.' I informed Mr. Praeger that I had not decided at what figure to place the flora of Donegal, as it depended on how far *Rubi* and *Hieracia* were to be admitted as counting towards the total. If I count each form of bramble and hawkweed as a 'species,' my total will very considerably exceed Mr. Praeger's estimate."—EDS.

Mr. Hart wrote me, *re* flora of Donegal, under date September 23rd, 1892—" If I adopt new London catalogue, it would be a good lot over 700, if I adhere to Hooker it would reduce the total, but certainly not below the 700." The figure I quoted (720) was based on this statement, coupled with Mr. Hart's numerous published papers on the Donegal flora; I regret if it is below the mark. My phrase "I am informed by Mr. Hart," should read " I infer from information supplied by Mr. Hart."—R. LLOYD PRAEGER.

ZOOLOGY.

MOLLUSCS.

Additional Localities for Irish Land and Freshwater Mollusca.—I record a few localities in which I have taken Land and Freshwater Mollusca, not included in Dr. Scharff's most interesting articles (*I. N.* vol. i.). I am much indebted to Dr. Scharff for help in identifying specimens of which I did not feel sure. *Vitrina pellucida* occurs in Districts I. and XI. From my experience of the variety of surroundings in which this is found, I am sure District III., the only blank at present, will speedily be included in its distribution; *Hyalinia cellaria* is abundant in XI.; *H. crystallina* occurs not rarely in XI.; *H. fulva*, abundant in certain localities in II.; *H. excavata* occurs in II.; *Arion hortensis* is abundant in X., the blank districts of this widely-distributed slug almost certainly indicate simply that it has not been looked for; *A. intermedius* occurs in II. on Waterford side of river Suir; *Limax flavus* I found in my lodgings in X., a decidedly unpleasant fellow-lodger; *Amalia sowerbyi* is not uncommon in X.; *Helix pulchella* occurs in District X., as usually, in my experience, on sand-hills; *H. aculeata*, half a dozen specimens in Strabane Glen, X.; *H. lamellata* is abundant in one small glen in X., similar glens close by seemed destitute of it; *H. hortensis* occurs abundantly as a recent fossil in marl in District II, I have taken it alive in XI., which Dr. Scharff marks (?); *Buliminus obscurus*, I saw and examined one specimen of this taken in II., but entirely failed to procure specimens myself; *Balea perversa* is widely distributed in II.; *Succinea elegans* is, I think, quite as common as *S. putris* in II.; *Carychium minimum* occurs in X.; *Limnaea stagnalis* abounds in Co. Tipperary (II.) in certain small isolated ponds, it also occurs in River Suir; *L. auricularia* is found in one pond in Co. Tipperary (II.), it abounds (or used to) in the water-lily tank in Glasnevin Botanic Gardens; *Bythinia tentaculata* occurs in Killarney lower lake (I.); *Valvata cristata* in several running streams in II.; and *Pisidium amnicum* is common in River Suir (II.). From my own experience I have little doubt that close search would show that the distribution of Irish molluscs is by no means as local as the present state of these records would imply. For example, it is surely rather from lack of observation, than poverty in molluscs, that District III. makes so few appearances in these lists. I hope that a series of papers may appear ere long in *The Irish Naturalist* dealing with our marine mollusca. Such if written in a popular form would be a great boon to collectors who are unable to procure the expensive authorities on this subject.—A. H. DELAP, Fannett, Letterkenny.

AMPHIBIANS.

The Frog in Ireland.—With reference to Dr. Scharff's very interesting paper in the *Irish Naturalist* for January, he may be interested to know that the late Mr. Gage, of Rathlin Island, in answer to my enquiries, told me that the Frog had been introduced into Rathlin several times, but had always died out, although there are many bogs and swamps which would seem suited to it. Both spawn and adult frogs had been brought over from the mainland at different times, but neither succeeded.—ROBERT PATTERSON, Belfast.

An article on the Frog in Ireland by Mr. W. F. de V. Kane will appear in our next issue.

BIRDS.

Waxwings (Ampelis garrulus, L.) in Ulster. Two specimens of this rare winter visitor have been recently shot. Mr. D. C. Campbell of Londonderry writes us:—" On 31st January my neighbour, Mr. Ezekiel Bredin, slightly wounded and captured a bird which I found on examination to be a Waxwing in fine plumage. This is the first time I have met with the bird in this district."

Dr. A. M. D'Evelyn of Ballymena sends us, under date 6th January, a sketch and description of a second Waxwing, recently shot at Newferry, on the River Bann.

Autumnal Disappearance of Woodcock (Scolopax rusticula). Previous to the year 1889, I firmly believed that all our homebred Woodcocks deserted us in autumn, although it often struck me as being very strange that a certain locality should suit a bird, both as a breeding haunt, and also as a winter resort, and at the same time be found unsuitable in August and September. In that year I had discovered that I had never found Woodcocks during these months, simply because I had never taken sufficient pains in looking for them.

Within about four miles from the place where I live, there is a typical cock covert. It consists of a dense growth of birch, holly, stunted oak, etc.; one portion, having a southern aspect, slopes down to a narrow strip of bog, which separates it from the heather. Every year some birds breed in this wood. For the past three seasons I have visited it early in August, in order to find out how many clutches there were; I do this with the aid of my spaniel, and at the same time I calculate from the appearance of the young how soon they will be fit to shoot. I generally make my first bag about the middle of September. The old birds are not fit to shoot then, but it is very easy to distinguish between them, as the young are much brighter in colour. I sometimes, though rarely, do make a mistake on a snap-shot, and then what a wretched looking object my dog brings to my foot! I do not know any bird which, in moulting, casts its feathers as freely as a Woodcock; sometimes a bird will show a perfectly bare patch on the back. It is no wonder these birds, at this time of year, prefer to skulk in the thickest cover, and depend on their wit rather than their wings for safety; in fact, until their wing-feathers are grown, it is almost as hard to flush a Woodcock as a Water-rail. The young birds, observing their parents' tactics when menaced by danger, naturally act in a similar manner, and continue to do so until the withering of the Bracken renders concealment impossible.

In the covert to which I have alluded, an observer might tramp to and fro from morning till night any day in August, or early September, and, unless assisted by a good dog, he will probably go away under the impression that there was not a single Woodcock about the place. A steady close-beating cocker spaniel is the best dog to put up cock during these months; such a dog will not over-run a bird through excitement, nor lose time with a series of fruitless sets. When I first found our home-bred birds staying on till over-lapped by winter migrants, I mentioned the matter to a friend; he merely ridiculed the idea, and since then I have permitted every man to hold his own belief. Now, however, that I have had three seasons' experience—and indeed I might say four—I would not consider myself justified in keeping silent any longer on the subject.—JAMES JOHNSTON, Novara, Bray.

Buff-Coloured Snipe (Gallinago cœlestis).—Mr. W. A. Hamilton, J.P., Ballyshannon, writes us that his brother shot near that town in December last, a buff variety of the Common Snipe. We notice in the current number of the *Annals of Scottish Natural History* a note on a similar specimen shot on the banks of the Tay, in October last.

A White Curlew (Numenius arquatus, L.) A specimen of the Common Curlew, nearly pure white, has been shot by Mr. R. Murray, of Ballyhaunis, Co. Mayo. The bird has been preserved and presented to the Dublin Museum.—*Land and Water*, Dec. 31st.

Bittern (Botaurus stellaris, L.) in Co. Clare. A fine example of the Bittern has been shot by Lieutenant-Colonel Oakes in the vicinity of Kilkee, Co. Clare. This is the first that has appeared this year in Ireland.—*Land and Water*, Dec. 31st.

Goosander (Mergus merganser) in Co. Cork. On December 22nd a male Goosander was shot near Timoleague; I have often heard of these birds being procured near the coast. Is their occurrence here rare?—G. F. DONOVAN, Timoleague, Co. Cork.

THE SHAMROCK—NOTICE.

Readers of *The Irish Naturalist* throughout Ireland are earnestly requested to forward to Mr. Colgan *rooted plants* of Shamrock to enable him to complete his inquiry into the species of the national badge (see paper in our volume for 1892). Each plant should be gathered in a rural district on or shortly before the 17th of this month by an Irish peasant, who can certify the specimen to be *real shamrock* proper to be worn on St. Patrick's Day. The specimens, labelled with their places of origin and accompanied by a statement that they have been duly certified, should be forwarded, packed in damp moss to

NATHANIEL COLGAN,
1 Belgrave-road,
Rathmines,
Dublin,

who has undertaken to cultivate the plants, and publish the results in these pages. It is hoped that this appeal may meet with a willing response from readers of this journal and their correspondents in all parts of the country, so that a complete and full collection of *real shamrocks* from every county on the mainland, and every island round the coast may be submitted to examination.

The Irish Naturalist.

AMERICAN BIRD-VISITORS TO IRELAND AT HOME.

BY W. E. PRAEGER, OF KEOKUK, IOWA.

II. THE PURPLE MARTIN (*Progne subis*).

THE Purple Martin is one of those American birds whose occurrence in Ireland certainly cannot be attributed to escape from confinement; especially in 1840 (when a specimen was secured near Dublin), it was hardly likely that an attempt to transport such a purely insectivorous bird across the Atlantic could have been successful, as that was long before the days of ocean racers. That a bird of such great powers of flight and migratory habits should sometimes wander far from its native land is to be expected, and as this species is very abundant on the North American continent, it is not so surprising that wanderers should occasionally reach the western coasts of Europe.

The Martin spends the winter in Central and South America, none remaining in any part of the United States; but before the winter is well over, the northern movement has commenced, and they advance rapidly, long before the bulk of the insectivorous birds, and reach this latitude (Iowa) about the 1st April, and may occasionally have to endure snows or sharp frosts that not unfrequently occur at that time of year.

They do not seem to nest, however, till they have been with us some time, and I observed two pairs closely a few years ago which did not have eggs till the middle of June, but this was certainly unusually late. The Martins have now all forsaken their old nesting-places in holes in trees, or crevices in rocks, and take advantage of the houses that their friend man has provided for their comfort. The birds are such universal favourites that all over the country boxes are placed under the eaves or on some convenient tree or post for them to build in,

A

and the Martins often use the crevices about the eaves of the buildings themselves, and even make their homes among the factories and warehouses of the cities, where they may be heard twittering overhead, or seen gliding swiftly through the crowded business thoroughfares. No bird is more of a favourite with men, and even the Indians and Negroes in the south hollow out gourds and hang them on trees for the Martins to nest in, so that they may have them around their primitive homes.

The nest is rather a rough structure, built of straws and other rubbish, and lined with feathers. The eggs are four to six in number, pure glossy white; they are about the length of an English Swift's, but average a tenth of an inch more in breadth, and are much more glossy. During the nesting season the pair of birds keep close to their home, and the male assists the female; fights with the introduced English Sparrows are now common, and one of our worst charges against the strangers is that they drive away our beloved Martins. Individually the Martins seem more than a match for the Sparrows, but the latter are so numerous, so persistent, so cunning, and so unscrupulous in their methods of warfare, that in the long run the Martins have the worst of it. Sparrows will destroy the Martins' eggs if they are left unprotected, and it is not unusual for a number of the rascals to keep the parent birds engaged in a hot fight while others sneak in and destroy the nest and eggs. Is it any wonder that the governments of many of our cities, and even some of our States, have taken the matter up, and that in many places bounties are now offered for dead Sparrows?

In fair fight, few birds are a match for the Martin, and should a hawk, crow, or even eagle, come near the martin-house it will be instantly attacked, the smaller bird relying on its powers of flight for victory. Some farmers even say that the Martins are a protection to their poultry yards, giving warning as soon as a hawk comes in sight, and harassing the marauder should he approach too near.

The Purple Martin cannot be confused with any other swallow of Europe or North America. It might be said to be the least swallow-like of them all. It is quite large, seven and a-half inches long by fifteen and a-half in extent, of robust build, with strong feet and bill, the latter half an inch in length.

The wings are far from scythe-shaped, as usual in other swallows, and still more in the swifts, but have both edges rather straight, and approaching a triangle in shape. The bird nevertheless can match the best of them in speed, and graceful movements on the wing. Its food consists not only of flies and gnats, but also of bees, wasps, and beetles. Its note is a loud and varied twitter, almost amounting to a song. It is the only swallow of Ireland or the United States in which the two sexes differ decidedly in colour. The male is entirely a beautiful glossy purplish black, the female greyish brown, lighter or almost white on the breast, glossed with steel-blue on the back and head. Young birds are like the female, the young males being somewhat the darker, and soon showing traces of purple.

On the 17th October, 1887, when steaming down the Mississippi, near Burlington, I saw a flock of Martins, estimated at one hundred and fifty birds, in a dense cloud over the water, apparently feeding on a swarm of insects. The occurrence was remarkable, as I never saw so many Martins together before or since, and all Martins were supposed to have left this part of the country fully a month previously.

THE EARTHWORMS OF IRELAND.

BY REV. HILDERIC FRIEND, F.L.S.

(*Continued from page* 43).

WE are now to take the four groups into which the genus *Allolobophora* has been divided, and discuss the species which they respectively contain.

GROUP I. Lumbricoidea.

Allolobophora longa, Ude.—LONG WORM. This species is the type of this section, and the only British representative at present known. Although it is even more ubiquitous than the common earthworm (*L. terrestris*, Linn.), and has been known to the angler for ages past as the Black-head, yet it was only recognised as a distinct species seven years ago, when Ude described it in the *Zeitschrift für Wissenschaftliche Zoologie*(1886, vol. xliii., p. 136), from specimens found in rich soil at Göttingen. It had never, I believe, been recognised as a British worm, till I found it three years ago around Carlisle, although it is so common that university professors and others have frequently used it as their type when giving lectures on biology! In more than one recent text-book it is apparent that the learned author had not the faintest idea that the Long Worm was different from the typical earthworm. It may be found in every part of Great Britain, and is as widely distributed in Ireland as in England.

The Long Worm is rightly so named. It is usually about six inches in length, but varies a good deal both in size and colour. I am making notes on these variations as opportunity permits, because of their important bearing on many points of interest. Taking the species as a whole, I have observed already four well-marked forms of variation. First, there is the milky variety (var. *lactea*), which, I believe, is the same as Oerley's *Octoclasian lacteum*, found in Italy. It is found in clay or gravel, and is creamy white. Next comes a graceful, slight, and much-extended form found by shaking the soil of pasture land with a garden fork. A third variety presents a striking contrast to the foregoing. It is found in gardens and cultivated soil, and is coarse, rough, and thick-headed—altogether quite a clod-hopper type of animal compared with the pasture-lover. A further form has sunken male-pores, very dark head, girdle deeply coloured, and seems very like a hybrid. The position of the *tubercula pubertatis* in the pasture form suggests the possibility of its being a quite distinct variety, but the whole subject needs very careful study. There is something very characteristic about the shape of the prostomium when extended, exactly corresponding with a figure given some years ago by Lankester to a worm which he named *Lumbricus agricola*.

What may be regarded as the typical form of the Long Worm is marked by the following characteristics. The body is cylindrical, tapering in front and flattened behind. This flattened form of tail is indicative of the habits of the worm. It crawls forth at night and lies partly exposed on the soil, while the posterior extremity retains a grip of the burrow. In colour the worm is a deep sienna brown, not ruddy or brick-red, as the various species of *Lumbricus* are, though there is usually a small amount of iridescence present. The anterior portion is frequently so intensely dark as to suggest the angler's name of Black-head. The segments number from 150 to 200 in a full-grown specimen. The setæ are disposed, as in *Lumbricus*, in four couples, the individuals of which are nearly close together. The under-surface of segments 9, 10, 11, where the principal organs are located, is tumid and pale, while the male pores are readily observed on segment 15 situated on conspicuous pale papillæ. The lip can be greatly extended forwards, while posteriorly it cuts the first ring or peristomium only in part. In *Lumbricus*, it will be remembered, the lip completely bisects the first segment. (Fig. 8, p. 10). The first dorsal pore is found between the 12th and 13th segments. Ude was one of the first to draw attention to the value of this character, and it will be seen by the diagnoses which we shall supply, that there is usually a distinct relationship between the various members of the several groups in this respect.

The girdle of the Long Worm extends over the segments 28–35, three of which (32, 33, 34,) carry the so-called clitellar papillæ (*tubercula pubertatis*). I have observed in some varieties a divergence from this rule, but shall not at present puzzle the reader by the introduction of exceptions.

This worm is more liable than any other British species to "sport." I have received from different localities, and figured in *Science Gossip, Nature*, and elsewhere, several of these monstrosities. They usually take the form of a double head or bifurcate tail. As much is yet to be learned by the study of abnormal forms, I shall be gratified for any specimens which seem to be peculiar.

As I am constantly receiving fresh supplies of earth worms from Ireland—thanks to the industry of the readers of this journal—I shall have to give a special paper on the subject of distribution at the end of the series, when it will be possible to give a fuller and more accurate list of localities and collectors than at present. It may be stated, however, that up till the present I have received specimens of the long worm from the following localities:—

DISTRIBUTION IN IRELAND. Cashel, Co. Tipperary (Lieut.-Col. R. E. Kelsall); Blackrock, Co. Dublin (Miss E. J. Kelsall); Malahide (Mr. Trumbull); Glasnevin (Mr. J. R. Redding); Loughbrickland, Co. Down (Rev. H. W. Lett); Newcastle, Co. Down (Mr. Praeger); Cork (Miss A. N. Abbott); Carrablagh, Co. Donegal (Mr. H. C. Hart); Piperstown, Co. Louth (Miss S. Smith). (TO BE CONTINUED.)

THE FLORA OF COUNTY ARMAGH.

BY R. LLOYD PRAEGER, B.E., M.R.I.A.

(*Continued from p. 62*)

ANNOTATED LIST OF RARER PLANTS.

*Clematis vitalba, Linn. N. — ‐
   In hedges in several places about Armagh; W. F. J., and R. Ll. P.—an escape.

(Thalictrum minus, Linn., var. **montanum,** Wallr. — — S. ?
   "*Thalictrum flavum*, or meadow rue, which I found on the lake side near the summit of Slieve Gullion, and on the river side near the village of Middletown."—*Coote's Armagh*. The Middletown plant is undoubtedly rightly placed under *T. flavum*, but if the S. Gullion plant was a *Thalictrum*, it must have been *T. montanum*. I searched the locality indicated without success; it is the little lough of Calliagh Berras, lying at an elevation of about 1,800 feet).

T. flavum, Linn. N. — —
   On the river side near the village of Middletown, *Coote's Armagh*. Frequent in meadows near the Blackwater (Campbell), *Flor. Hib.* Near entrance of Lagan canal at Lough Neagh (Hyndman), and shores of Lough Neagh near Maghery (G. R.); *Flor. Ulst.* By the Blackwater at Maghery, S. A. S. Mullinure meadows near Armagh, W. F. J.! Wet meadows by the railway south of Portadown, R. Ll. P.

Anemone nemorosa, Linn., var. Mr. More records (*N. H. R.*) a state of this plant, with the petals of a rich dark purple colour, in an open meadow at Loughgall.

Ranunculus trichophyllus, Chaix. N. — —
   Crowhill, B. N. F. C., 1871, and Herb. N. H. P. S. spec.!

R. heterophyllus, Fries. N. — S.
   In Lough Neagh at Ardmore point, and plentiful in Camlough river between the lake and the village, R. Ll. P.

R. circinatus, Sibth. N. — —
   Entrance of Lagan canal; flax-hole on lake-shore near Ardmore glebe; in the greatest abundance in Lough Neagh at Derryadd bay, covering the water with a thick mat over a space of several acres, R. Ll. P. New to Ulster.

R. penicillatus, Dum. N. — S
   Lough Neagh at Maghery, S. A. S.! Callan river at several places near Loughgall, and abundant in stream at Forkhill, R. Ll. P.

R. lingua, Linn. N. — —
   Lake side at Loughgall, More *N. H. R.*! Closet river, H. W. L.! Entrance of Lagan canal, R. Ll. P.

*Aquilegia vulgaris, Linn. N. — —
   Lane at Killooney near Armagh, W. F. J. spec.! Frequent in hedges about Ardmore, H. W. L.

Papaver argemone, Linn. N. — —
   Gravel-pit at Killaghy corner near Lurgan, and gravel-pit by the railway two and a-half miles N.E. of Armagh station, R. Ll. P.

P. rhœas, Linn. N. — [S.]
   Armagh, abundant, S. A. S.! Cornfields near Armagh, W. F. J. spec.! Abundant on the limestone area lying between Armagh, Richhill, and Loughgall; not found anywhere else in the county, except as a casual on the railway at Wellington cutting south of Bessbrook, at Newry, and south of Portadown, R. Ll. P.

Papaver dubium, Linn. N. — —
Sparingly, on roadsides, chiefly, near Portadown, Lurgan, Armagh, Loughgall, and Maghery. The only spots where more than an odd plant was found were the two gravel-pits where *P. argemone* grew. Not seen anywhere in the centre or south of the county.

†**Chelidonium majus,** Linn. N. M. S.
Near Loughgall, More *N. H. R*! Hedge-banks near Tynan, B. N. F. C., 1889. Navan Fort! and between Armagh and Loughgall! W. F. J. Seagoe, H. W. L. Tartaraghan, Lurgan, and Armagh, S. A. S. Roadside by Lough Ross near Crossmaglen, and old walls in Tanderagee upper demesne, R. Ll. P.

Fumaria pallidiflora, Jord. N. M. S.
Rare. Noted from roadsides near Portadown, Armagh, Tartaraghan, Loughgilly, and Newry, R. Ll. P.

F. confusa, Jord. N. — S.
Near Armagh and Newry—probably frequent, R. Ll. P.

F. muralis, Sond. N. — S.?
Gravel-pit near Armagh (fide A. Bennett); near Newry (? A. Bennett), R. Ll. P.

F. densiflora, DC. N. — —
Gravel-pit by the railway near Grange N.E. of Armagh, R. Ll. P. (fide A. Bennett). The only previously recorded Irish station is Portmarnock (Druce, *Journ. Bot.*, 1891).

Nasturtium palustre, DC. N. M. S.
Maghery (G. R.), *Flor. Ulst.* (as *N. terrestre*); and subsequently, S. A. S., W. F. J., and R. Ll. P. Lurgan, S. A. S. Mullinure meadows near Armagh, W. F. J. Lough Gullion, bog south of Portadown, near Markethill, Mullaghmore lake, and Camlough, R. Ll. P.

N. amphibium, R. Br. N. —'—
Blackwater at Maghery, S. A. S.! Various places along Lough Neagh shore, such as mouth of Lagan canal, marsh south of Morrow's point, Bird Island, Closet river, and shore east of Maghery; also bog-drains south of Portadown, and in the canal south of Charlemont, R. Ll P.

Barbarea vulgaris, R. Br., var. **arcuata,** Reich. N. — —
Roadsides in several places near Loughgall, More *N. H. R.*! I found it by the roadside a little north and a little south of Loughgall; Mr. Bennett writes of my specimens "seems really Syme's plant;" Syme considered the Loughgall plant the only typical *arcuata* he had seen in Britain.

‡**B. intermedia,** Bor. N. — —
Near Armagh, *Eng. Bot.* Abundant in some cultivated fields near Tartaraghan, More *N.H.R*. Not uncommon in the county, especially in the north, as at Lurgan, Portadown, and Armagh, R. Ll. P.

Sisymbrium thalianum, Gaud. N. — —
Ardmore, H. W. L. North wall of Lurgan demesne, and luxuriant on railway ballast near to, and also three miles south of Portadown, R. Ll. P.

S. alliaria, Linn. N. — —
Lurgan, S. A. S. Ardmore, H. W. L. Roadside north of Loughgall, and near Castlerow, which is N.E. of Loughgall; roadside at Maghery ferry, and at Derryadd bay on Lough Neagh, R. Ll. P.

‡**Diplotaxis muralis,** DC. — — S.
On gravel ballast on main line of G. N. Railway at Wellington cutting, south of Newry, R. Ll. P. This rare plant, whose only known stations in Ireland are by the sea in the counties of Water-

ford and Dublin, grows in the present station along with *Sper­gularia rubra, Carum carui, Papaver rhœas*, and *Festuca rigida*. Its known occurrence in the Dublin district, and its association with *P. rhœas* and *F. rigida*, which are extremely rare in the north-east, but abundant in Co. Dublin, made me suspect that *Diplotaxis* might have been imported with the gravel from some station to the southward, and, an examination of the composition of the gravel having strengthened these suspicions, I applied to a friend of the engi­neering staff of the railway, who informed me that the material used on this portion of the line was brought partly from Goragh­wood, partly from a pit south of Dundalk, and partly from Skerries, which is situated by the sea at the northern end of Co. Dublin. A visit to the last-mentioned place, which appeared the most likely, was kindly undertaken at my request by Dr. E. J. M'Weeney, President Dublin Nat. Field Club, and Mr. David M'Ardle, of Glasnevin Botanic Gardens, with the result that *Diplo­taxis* was duly discovered growing in the gravel-pit there, along with *F. rigida* and *P. rhœas*, thus extending the known range of the plant some ten miles to the northward; and there can be little doubt that the plant has spread to Co. Armagh from its Co. Dublin stations. But, at least, it may rank as a colonist, since the railway at Wellington cutting has not been re-ballasted for many years.

[**Draba incana,** Linn. N. — —
A single plant on the gravelled edge of an avenue in Loughgall Manor demesne, W. F. J. spec! It is difficult to understand how this rare plant can have come here, but it must have been by some chance. Its nearest station is Magilligan, Co. Derry].

D. verna, Linn. N. — —
One station only. Sheep-walk near Armagh (Admiral Jones), *Flor. Ulst.*; and recently, W. F. J. spec.!

Cochlearia officinalis, Linn. — — S.
Estuary of Newry river, common.

C. danica, Linn. — — S.
With the last.

Thlaspi arvense, Linn. N. — —
Cultivated ground at Loughgall, More *N. H. R.* Roadside be­tween Portadown and Tartaraghan church, R. Ll. P.

*****Lepidium draba,** Linn. — — S.
In some abundance on waste ground below Newry docks, no doubt accidentally imported. R. Ll. P.

L. campestre, R. Br. N. — —
Among crops at Tartaraghan, and in a cultivated field near Loughgall (var. *longistylum*), More *N. H. R.* Mr. More writes me that he does not consider the latter form of any importance as a variety. Co. Armagh (G. R.), *Flor. Ulst.* Roadside near Lurgan (S. A. S.), Herb. N. H. P. S., spec.! Tannaghmore near Lurgan, R. Ll. P.

L. smithii, Hook. — M. S.
The distribution of this species is the reverse of the preceding. It is absent on the trap, limestone, etc., of the Northern district, but of frequent occurrence throughout the Silurian and granite areas.

(Subularia aquatica, Linn. (N.) — (S.)
Said to have been found in Lough Neagh by Sherard, *Flor. Hib.* In Lough Neagh, Co. Armagh (D. M.), *Cyb. Hib.* In the canal at Newry (Thompson), *Flor. Ulst.* Not found in Lough Neagh since the lake was lowered by drainage in 1855, but it is improbable that a plant which appears to have been abundant there has been exter­minated by this cause. The water in the canal at Newry is nowa-

days so impure that I was not surprised at my failure to re-discover it at that station).

†**Viola odorata,** Linn. N. — —
Co. Armagh (G. R.), *Flor. Ulst.* Grange! Loughgall! Tyross Hill, Tynan, W. F. J. Near Loughnashade, R. Ll. P. Doubtfully native in this county.

V. canina, Linn. N. — S.
Banks of Lough Neagh, More *N. H. R.*! Maghery, S. A. S.! Common along the Lough Neagh shore; on shores of Lough Ross, near Crossmaglen, R. Ll. P.

Drosera intermedia, Hayne. N. — —
Moyntaghs bogs (Hyndman), *Flor. Ulst.* Abundant on the extensive bogs south of Annagarriff lake, where it almost entirely replaces *D. anglica*, R. Ll. P.

D. anglica, Hudson. N. — —
Moyntaghs bog (Hyndman), and bog at Annaghmore (G. R.), *Flor. Ulst.* Bog near Maghery, W. F. J. spec.! Montiaghs bogs, H. W. L. spec.! Annaghmore, S. A. S. In many places, and often abundant, on the bogs which lie along the Lough Neagh shore between the Blackwater and Ardmore point, and sparingly on a bog south of Portadown, R. Ll. P. Not seen on the southern mountains.

(Elatine hydropiper, Linn. — — (S.)
In the canal at Newry (Thompson), *Flor. Ulst.* Not found there since, and probably not there now. The Lagan canal records of *Flor. Ulst.* and *Cyb. Hib.* are just outside our district).

*****Saponaria officinalis,** Linn. N. — S.
Montiaghs and Derryadd, H. W. L. spec.! Railway embankment near Tartaraghan glebe, and by the railway at Dublin bridge, Newry, R. Ll. P.

Silene noctiflora, Linn. N. — —
In a gravel pit near the railway 2½ miles N. E. of Armagh station, R. Ll. P.

Lychnis diurna, Sibth. N. M. —
Shore of Lough Neagh at Maghery, W. F. J. spec.! Raughlan, H. W. L. spec.! Banks of Closet river, and in Tanderagee upper demesne, R. Ll. P.

Sagina maritima, Don. — — S.
At the canal locks below Newry, and abundant on marshy ground near Newry docks, R. Ll. P.

S. nodosa, E. Meyer, N. — —
Near Navan Fort, W. F. J. spec.! Shore of Lough Neagh near Ardmore, H. W. L. spec.! Lowry's Lough, bog of Annaghmore, Lough Neagh shore near Reedy Island, and by a lakelet east of Middletown, R. Ll. P.

Arenaria trinervis, Linn. N. — S.
Hedges about Loughgall, More *N. H. R.* Tynan, S. A. S. Hedgebank near Lagan canal, old fort at Crowhill, and abundant under trees at Bessbrook viaduct, R. Ll. P.

A. serpyllifolia, Linn. N. — S.
Legarhill near Armagh, W. F. J. spec.! On the railway two miles south of Portadown, and frequent about Newry, R. Ll. P.

A. leptoclados, Guss. N. — —
Old limestone quarry near Grange N.E. of Armagh, and in a gravel-pit near mouth of Lagan canal, R. Ll. P. Mr. More writes me that he does not consider *A. leptoclados* specifically distinct from *A. serpyllifolia*, but only a slight variety, and that he has found intermediate forms. In Armagh both species occur in various situations, and they appear to me distinct.

Cerastium tetrandrum, Curtis. S.
On the G. N. Railway at Wellington cutting, R. Ll. P.

Spergularia rubra, Pers. N. S.
On the G. N. railway a mile south of Portadown, and at Wellington cutting near Newry, and abundant on the Greenore Railway near Narrow-water. Found, strangely enough, on railway ballast only, but the plant is certainly a native in the county, and not imported, since the Narrow-water and Portadown ballast at least is local material; the plant does not grow in the gravel-pit at Skerries, where the Wellington cutting ballast was presumably obtained.

S. media, Pers. — — S.
Estuary of Newry river, abundant.

Malva moschata, Linn. N. M. S.
Tanderagee (Templeton), *Flor. Ulst.*! Fields on Lough Neagh shore at Derryadd and Raughlan, H. W. L. spec.! Roadside near Lurgan (S. A. S.), Herb. N. H. P. S.! Hedge-bank a mile north of Newry, and in the upper and lower demesnes of Tanderagee, R. Ll. P.

(TO BE CONTINUED).

IS THE FROG A NATIVE OF IRELAND?

BY W. F. DE V. KANE, M.A., F.E.S.

DR. SCHARFF'S paper on the origin of this ubiquitous batrachian in Ireland seems to imply that an undoubted naturalization of some 200 years in this country does not confer the title of "native." But, joking apart, I would wish to examine the interesting problems suggested, and, no doubt, Dr. Scharff's remarks are more in the nature of a challenge for discussion than an attempt to press the interesting evidence he has collected in disproof of the tradition generally accepted against its indigenous origin, which tradition I, as an undoubted native, maintain. Now, with respect to the introduction of a colony of frogs before the year 1700 into the grounds then lying about Trinity College, Dublin, there is a collection of MSS. preserved in the College Library, formed by Dr. Thomas Molyneux, a portion of which was utilized in the volume published in 1755, entitled "A Natural History of Ireland, by Dr. Gerard Boate, Thomas Molyneux, M.D., F.R.S., and others." From one of these MSS. it would appear that, previous to the year 1700, there was projected a more comprehensive scheme than the meagre result above mentioned, and I find that to Dr. Gwithers was assigned the collection of information as to Irish quadrupeds, to the Provost and Dr.

Foley as to fishes, to the Lord Archbishop of Dublin and Sir R. Bulkeley as to insects; while Dr. Scrogs and Mr. Cox took in hand the botanical, and Dr. Molyneux the mineralogical sections.

In another paper we have short memoranda as to birds, by which it appears that the "cock of ye wood, *Urogallus major*," and "ye great Irish owle," were found then in Ireland and not in England; while the "magpye" was rare in Ireland and common in England; as also "ye comon black crow cornix, quære whether it be found at all in Ireland?" is a noticeable entry. But to come to the Frog. Under "Quadrupeds in England and not in Ireland" are noted "Frogg, toad, mole, water rat (vole), and roe in Scotland." From this we learn that Dr. Gwithers was not able to learn of the existence of the Frog at that time in Ireland, and certainly thought he was introducing a new animal. It is also well known from contemporary notices that after twenty-five years the colony spread rapidly far and wide. But if we are to accept Dr. Scharff's proposition, we must conclude that since 1700 the Frog has extended itself from Achill to Dublin, rather than *vice versa*. Now, if we examine the evidence brought forward in favour of its being indigenous, we find Stuart quoting Colgan to the effect that one specimen was first noticed in a pasture field near Waterford about 1630, and that Giraldus Cambrensis records in 1187 another, also in a locality near Waterford. We also have to note that in both cases they were viewed with unfeigned surprise by the inhabitants of the country. Now, if I might be allowed to conjecture that Giraldus's green Frog was the indigenous Natterjack, which, from its colour and more slender proportions, differs greatly from the Common Toad, and might well be taken for an Irish Frog, we should at once have a solution of the mystery; as the retiring habits of the former animal, its peculiar localisation, and its failure to propagate its species in such numbers as to spread widely either here or in England, would quite account for its not having been historically recorded since 1630. I think, too, the remarks of Giraldus are very convincing, when, attempting to prove his remarkable aërial germ theory, or the bacterial embryology of his specimen, he points out most cogently that if it had had been engendered by Irish mud "they would have been found more frequently and in greater numbers, both before and after the time mentioned." So it is evident that, after this single apparition, the land did not bring forth frogs abundantly, owing, Dr. Scharff suggests, to the ducks, an explanation which did not suggest itself to Giraldus. Nor does the frog sculptured on the Drumcree cross, as Dr. Scharff freely acknowledges, prove much. For, on the same most interesting but much weather-worn relic there is the representation of a camel (so most archæologists hold, though others have declared it "very like a whale"), but no one would thence infer that the camel was indigenous to Ireland.

To me the two real cruxes propounded in the interesting paper I am discussing seem to be the following:—Firstly, the presence of the bones of a frog in the deposits of the Ballynamintra caves. Now, if it be beyond question that the stratum in which these were found was extremely ancient, and not a surface deposit, it would be very convincing, but would it be possible to ascertain whether the remains might not be that of our undoubtedly indigenous Natterjack? The second difficulty put forward is the present wide distribution of *Rana temporaria*, which occurs more abundantly, we are assured, in the west than in the east of Ireland; while its introduction has been alleged to have taken place not more than 200 years ago. Now, as to its greater abundance in the marshes and mountains of the west, this is only to be expected, once it became naturalised there. It could not well be more numerous, however, in the fens of Wicklow than it is, and in such ponds and streams as exist in the county of Dublin. And when we consider that about twenty-five miles up the stream of the Liffey we reach the confines of the Bog of Allen, which extends almost continuously to the placid floods of the Shannon, and the series of lakes and lakelets of its upper reaches which drain the extensive bogs of Leitrim, Longford, and Roscommon, I do not think that it would be at all surprising if the spawn of so prolific an animal placed on the banks of the Liffey in the then marshy recreation fields of Trinity College, outside of Dublin, should find its way to Achill in, say, 100 years. For the aquatic birds which Dr. Scharff arrays on his side of the question to keep the batrachian hosts in check do undoubtedly aid in its distribution by carrying the spawn from marsh to marsh, and so probably to Achill. While conceding their probably larger numbers in former times, we must, at the same time, remember that the dripping forests and woodlands which, so late as Spenser's time, *i.e.*, about 1600, and later, as may be seen from maps, covered vast tracts of Ireland, would shelter the slimy victim from his winged foe, and aid his secure peregrinations.

So, if it is not an indigenous animal it had everything in favour of its rapid multiplication. Further, we may take into account the well ascertained and acknowledged phenomenon of the extraordinarily rapid multiplication of newly-introduced creatures in a suitable habitat.

In explanation of the difficulty which militates against Dr. Scharff's contention, arising out of the modern character of the Gaelic name for the Frog, he suggests that some more general term might have been used for an obscure animal which was not of use to man, etc. But I believe it is a remarkable fact, and has been frequently commented upon, that the Irish vocabulary is surprisingly rich in special and significant names of every sort of natural object; and that a considerable number of birds and plants were well recognised by specific names at a very early date in Ireland, so much so as to challenge the surprise of investigators, more than one of whom have pointed out that, notwithstanding the rude conditions of their existence, the Irish showed a keen perception of natural phenomena, and seized upon the characteristic features of any natural object with peculiar quickness. The very fact that any animal like a Frog was, as Dr. Scharff points out, looked upon as uncanny, even if not poisonous, would have rivetted attention to it, and secured it a place in the vocabulary if at all known. The caterpillars of Sphinx moths were noted, named, and a mass of fables were invented for them, as well as for the Newt or "Delicaluchre," as it is called. The "Dordeil" or uncanny-looking beetle *Ocypus olens* was also well known, sadly slandered, and cruelly ill-treated. I will not multiply instances, but end by asking whether there is any instance known of the common Frog inhabiting any country so suitable for its habitat and multiplication as Ireland, and being able nevertheless for centuries to exist in such small numbers, or under such circumstances as to escape the notice of intelligent inhabitants?

WATER SPIDERS IN CAPTIVITY.

BY REV. W. F. JOHNSON, M.A., F.E.S.

ON September 5th, 1892, a kind friend drove me down to Clonmacate, on the shores of Lough Neagh. Having arrived, I made for the shore of the lake, where, on a former visit, I had had some success in capturing Coleoptera. I soon came to a very promising looking drain covered with *Potamogeton*, etc. In went my water-net, and when I drew it forth I gave a howl of delight (there was no one near but two young lady friends who were watching my operations with great interest, so my antics did not matter), for here were two *Argyroneta aquatica*. I should, perhaps, explain that *Argyroneta aquatica* is an interesting and somewhat rare spider. It lives under water, thus differing in its habits from other spiders, and usually hides itself in the recesses of deep drains, only coming to the surface occasionally for air, and is, consequently, not easy to catch. This will explain my excitement on the present occasion. Having duly exhibited them, I secured them in boxes, such as one usually uses for Lepidoptera. I had forgotten my spider-tubes, so I had to put up with a substitute. In went the net again, and out came more *Argyroneta*, and with every plunge of the net there were more; in fact, I could have taken thirty or forty if I had so wished. Evidently I had come upon a regular rendezvous, the head-quarters of these spiders in that locality. I tried just skimming with the net, only a couple of inches below the surface, and took the spiders that way as well as when I plunged deep down into the drain. I secured as many as I thought would suffice Mr. G. H. Carpenter, and a couple for myself, and let the rest return to the maxillæ of their family. When I got home, I duly introduced those intended for Mr. Carpenter to a phial of spirits, and finding that two which I had put into one box had travelled without quarrelling and eating each other, I placed them in my aquarium, in hopes that they might condescend to live a little time therein, and give me an opportunity of studying their habits. I felt rather doubtful about this, for I had tried the same experiment with one caught in the Mullinures, but it had incontinently died. However, to my delight, the present pair seemed to have no intention of dying, and soon established themselves in the rock-work of the aquarium, and I had the pleasure of seeing each with a silvery web full of air. I was very curious about this web full of air, for I had been told that there were various theories as to the way in which it was filled, consequently I was much delighted one day at seeing the process. I noticed the smaller of the two spiders going backwards and forwards from a point below to the surface. Looking closer, I saw that it had spun a web, and was occupied in filling it with air. It would run up to the surface, fill its air sac, and run down to its web and empty its cargo of air, and immediately return for more, until the web was fully distended. For some days the two spiders kept their respective quarters, but one morning the smaller had disappeared, and I came to the conclusion that the larger spider had yielded to the worst instincts of its nature, and devoured its companion. I was consequently much surprised and pleased a few days ago, to see the small spider again, after losing sight of it for fully two months. The large spider had left its usual haunt, and the small one was coolly sitting there. It has since disappeared again, so I conclude it ensconces itself in some hole or corner where its bigger brother cannot intrude.

I was somewhat puzzled at first to understand what use the spiders made of the bags of air which they accumulated, but careful observation revealed the secret. The spider weaves its air-bag in some suitable position, and then sits with the opening of its own air sac in the woven bag of air, and is thus able to remain under the surface for a long time, and pounce upon any unwary denizen of the waters that comes within its reach. When the air in the web is exhausted, the spider does not seem to use the same web again, but to make a new one. Owing to this habit, the hole in which the big spider lives has got quite full of discarded webs. These, of course, are useful for entangling passing insects. Most of the time the spider sits motionless in its web like its congeners who live above water. I was much amused the other day at the big spider. I was poking about with my pincers, and put them near it, when immediately it made at them in most fierce fashion, and followed them out of its lair up to the surface. It then retreated, but on my putting the pincers down again, it again rushed out to the attack. I have not yet seen either spider in the act of capturing any prey, but as the number of water-beetles in the aquarium steadily decreases until renewed, and the spiders are plump and lively, I conclude that *Hydroporus palustris* and Co. furnish the arachnid dinner-table with sumptuous repasts. I found one cast skin, but of which spider I could not tell, probably the larger one.

As far as I can judge, the spiders are most active at night, and they choose for their residence the darkest corners of the aquarium. As the spiders are very well, I am in hopes that they will live for some time longer, and possibly enable me to add some further observations to the present notes.

Since writing the above (in December last), I have made some further observations

When travelling over the bottom, or on the rock-work, they move like other spiders, but when swimming they turn on their backs, and paddle with their legs, the hairs on which must assist this process. They look very funny when thus swimming, as they appear to be making vast exertions to walk upon nothing. They are able to remain below the surface, without renewing their stock of air, for a considerable time. I timed the smaller spider one day, and it was forty-five minutes without renewing its stock of air. During the most of this time it was running about on the bottom of the aquarium. This, coupled with their habit of remaining motionless in one spot for an hour or more, would account for the difficulty usually found in meeting with them. On 22nd December, the big spider was very busy with a new web, which it was filling with air. To introduce the air from its sac into the web, it applied the apex of its abdomen to the opening in the lower part of the web, and pressed the air backwards with its two hindmost legs so as to pass it into the web. It spent from 7 p.m. till 7.30 in this occupation, and then after a great rubbing of its legs against each other, got into the web, and sat there evidently in a great state of contentment. I have discovered the abode of the smaller spider. It is in a hole in one of the stones, from whence it is very difficult to dislodge it. It seems probable from what Mr. Carpenter tells me, that the large spider is a male, and the small one a female. This will, of course, account for their amiability, and as they are at the present time (March) still well, I may have an opportunity of seeing them rear a family.

THE SILICIFIED WOOD OF LOUGH NEAGH.

BY WILLIAM SWANSTON, F.G.S.

(*Concluded from page* 66.)

DR. MACLOSKIE, in 1873, gave an elaborate paper to the Belfast Natural History and Philosophical Society on the silicified wood, and expressed his opinion that the specimens found in the drift were derived from beds of Miocene age, and gave a fancy picture of a vast river flowing southward over a continent of which the Hebrides and Western Islands of Scotland form but a remnant, and this river brought the partially silicified wood, and scattered it along its course.

In the same year, 1873, the coal question was the all-absorbing topic, and Mr. Wm. Gray, M.R.I.A., then Senior Honorary Secretary of the Belfast Naturalists' Field Club, gave a valuable paper on "The Lignites of Antrim and their relation to true Cal." The subject was thoroughly gone into, and many new facts were brought forward; perhaps one of the most important being the discovery of silicified wood in the basalt at Laurencetown, where, he states:—

"There is a bed of lignite in the basalt about thirty feet from the surface, and in this lignite there are layers of wood charged with siliceous matter, and resembling the wood erroneously supposed to be petrified by the waters of Lough Neagh. This fact supplies the evidence Captain Portlock admitted was wanting."

After summing up all the evidence, which Mr. Gray puts into a concise form, he comes to the conclusion that we cannot escape the deduction that the beds of Ballypalady, Isle of Mull, those near Shane's Castle, and at Laurencetown, together with the silicified wood, and their associated lignites of Lough Neagh, are of the same age,—namely, Miocene, as supposed by various writers.

Taking the literature of the subject in its order, the next reference we have to these Lough Neagh beds is that made by the officers of the Geological Survey, and as their opinions are of great weight, it is necessary to examine them carefully. Sheet 47 and its explanatory memoir, describing the neighbourhood of Armagh, was issued in 1873. Sheet 35 and its explanation, descriptive of the Tyrone Coal-fields, and the south-west corner of Lough Neagh, appeared in 1877; these clay beds are there described fully, under the head of *Pliocene Clays*, their thickness being estimated at above 500 feet. The results of many borings and sections obtained in pits are given. Nearly all of these have records of lignites and ironstone nodules, the latter in one place containing reed-like plants. The writers are careful however to note that " in no instance has any specimens of the celebrated silicified wood of Lough Neagh been found in them, although a good opportunity for its discovery has thus been afforded over an extensive area."

The memoirs and sheet 27 appeared in 1881, and there is again another chapter on the Pliocene clays continued into the area which they represent. The author says—"That the fossil wood is more or less directly connected with the lignite seems to be generally admitted, but there has existed diversity of opinion as to the nature of this relation;" and he then proceeds to give one of Dr. Barton's definite statements, and quotes the paragraph describing his digging into the lignite deposit where some of his largest specimens where found, and concludes with the following paragraph:—" Mr. Hardman, one of the surveyors, supposes that the silicified pieces of wood had their *locus* in the basalt, and that the silicification is due to the percolation of water through the porous and easily decomposible rock. That this process does take place, at least to some extent, appears from a note to Dr. Macloskie's paper, referring to a specimen of partially silicified lignite found intercalated between beds of trap at Knocknagor, near Banbridge; and specimens are said to have been found in the heart of silicified blocks at Lough Neagh, resembling lignite of Knocknagor and the Giants' Causeway." Thus to a great extent, all the definite statements based on the observations and research of previous writers, that the silicified wood has its source in these clays, are ignored.

In company with Mr. Starkie Gardner, the writer visited the Lough shores frequently in the summer of 1884, when the waters were low, and while admitting the probability of silicified wood being found in the basalts, we were quite satisfied from what we saw, that the Lough Neagh examples and the numerous specimens scattered about that area are associated with the ironstone nodules, and are derived from the lignite-bearing clays in question, but no positive proof could then be gained, and the older writers stood unsupported. In December 1884, however, Mr. S. A. Stewart, of Belfast, and the writer again visited the ground, and found that a pit had been sunk on the margin of the lough at the spot so precisely indicated by Dr. Barton, that is to say Ahaness, half a mile south of Glenavy river. The pit had been sunk to obtain lignite for trial in some manufacturing process. We found the hole, about three feet deep, full of water, but after no small labour we cleared it. Under a foot of surface gravels, and some of the white tenacious clay which characterises these beds, was a solid stratum of lignite, that is, vegetable matter such as branches and roots of trees, twigs, and earthy matter, probably leaves, etc., much decomposed and all greatly compressed, and of a black or dark-brown colour. With a good deal of difficulty it could be dug, as so accurately described by Dr. Barton. We could not work long at the digging, as the water could not be kept out, but after throwing out several hundredweight had to abandon the work. On asking the very intelligent farmer who assisted us if he could tell us where the silicified wood came from, he at once said it came from the lignite, and could prove it. He said he had carted several loads of the lignite to his house for fuel, and on burning a large woody piece he found the heart of it was stone. The calcined remains of this important specimen he gave the writer, and pointed out the heap he had carted up, and in it was then found a piece, part wood and part stone, that had not reached the domestic hearth. Resident for a long time on the spot, he said there could be no doubt but the specimens found along the lough side had originally come from the lignite beds. Several pieces on his garden wall showed part still wood, although they had been there exposed for years.

All this is, after all, only corroborating what has already been described by Dr. Barton, and re-asserted by Dr. Scouler, our wish being to place it again on record, believing it to be the proof necessary to show the relation between the fossil wood and the lignites, as required by the writer of "Explanatory Memoir to Sheet 27" of the Geological Survey.

Having thus pointed out the source of what for accuracy may be termed the Lough Neagh wood, and at the same time admitting the occurrence of examples from the basalt, it is necessary to endeavour to define the position or geological age of the beds to which they belong.

The officers of the Geological Survey[1] have assigned them to Pliocene age, evidently from stratigraphical evidence only. In 1883 and 1884 Mr. J. Starkie Gardner, F.L.S., F.G.S. paid several extended visits to Belfast in furtherance of his researches in Tertiary floras. The writer had the advantage of accompanying him to the best fossil localities. On the visits to Lough Neagh large collections of the silicified wood and the ironstone nodules associated with it were made; many of these nodules were exceedingly rich in plant remains, in beautiful preservation, and they afford a key not previously examined, to the age of the beds. The plant-bearing beds interstratified with the basalts also received close attention, Ballintoy, Ballypalady, and Glenarm yielding a vast store of fossil evidence. To be brief, the results of Mr. Gardner's examinations of these, in the light of experience gained by working in all the English Tertiary deposits, as well as many on the continent, in Scotland, Iceland, and Madeira, will perhaps be best summed up by an extract from a paper which he read:—

"The plants which these nodules contain are most diversified, though usually small-leafed dicotyledons, which at first sight seem of very modern aspect. On closer examination, however, many are found to be characteristic of English Middle Eocene, and others of Lower Eocene. Others are common to Ballypalady, to Mull, and to Greenland. This mixture of types so separated elsewhere would be difficult of explanation did the thickness of the deposit not warrant the belief that it may have been continuously forming throughout more than one period of the Eocene. Most of the plant-remains come probably from the higher horizons now exposed on the shores of the lough; but some of them from the Boulder clay may come from much lower zones in it. The flora, however, is by far the most important link yet discovered between the Eocenes of England and those of high northern latitudes, and as such is deserving of most attentive study."[2]

To summarise, the Lough Neagh silicified wood (as distinguished from the few examples found in the basalt, which bear but little outward resemblance to it) is found in the lig-

---

[1] Memoirs of the Geological Survey; Explanatory Memoir to sheet 35, page 72.
[2] The Lower Eocene plant beds of the basaltic formation of Ulster, by J. Starkie Gardner, Esq., F.L.S., F.G.S.—Q.J.G.S., February, 1885.

nite beds of the clays, associated with ironstone nodules containing a rich assemblage of plant-remains, which point to a Middle or Lower Eocene age for the containing deposits. As all the fossil evidence obtained from the plant-bearing beds intercalated with the basalts of Antrim also points to the same horizon, some of the fossils being common to both, we cannot escape the conclusion that the basalts are of the same age, which is one much earlier than that previously assigned them; and they thus rank with the famous deposits of Mull and Greenland, and form perhaps part of the remains of the same stupendous volcanic outbursts. During the intervals in these outbursts, dense vegetation flourished, lakes and mountain tarns received deposits of detritus and vegetable matter from highlands, the position of which we cannot now even conjecture. Succeeding lava-outbursts overwhelmed most of these lakes, and their sediments were by heat and pressure converted into what are now the plant-bearing iron-ores of Antrim. The lignite beds of Lough Neagh, lying just outside the south-western fringe of these immense lava sheets, escaped the fate which overwhelmed the more northern deposits, and thus they still retain their unaltered plastic character. Infiltration of silicious waters, such as often accompany volcanic activity, reached some of the buried wood, altering its woody structure and forming the silicified wood of Lough Neagh. Students of geology in this age of enquiry would probably never have known of the existence of this interesting fossil, had not the ice of a Glacial Epoch cut deeply into the deposits, scattering their contents far and wide to delight and puzzle them.

NOTES ON THE FLORA OF THE ARAN ISLANDS.

BY NATHANIEL COLGAN.

(Concluded from page 78).

THE third day's work in Aranmore was the most successful of all. Traversing the island from Kilronan to Bungowla, in the extreme west, and returning by the shore through Port Cowruck and Monastir, I noted the range of the Aran form *vineale* of *Helianthemum canum*, found three additional stations for *Astragalus hypoglottis* in the neighbourhood of Kilmurvy, added to the flora of the islands one sedge, *Carex præcox*, abundant in a very dwarf form near Bungowla, found in Oorgowla lake the *Hippuris vulgaris* and *Myriophyllum*[1] of Mr. Hart, which Messrs. Nowers and Wells had failed to trace, and, as a crowning piece of good fortune, discovered a solitary plant of the long-desiderated *Ajuga pyramidalis* in a shady nook of rock close by the hamlet of Creggacareen.[2] The *Helianthemum* occurred, at intervals, from near Oghil on to Bungowla, over a stretch of about five miles, profusely in many places, and appears confined to that northern strip of the island lying between the high road and the sea, so that its upper limit here must be placed at a height of not more than 180 feet. In Lough Oorgowla I found *Ranunculus trichophyllus*, first reported from the islands by Dr. Wright, and on the way back to Kilronan observed several plants of *Thalictrum minus*, and a few of *Hieracium anglicum* on a rocky tract, strewn with granite and conglomerate erratics, close by the shore between Kilmurvy and Port Cowruck.[3] This station seems to be distinct from those recorded for these species by Mr. Hart. Near Port Cowruck *Chrysosplenium oppositifolium* was found, at Monastir Kieran the Male Fern, and at Creggacareen *Oxalis acetosella*. These three species, which seem to be among the rarest in the islands, were first added to the flora of the group by Messrs. Nowers and Wells from other stations in Aranmore.

A swift run of less than three-quarters of an hour in a large native *curragh*, or canvas canoe, manned by three islanders, took me next morning across the four miles from Kilronan to Inishmaan, or Middle Island, where I landed for a couple of hours before pushing on to Inisheer, or South Island, four miles farther to the south-east. Inishmaan seems to remain

---

[1] The plant was not sufficiently developed to admit of the species being determined.

[2] See note in *Journal of Botany*, of Oct., 1892, for details of this re-discovery.

[3] On the shores of this small creek opening N. W., great quantities of the *Laminaria* weed, the "Cowlyock" of the islanders, and of the western Irish in general, are thrown up by western gales, and kelp-burning is in consequence very actively carried on here. The *Slawth rawré*, or sea-rods, as the *Laminaria* stems are called, are highly esteemed for kelp-making, so long as their rind remains unbroken.

to-day what Mr. Hart found it in 1869, the most primitive of the three islands, and the visit of a stranger is still regarded as an event. As I strolled up from the landing-place towards the fine old cyclopean fort in the centre of the island, peering into the fissures of the limestone, and pausing now and again to jot down the species observed, I soon found that I was not the only one engaged in taking notes. I had only to raise my head sharply to set other heads ducking behind stone walls, or to catch glimpses of red petticoats flashing into ambush round the corner of some boreen. The net result of the two hours spent in Inishmaan was the addition of three species to the flora of the islands, *Erophila verna* from the old fort, *Pyrus malus* from the track to Ballintemple, one tortured shrub spread flat like a juniper over the limestone, and *Ranunculus baudotii* from shallow rock-pools north of Ballinlisheen. Maiden-Hair was rather frequent in the north-west of the island, and *Ceterach officinarum* less rare than in Aranmore and Inisheer. No trace of *Helianthemum canum* or *Astragalus hypoglottis* was observed either here or in Inisheer, though the latter was found in Inishmaan by Mr. Ball in 1835. As no botanist, of the many who have visited the islands, has reported the *Helianthemum* from Middle or South Island, it may fairly be set down as confined to Aranmore.

We landed at Inisheer soon after two o'clock, and here I secured very comfortable rooms in the house of Mr. Michael Costello, a retired constabulary sergeant, who takes an intelligent interest in his native Irish tongue. Two days were very pleasantly spent in exploring Inisheer, without, however, making any additions to the flora of the islands. Most of the prevalent limestone species of Aranmore were equally abundant in Inisheer. *Gentiana verna*, now almost past flowering (May 28th), occurred frequently, as in the other two islands, though apparently nowhere so abundant as on the limestone drift of Gentian Hill, and the promontory on the opposite shore of Galway bay, where it grows so freely down to sea-level, associated with another alpine species, *Dryas octopetala*. These curious isolated masses of drift, with their distinctly alpine flora, resemble nothing so much as slices of dead *moraine*, slid down bodily from some snowy range, carrying with them their freight of alpine plants.

Maiden-Hair in some parts of Inisheer is abundant and

luxuriant, the individual pinnules of some old fronds which I plucked measuring fully one three-eighth inches in their largest diameter. This fern is rather capriciously distributed over the island, and it seemed to me as if the absence or presence of the species depended largely on the direction of the limestone fissures with relation to the prevailing winds, though on this point my observations were not numerous enough to enable me to speak with confidence. *Arabis hirsuta* was plentiful in many parts of the island, and curious pads of *Carex pulicaris* were found here and there filling up hemispherical basins in the limestone, where, like sponges, they hold the rain water with sufficient tenacity to carry the species alive through the droughts of summer. A single plant of Juniper was known to grow in the island when I arrived there, and my discovery of a second plant, near the light-house in the south, gave deep satisfaction to the Inisheer boy who accompanied me in my rambles.

For the first-known Juniper had almost succumbed under the severe strain of recurring Palm Sundays, when it has been forced to furnish the island population of some sixty families with their emblematic palm. Throughout Ireland, as is well known, the Yew does duty for the eastern palm on such occasions; but the tree is nowhere found in the islands at present, though clear evidence of its former existence in Aranmore is afforded by the place-name, Oghil.

The boy, Peter Donohoe, who *assisted* at the discovery of this second Juniper, was well versed in Irish plant-lore, and I was able to get from him an Irish name for *Sedum anglicum*, a species I had never previously heard named in the native tongue. This stone-crop is known in Inisheer as *Poureenshingan*, or the Ant-fold, a name which is far from being so obviously appropriate as the Aran name for the Maiden-Hair, *Dubh-chosach*[1] or Black-footed (plant). The fitness of this native name for the stone-crop was however fully vindicated, when the boy, lifting up a large pad of the plant from where it grew on a slab of warm limestone, showed me underneath a swarm of ants scurrying over the rock in a comic state of panic. *Scangan* is the common Irish word for ant, and *poureen* the local name for a peculiar kind of roofed pen or fold made

---

[1] Pronounced almost as *Dhoo-hussock*.

of slabs of limestone, and used in Inisheer to shelter young lambs.[1] It is much to be regretted that no Irish botanist with an adequate knowledge of the old language of his country has ever been found to take in hand the preparation of an exhaustive lexicon of Irish plant-names, founded on personal research among the Irish-speaking peasantry.

Taking advantage of a favourable breeze on the 30th May, I took passage from Inisheer in one of the Connemara turf hookers, which constantly ply with fuel between the mainland and the islands, and after a run of an hour and a-half landed at the nearest point of the Iar-Connaught coast, to the east of Cashla bay, and just twelve miles north of Inisheer. I had failed after the closest search in the likeliest places to find any trace of *Neotinea intacta*, the discovery of which had been one of the chief objects of my visit to the Aran isles. But however modest were the results achieved during my short stay, I had no cause to regret the time and labour spent; for no one who takes the least interest in botany, or archæology, or folk-lore, can fail to find congenial food for his tastes in a survey of this most attractive group.

Before bringing these disjointed notes to a close, a few words may be said on the Aran flora as a whole. The total of species for the islands, brought up to date, and retaining in the list some three or four which have not been verified for many years, amounts to 419.[2] Compared with the total of the Howth flora, 547 species for an area of only one-fourth the extent,[3] the Aran district would appear to be decidedly poor.

But compared with Ben Bulben, and the similarity of the rock formation here to that of the Aran isles makes the comparison a much fairer one, the Aran flora appears to be decidedly rich.

---

[1] There seems to be no record of their poetic name for the Stone-crop in the Irish Dictionaries of O'Brien or O'Reilly; Cameron in his excellent *Gaelic names of Plants, Edinburgh*, 1883, omits the species altogether, and Wade, in his Latin Catalogue of Co. Dublin plants—a work which is very full in Irish plant names—leaves a blank under *Sedum anglicum* in the space for the equivalent native name.

[2] Or 420, adding in *Primula veris* (Cowslip), a species which no botanist has hitherto noticed in the islands, though Miss Kilbride, of the Rectory, Kilronan, assures me that she has found it growing sparingly near Kilronan and Killeany, where it flowers much earlier than the Primrose, which latter is abundant in the islands. N.C.

[3] See Mr. H. C. Hart's excellent *Flora of Howth*.

For the total of species recorded by Messrs. Barrington and Vowell[1] from the Ben Bulben district of fully four times the extent of the Aran islands, is only 430, or eleven in excess of the insular flora. And Ben Bulben, it must be borne in mind, is not only, relatively to the Aran islands, a continental area, but rises over a large part of its surface to a height which places it within the zone of alpine vegetation in Ireland.[2]

NOTES.

BOTANY.

LIVERWORTS.

Rare Hepaticæ at Leixlip, Co. Kildare.—On the excursion of the Dublin Naturalists' Field Club, 18th June, 1892, a hurried visit was paid to a narrow strip of marsh-land and shallow soil on limestone and diatomaceous deposit, which slopes on each side of the margin of the Ryewater river. It is on the south-west side of the railway station, and is excellent collecting ground for flowering plants, etc. (*Irish Naturalist*, vol. i., p. 101.) On July 2nd, in company with Dr. Scharff and Dr. M'Weeney we paid it a second visit, of more extended duration, when I collected the following liverworts, most of them in a fertile state. *Preissia commutata*, Nees; *Frullania dilatata*, Linn.; *Lophocolea bidentata*, Linn.; *Jungermania turbinata*, Raddi; *J. turbinata*, Raddi, var. *acutiloba*; this form which was quite new to me I fortunately found in fruit; I sent a portion to Mr. Slater, Yorkshire, an excellent authority on Hepaticæ, who says he compared the Leixlip plant with continental ones of *Jungermania corcyræa*, Nees, and they are identical. Dumortier in his last "Hepaticæ Europœæ," 1874, gives *J. corcyræa*, Nees, as a synonym of *J. turbinata*, Raddi (p. 79). He also gives on page 65 of the same work *Gymnocolea affinis*, Dmrt.; the two are, however, forms of the same plant, the latter being the obtuse-lobed form of his *J. turbinata*, Raddi, and the Leixlip plant the var. *acutiloba*; it is abundant in this station, I am not aware that this form has ever been found by any person in Ireland before; *Blasia pusilla*, Linn., plentiful (this is a new locality); *Pellia epiphylla*, Dill.; *P. calycina*, Nees, very fine, often immersed in water (this is a new locality); *Riccardia multifida*, Dill.; *R. pinguis*, Linn.—DAVID McARDLE, Glasnevin.

PHANEROGAMS.

Inconstancy of Colour in Flowers.—Recent references in these pages to the occurrence of White-flowered "Sports" of the Centaury (*Erythræa centaurium*) and other species have no doubt aroused interest in the general question of variability of colour in flowers. The question is one which has attracted the attention of botanists from early times; but so far as I am aware no law of variability has ever been established. Plukenet in his "Almagestum Botanicum," 1696, notes the White Cen-

---

[1] "Flora of Ben Bulben"—*Proc. R. I. Academy* 1885.
[2] Those desirous of learning more about the flora of the Aran islands are strongly recommended to read Mr. H. C. Hart's *List of plants found in the Islands of Aran*, Dublin, 1875.

taury; Caleb Threlkeld, too, the father of Irish botany, as he may be called, in a note in his "Synopsis Stirpium Hibernicarum" (Dublin 1727) observes:—"that many plants which commonly bring forth purple or blew flowers do vary into white or flesh-coloured, as *Bugula, Digitalis, Centaurium minus*" (*Bugula* and *Centaurium minus* being here old synonyms for *Ajuga reptans* and *Erythræa centaurium*); while Haller, in the second edition of his splendid work on the Swiss flora—"Historia Stirpium Indigenarum Helveticæ"—Berne, 1768—records the occurrence of White Centaury at two stations in northern Switzerland.

As for the sports of *Ajuga reptans* and *Prunella vulgaris* noted by Mr. Moffat in the January issue of the *Irish Naturalist*, they have been long recognized by botanists. Haller quotes Jerome Tragus of Strasburg, who wrote about the middle of the 16th century, as having recorded the red variety of *Prunella*, and Tabernæmontanus (A.D. 1590) the white, both of these varieties having been observed in Switzerland by Haller himself, the white, as he tells us, in hilly stations, the red in gravelly tracts.

Every practical botanist must early have noted in flowers the superior permanence of yellows to blues and purples, and will agree with the opinion expressed by Haller in the preface to his Swiss flora, where, discussing the value of colour as a specific mark, he lays it down that while yellows are rarely deceptive, blues and purples are frequently so. Increase of elevation above sea-level, I have myself frequently observed to be accompanied by a blanching of blue and purple flowers, as in the Field Gentian (*G. campestris*) and the common Marsh Thistle (*Cnicus palustris*) which, purple, as a rule, in the lowlands, are often white in the hills. Any attempt, however, to connect this blanching with one or more of the many changes of conditions necessarily or accidentally attendant upon change of elevation would soon lead the inquirer beyond the domain of botany pure and simple into the fields of biology and organic chemistry.

Perhaps some reader of *The Irish Naturalist* with the necessary attainments in these provinces could throw light on this very interesting subject. Field botanists by systematic observation of the obvious changes of condition accompanying changes of colour, would, no doubt, help towards the solution of the problem.—N. COLGAN, Dublin.

The Tree Mallow (Lavatera arborea) in Ireland.—As Mr. Praeger mentioned (*Irish Naturalist*, vol. ii., page 53.) the Tree Mallow, as growing on isolated and precipitous rocks on Rathlin Island, on the north coast, it may interest readers to hear of the same plant in similar situations off the south-west coast. Large bushes of it may be found growing on the "Little Skelligs Rock," which is fully eight miles from nearest point of mainland, and ten, at least, from nearest houses on mainland. The Little Skelligs is very precipitous, rising in broken pinnacles to about 600 feet; it is and always has been uninhabited, except by the myriads of sea-birds which frequent it in the breeding season; so far as I have noticed on various visits it is totally unfrequented by any *seed-eating* birds.

Another plant I may mention which grows in great luxuriance is known here as "Skellig Spinach," and used as such—I think it is known as "Good King Henry"—and yet another very abundant growth there, is a very large-leafed Sorrel. These with great tufts of Thrift, both pink and *white* grow above the wash of the heavy Atlantic rollers that incessantly break round the foot of the cliffs.—ALEX. DELAP, Valencia Island.

ZOOLOGY.

MOLLUSCS.

Valvata cristata in Co. Cork.—It is stated in the December number of *The Irish Naturalist* (vol. i., p. 178) that the above shell seems quite absent from the south-west of Ireland. I have, therefore, much pleasure in recording it from this district, having collected specimens in the slow streams near Cork park, about one and a-half miles from the city.—R. A. PHILLIPS, Ashburton, Cork.

INSECTS.

Sirex gigas in the North of Ireland.—This fine Saw-Fly, though not yet known as a permanent resident in the North of Ireland, is apparently on the increase in that district, owing either to a greater number of imported specimens, or to the establishment of small colonies in spots which have not yet been discovered. While a number of the recent local captures of this animal point to its introduction in timber or otherwise, other specimens were taken in the open country, and many have had a local origin. As the Irish records of this species are few, possibly a note of its recent occurrences in the north-east may be of interest. Between 1885 and 1888 several specimens were taken in the neighbourhood of Belfast, of which no note was kept. In 1888 one was taken in a timber yard in Armagh, and another in a shop-window in the same city (see *Entomologists' Monthly Mag.* vol. xxv., 1st series, p. 132). In 1889 three were found in Lord Lurgan's vinery at Lurgan. In 1890 one was taken at the Sirocco Works at Belfast. The following year yielded a number of specimens. Mr. John Hamilton received one which was captured in a Belfast warehouse; two Armagh timber yards yielded a specimen each; one was taken at Conlig, Co. Down, by Mr. G. B. Coulter, and several in the neighbourhood of Holywood. In 1892 Mr. J. H. Davies captured two in the open air at Lisburn; Lady Clanmorris forwarded a Bangor specimen to the Belfast Museum; one occurred in Messrs. Martin's timber yard in Belfast; Dr. J. S. Darling forwarded me a specimen taken on a grocer's window in Lurgan; and a very fine example was found by Mr. H. T. Mercer crawling on a road at Cultra, near Holywood. All the specimens which I have seen, or which were described to me, were females. I have heard of several other occurrences, of which, however, I have not been able to procure authentic information. I have to thank Rev. W. F. Johnson, M.A., Dr. J. S. Darling, and Messrs. S. A. Stewart, R. M. Young, John Hamilton, and J. H. Davies, for assisting me in the above compilation.—R. LLOYD PRAEGER.

BIRDS.

The Eagle Owl (Bubo maximus) in Ireland, and former scarcity of the Magpie (Pica rustica).—No record of the capture of this large Owl in modern times in Ireland has been substantiated, I believe, but the following memoranda may be of interest, as it is quite possible that when natural history pursuits become more generally in favour, many rare species may be discovered. When in conversation lately with Robert B. Evatt, Esq., of Mount Louise, Monaghan, now a very old man, he assured me that many years ago he had seen two Eagle Owls at rest in the daytime on a wooded island in upper Lough Erne, belonging to Mr. Porter of Belleisle, and was deeply impressed by their size and noble appearance. Mr. Evatt is a practical naturalist of long and wide experience, and Mr. Williams, senior, the well known taxidermist of Dublin, owes his first lessons in bird-stuffing to his instructions. He is thoroughly conversant with our common species of Owl such as the Long-Eared and Woodcock Owls, so that his testimony cannot be well ignored. But, in the absence of a specimen, and of further corroboration it is insufficient to entitle the species to a place in the category of modern Irish birds. The bird appears, however, anciently to have been acknowledged indigenous here, as in the MS. preserved among the Molyneux documents, and referred to in my remarks under the heading of "Is the Frog a Native of Ireland," I find "ye cock of ye wood *Urogallus major*," and "ye Great Irish Owle," set down as "Birds found in Ireland, not in England." With reference to the Magpie which is entered as "rare in Ireland but common in England" (*i.e*, about the year 1700), there is also an interesting record of a flight of Magpies from England in 1670 "landing where the English first did (Barony of Forth)," Co. Wexford.—WM. FRAS. DE V. KANE, Drumreask, Monaghan.

Mealy Redpolls (Linota linaria) on Achill Island.—In the early part of February a specimen of the Mealy Redpoll was shot on Achill island, Co. Mayo, and has been presented to the Dublin Museum through Mr. Williams. It appears that a small flock of about eight had remained on the island during the whole winter, having evidently then been on their way south from their northern summer quarters. The track of this bird's migration from northern Scandinavia, where it breeds, to the south, is supposed to pass down the east coast of Scotland and England, and the appearance of the species on the west coast of Ireland, must, therefore, be looked upon as a quite exceptional occurrence. Mr. A. G. More gives only a single Irish record in his "List of Irish Birds."—R. F. SCHARFF, Dublin.

The Serin (Serinus hortulanus) in Ireland.—Mr. E. Williams writes to the *Zoologist* for March:—On the 2nd of January one of our local bird-catchers brought me a bird which he described as a "Mule Siskin." I was much pleased to identify it as a Serin, *Serinus hortulanus*, in adult winter plumage, the first occurrence in Ireland. From the fact of never seeing a caged bird of this species here, and the capture of upwards of a dozen in England, I think there can be little doubt that this was a genuine wild bird, and as such, entitled to be added to our Irish list.

Waxwing (Ampelis garrulus) in Co. Wicklow.—A specimen of the Waxwing, *Ampelis garrulus*, was shot in the village of Delgany, Co. Wicklow, in the early part of January last. It was exceedingly fat, and had been feeding on holly-berries.—E. WILLIAMS in *Zoologist* for March.

Waxwing in Co. Antrim.—A Waxwing was shot at Ballinderry, Co. Antrim, a day or two ago, by a farm labourer.—"J. A. B.," in *Land and Water* of 4th March.

Waxwing near Londonderry.—Another specimen of the Waxwing was shot near Londonderry during the last week of January, by Mr. Lawrence Nash.—D. C. CAMPBELL, Londonderry.

Bittern (Botaurus stellaris) in Ireland.—Seeing a notice in last month's *Irish Naturalist*, p. 86, that the only Irish specimen of the Bittern obtained last year was one shot by Lieut.-Col. Oakes, Kilkee, Co. Clare, I mention that Thomas Plunkett, Esq., Enniskillen, has written to me that he obtained a fine specimen of the Bittern on the 5th January, 1893, about seven miles from that place. I did not think this of sufficient interest to record earlier.—ARTHUR J. COLLINS, Belfast.

Bewick's Swan (Cygnus bewickii) in Co. Armagh.—These swans appeared to be more numerous near Loughgilly than usual this winter. The first record I received was on January 15th, when five "swans" were reported flying south. On the 18th five were again reported northwest. On the 26th I was informed that five birds were feeding on a piece of marshy land that had been flooded over by the heavy rains, and they were reported to be still there on the 28th. On the 2nd of February I received a message that twelve birds were on the same bog, and on the 4th I was informed that "four or five" were on a small lake known as Mulloughmore. On the 7th, seventeen were on the bog first mentioned; I was told they went away when shot at. They were heard calling by my informant the same night.

On the 8th fifteen birds passed over in an easterly direction, which from their voice I identified as Bewick's. On the 9th I found five birds on Mulloughmore lake which were also undoubtedly Bewick's Swans.

In previous winters we only had small flocks of four to eight, which seldom remained for long.—H. LYSTER JAMESON, Killincoole, Castlebellingham.

Ferruginous Duck (Nyroca ferruginea) near Athlone.—Mr. E. Williams writes in the *Zoologist* for March, that a specimen of this duck was shot on the Shannon, near Athlone, on 21st January last, by Mr. R. Surtington.

GEOLOGY.

Supposed Animal Footprints in Old Red Sandstone Rocks.—A paragraph in the *Tuam Herald* of 3rd February, seems to demand attention. It states that "on the old road between Molranny" (Malaranny of the one-inch Ordnance Map) "and the village of Bonnyglan" (Bolinglanna of the map?), "and within a mile of the latter old mining station, there are imprinted on the solid rock footprints of huge animals." These places are on the mainland, east of Achill island, and at the foot of Curraun Achill. The Geological Survey have here mapped and described (sheet 74, and memoir to sheets 63 and 74) a tract of Old Red Sandstone lying on the schists and quartzites, the latter being possibly Precambrian. If there are genuine footprints in this rock, the fact would be of great importance, though there would be no reason to ascribe them to a mammal, as is hinted by the writer in the *Tuam Herald*. This writer, however, is clearly familiar with geological terminology, and it becomes imperative for some one to set the question of these alleged footprints at rest. They may be footprints of a "quadruped" with its "calf" running beside it, as suggested by the writer in the *Herald*, or rain-pittings, gradually enlarged; or the hollows from which a number of concretions have fallen away. If there is any likelihood of their being footprints, such as occur in the Triassic sandstones of England, it is to be hoped that some one will be able at once to photograph them, to measure them and the distances between them, to draw them accurately in plan, and even to take plaster impressions from them. Any investigation of them will be awaited with interest by the readers of *The Irish Naturalist*. If the writer in the *Tuam Herald* is recording what he himself has seen, it becomes his scientific duty to prove his statement at the earliest opportunity; since the occurrence of true footprints in this sandstone may give us evidence of the existence of amphibians in the lowest Carboniferous of Ireland, or even in the upper Devonian series. This is, perhaps, too much to hope for.—GRENVILLE A. J. COLE, Dublin.

PROCEEDINGS OF IRISH SOCIETIES.

ROYAL ZOOLOGICAL SOCIETY.

Recent donations comprise a Japanese Deer from Sir Douglas Brooke; a pair of Bramble-Finches from Miss Roberts; four Wild Ducks from J. H. Sutton, Esq.; and a monkey from C. G. Fitzgerald, Esq.

4,300 persons visited the gardens in February.

At the Annual Meeting on January 31st, Dr. S. Gordon was elected President, and Dr. A. Traill, Rev. Dr. S. Haughton, Mr. W. Findlater, Prof. Haddon, and Mr. S. U. Roberts, Vice-Presidents for 1893. Rev. Dr. C. W. Benson, so well known for his ornithological work, was elected an Honorary Member of the Society. The Report for 1892 states that the year has been a very successful one, the number of visitors having increased, and a sum of £264 being balance to the credit of the Society. An outdoor aviary will shortly be commenced and should prove an attractive feature. Two very fine lion cubs (male and female) were born in the gardens during 1892. It is possible that hybrids between a tiger and a lioness may be produced during the present year; an interesting account of the former production of such hybrids is given in an appendix by the Secretary, Dr. V. Ball, C.B., who has since the publication of the Report obtained new information on the subject.

DUBLIN MICROSCOPICAL CLUB.

FEBRUARY 15th.—The Club met at MR. A. ANDREWS. *Specimens of Epicoccum purpurascens* were shown by MR. GREENWOOD PIM. This fungus occurred on young leaves of *Congline australis*, recently killed by frost in his garden. The species was somewhat striking both to the naked eye and under the microscope, on account of the vivid red mycilium which in large quantities surround the spores, which do not very materially differ from those of *E. neglectum*.

Venturia sp. was exhibited by MR. F. W. MOORE. The specimens were found growing on the leaves of *Nardla scalaris*, collected in Co. Wicklow. They have been submitted to Dr. M. C. Cooke, who stated that this must be a new species of *Venturia*. Hitherto only one species has been found on cryptogams, and this is much larger than the species which was submitted.

Rhopalorhynchus clavipes was shown by MR. G. H. CARPENTER. This is a pycnogon discovered by Prof. Haddon in Torres straits, and described and figured by exhibitor (*Sci. Proc. R.D.S.*, n.s. vol. viii.); it is remarkable for the extreme attenuation of the body, this character of the group being specially developed in the present genus. The femora are swollen distally, a character from which the species is named. A false leg was shown under the compound microscope. This appendage is ten-jointed, the terminal joints bearing scythe-shaped spines. The complicated series of muscles for moving the joints was well shown in the preparation.

Anthelia juratzkana, Limpr. (*fertill specimen*) was shown by MR. D. M'ARDLE, who had collected it amongst the rocks at the Bailey Lighthouse, Howth, in 1891, and had since found it growing in small quantity on Ireland's Eye and Dalkey island. (See "The Plants of Dalkey island," *Irish Nat.*, vol. i., p. 134, where a list of the localities known for the plant is given). He also exhibited a figure of the plant drawn by Mr. W. N. Allen.

BELFAST NATURALISTS' FIELD CLUB.

FEBRUARY 21st.—The President (MR. J. VINYCOMB, M.R.I.A.), in the chair. MR. FRANCIS JOSEPH BIGGER, M.R.I.A., read a short paper on "Some Local Folk-lore." MR. WILLIAM GRAY, M.R.I.A., delivered an interesting lecture on "Worked Flints, Ancient and Modern."

BELFAST NATURAL HISTORY AND PHILOSOPHICAL SOCIETY.

FEBRUARY 17th.—The President (PROF. FITZGERALD, M.I.C.E.), in the chair. MISS ALICE MILLIGAN read a paper entitled "Historic Ulster," illustrated by limelight views.

MARCH 7th.—The President in the chair. DR. SHELDON, M.A., read a paper on "Education—a Critical Examination of the Theory and Practice of Dr. Arnold, of Rugby." MR. W. H. PATTERSON, M.R.I.A., read a paper on "Hints on collecting Irish Folk-lore."

ARMAGH NATURAL HISTORY AND PHILOSOPHICAL SOCIETY.

MARCH 6th, 1893.—REV. W. F. JOHNSON, M.A., F.E.S., President, in the chair. The President exhibited specimens of *Sphinx convolvuli* from Armagh and Gloucestershire, and of *Deilephila galii* from Wallasey, Cheshire, and remarked on the various theories as to their sudden appearance in numbers in particular years.

CORK NATURALISTS' FIELD CLUB.

FEBRUARY 15th.—The President, PROF. MARCUS HARTOG, in the chair. MISS H. A. MARTIN, M.R.C.P., read a paper on "Mushrooms and Toadstools," explaining the propagation of these curious and interesting organisms, and the mode of growth, shape, and peculiarities of those species most frequently brought under our observation. She also showed the fatal beauties and brilliant colourings of the poisonous kinds when compared with those which are edible. Her personal observations on fungi in fish were most interesting. Mr. O'Sullivan gave his experiences of rust on wheat.

MARCH 15th.—The President, PROF. MARCUS HARTOG, in the chair. The President called attention to the microscopic appearance of fish-scales as a means of identifying fish, and referred to a case reported in the last number of the *Field*, where, at Youghal, a number of salmon poachers were convicted, the microscope being used in court to demonstrate the characters of the scales to the bench.

MR. BENNETT exhibited *Hymenophyllum tunbridgense* from Glengariffe.

MISS MARTIN exhibited a rare coral dredged by the Rev. W. S. Green, off the coast of Cork in 1890.

The President announced that Mr. T. Dillon had undertaken to edit notes for a paper on the "Earthworms of Cork," kindly sent by the Rev. Hilderic Friend.

MR. T. FARRINGTON, F.C.S., read a paper "On the Dolomite or Magnesian Limestone of Cork," giving a full description of its mode of occurrence, characters, and chemical analysis. He suggested that in post-Carboniferous times, probably Permian, after the denudation of the Coal Measures, and the dynamic action which had determined the present ridges and troughs, the fissured exposed surface of the limestone was depressed below the Permian sea, and then filled by magnesian deposit. Glacial erosion was probably the cause of the removal of this Permian dolomite from the general surface of the land. After observations from the President and Dr. Knight, Mr. Shaw, C.E., criticised the assumption that gaping fissures could be formed in a synclinal trough like that of the Cork limestone. In support, however, of the author's views he referred to Permian beds at Dingle, which he had visited. Mr. Porter dissented from the view that the dolomite was Permian; he thought that the limestone had been dolomised *in situ*, possibly by the action of humic acid, etc., in the neighbourhood of faults. Mr. Bergin also took part in the discussion. Mr. D. O'Mahony, F.C.S., called attention to the remarkable absence of magnesia in the limestone rock in the neighbourhood, and in the water derived therefrom.

At various meetings of the Club, PROF. M. M. HARTOG has mentioned the following rare or interesting finds in "Pond Life"—

SCHIZOMYCETES:—*Beggialoa roseopersicina*, Zoff., in tanks at Queen's College—Lankester's "Peach-coloured Bacterium," the Clathrocystis form appearing as specks visible to the naked eye.

SAPROLEGINEÆ:—*Aphanomyces sp.*, Bennet's lough, two miles north-east of Cork.

DESMIDIACEÆ:—*Didymoprium grevillei*, Kütz., Bennet's lough.

RHIZOPODA:—*Pelomyxa palustris*, Greep, tanks at Queen's College. This gigantic multinucleate amœboid attains here a diameter of over one-twelfth inch.

CILIATA:—*Urocentrum turbo*, Müll., *Loxodes ehrenbergii*, tanks at Queen's College.

TURBELLARIA:—*Catenula lemnæ*, Dugès, *Microstomum lineare*, O. F. Müll., *Mesostomum rostratum*, Ehrb., *Planaria torva*, Bennet's lough; the first two species show fission exquisitely.

ROTIFERA:—*Floscularia longicaudata*, Huds., tanks at Queen's College; this rare species is only recorded from Scotland; *Taphrocampa sp.*, lower pond at Queen's College, this species has both a malleoramate mastax and two distinct pink eyes, thus differing from either species described by Hudson.

OLIGOCHÆTA LIMICOLA:—*Chætogaster crystallinus*, a large species revealing its structure under a pocket-lens, in tanks at Queen's College;

Ælosoma varians, Bennet's lough and tanks at Queen's College; *Æ sp.* with granules colourless instead of green or red, Bennet's lough; *Bohemilla ornata*, Vejd., Bennet's lough, this species has tufts of as many as seven dorsal setæ, which are frayed or plumose, giving the worm a very polychæte appearance.

LIMERICK NATURALISTS' FIELD CLUB.

MARCH 14th.—The President, MR. A. MURRAY, in the chair. MR. ROBERT GIBSON read a paper entitled "An Introduction to the Study of Geology," illustrating it with coloured diagrams and maps, and examples of local rocks and fossils. Mr. Murray, Mr. Taylor, Mr. Gibson, Mr. Belshaw, and Dr. Todd took part in the discussion which followed.

MR. F. NEALE showed specimens of the Greasy Fritillary *(Melitea aurinia* var. *hibernica)*, and a colony of its young gregarious larvae spun up in their winter domicile, or web. This insect appears to occur plentifully at Cratloe, and Mr. Kane states that it is the distinctively Irish type, and as such is an interesting record.

ROYAL DUBLIN SOCIETY.

JANUARY 11th.—PROF. SOLLAS in the chair. DR. J. JOLY read a paper entitled "A Suggestion as to the cause of the bright colour of Alpine Flowers." Flowers growing at high altitudes are much brighter than those of the same species in valleys. This has been explained by Helmholtz and others as due to the brighter sunlight; but Dr. Joly considers it to be the result of a process of natural selection of the brighter flowers, which alone succeed in attracting insects, and so securing fertilisation; as the short seasons, and great destruction of insects by cold in alpine regions must render the struggle for existence among flowering-plants severe. Prof. T. Johnson and Rev. W. S. Green took part in the discussion, the latter remarking that in the New Zealand Alps the flowers at high elevations are very pale.

PROF. G. A. J. COLE gave a paper on *Hemitrypa hibernica*. This interesting fossil will be described for readers of *The Irish Naturalist* in his forthcoming paper on the Irish Fenestellidæ.

FEBRUARY 21st.—A paper on Human Sacrum was communicated by PROF. PATERSON.

ROYAL IRISH ACADEMY.

FEBRUARY 13th.—PROF. M. M. HARTOG read a paper "On the Cytology of the Saprophytæ."

FEBRUARY 27th.—DR. C. R. BROWNE read a paper "On some Crania from Tipperary." A grant of £20 was voted to a Committee consisting of Dr. Scharff, Mr. R. Lloyd Praeger; Mr. A. G. More; Mr. R. M. Barrington; Mr. Greenwood Pim; Mr. H. Dixon; Dr. M'Weeney; Mr. G. H. Carpenter; Professor T. Johnson; and Professor E. P. Wright, to aid them in framing a Report on the present state of our knowledge of the Flora and Fauna of Ireland, and as to what is needed to bring this knowledge up to date.

This Committee held its preliminary meeting on March 18th. Dr. Scharff was elected chairman and treasurer, and Mr. Carpenter convener. Prof. E. P. Wright explained the objects for which the Committee had been formed. The section appointed to prepare the preliminary report on the Irish Flora consists of Mr. H. H. Dixon, Prof. T. Johnson (convener), Dr. M'Weeney, Mr. A. G. More, and Mr. Greenwood Pim. The section to report on the Irish Fauna, including Tertiary Palæontology, consists of Mr. R. M. Barrington, Mr. G. H. Carpenter, Mr. R. L. Praeger, and Dr. Scharff.

The Irish Naturalist.

Vol. II. MAY, 1893. No. 5.

THE HUMP-BACKED WHALE ON THE IRISH COAST.

BY ROBERT WARREN.

I HAVE much pleasure in bringing under the notice of Irish naturalists an interesting addition to the list of Irish mammals, by the occurrence on our shores of that rare visitor to British waters, the Hump-backed Whale, *Megaptera boops*, Fab., (*longimana*, Rud.), a fine female specimen having come ashore on the sands of Killala bay, at Enniscrone, Co. Sligo, on the 21st March. The animal had probably been feeding too close to shore in the shallow water, and on taking the ground, was overpowered by the surf, and cast upon the sands; it lived for some hours, lashing the water furiously with its tail, and spouting from its blow-holes, and from time to time, opening and shutting its mouth, occasionally giving vent to great sighs or grunts. The body was very clumsy-looking, and so thick, as to look out of all proportion to its length, and was probably between twenty and thirty feet in circumference. Black in colour all over the upper parts (the under being buried in sand were not visible) except the long, narrow flippers, which were white, with a few black spots on the upper sides, and a few patches of white on the margins and under the side of the flukes, and also on the longitudinal folds, or pleats of skin, on the sides of the throat, giving the latter a marbled appearance. To the edges and under sides of the flippers and flukes, and to the under part of the lower jaw were attached a large number of that barnacle (so like a gigantic *Balanus*), *Coronula diadema*, varying in size from an inch and a-half to two inches in diameter, and an inch and three-quarters in height; and so firmly fastened to, or embedded in the skin, that both blubber and skin had to be cut away before the shells could be removed from their position. The long, narrow, straight flippers, with scarcely a curve perceptible, were notched or scalloped along the edges, as was also the posterior margin of the flukes. The head was broad and flat; the upper jaw very flat, and depressed between the lower jaw bones, which rose above it when the mouth was closed. On the upper jaw were three rows of tubercles; one of seven, in the centre, running from end of snout to blow-holes, from six to seven and a-half inches apart in the row, and varying from half to an inch in height; one of eleven on each side, just above the lips, reaching almost to the eyes; and in two places in each side row, for a space of six or seven inches, the line of tubercles was double; also a row of six or seven, each side of the lower jaw, just below the lips. The baleen, as well as I could judge, without measuring, appeared to be from twelve to fifteen inches in length, was black in colour, and fringed at the ends with coarse, greyish-brown hairs. The small dorsal fin, placed very far back, was between six and seven inches in height. The dimensions, carefully taken with a string, are as follows:—

Length from fork of tail to dorsal fin,	10 feet 3 inches.
From dorsal fin to end of snout,	18 ,, 10 ,,
Total length over round of back, ..	29 ,, 1 ,,
From end of snout to blow-holes, ..	4 ,, 7 ,,
Breadth of flukes, ...	9 ,, 0 ,,
Length of flippers from humerus, ..	9 ,, 2 ,,

Although so common on the coasts of Norway and Iceland, this whale appears to be of rare occurrence in British waters, this being the first of the species known to have visited the Irish coast; while Flower and Lydekker, in their "Mammals," published in 1891, mention only three examples as having visited the British coasts, one at Newcastle in 1839; a second at Dee in 1863; and a third at the mouth of the Tay in 1883-4, thus showing the extreme rarity of its occurrence on our shores; though, of course, it is not improbable that some specimens may have been unrecognized, or mistaken for other species when thrown ashore. However, the unusually long white narrow flippers, thick, robust body, and flat depressed tubercle-covered head, should always identify this whale and distinguish it from others.

The skeleton has been secured for the Dublin Museum.

THE EARTHWORMS OF IRELAND.

BY REV. HILDERIC FRIEND, F.L.S.

(*Continued from page 90.*)

GROUP II. **Disjuncta**.

As in the last group we had only one indigenous species of worm for examination, so in the present instance. The paucity of species, however, is balanced by the interest and peculiarity of this solitary illustration; and from facts which have come under observation recently, it would appear as though the Irish representative of the group had begun to diverge from its English and European type.

Allolobophora profuga, Rosa.—THE RAMBLER. A fine, steel-blue worm, unlike any other British species in colour. The girdle and last half-dozen segments of a yellowish hue, the latter owing to the presence of turbid fluid, such as is secreted in great quantities by the Brandling (*A. fœtida*, Savigny), and others. When living, it is from five to eight inches in length, averaging six. There is a total number of from 120 to 160 segments in the body. The worm is cylindrical, tending to octagonal, owing to the disjuncted arrangement of the setæ, which are much wider apart than in the groups previously studied. The tail tapers rapidly to a point, and is conspicuous, by reason of the striking difference in colour existing between it and the rest of the body. The girdle normally occupies segments 30 to 35, along the innermost four of which the band is stretched. Thus, this species closely resembles the true *Lumbrici*, with their six-segment girdle, and four-segment band. There is a tendency in this species, however, for the band to project beyond the four segments, or run into the two outermost. Well marked and prominent papillæ on segment 15 carry the male pores. A peculiar odour, as of garlic, or some similar vegetable, is given off when the worm is irritated, just as the Brandling raises a recollection of boiled cabbage under similar circumstances. I find this worm is not averse to very poor, clayey, cold soil. Here it is undoubtedly of great service, and, as it does not come out of its burrow, like the *Lumbrici*, it does not possess the flattened tail.

Mr. Trumbull, of Malahide, has recently found several specimens of the Rambler, and observes that the girdle and band are shifted forward one segment, beginning on the 29th, instead of the 30th. As specimens have been submitted to me for examination, I am able to confirm the observation, and prove the identity.

GROUP III. **Mucida**.

The next group of the genus *Allolobophora* contains a larger number of species than any other. We shall discuss the different species in order, a diagnosis of the group having been already given (p. 42). The worms are not usually addicted to burrowing, or casting up mould, so that these species are, to a large extent, out of the reckoning in such a work as Darwin's "Vegetable Mould and Earthworms." There are close affinities with the other groups, the arrangement of the setæ linking these species with those already studied, while the habitat, exudation, and shape, lead us naturally on to the groups which follow. There is no fixed number of segments composing the girdle, as in *Lumbricus*, neither do the clitellar papillæ (*tubercula pubertatis*) follow any definite law. They may occur on contiguous or alternate segments, and be band-like, or papillose.

Five species fall under this heading, the name of the group having special reference to the peculiar exudations.

Allolobophora turgida, Eisen.—TURGID WORM. Very common, and widely distributed. Variable in size and colour; sometimes six inches in length, and considerably larger in the region of the essential organs (segments 8 to 12) than elsewhere. Of a dull flesh-colour, exuding slime, or turbid fluid, when irritated. Girdle covering the 28th to the 34th segments, the papillæ being on the alternate segments 31 and 33. Often when the worm is adult these seem to form a band which extends across the intervening segment, so that it may easily be mistaken for the much rarer species which follows.

DISTRIBUTION IN IRELAND. Cork (Miss Martin and Miss Abbott); Valencia, Co. Kerry (Miss Delap); Knocknacarry, Co. Antrim (Rev. S. Brenan); Cashel, Co. Tipperary (Lieut.-Col. R. E. Kelsall); Killencoole, Co. Louth (Mr. Jameson), etc.

Allolobophora trapezoidea, Dugès. — TRAPEZE WORM.—Very similar to the last, with which it has been repeatedly confused. Rosa was the first to thoroughly disentangle them. Much rarer than the foregoing. I have only one well-authenticated Irish locality at present. The girdle covers segments 27 to 34, and the clitellar band extends over three consecutive segments (31, 32, 33). Rosa has correctly pointed out that the shape of the segments, and the number in any given length, differentiate this species from the last.

DISTRIBUTION IN IRELAND. Valencia, Co. Kerry (Miss Delap).

Allolobophora mucosa, Eisen.—MUCOUS WORM. Readily distinguished from the others by its bright, fleshy-red colour, and the white granular deposit from the exudation when placed in spirits, as well as by the position and shape of the girdle. The worm is usually the smallest of the group, two or three inches long, and much more delicate than its allies. The girdle usually extends from the 26th to the 32nd segments, on the 29th, 30th, and 31st, of which the band is seen so placed as to extend the girdle ventrally, and give it the characteristic appearance which Eisen has figured with such truth and accuracy. Mr. Trumbull has sent some small specimens from brick-clay, taken at Malahide. The longest adult did not exceed one and a-half inches, and it is evident that habitat has a great deal to do with their size.

DISTRIBUTION IN IRELAND. Cashel, Co. Tipperary (Lieut.-Col. R. E. Kelsall); Valencia, Co. Kerry (Miss Delap); Dublin (Dr. Scharff), etc.

Allolobophora chlorotica, Savigny.—GREEN WORM. Often looking, when coiled up in its sulky, sluggish fashion, exactly like the dirty larva of some large fly. The most common and variable of all our indigenous species. Several well-marked varieties might be enumerated, if colour, shape, and habitat were sufficient to form a basis. In every case, however, the specific characters are the same—viz., girdle extending from segment 29 to segment 37, and three pairs of papillæ situated on segments 31, 33, 35. The colour varies from dirty green to dull yellow, and from clay-brown to fleshy-red. Occasionally a bright emerald green is met with. It lurks under stones and refuse, moves indifferently, and exudes an unusual amount of dirty yellow, turbid matter.

DISTRIBUTION IN IRELAND. Cork, Dublin, Tipperary, Louth, and wherever specimens of worm-fauna have been collected.

Allolobophora cambrica, Friend. — WELSH WORM. Has the colour and general appearance of the Mucous Worm, and the girdle arrangement of the Green Worm. To determine its specific character dissection is necessary, when it will be found to present features which differ from each of its nearest allies. First found in 1891 in Wales, and recently received from Ireland. Probably fairly distributed, but apt to be confused with one or other of the better-known species.

DISTRIBUTION IN IRELAND. Blackrock, Co. Dublin (Miss Kelsall).

(TO BE CONTINUED.)

THE SELBORNE SOCIETY.
BY GEORGE A. MUSGRAVE, F.R.G.S., F.Z.S.

IT is rather a bitter satire on our civilisation that a society for the protection of the harmless objects of wild nature from unnecessary destruction should be "a want of the day." Yet such is the fact. With the facilities now afforded for locomotion, thousands of excursionists, in the place of half a dozen quiet visitors, are hurled periodically upon a limited tract of country remarkable for its beauty or associations, and instead of doing their utmost, as intelligent beings, to preserve the objects, such as trees, flowers, ferns, birds, or architectural remains, enhancing the beauty, or giving additional interest to the spot, they destroy them.

The evil thus wrought, in great measure thoughtlessly, is a novel one, hence the necessity for seeking to overcome it by a novel method. Those who founded and built up the Selborne Society felt that individual protests made against the evil were a mere waste of strength, which could only be obtained in fulness by the united action of representatives of all classes, and by the free use of the local knowledge and tact possessed by members of branches. The adherence of sympathetic members was not difficult to obtain, because the objects of the association are such as interest the naturalist, the artist, the poet, the wise lover of nature, and the archæologist; whilst the co-operation of owners and occupiers of land, gamekeepers, woodreeves, and others engaged in rural occupations, was not wanting.

Such, in brief, is the history of a union for the protection of harmless birds and other creatures, a society for the preservation of trees and plants, a coadjutor in the good work of the Kyrle, Footpath, Ancient Buildings, and other kindred Associations. One fact concerning the society is peculiarly interesting, and that is, that several of the collateral descendants of Gilbert White, the author of "The Natural History of Selborne," in whose honour the society is named, take an active part in promoting its objects.

Primarily its energies were chiefly devoted to the collection and circulation of reliable information respecting the excessive destruction of birds for ornamental purposes, with the result, that the Audubon Society was founded in the United States, and, recently, the Birds' Protection Society in England, under the patronage of the Duchess of Portland; and also that a more willing and hearty support was given in the Colonies and elsewhere to the Birds' Protection Acts. The Society has based its appeal for preservation on scientific, æsthetic, and economic grounds, and has a due regard for sentiment, without which our daily life would be a dreary and monotonous toil. Still, appeals to uninstructed persons do not always prove successful, therefore, in order to obtain voluntary co-operation, it seemed desirable to encourage the study of natural history. If an interest can be excited in young people in the structure and habits of an animal, or plant, by hedgerow and field, then one long step in the right direction has been taken towards creating in them a lasting taste for a pursuit demanding no costly appliances, and dealing with an inexhaustible store of material always at hand.

With the acquisition of a certain amount of elementary knowledge, the habit of accurate observation and careful investigation is fostered; thus a faithful follower of Gilbert White is developed, ever on the alert for note-making, and always capable of writing an intelligible and truthful account of some occurrence likely to interest the readers of the Society's organ, *Nature Notes*. This magazine is like the sisters' only doll in *Punch*—"it's all of our magazine," containing, from its most learned articles to the shortest paragraphs, in "stuff" voluntarily contributed by members of all sorts and conditions, and of all ages.

The Editor, Mr. James Britten, F.L.S., a well-known botanist, is especially grateful to persons who will, without regard for fine writing, send him short accounts of what they themselves see and hear. We live in an age of close observation, looking forward to a time when much valuable knowledge will be derived from collections of even the humblest notes, provided that they have been recorded simply and truthfully.

In almost every branch of the Society there are members who, being expert naturalists, find time in which to give short addresses to children or unskilled members, as well as to the general public, and there also gradually arise ladies and gentlemen who, with an aptitude for imparting information, try to follow successfully in the direction so ably indicated by Kingsley in his lectures, and in " Madam How, and Lady Why?"

The progress, however, of such a society must be necessarily slow, so great, alas! is the indifference, even amongst educated people, to anything demanding a little attention and mental effort. University extension lecturers find subjects which are not "amusing," fall very flat.

Take it altogether, however, the Selborne Society has steadily increased in influential and numerical strength, and branch after branch has been formed, and the area of voluntary guardianship of the fauna and flora of fresh neighbourhoods secured. There is no reason why branches should not quickly fill up, swarm, and make others in the same way in Ireland.

Unfortunately, obscured by political storm-clouds, Ireland, one of the most delightful countries in the world for the tourist, artist, and sportsman, with all its capabilities for rapid development, with its winter and summer health-resorts derelict, or checked in healthy growth, has almost dropped out of the list of the playgrounds of Europe. But the day will come when it will be "fashionable," and then the Irish Selbornians will rejoice that they have protected all that material which once made many a favourite spot in England so attractive, and which has been sacrificed to greed and stupidity.

The first step is to get a few kindred spirits to agree to form a branch, and then to direct the secretary *pro. tem.* to write to the Secretary of the Selborne Society, 9 Adam-street, Adelphi, London, W.C., for the leaflet "How to form a Branch," and a form of application for a warrant. When the branch is formed, it is useful to get some local land-owner to follow the example of Mr. Skrine, of the Bath Branch, Lord of the Manor of Claverton, by giving a "Selborne at Home," when local botanists, naturalists, and archæologists, can improve the occasion, and do a great deal towards directing usefully the energies of the members. Ireland being particularly rich in rare plants, a voluntary guardianship of their habitats will, of course, suggest itself.

The great thing, however, to impress on old and young is that, true to Gilbert White, the Society is essentially an observing rather than a collecting one.

The minimum subscription has remained the same as when the writer of this article and his wife originated the Society; for those who assisted in the organization hoped that half-a-crown would be within reach of National and Board School teachers, factory hands, and others. Unfortunately, however, it has been found to be not low enough for persons receiving small incomes, and not large enough to comfortably bear the cost of issuing the Society's organ, *Nature Notes*, which, of course, considering the limited circulation of all scientific periodicals, is absurdly cheap—2d. per part! Owing to larger subscriptions and donations from wealthy people and the contributions from the branches, the Committee have been enabled to defray the cost of the magazine, the rental of office, and the honorarium of the Secretary, but not to print leaflets for free distribution broadcast in the way originally contemplated. This is a pity, because cyclists, fishermen, and other wanderers, could do a great deal amongst people prone to kill every rare bird, uproot rare plants for sale, and otherwise do mischief. Every year it is getting more difficult to obtain specimens of particular birds for local museums, and what makes it more annoying is that the birds are shot and carried away by private persons for the pure love of acquisition, and eventually lost in some distant auction.

A capital plan in starting an association such as the Selborne Society, is to get each member to secure ten others, and then the society "snow-balls" on in that way, and cheereth the hearts of the Committees.

Amongst the very earliest adherents of the society were Lord Cork's sister-in-law, the Hon. Mrs. R. C. Boyle, well known as E. V. B., without whose artistic and literary powers and influence very little progress would have been made. Through her, H.R.H. Princess Christian became chief Patroness, and the lamented Laureate, President. Louisa, Marchioness of Waterford, a lady of extraordinary abilities, Lady Muncaster, Professor Haddon, Mr. Burbidge, and others also lent a helping hand.

The Committee in England cordially wish every success to the efforts now about to be made in Ireland to establish branches of a society which admittedly is not only doing a good work, in the prosecution of its various objects, but offers a common ground of fraternization between resident naturalists and visitors from distant parts, who are sure of finding in a Selbornian, a guide, philosopher, and friend.

THE FLORA OF COUNTY ARMAGH.

BY R. LLOYD PRAEGER, B.E., M.R.I.A.

(*Continued from page* 95).

Hypericum dubium, Leers., var. **maculatum,** Bab.   N. M. S.
   Throughout the county, and as common in Armagh as *H. perforatum*. Ardmore, H. W. L. spec.! By the railway near Lurgan station, old quarry two miles S.W. of Lurgan, roadside at Glen Eyre near Portadown, Tynan Abbey grounds, lane two miles south of Killilea, roadside a mile S.E. of Tanderagee, roadside two miles west of Tanderagee, by the railway south of Poyntzpass, roadside between Poyntzpass and Scarva, abundant by the railway between Goraghwood and Newry, and by the Warrenpoint railway below Newry; about Armagh *H. dubium* is absent, and *H. perforatum* common, R. Ll. P. The abundance of this species in Armagh contrasts strangely with its extreme rarity in Antrim and Down.

H. humifusum, Linn.   N. — S.
   Very rare in the county. On the railway near Narrow-water, and roadside near Lislea south of Armagh, R. Ll. P.

‡**Acer campestre,** Linn.   N. — —
   About Loughgall, More *N. H. R.*! In Mr. More's paper and *Cyb. Hib.* this tree is admitted as a native at Loughgall. I did not find it anywhere in the county in such situations as to justify an unquestioned admission to the indigenous flora.

*****A. pseudo-platanus,** Linn.   N. M. S.
   Occasionally apparently wild, and frequent in hedges, etc., but not native, R. Ll. P.

*****Geranium phœum,** Linn.   — M. —
   In a hedge near Mullaghmore lake, escaped, R. Ll. P.

*****G. nodosum,** Linn.   N. — —
   On a hedge-bank by roadside near Linenhill House south of Armagh, quite naturalized, R. Ll. P.

(*****G. perenne,** Huds.   N. — —
   "A few plants only on the roadside, by the hedge-bank, not far from a cottage a little north of Loughgall: not, I believe, wild here," More *N. H. R.* I could not find the plant at the spot indicated, and it was apparently an escape which did not maintain its hold).

Radiola linoides, Dc.   N. — —
   Abundant on a bog two miles south of Portadown, R. Ll. P.

Ulex gallii, Planch.   — M. S.
   Abundant on the southern mountains, and on the high ground around Carrigatuke and Deadman's Hill, in the centre of the county; absent from the northern bogs and the rest of Armagh, R. Ll. P.

Trifolium medium, Linn.   N. — —
   Very rare. Only observed at Navan Fort and the adjoining lakelet of Loughnashade, R. Ll. P.

*****T. hybridum,** Linn.   N. M. S.
   In fields of grass and pastures occasionally throughout the county; R. Ll. P. Not considered a native in Britain.

T. filiforme, Linn.   N. — —
   One station only. Tynan Abbey, B. N. F. C., 1873 and 1889; also Herb. N. H. P. S. (S. A. S.)! The plant grows sparingly here on lawns near the house.

B

*Medicago sativa, Linn. N. — —
  Fields near Armagh, W. F. J. spec.! Field near Richhill, R. Ll.
  P. Introduced with grass-seed.
[Melilotus parviflora, Desf. — — S.
  Waste ground at Newry docks—a casual; R. Ll. P.]
Anthyllis vulneraria, Linn. N. — S.
  Very local, but frequent by the estuary of the Newry river, and
  on limestone about Armagh, R. Ll. P.
Lathyrus palustris, Linn. N. — —
  Islets in the Closet river (Lett), *Flor. N. E. I.*! I saw the plant
  in abundance on these islets, which lie where the river debouches
  into Lough Neagh, and also obtained it on the reedy banks of the
  stream half a mile from its mouth. More's note on Rev. G.
  Robinson's authority (*N. H. R.* and *Cyb. Hib.*) is a mistake: Scawdy
  Island in Tyrone is the spot intended; the plant formerly grew
  there, but is now extinct.
†Prunus cerasus, Linn. N. M. S.
  In field hedges about Loughgall, but not wild, More *N. H. R.*!
  In hedges, copses, and thickets throughout the county, as com-
  mon or commoner than *P. avium*, and, although frequently planted,
  having equally the appearance of a native, R. Ll. P.
*Spiræa salicifolia, Linn. — M. —
  Abundant in hedges between Newtownhamilton and Ballymyre,
  but planted, R. Ll. P.
Alchemilla vulgaris, Linn., var. **minor,** Huds. N. — —
  Near Tynan, B. N. F. C., 1889. Abundant on a lawn in Tynan
  Abbey demesne, R. Ll. P.
Rubus plicatus, W. and N. N. — —
  Church Hill, R. Ll. P. "Perhaps best under var. *hemistemon*,
  P. J. Muell"—W. M. R.
R. rhamnifolius, W. and N. N. — —
  Near Armagh, R. Ll. P.
R. nemoralis, P. J. Muell., var. **pulcherrimus,** Newm. ? N. M. —
  My specimen was gathered, I think, in North Armagh; the
  label bearing locality was unfortunately lost. One of Mr. Lett's
  Ballymore *Rubi* belongs here also.
R. villicaulis, Koehl. N. M. S.
  Ballymore, H. W. L. spec.! At Derryadd bay on Lough Neagh,
  and at Newry, R. Ll. P.
R. lindleianus, Lees. N. — —
  Near Lurgan and Armagh, R. Ll. P.
R. rusticanus, Merc. N. M. S.
  "Armagh; Prof. Oliver," *Cyb. Hib.* Perhaps the commonest
  bramble in the county, being abundant nearly everywhere. Speci-
  mens from Tartaraghan and Armagh were confirmed by Mr.
  Rogers.
R. macrophyllus, W. and N., var. **schlectendalii,** Weihe. — — S.
  Near Newry, R. Ll. P. "Or between this and *R. macrophyllus*,
  W. and N. Panicle exceptionally weak."—W. M. R.
R. salteri, Bab. — — S.
  Newry, R. Ll. P. "Probably best under *R. salteri*, Bab., though
  in that the leaves are usually less rounded and more deeply cut,
  and the fruiting sepals erect."—W. M. R.
R. pyramidalis, Kalt. N. M. —
  Ballymore, H. W. L. spec.! Roadsides near Lurgan, R. Ll. P.
  "Armature of panicle-rachis unusually mixed."—W. M. R. Of
  another Lurgan specimen Mr. Rogers writes :—" Probably *R. pyra-
  midalis*, Kalt., *growing in sunshine.*"

Rubus leucostachys, Schleich. N. — —
Near Lurgan, R. Ll. P.
R. mucronatus, Blox. N. — —
Near Armagh, R. Ll. P.
R. anglosaxonicus, Gelert. N. — S.
Tartaraghan and Newry, R. Ll. P. Of the latter plant Mr. Rogers writes:—"Not a typical specimen," and of the former, "or between *R. anglosaxonicus* and *R. echinatus; near* my var. *raduloides, vide Journ. Bot.* 1892, p. 269."
R. borreri, Bell-Salt. — — S.
Beside a rivulet by the Dundalk road, a mile from Newry, R. Ll. P. "True *R. borreri*, Bell-Salt, beyond a doubt. I have before seen it only from Dorset and Somerset (abundant), Glost. and Wight, so this extension of it to Ireland is very interesting."—W. M. R.
R. drejeri, G. Jensen. — M. —
Ballymore, H. W. L. spec.! "Must go to *R. drejeri,* G. Jenson, I suspect, but that, *when typical,* has the leaves almost simply serrate and the sepals patent or clasping in fruit. In colouring, armature, etc., however, this just fits."—W. M. R.
R. radula, Weihe.
Ballymore, H. W. L. spec.! "Apparently."—W. M. R.
R. scaber, W. and N. N. — S
Lurgan ("apparently the typical plant."—W. M. R.), Armagh ("?"—W. M. R.), and Newry ("apparently a strong form, with hirsute panicle and leaves softly hairy beneath."—W. M. R.), R. Ll. P.
R. rosaceus, Weihe. — M. —
Ballymore, H. W. L. spec.! "Apparently a *rosaceus* form, but not typical."—W. M. R.
R. corylifolius, Sm. N. — —
Near Armagh, R. Ll. P. Apparently not so common in Co. Armagh as in Co. Down.
R. corylifolius, Sm., var. **cyclophyllus,** Lindeb. N. — —
Tartaraghan, R. Ll. P.
*****R. laciniatus,** Willd? N. — —
In a lane near Tartaraghan glebe, R. Ll. P. "A garden escape; I think the name has been given to divers laciniate-leaved forms."—W. M. R. This plant grows quite away from cultivation; I took it to be a wild sport of *R. rusticanus.*
Rubus saxatilis, Linn. S. — —
North side of Slieve Gullion at 1,500 feet, R. Ll. P.
Geum intermedium, Ehr. — — S.
Copses in the park at the Manor, Loughgall, accompanied as usual by *G. rivale* and *G. urbanum,* More *N. H. R.*
G. rivale, Linn.
Loughgall Manor, More *N. H. R.* Mullinure meadows and Loughnashade. W. F. J. spec.! Rare in Co. Armagh.
Rosa spinosissima, Linn. — M. —
Very rare in the county; observed in one spot only near Poyntzpass, R. Ll. P.
R. mollissima, Willd. N. — S.
Frequent on the limestone about Armagh, where I noted it in a number of spots; shore of Lough Ross near Crossmaglen, R. Ll. P.
†**R. rubiginosa,** Linn. N. M. S.
Occurs mostly as stray bushes, and sometimes probably escaped, but apparently native on Lough Neagh shore. By Ulster canal

near Eglish, and between Charlemont and Blackwatertown; shores of Lough Neagh west and south of Ardmore point; roadsides south of Markethill; by the canal below Newry, R. Ll. P.

R. arvensis, Huds. — M. —
Extremely rare; a single bush in the hedge by the roadside close to Scarva bridge, R. Ll. P.

Peplis portula, Linn. — M. S.
Rare. Shores of Camlough and Lough Ross; marsh at base of Carrigatuke, R. Ll. P.

*****Epilobium angustifolium,** Linn. N. M. S.
Frequent in cottage gardens, and occasionally escaped. Perhaps originally a native.

Circæa alpina, Linn. N. — —
Shore of Lough Neagh south of Ardmore point, H. W. L. spec.!

Myriophyllum spicatum, Linn. N. — —
Frequent in the northern portion of the county; noted from near Lurgan, Portadown, Armagh, and in pools along the Lough Neagh shore, R. Ll. P.

†Sedum telephium, Linn. N. — —
Copse in Armagh Palace demesne, R. Ll. P.

*****S. album,** Linn. N. M. —
Occasionally on old walls, etc., no doubt escaped, R. Ll. P.

*****S. dasyphyllum,** Linn.
Co. Armagh, *Flor. Ulst. Supp.*—an escape.

S. anglicum, Huds. — — S.
Very rare; rock at western base of Slieve Gullion, and rocks on a hill near Milltown chapel west of Camlough, R. Ll. P.

S. acre, Linn. N. — —
Near Navan Fort, W. F. J.! (only as an escape here, R. Ll. P.). Sandy banks by Lough Neagh west of Ardmore point, R. Ll. P.; this was the only native station I observed for this species; it is occasionally grown in cottage gardens.

*****S. sexangulare,** Linn. N. — —
Sandy spots on Lough Neagh shore at Raughlan, H. W. L. spec.!

*****S. reflexum,** Linn. N. M. S.
On limestone rocks by the Dungannon road three miles from Armagh; planted on cottage roofs in various parts of the county, R. Ll. P.

*****S. rupestre,** Huds. — M. —
Old walls near Keady—escaped, R. Ll. P.

Saxifraga granulata, Linn. N. — —
Sparingly on the mound at Rathtrillick, near Middletown, B. N. F. C., 1873, and Herb. N. H. P. S. spec.!

Parnassia palustris, Linn. N. — —
"The parnassia, or grass of parnassus, a plant of extreme elegance and beauty, grows in the vicinity of Lough Neagh, and on the banks of the Tynan river,—*Coote's Armagh*. Loughnashade and Mullinure meadows near Armagh, W. F. J. spec.!

Cicuta virosa, Linn. N. M. S.
Near foot of Blackwater (Templeton)! and shores of Lough Neagh (G. R.)! *Flor. Ulst.* Closet River, H. W. L. spec.! Several places along Lough Neagh shores from Lagan Canal to Maghery, in the Newry canal and pools near, at many spots between Portadown and Goraghwood, Mullaghmore Lough, Lough Gilly, R. Ll. P.

Apium graveolans, Linn. — — S.
By the river at Newry, and by the canal below Newry, R. Ll. P.

Apium Inundatum, Reich., var. **moorei,** Syme. N. — —
   In the Blackwater at Maghery; near mouth of Closet River; and in a marsh near Morrow's Point in the S.E. corner of Lough Neagh, R. Ll. P. Confined to the Lough Neagh borders.

*****Carum caruí,** Linn. — — S.
   Common on the G. N. railway for several miles south of Bessbrook; apparently naturalised here, R. Ll. P.

Œnanthe fistulosa, Linn. N. M. —
   Moyntaghs bogs (Hyndman), and Armagh (G. R.), *Flor. Ulst.* Closet River, H. W. L.! By Lough Neagh near Maghery, Milltown, and Lagan Canal, and abundant in Newry Canal between Portadown and Tanderagee, R. Ll. P.

*****Peucedanum ostruthium,** Koch. N. M. S.
   Roadsides and hedgebanks—no doubt introduced or escaped. Noted near Lough Gullion, Ballymyre, Camlough and Jonesborough, R. Ll. P.

Torilis nodosa, Gaert. N. — S.
   Sparingly by the roadside at Drumintee chapel west of Jonesborough, and on bridge over the Bann on the borders of Down and Armagh, R. Ll. P.

Chærophyllum temulum, Linn. N. M. —
   Dry hedgebanks, chiefly along the Lough Neagh shore. Close to Maghery ferry, roadside quarter mile east of Milltown, roadside a short distance S.W. of Ardmore church, in a lane by the main road at Derryadd Bay, and roadside south of Temple national school near Keady, R. Ll. P.

†**Smyrnium olusatrum** Linn. N. — S.
   Near Loughall, but, as in most of its habitats, liable to suspicion, More *N. H. R.!* Ardmore Glebe, H. W. L.! Near Newry, very rare in the county, R. Ll. P.

*****Myrrhis odorata,** Linn. N. M. S.
   Tanderagee (G. R.), *Flor. Ulst.* Roadsides near Eglish church, at base of Camlough mountain, and at Ballymyre, R. Ll. P.

(*****Cornus sanguinea,** Linn.
   On a small islet in the Loughgall lake, More *N. H. R.* Is not there now, and as it does not grow elsewhere in the county, I have no doubt it was planted, R. Ll. P.)

†**Sambucus ebulus,** Linn. N. — —
   About the ruins of an old building close to Lough Neagh, More *N. H. R.* Armagh (G. R.), *Flor. Ulst.* Near Eglish church, and roadside east side of Loughgall demesne, R. Ll. P.

Galium boreale, Linn. N. — —
   Lough Neagh shore only. Banks of Lough Neagh, More *N. H. R.!* Ardmore Glebe, H. W. L.! Bird Island, R. Ll. P.

G. mollugo, Linn. N. M. —
   Near Armagh, W. F. J. spec.! In several places in Tanderagee upper demesne, R. Ll. P.

Valerianella dentata, Poll. N. — S.
   Corn-field between Armagh and Loughgall, W. F. J. spec.! Gravel-pit east of Grange, near Armagh; fields near Beech Hill House, Armagh; fields east of Middletown, and at Lough Ross near Crossmaglen; and on the Warrenpoint railway below Newry, R. Ll. P.

Eupatorium cannabinum, Linn. N. — —
   Loughgall manor grounds, by the lake, W. F. J.!

Astertripolium, Linn. — — S
   Estuary of Newry river; abundant and luxuriant by the stream in the town of Newry, growing in groves four feet high, R. Ll. P.

Solidago virgaurea, Linn. — — S.
Sparingly on Slieve Gullión, R. Ll. P.

‡**Inula helenium,** Linn. N. — S.
Derryadd, H. W. L. spec.! In a lane west of Goraghwood, R. Ll. P.

Filago germanica, Linn. N. — S.
Shore of Lough Neagh at Raughlan, H. W. L. spec.! On a ruined cottage at the western base of Slieve Gullion, R. Ll. P.

F. minima, Fries. N. — —
Sandy ground near Lough Neagh, More *N. H. R.* Shore of Lough Neagh at Raughlan, H. W. L. spec.! Sandy shore of Lough Neagh near Charlestown, R. Ll. P.

Gnaphalium sylvaticum, Linn. N. — S
Derryadd, H. W. L. spec.! Frequent among the hills south of Newry, R. Ll. P.

Antennaria dioica, Gaert. N. — —
Raughlan Point and Croaghan Island, Lough Neagh, H. W. L. spec.! Stony Hill near Retreat N.E. of Armagh, R. Ll. P.

Anthemis nobilis, Linn. N. — —
Near Maghery, W. F. J. spec.! Near Tartaraghan Church, but cultivated, R. Ll. P.

Matricaria inodora, Linn., var. **salina,** Bab. — — S.
Estuary of Newry River, R. Ll. P.

‡**M. chamomilla,** Linn. N. — S.
Roadside at Woodview post-office near Richhill, and on railway at Newry, R. Ll. P.

*__M. parthenium,__ Linn. N. — S.
Near houses, escaped. Tartaraghan, S. A. S. Portadown and Newry, R. Ll. P.

*__Doronicum pardalianches,__ Linn. N. — —
Roadside near Tynan, B. N. F. C. 1889. Roadside from Armagh to Tynan, W. F. J. spec.! Roadside between Tynan and Middletown, R. Ll. P. Apparently naturalised about Tynan.

‡**Tanacetum vulgare,** Linn. N. — S.
" If a stubble-field should be left a year in cashier fallow, which is very seldom the case, the crowfoot and tansy soon overspread it, and are very difficult to be eradicated," *Coote's Armagh.* Derryadd Bay, H. W. L.! Near Loughgall, Blackwatertown, Charlemont, Portadown, and Camlough, but not having the appearance of a native, R. Ll. P.

Senecio sylvaticus,, Linn. N. — —
Ardmore, H. W. L. spec.! On the Lough Neagh shore, at Maghery, Milltown, and Charlestown; on bog east of Lough Gullion; by Dungannon road three miles from Portadown, R. Ll. P.

*__S. saracenicus,__ Linn. — M. —
Banks of a stream 1½ mile N.W. of Keady—an escape, R. Ll. P.

Bidens tripartita, Linn. N. M. —
Armagh (G. R.), *Flor. Ulst.* Lough Neagh shore, west of Bannmouth; bogs by Bann below Portadown; shores of Lough Gullion, Marlacoo Lake, Ballynewry Lake, and Mullaghmore Lake, R. Ll. P.

B. cernua, Linn. N. M. S.
Armagh (G. R.), *Flor. Ulst.* Canal at Portadown, S. A. S.. Mullinure meadows, and Maghery, W. F. J. spec.! Ardmore, H.W. L. spec.! Frequent on the northern bogs; shores of Portnelligan and Mullaghmore Lakes; canal near Tanderagee; bog south of Portadown, and bog near Forkill, R. Ll. P.

Arctium nemorosum, Lej. N. — —
Near Tynan, B. N. F. C. 1889. Near Navan Fort, R. Ll. P. Mr.

Bennett writes of my specimen "*A. nemorosum* Bab. *non* Lej; the plant *Babington* names as *nemorosum* (= your plant!) is not the *A. intermedium* Lange, with which Lange says *A. nemorosum*, Lej. is synonymous."

Arctium majus, Schk. N. — —
 Roadside two miles east of Loughall, R. Ll. P. (*fide* A. Bennett).

[Centaurea scabiosa, Linn.
 In County of Armagh, *Flor. Ulst. Supp.* A mistake.]

Carduus crispus, var. **acanthoides,** inn. N. — —
 Common in the limestone district, and occasionally on the New Red Sandstone; absent from the rest of the county, R. Ll. P.

C. pratensis, Huds. — — S.
 Sparingly on the N.W. slope of Camlough mountain, R. Ll. P.

*Silybum marianum, Gaert.
 In small enclosures, waste ground, etc., always near buildings, More *N. H. R.* Maghery, W. F. J.! Seagoe, H. W. L. spec.!

Leontodon hirtus, Linn. N. — —
 Frequent in the northern portion of the county, on boggy and wet gravelly ground; noted from Loughadian near Armagh, lakeside at Loughgall, shore of Derrylileagh Lake, bog two miles south of Portadown, gravel pit two and a-half miles N.E. of Armagh, and abundant on a stony hill near Retreat between Armagh and Richhill, R. Ll. P.

†Crepis biennis, Linn. N. — —
 Abundant in a field at Armagh workhouse, about 1886, A. G. More *in litt.* I found it growing plentifully on the lawn of the Shiels Memorial Buildings, adjoining the workhouse, which is no doubt Mr. More's station; it does not appear to have spread. Introduced with seed?

C. paludosa, Moench. — M. S.
 Observed at one or two spots in the centre and south of the county, but rare, R. Ll. P.

*C. nicæensis, Balb. N. — —
 Sparingly on railroad track south of Drummanmore Lake, near Armagh, R. Ll. P. The specimens were poor and apparently not characteristic. Mr. Hanbury writes of my plant "I have little doubt but that it is *C. nicæensis*, Balb.; it agrees well with my specimens." Mr. Bennett says: "Your plant differs from typical *nicæensis* by the want of pubescence on the stems, etc., which is sometimes very marked, but I suppose it must go to it." This is a S. European species, and was probably introduced with grass seed; it has not been previously detected in Ireland, so far as I am aware.

Lobelia dortmanna, Linn. N. — S.
 Junction of Lagan canal and Lough Neagh (Hyndman) *Flor. Ulst.*; this is on the borders of Armagh and Down. In Lough Neagh at west side Raughlan Point! and shores of Derrylileagh Lake, H. W. L. In Lough Neagh north of Bird Island, and abundant at the east end of Lough Ross, near Crossmaglen, R. Ll. P.

Jasione montana, Linn. — — S.
 Abundant in the southern hill district; not seen elsewhere, R. Ll. P.

Campanula rotundifolia, Linn. — M. S.
 Centre and south of the county; not common, R. Ll. P.

Andromeda polifolia, Linn. N. — —
 Bogs in Armagh (G. R.), *Flor. Ulst.* Tartaraghan (G. R.), *Cyb. Hib.* "Bog near Tartaraghan, Rev. G. Robinson, spec.!" More *N. H. R.* Must be very rare; I passed over miles of likely ground without seeing it.

Vaccinium vitis-idæa, Linn. N. — S.
At south end of Lough Neagh (Templeton), *Flor. Ulst.* Summit of Slieve Gullion (1,893 feet), and for several hundred feet downwards, R. Ll. P. The Loughgall record of *Flor. Ulst.* was an error; *V. oxycoccos* was the plant, and Tartaraghan the station intended. I did not succeed in refinding this plant on the northern bogs, although I kept a look-out for it, in view of Mr. More's recent remarks in *Journal of Botany* (1892, p. 88); these bogs lie at an elevation of only fifty to one hundred feet, but to judge from the presence on them of such mountain plants as *Listera cordata* and *Lycopodium selago*, the occurrence of *V. vitis-idæa* does not appear unlikely.

V. oxycoccos, Linn. N. — —
Bog near Tartaraghan, More *N. H. R.* Bog at Annaghmore (G. R.), *Flor. Ulst.* Bog between Annaghmore and Maghery, B. N. F. C. 1871. Wet bog, Annaghmore (S. A. S.), Herb. N. H. P. S. Montiaghs bogs, H. W. L. spec.! Abundant on bogs south of Annagarriff Lake, north of Lough Gullion, and near Ardmore Point, sometimes forming a dense mat on quite dry turf, R. Ll. P.

***Ligustrum vulgare,** Linn. N. M. —
Common near Armagh, W. F. J. spec! Occasionally in wild-looking stations, but no doubt escaped, R. Ll. P.

Convolvulus arvensis, Linn. N. — S.
County Armagh (G. R.), *Flor. Ulst.* Mullinure near Armagh, W. F. J. spec.! Lanes west of Armagh, railway near Richhill, roadside near Loughgall, and rather common in the Newry neighbourhood, R. Ll. P.

C. sepium, Linn., grows abundantly in the Closet river in one to two feet of water, twining up the stems of *Scirpus lacustris*, among such plants as *Nuphar*, *Armoracia*, and *Cicuta*. I do not find any notice of this aquatic habit in the text-books.

*****Anchusa sempervirens,** Linn. — M. —
Tanderagee, *Flor. Ulst. Supp.*

Lithospermum officinale, Linn. N. — S.
In hedge banks in several places near Loughgall, but sparingly, More *N. H. R.*! Where I observed it was on roadside between Loughgall and Richhill, R. Ll. P. Grange near Armagh, W. F. J. spec.! Ruins of Killeavy church near Slieve Gullion, H. W. L. spec.!

L. arvense, Linn. N. — —
Tartaraghan, in cultivated ground, More *N. H. R.*

Myosotis repens, Don. — — S.
Abundant in the southern hill district; absent from the rest of the country. The distribution of *M. palustris* is just the reverse of this, that species being abundant on the northern bogs, and by the low-lying lakes, streams, and canals of the north and centre of the county, and extremely rare in the south, R. Ll. P.

Solanum dulcamara, Linn. N. — —
Shores of Lurgan lake, H. W. L. spec.! Armagh Palace demesne, R. Ll. P. Frequently grown in cottage gardens.

Hyoscyamus niger, Linn. N. — —
Near Armagh Cathedral (Thompson), *Flor. Ulst.* Not seen recently, but is a very uncertain plant.

Lathræa squamaria, Linn.
Armagh (G. R.), *Flor. Ulst.*; this record refers to the succeeding station. In a small copse within the park at Loughgall manor, More *N. H. R.*, and subsequently, G. R.

(TO BE CONTINUED.)

THE MAGNESIAN LIMESTONE OF THE CORK DISTRICT.

BY THOMAS FARRINGTON, M.A., F.C.S., F.I.C.

[Read before the Cork Naturalists' Field Club, March 15th, 1893.]

THE beds of dolomite, or magnesian limestone, existing in the neighbourhood of Cork, though inextensive, are not alone important in connection with our local manufacturing industries, but as having also considerable interest from a geological point of view. Almost the whole surface of the county is occupied by the various subdivisions of two formations, viz., the Old Red Sandstone and the Carboniferous limestone; anything, therefore, that opens the door for a wider study of the science ought to be welcome to its students here.

The presence of dolomite, in association with the Cork limestone, has been somewhat of a puzzle to geologists, and one eminent exponent of the science, Professor Harkness, has attributed its origin to the action of sea-water upon the ordinary limestone. In a paper on "Jointing," read before the Geological Society of London, June 9th, 1858, he says:—

"The mode in which the magnesian limestones make their appearance in the district under review leads to the inference, that the dolomites were not deposited by the ordinary action of water as sedimentary rocks, but that they are superinduced structures, which have not only arisen from the action of forces operating subsequent to the deposition and consolidation of the limestones in which they occur, but have had their origin after the operation of that force which has produced joints among these limestone strata."[1]

The object of the present communication is to adduce some facts which seem inconsistent with a portion of this statement, and to bring forward another theory which seems to accord better with all the facts of the case. As the greater part of the above quotation fits in as well with this latter theory as with the Professor's own, the only portion of it directly traversed is that which asserts "that the dolomites were not deposited by the ordinary action of water as sedimentary rocks, but that they are superinduced structures." So far from confirming this view, my observations have led me to an opposite con-

---

[1] *Quarterly Journal Geol. Soc. London*, vol. xv. (1859), p. 100.

clusion, viz., *that the dolomites of this district, instead of being superinduced structures, are the remnants of sedimentary rocks of the Permian formation, resting unconformably on the denuded, fissured, and excavated limestone.*

The principal grounds on which this opinion is based are as follows :—

1. The dolomitic bands which have come under my notice have a general east and west direction; this is such an evident fact, that it has been customary, in connection with the magnesia manufacture, to search for the rock in a direct line east or west of the points at which it had been previously found.

2. These deposits invariably show at the top surface of the rock-formation, either overlying the limestone, or being wedged in between masses of that rock which also show at the surface on either side of them.

3. Though in many cases they penetrate the limestone for a considerable depth, there is a general diminution of breadth downwards, the horizontal section meanwhile widening or narrowing in an irregular manner. Figure 1, *a* shows the

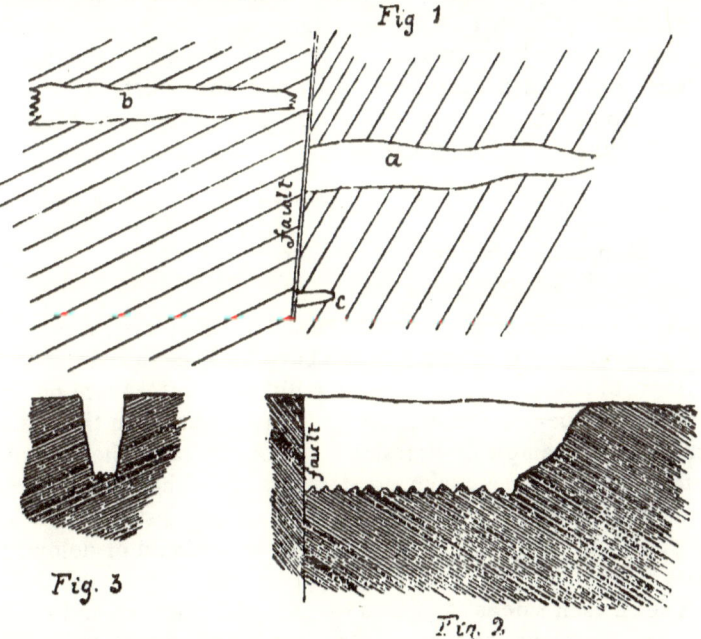

plan, or horizontal section; *fig.* 2, the longitudinal section; and *fig.* 3, the cross section of a small quarry which was worked for the "Magnesia-stone" only, the space left by the stone removed consequently representing the original dolomitic deposit.

4. The upper surface of both the limestone and dolomite is found to be eroded by the action of water or ice, and is often covered by deposits containing sand, gravel, or rounded stones. I have obtained a sample of gravel from over a long band which was found to the westward of the fault, but not in line with it (*fig.* 1, *b*); it has not yet been ascertained whether this is a continuation of the aforementioned strip (*a*) or no; at present it seems more in character with another (*c*) which runs parallel a short distance to the south.

5. The line of demarcation between the magnesia and limestone when found in juxta-position is always sharp; even when the minerals are nearly of the same colour and general appearance, it is plain to a practised eye; and while they often adhere, so that a hand-specimen containing both may be obtained, they, on the other hand, can in general be readily separated at the surface of junction.

The following analyses of samples taken from the same stone, not a yard apart, will illustrate the great difference of composition between rocks which an ordinary observer would take to be identical:—

	Dolomite.	Limestone.
Foreign matter,	2.5	1.7 per cent.
Magnesium carbonate,	42.9	1.7 ,,
Specific gravity,	2.83	2.71 ,,

6. The dolomite is generally less pure than the limestone. This point is also shown by the above analysis (although the sample of dolomite is an exceptionally pure one), there being nearly fifty per cent. more foreign matter present in the latter than in the sample of limestone. In many cases the amount of foreign matter is much greater, and often there is so much iron present as to produce a very dark-coloured stone.

7. In the cavity left by the removal of the band of dolomite last mentioned (*fig.* 1, *c*), there appear adhering to the limestone on each side, slaty scales—some light-coloured and some of darker colour, and greasy to the touch,—which will probably repay a careful examination. Apart, however, from their composition, they form a strong link in the chain of evidence which goes to prove that the magnesia-stone was

deposited in its present position, and that the latter is not the result of the tilting-up of strata originally horizontal.

In addition to denudation, it seems as if the strata had been subjected to a degree of heat sufficient to weld them together without such fusion as would completely destroy the previous arrangement of their parts. The presence of large crystals of iron pyrites in the magnesia-stone seems to favour this view, as also its crystalline structure. Prof. M. M. Hartog, of Queen's College, Cork, who has kindly examined for me a mounted section of the minerals in juxta-position, says the dolomite is in the form of saccharine marble, while the limestone is not nearly so much metamorphosed.

To ascertain the character of the organic remains will, no doubt, help much in elucidating the question of the common or distinct origin of these rocks. This is, however, rendered somewhat difficult by the consideration just alluded to, and it is only rarely that distinct fossils are obtained from the dolomite-bearing limestone of the district. In only one or two cases have I found signs of life in the dolomite—viz., some small crinoids, and some tiny shells in a few weathered specimens. More distinct and larger fossils may be found in the pure limestone, but not to anything like the extent that obtains in other parts, the Little Island quarries for instance. Judging from these limited materials, the palæontological evidence is not adverse to my theory, but it can hardly be of much value until a closer examination has been made.

The theory of the origin of these deposits to which the foregoing among other facts have led me, may be briefly stated as follows:—After the deposition of the Old Red Sandstone, the Carboniferous limestone, and the Coal Measures, these strata were distorted by terrestrial disturbance, and thrown into the succession of parallel hills and valleys which we find now forming an important feature of our southern Irish scenery. A period of denudation then set in which cleared away nearly all the Coal-Measures, carried off the limestone from the hilltops, and exposed the Old Red Sandstone over most of the countryside.

As the result of upheaval, long cracks and fissures may have been formed in the limestone, in a direction parallel to the lines of hills, *i.e.*, east and west, or rapid streams running down the valleys, and possibly charged with solvents, may have made deep channels in this soft and easily-solved rock. Then succeeded the so-called Permian period, with its lagoons of concentrated sea-water, from which the dolomite was deposited over the limestone still remaining, and also down deep in the parallel cracks which scored its surface. Later on, another period of denudation ensued, viz., the Glacial epoch, which has left such enduring marks upon the geological features of the district, and the soft Permian strata were all cleared away, with the exception of that portion deposited in the limestone fissures, and which, under the name of the Magnesian Limestone of the Cork District, forms the subject of these notes.[1]

THE COLEOPTERIST IN IRELAND.

BY W. E. SHARP.

DUBLIN COUNTY—NORTH COAST.

To the present writer, whose misfortune it is to be a native of the larger of the islands of the United Kingdom, Ireland had always seemed, viewed from an entomological stand-point, to be a land not so much of definite promise as of vague possibilities. In earlier days we had no authentic list of Irish Coleoptera (a want, now how well supplied as regards the north, by the Rev. W. F. Johnson, the readers of this serial know). What might be discovered in a land which cultivation had so little altered—a land of undrained bogs, wild, rough mountains, lakes, and moors, and wildernesses, and one withal of so singularly mild and equable a temperature—it was impossible to conjecture. There were the theorists, who suggested that the remnants of that arctic, or glacial fauna, restricted in England to the highest altitudes, whose places had been occupied by newer races from the Continent, adapted to a more temperate era, had been driven ever westward by that incursion from the east, and might even now be found, perhaps, more abundantly in the west of Ireland than anywhere on this side the channel. Then there was that idea of a former land-

---

[1] Since the above theory was conceived, it has received confirmation, by the discovery that the observations of others in the North of Ireland had led them to the conclusion that Permian beds existed there also. See Hull's *Phys. Geol. and Geog. of Ireland*, second edition, pp. 67-70.

connection between Kerry and the Spanish peninsula, to which the occurrence of the spotted slug, *Geomalacus maculosus*, among the rocks of the south-west, gave some colour; and our imagination was fired by the fancy of ancient Iberian forms still lingering on among the sheltered valleys of the Kerry hills, or sporadic among the islands that fringe that tumultuous coast. Thus Ireland, to the young and imaginative coleopterist, became an enchanted island, where might lie buried unheard of rarities, archaic types of the days of the retreating ice—species new to Britain, or even, exciting thought, new to science, and only describable in the most formal Latin. Nor, indeed, are such dreams even now proved to be of the ivory gate. It is true we have in the north and east of Ireland observers who are unlikely to leave much undiscovered. We have also many records from Cork and Waterford by the late Dr. Power; but all the extreme south, and the best part of the west, and the region of the midland bogs, are still virtually a *terra incognita*, and among these mountains and fens, doubtless there still lies hid much worth the capture.

After this exordium, we fear the reader will experience some disappointment in discovering that the following notes chronicle no exploration into these wilds, but merely a simple walk along the northern coast of Dublin county, and that of the species captured on that occasion, not one can, by any stretch of credulity, be called rare, and that nearly all are probably well known as occurring in Ireland as well as in England.

Not far southward from the town of Drogheda are certain islets called by the generic term of Skerries, and hard by, on the mainland, is a village, perhaps more properly a town, of the same name. The derivation of this word seems interesting, and we hazily conjecture that it may possibly be akin to Skelligs, as similar rocks on the west coast seem to be called. The point, however, is undetermined, and the town of Skerries not particularly interesting. On this bright, windy, May morning we are glad to get free from its long rows of white cottages, and strike the beach at the south end of the town. The shore here is shingly high up, rocky lower down, and a low cliff terminates the cultivated land beyond. If you are a geologist, you may notice there exposed a section of drift, sandy or gravelly in some places, and you may see, in scratched stones and pebbles, tokens of the long since melted ice.

But being more especially of the coleopterist's cult, a dead gull on the shore proves more attractive, and we proceed to investigate the corpse. Alas, it is but a skeleton, and tenanted apparently only by multitudes of a species of *Homalium*, that the long elytra and shining chesnut colour at once declare; but the species is another matter, so we convey a few of them to the laurel-bottle for further examination with a lens. Now, it is this delightful uncertainty which lends such a fascination to the coleopterist's outdoor work. So many of the species are so minute and so obscure, that not even the most experienced veteran can feel absolutely sure what *Homalota*, *Homalium*, *Atomaria*, or *Trichopteryx* he may have got. Probably patient investigation will ultimately disappoint our hopes, and resolve our unknown into the commonest of the genus; but there is always the chance of the prize, and although this uncertainty entails a vast amount of superfluous labour in securing almost everything small from likely localities, yet it invests them all with the interest of their possible value. So it was with these *Homalia* shaken out of this skeleton sea-fowl; they looked good, but they turned out nothing better than *H. rivulare*, probably the most frequent member of the group.

Strewn about among the shingle are bunches of tangled, sand-coloured seaweeds, and moister olive-green masses; beneath the former we find a small *Alcochara*, ashy-grey, instead of shining like the so common *A. languinosa*, and this proved to be *A. algarum*, a species of exclusively maritime habits; we also found a few specimens of *Cercyon littoralis*, a form which a beginner might readily mistake for *C. hæmorrhoidalis*, the most plentiful of this group, but besides the completely different habitat, if the two insects are held up on a level with the eye, so that one can view their contour in profile, this *C. littoralis* is at once distinguished by its flattened back as contrasted with the boldly convex profile of *C. hæmorrhoidalis*.

Under the heavier and wetter masses were great numbers of *Cafius xantholoma* and *C. fucicola*, the latter rather a rare, or at any rate, a local insect. All the members of this genus of *Cafius* inhabit seashores and the margins of tidal rivers, and, indeed, seem to be met with nowhere else. There is a peculiar look about these insects which renders them unmistakable after being once seen. Probably their food consists of the small, or immature sandhoppers, which rise up in a cloud from beneath these masses of tangled *Fucus* when they are moved.

Proceeding onward along the shore, we cannot but notice those unfamiliar rocks which run out in points and masses opposite Lambay island. Had we at that time read Professor Cole's series of articles which have appeared in *The Irish Naturalist*, in "Co. Dublin Past and Present," we should have examined these rocks with more curiosity, and looked out for some of the silicified fossils, the brachiopods, gastropods, and the rest, which the Professor describes as occurring along this part of the coast; as it was, with undiscerning eye, and to avoid the wet and contorted surface which those interesting Ordovicians present, we left the actual beach, and mounting the low cliff, continued our way by a path through the meadows which there border the shore. Scattered along by the side of this track were many boulders and fragments of stone. These being inverted, disclosed a few beetles, mostly, however, valueless. There were the common *Philonthus varius*, *P. politus* and *P. marginatus*; a *Quedius* or two, such as *Q. tristis* and *Q. molochinus*; *Lathrobium fulvipenne*, and *Xantholinus linearis*. These one finds everywhere, but this shining brown *Silpha*, which tumbles into the cavity exposed by the uplifting of one of our stones, one does not find everywhere. In fact, this is the first insect which tells us that we are in Ireland, and nowhere else. The thing is generally described as a variety of *Silpha atrata*, under the name *subrotundata*, and to the present writer is a beetle of considerable interest. It differs so materially from the type-form common in England, that there seems no good reason to deny to it the rank of a separate species. That is to say, the two differ not only in colour (which is comparatively unimportant), but also in structure, and there are among the Geodephaga many differences apparently smaller and less distinct, which are held to divide true species, such are *Notiophilus biguttatus* and *N. substriatus*, *Nebria brevicollis*, and *N. gyllenhali*, *Bembidium tibiale* and *B. atrocœruleum*. Again, there are no connecting links so far in evidence between *S. atrata* and *S. subrotundata*, although, perhaps, the var. *brunnea*, found amongst the Welsh hills, might suggest a common origin; but *brunnea* does not differ in *structure* at all from *atrata*, while this *subrotundata* does. Of course, we all know how difficult—nay, impossible, it is, accurately to define what we mean by "a species," and whether we call any particular form a species, or a racial variety matters but little; the really interesting point about this oily-looking light-brown *Silpha*, which lies kicking in our laurel bottle, is, that the form is almost exclusively restricted to Ireland and the Isle of Man. There are a few, possibly doubtful, English records, as the form *brunnea* might easily have been mistaken for it; whether the type-form has ever been taken in Ireland we cannot say,[1] but if it had never been discovered, that is no proof that it does not exist there; but whether it exists or not, roughly speaking, *S. atrata* is the English, and *S. subrotundata*, the Irish form, and the question at once arises—why should this be? Has the insect been differentiated since the complete disruption of Ireland from Great Britain? or was *S. subrotundata* the original form which in England has been supplanted, and, indeed, exterminated by a younger rival, *S. atrata?* And where does our mountain *S. brunnea* come in? Can that be older than either of the other two, or have all three been synchronously differentiated? Such are some of the problems which this small beetle suggests. It may possibly also occur to us that this insect is rather a stumbling-block in the way of current theories of melanism. Upland forms being presumably relics of the age of the passing glaciers, ought according to such theories to be black, or at least, darker than exclusively lowland forms; and many Geodephaga, such as *Carabus arvensis*, *Notiophilus aquaticus* and *N. palustris*, and *Calathus melanocephalus*, by their melanic alpine variation are consistent evidences of such a principle, but here we have a beetle whose lowland form is black, and upland (*brunnea*) form pale! Such questions as these can only be answered by careful record of the occurrence of the particular species we may be investigating, its varieties, and allied species, over the whole Palæarctic zone, and such records seem at present too fragmentary and indefinite to be of much service, while such as do exist

---

[1] Both *Silpha atrata* (type), and its variety *brunnea*, occur in Ireland. It is worthy of remark that *S. subrotundata*, though generally brown, is sometimes black.—EDS.

are too often inaccessible to the ordinary student. With our present knowledge, questions such as these are clearly insoluble, and so having taken a sufficient number of this engaging insect (and they seem rather plentiful under these stones), let us note some of the other species which occur there.

(TO BE CONCLUDED.)

REVIEWS.

An Account of British Flies (Diptera). By F. V. THEOBALD, M.A., F.E.S. Vol. i. London: Elliot Stock, 1892. 10s.

This is the first volume of a work which will be valuable to students of this most difficult order of insects. It contains chapters on fossil Diptera, the classification of the families of the order, and descriptions of the British genera and species of the *Pulicidæ* (Fleas), *Cecidomyidæ* (Gall-Gnats), *Mycetophilidæ* (Fungus-Gnats), *Bibionidæ*, *Simuliidæ*, and *Chironomidæ* (Midges). There is often great difficulty in determining what species really occur in Britain; Mr. Theobald has given to the commoner and certain species the longest descriptions. Tables of genera and their species are given in some families but not in all; the localities in which species occur are rarely indicated. The larval and pupal stages of the flies are, however, dealt with fully; the book in this respect contrasts most favourably with many entomological works, whose authors consider the perfect insect alone worth consideration. Agriculturalists will be interested to know that species which injure crops are described in special detail.

In the earlier decades of the century, the great Irish naturalist, Haliday, was a pioneer in the study of Diptera. We hope that some of our present-day entomologists may be induced to work at this obscure but most interesting order.

Blue, White, and Blue. Edited by JOHN CHARLES BENSON. Vol. ix., No 1. Dublin, February, 1893. 6d.

We have received the current number of the Rathmines School Magazine, and note with pleasure the prominence given to natural history subjects.

There are some interesting "Bird Notes" by the head master, Rev. Dr C. W. Benson, and we believe that the record of our latest visitor, the Serin Finch, appeared earlier here than in any other journal. In an article on "Dublin in 1805," there is a reference to the introduction of the Frog, and the writer evidently agrees with Mr. Kane rather than with Dr. Scharff. We are a little surprised to read, in an article on the Bailey Lighthouse, of the Sugarloaf and "its volcanic glories of a bygone age." We thought it generally known that this mountain is not an extinct volcano, and that its conical shape is due to the even weathering of the quartzite of which it is composed.

It is gratifying to know that a taste for observing natural objects is being so well developed in Rathmines School, and we confidently look for new recruits from its pupils to the ranks of Irish naturalists.

PROCEEDINGS OF IRISH SOCIETIES.

Royal Zoological Society.

Recent donations comprise a Sparrow-Hawk from Master Phillips; two gulls from A. M. Harper, Esq.; a Guinea-Fowl from Mr. Brady; a Golden-headed Marmoset from Miss S. Roberts; and some freshwater fish from A. Godden, Esq. A Bactrian (two-humped) Camel, an Axis Deer, and a Nylghaie, have been purchased.
7,500 persons visited the Gardens in March.

Armagh Natural History and Philosophical Society.

MARCH 20th.—The President (REV. W. F. JOHNSON, M.A., F.E.S.) in the chair. MR. R. LLOYD PRAEGER, M.R.I.A., delivered a lecture on "Botanical Rambles in Co. Armagh." The results of Mr. Praeger's investigations are at present appearing in these pages.

Belfast Naturalists' Field Club.

MARCH 21st.—The President (MR. JOHN VINYCOMB) in the chair. The evening was devoted to a display of microscopical objects and apparatus. This being the second Annual Meeting of the Microscopical Section, the Secretary (MR. H. M'CLEERY) presented the report of the section, which was adopted. The microscopes then claimed attention. The exhibitors were—Miss C. M. Patterson, Messrs. J. J. Andrew, S. Cunningham, Henry Davis, W. D. Donnan, Wm. Gray, M.R.I.A.; P. F. Gulbransen, W. Hanna, B.A.; Adam Speers, B.Sc.; Alex. Tate, C.E.; R. Welch and Joseph Wright, F.G.S. At nine o'clock a short business meeting was held, at which a number of new members were elected.

APRIL 5th.—The President in the chair. The evening was devoted to Irish folk-lore. The following papers were read:—"Pishogues from Tipperary," MISS LILY S. MOLLAN; "A Notice of Irish Fairies," MR. W. H. PATTERSON, M.R.I.A.; "Notes from Co. Down," MRS. BLAIR.

Dublin Naturalists' Field Club.

MARCH 21st.—The REV. MAXWELL CLOSE, M.A., in the chair. DR. VALENTINE BALL, C.B., F.R.S., gave a lecture entitled, "Notes on some Animals and Plants observed in the Valley of the Nile." Having described the natural features of the country, its geology, climate, and irrigation, and illustrated his remarks by means of limelight photographs, which included many views of architectural ruins and animal life in the Nile Valley, Dr. Ball referred to the influence which the inroad of the Camel has had on the nature of the soil in destroying the herbage, and rendering the land a desert. He then alluded to the customs of the ancient Egyptians, and showed how certain animals, such as the Ibis and the Cat were worshipped, only by certain sections of the people—one creature being held sacred in one region, and another in a different one. The Chairman having thanked Dr. Ball for his lecture, discussed several points of the geology of Egypt, and then spoke of the worship of the ancient Egyptian peoples, showing that it is very probable that they possessed other obscure religious ideas than those commonly credited to them.

MR. H. LYSTER JAMESON exhibited a variety of the Swallow (*Hirundo rustica*) as an example of albinism.

MR. D. M'ARDLE exhibited specimens of *Saracenia flava maxima*, a hybrid, being the first production of this variety in Ireland, and having been grown in the Glasnevin gardens.

Mr. Duerden exhibited a mounted specimen of *Crisia ramosa*, Harmer, a polyzoon new to Ireland, from Dublin bay; the species has recently been described by Mr. S. F. Harmer, who obtained it abundantly at Plymouth.

April 11th.—The President (Dr. M'Weeney) in the chair. Mr. H. K. G. Cuthbert read a paper on "Some Destructive Weevils," giving an account, illustrated by lantern diagrams, of the more important species of Weevils which injure garden plants, fruit and timber trees, and stored grain. The President, Mr. G. H. Carpenter, and Mr. J. M. Browne, took part in the discussion.

Mr. H. Lyster Jameson read a paper on "Some Coleoptera from Loughgilly, Co. Armagh," and exhibited specimens in illustration thereof.

Mr. J. N. Halbert exhibited *Hæmonia appendiculata*, a chrysomelid beetle new to Ireland (see note, p. 148) from the Royal Canal.

Dr. M'Weeney exhibited a fungus, *Cordyceps entomorrhiza*, new to Ireland, from Woodenbridge, Co. Wicklow. This remarkable fungus was growing on the two-winged fly *Polietes lardaria*.

Rev. M. H. Close showed a piece of coal with fracture-planes resembling the faces of a rhomboidal crystal.

NOTES.

BOTANY.

FUNGI.

Fungi from Woodenbridge, Co. Wicklow.—In company with Dr. Scharff I spent several hours collecting in the above locality during the Easter vacation. The following is a list of the chief species met with. They would doubtless have been much more numerous had the weather not been continuously dry for nearly a month previous to our excursion, dryness being, as is well known, unfavourable to the development of most Fungi:—

Three agarics, all belonging to the indistinct purple-spored groups, *Psilocybe* and *Psathyra*. As there was only a single specimen of each species to be found, complete identification was quite impossible; *Polyporus armeniacus*, Berk., or some closely-allied species, on dead fir-trunk; *Dædalia quercina*, Fr.; *Stereum hirsutum*, Fr.; *Peronospora pygmæa*, Ung., and *Urocystis anemones*, Pers., both abundant on *A. nemorosa*, which was very plentiful along the banks of the Aughrim river; the two parasites sometimes occurred in company, the epidermis raised up and blistered by the *Urocystis*, being covered with a thin grey coating of *Peronospora;* sections through these places showed the oospores of the *Peronospora* lying in the parenchyma-cells close to where the spore-groups of the *Urocystis* were in process of differentiation; *Uromyces poæ*, Rabh., æcidiospores everywhere abundant on *Ranunculus ficaria;* *Puccinia phalaridis*, Plow., æcidiospores and pycnids on *Arum maculatum* (scarce); *P. glomerata*, Grev. on *Senecio jacobæa;* *Peziza stercorea*, Fr., and *Ascobolus furfuraceus*, Pers., on cowdung; *Reticularia umbrina*, Fr.; *Arcyria cinerea*, Schum.; *Rhyisma acerinum* in its typical ascigerous condition; *Acrospermum graminum*, Lib., in its only recently-recognized ascigerous state (kindly identified for me by Mr. Massee); *Cordyceps entomorrhiza*(?), Dicks, growing from a dead *Polietes lardaria*, Fab. (a dipterous fly, for the identification of which, I have to thank Mr. G. H. Carpenter). The two last-mentioned Fungi are new to Ireland, and of the highest interest. I do not know that this *Cordyceps* has ever been observed growing from a fly. Dr. Cooke in his recent work on these entomophagous fungi, states—"The only perfect *Cordyceps* yet recorded on Diptera in Europe is one *Cordyceps forquignoni* which has occurred in

France on a dung-fly, *Musca rufa* or *Dasyphora pratorum.*" ("Vegetable Wasps," etc., p. 224).—E. J. McWEENEY, Dublin.

LIVERWORTS.

Irish Liverworts.—To the *Journal of Botany* for April, Rev. C. H. Waddell, B.D., contributes a short paper on the distribution of *Lejeunea* in Ireland, remarking that in his opinion the extensive felling of timber and draining of land which have been carried out in recent times has had a marked effect on the moisture-loving species, and quoting some instances of the recent disappearance of such plants owing to these causes. He adds some new stations for North of Ireland *Lejeuneæ*.

ZOOLOGY.

ARACHNIDS.

Argyroneta aquatica in Captivity.—It is with much pleasure that I have read Mr. Johnson's most interesting article on this subject (p. 99). I myself kept a water spider for some time; but it did not live sufficiently long for me to make many notes on the subject. My aquarium consisted of a tumbler with a little fine gravel on the bottom, and a flat pebble supported on two others, under which the spider constructed a web after the manner described by Mr. Johnson. During its short period of captivity it killed a water-boatman *(Notonecta glauca)* which it pulled into its web. After the *Argyroneta* had died I removed the stone under which the web was constructed, and discovered that some small pebbles were attached to the edge of the web, and I at first thought that they had been suspended there by the spider to weigh down the edge; but I afterwards concluded that it had been originally attached to the bottom, and these pebbles had been buoyed up when it was filled with air.—H. LYSTER JAMESON, Killencoole, Co. Louth.

INSECTS.

A New List of Irish Lepidoptera.—In the *Entomologist* for February, Mr. W. F. de V. Kane commences a new list of the Butterflies and Moths of Ireland, which will be of the greatest use to naturalists, and meets a long felt want. We hope to record the progress of Mr. Kane's work, and to give a summary of his results in each group as it appears.

Lepidoptera of Londonderry.—Mr. Kane has pointed out an error in my list, the species *Geometra vernaria* must be deleted. Mr. Milne informs me that he reared a specimen of *Sesia tipuliformis* last June.—D. C. CAMPBELL, Londonderry.

Lepidoptera at Ardara, Co. Donegal.—Though I paid most attention to the coleoptera at Ardara, I did not altogether neglect other orders, and managed to pick up a few butterflies and moths. Of the latter I should have probably taken more species had not the cold that I caught prevented night work.

The butterflies were represented by the three "Whites," viz.: *Pieris brassicæ, P. rapæ,* and *P. napi; Vanessa urticæ; Satyrus semele,* fairly common on the sandhills, but only just coming out when I left; *Cœnonympha typhon,* a single specimen on the mountain; *C. pamphilus,* common on the mountain; *Polyommatus phlæas,* and *Lycæna icarus.* I almost forgot to mention the ubiquitous *Epinephile janira* which abounded in the meadows. Among the moths the following occurred; *Smerinthus populi,* a single male on the shore of the estuary; *Nudaria mundana; Cymatophora duplaris,* a single specimen at the Rectory; *Xylophasia monoglypha,* a couple of nice dark forms; *Charœas graminis,* on Ragweed; *Caradrina quadripunctata; Apamea didyma;* the paucity of Noctuæ is to be laid to the blame of the cold mentioned above. *Cidaria truncata, C. immanata*, both varying a good deal; *C. testata*, common on the mountain; *Larentia didymata*; *L. cæsiata*, among heather; *Hypsipetes sordidata*; *Emmelesia albulata*, very abundant; *E. adæquata* and *E. alchemillata*, single specimens of each by beating hedges; *Melanippe montanata*; *M. fluctuata*; *Camptogramma bilineata*; *Anaitis plagiata*; *Eubolia limitata*; *Metrocampa margaritaria*; *Hemithea strigata*; *Acidalia dimidiata*; *Eudorea atomalis*, among heather; *Stenopteryx noctuella*; *Pionea forficalis*; *Aphomia sociella*; *Crambus tristellus*; *C. perlellus*, some small varieties; *C. pratellus*; *C. culmellus*; *Tortrix viburnana*, a pale form; *Dichelia grotiana*; *Catoptria cana*; *Pamplusia mercuriana*, I got this beautiful little moth on the top of one of the highest mountains, but it was difficult to catch owing to the wind and the broken nature of the ground; *Grapholitha trimaculana*; *Lita marmorea*, very plentiful on the sandhills at the roots of *Ammophila*.

I am indebted to Mr. C. G. Barrett for kind aid in determining several species with which I was unacquainted.—W. F. JOHNSON, Armagh.

A Beetle new to Ireland,—Hæmonia appendiculata, Panz. in Co. Dublin.—While exercising the water-net in the Royal Canal, near Dublin, on the 8th April, I was fortunate enough to take a specimen of this beetle which is apparently of great rarity, I cannot find any records of its recent occurrence in Great Britain, and there are very few British records of any kind, all are from the south of England. The species is chiefly south European in its distribution.—J. N. HALBERT, Dublin.

MOLLUSCA.

Some Notes on the Irish Slugs.—It is to be hoped that by the publication of Dr. Scharff's monograph on the Irish Slugs, and his more recent series of articles in *The Irish Naturalist* for 1892, an impetus will be given to Irish conchology, and that a deeper and more careful study will be the result. With the exception of Dr. Scharff's admirable and exceedingly useful work, comparatively little or nothing has been done amongst the Irish slugs, and this is the more surprising when one considers the many interesting problems connected with the country geographically. Some of my friends, of a very sanguine nature, see in the systematic study of Irish Conchology a host of new and rare forms. Westerlund has recorded several species of *Sphæriidæ* peculiar to Ireland.

Regarding the slugs, I think future careful and systematic studies of their distribution will reveal a number of forms not as yet known to occur in any of the British Isles. I am indebted to the kindness of Dr. Scharff for many interesting consignments of Irish slugs, amongst which the following have been found: (1) forms very nearly allied to *Arion celticus*, Poll. (which species I now regard as a variety of *A. hortensis*, Fér.); (2) a very interesting *Arion*, much smaller than *A. empiricorum*, Fér., of a silvery-grey colour; possibly this may be only a colour-variation of a young individual. It might easily be mistaken for the British form of *A. fuscatus*, Nils. (*A. bourguignati*, Mab., and *A. circumscriptus*, Johnst.). I had only a single specimen, but from what I could make out by dissection it was closely allied to *A. empiricorum*. The reproductive organs were but slightly developed. In Dr. Scharff's work (p. 539) he makes mention of some *Arions* from the west coast, in which the retractor muscles of the oviduct and receptacular duct have their point of attachment on the *upper portion* of the oviduct and close to the receptaculum seminis. I have suggested to Dr. Scharff that this form may possibly be the *A. lusitanicus*, Mabille, in which species the muscles are so situated. This species has been found in England, and I can see no reason why it should not occur also in Ireland. It is quite possible that many of the slugs which, from external appearances, we at present regard as varieties of *A. hortensis*, Fér., may by careful anatomical investigations prove to be referable to some of the more northerly distributed continental forms. I hope, at no distant date, to publish in the pages of this

Journal, an account of the Irish Slugs I have examined, together with a list of the species and varieties, and shall much esteem any assistance from Irish malacologists.—W. E. COLLINGE, Mason College, Birmingham.

Mollusca from Woodenbridge, Co. Wicklow.—I spent a few days after Easter in the depths of the Co. Wicklow, at Woodenbridge, which I can strongly recommend as a promising collecting-ground. The weather was as fine as could be desired for collecting both land and fresh-water mollusca. Towards the end of my visit I was joined by Dr. M'Weeney, whose great power in detecting microscopic organisms enabled him to find many of the smaller *Helices*. Of the two rarities, *Helix lamellata* and *H. fusca*, we obtained a good number. I was most anxious to get some fine specimens of the fresh-water pearl-mussel (*Unio margaritifer*), which, although absent in some of the Wicklow rivers, is abundant in a few favourable spots in the Aughrim river. It has been stated that one pearl is found on an average in a hundred shells, and that only one in every twenty is of any value as an ornament. But this is a general average which is possibly much exceeded in the shells found in many of the Irish rivers, as I discovered several small pearls in about a dozen specimens. I am not aware that any organised pearl fisheries have ever been established in Ireland, but in Scotland the river pearl industry was of some importance in the 17th century, and British pearls were even spoken of by Tacitus and Pliny.

The following were the species we took at Woodenbridge:—*Vitrina pellucida*, *Hyalinia cellaria*, *H. alliaria*, *H. nitidula*, *H. pura*, *H. radiatula*, *H. crystallina*, *H. fulva*, *Arion ater*, *A. subfuscus*, *A. hortensis*, *A. circumscriptus*, *A. intermedius*, *Limax maximus*, *L. marginatus*, *Agriolimax agrestis*, *A. laevis*, *Amalia sowerbyi*, *Helix pygmaea*, *H. rotundata*, *H. lamellata*, *H. hispida*, *H. fusca*, *H. nemoralis*, *Cochlicopa lubrica*, *Pupa cylindracea*, *Vertigo edentula*, *V. substriata*, *Clausilia bidentata*, *Succinea putris*, *Carychium minimum*, *Limnaea peregra*, *L. truncatula*, *Ancylus fluviatilis*, *Unio margaritifer*.

The following species were obtained on the sand-hills at Arklow, Co. Wicklow:—*Vitrina pellucida*, *Hyalinia radiatula*, *Arion ater*, *A. subfuscus*, *Agriolimax agrestis*, *Helix rotundata*, *H. pulchella*, *H. hispida*, *H. intersecta*, *H. ericetorum*, *H. acuta*, *H. aspersa*, *Cochlicopa lubrica*, *Pupa cylindracea*, *P. muscorum*, *Vertigo pygmaea*.—R. F. SCHARFF, Dublin.

Planorbis riparius—A Correction.—I recently received genuine specimens of this species from Germany, and on comparing these with the Irish forms alluded to in *The Irish Naturalist* (vol. i., p. 192), I regret to inform the readers of this Journal that the latter do not belong to *Pl. riparius*. They are large specimens of *Pl. crista*, var. *nautileus*.—R. F. SCHARFF, Dublin.

AMPHIBIANS.

Arrested Development of the Frog's Tadpole.—Referring to Dr. Scharff's very interesting paper on Frogs in the January number, I should like to mention that I have in my possession some Tadpoles which have remained as such all through last summer and winter, and as I never before knew of the Frog remaining so long in its primitive form, I should be glad to hear if any of your readers have ever observed this peculiarity, and if so, under what conditions. In the case of mine, there is no hindrance to their getting out of the water when ready, as they are in a rough rock-built basin, with the water always nearly to the lip, but the water is not stagnant—a trickle of Vartry water always running into it, keeping it more or less fresh, but not so much as to prevent duckweed growing freely. Could it be possible that the freshness of the water might have such an effect upon their breathing apparatus as to retain them in their fishy state, and retard their otherwise natural development; or may it be the case that a number do remain over unobserved every year in the ditches without change? for what I have are only a small remnant of the number hatched out from the spawn. They lie in the mud at the bottom, but are quite lively when stirred up. Most of them have the two hind legs developed.—H. M. BARTON, Dublin.

BIRDS.

Crossbills (Loxia curvirostra) breeding in Co. Armagh.— Mr. George D. Beresford, of Castle Dillon, Armagh, informs me that he has on the 29th March seen a pair of mature Crossbills captured near Castle Dillon, by a boy, who on the 6th March found their nest containing four young ones, covered with down of a dark-grey colour characteristic of the unfledged nestling Crossbill. He put them into a cage, on which he placed some twigs with bird-lime, and thus caught the two old birds, which feed on fir cones and hemp-seed, but the young ones died three days after they were taken. I may remark that Crossbills which were plentiful here at Cappagh from 1869 to 1892, have now become very scarce.—R. J. USSHER, Cappagh, Co. Waterford.

[We hope naturalists will discourage the useless slaughter and capture of these most interesting birds, which would breed freely with us if undisturbed.—EDS.]

Early Arrivals.— The Chiff-Chaff (*Phylloscopus rufus*) was noted at Comragh in this county on the 19th March. I heard one on the 20th, and at Michelstown, Co. Cork, one was noted on the 21st.

A Swallow (*H. rustica*) was seen at Comragh on the 19th March, and up to the 30th it has been still observed there daily flying about the yard, etc., though only the one bird has as yet appeared.—R. J. USSHER, Cappagh.

In *Land and Water* for April 1st, the Chiff-Chaff is recorded as having been heard in the Downs, Wicklow, on March 23rd, and in Tyrone on the 24th.

Abundance of Wild Swans in Mayo, 1892-3.— I subjoin an extract on this subject from a letter I have received from Dr. Burkitt, late of Waterford, now in his eighty-sixth year, residing at Belmullet. He was the correspondent of Yarrell and Thompson, and collected birds at Waterford since 1830, where among the number of specimens that he preserved were the Waterford Great Auk, given by him to Trinity College Museum, the Gold-vented Thrush, and the South African Eagle-Owl, all obtained by him in the flesh from the locality. Of late years he has added to the Irish list the Barred Warbler, which he obtained at Belmullet in September, 1884. This with a County Waterford specimen of Baillon's Crake he has given to the Science and Art Museum.—R. J. USSHER.

"I had intended mentioning to you as an astonishing fact the unprecedented migration of swans during the winter 1892 to this district. This last winter has been mild, little or no frost or snow, but murky, foggy, wet or stormy, a damp miserable season, elsewhere reported as about the most intensely cold and severe winter on record. From about the middle of November swans appeared, from time to time, to visit this district the Mullet, until the second week in February, in enormous numbers, some thousands reported. Generally swans visit the Mullet in winter, in detached bodies of five, six, eight, or so, amounting to the total number of fifty to a hundred during the winter, but this season on the lake of Cross, about three miles from this, upwards of a thousand were seen together almost daily, for weeks in December and January, and some used occasionally to fly from it to a smaller lake about two miles from this, Turmon Carra, and if disturbed there go back again to Cross. This Turmon Carra, although a very small piece of water, was always a favourite resting-place for ducks, geese, and swans in hard weather, when they migrate to this district.

"The vast majority of these swans were *C. bewicki*. This bird has the receptacle in the sternum for the windpipe as the Whooper has, but not nearly so large nor deep. Mr. Moran shot one on February 6th, a young bird, some greyish feathers being on the head. It was in fine condition being very fat.—ROBERT J. BURKITT."

THE YELLOW-BILLED SHEATHBILL. (*Chionis alba*, Lath.)
(Shot at Carlingford Lighthouse, 2nd December, 1892.) [See p. 151.]
[*From a Photograph by Mr. Greenwood Pim.*]

The Irish Naturalist.

VOL. II.   JUNE, 1893.   NO. 6.

THE YELLOW-BILLED SHEATHBILL (CHIONIS ALBA, LATHAM) ON THE IRISH COAST.

BY H. LYSTER JAMESON.

OF the many rare birds that have within the last few years been added to the Irish list through the energetic researches of Mr. R. M. Barrington and his correspondents at the Irish lighthouses, none has caused more interest among ornithologists than the Yellow-billed Sheathbill (*Chionis alba*).

The specimen, of which a plate is given in this number, was shot by Mr. Richard Hamilton, lighthouse-keeper, Carlingford, Co. Down, on December 2nd, 1892. Mr. Hamilton describes the capture in his letter to Mr. Barrington (December 9th) as follows:—

"At 8.30 a.m. on the 2nd, I was at the Blockhouse (a small island about 800 yards from the lighthouse) shooting ducks, and saw the bird walking about on the highest part of it, which is not more than ten feet. I at first took it for a tame pigeon, as it seemed to take no notice of me, but observed that it walked differently, at an angle of about 45°, and was not picking at anything; so fired at it about thirty yards, and was surprised to see it go off. It took a half circle of the rock, and again alighted a few yards from the water. I again fired at about forty yards, still the bird stood steady as if not touched—and I consider myself a fair shot,—so I sent the dog to fetch it, and when about two yards from it, it again took to flight, as it seemed quite strong, but fell about fifty yards from the rock. I picked it up with the boat, and from its attitude on the water, I dare say it was a land bird. The wings were partly opened, particularly in front. The shot used was No. 2."

Mr. Benjamin R. Jeffers, assistant-keeper, who watched the proceedings from the lighthouse with a telescope, described the bird as being quite at ease on the water until the boat came up, when it assumed the attitude described by Mr. Hamilton.' He also said that it had a very "proud, bold

For this information I am indebted to Mr. Barrington.

A

walk," and that the flight resembled that of a Puffin, the motion of the wings a little less rapid. The opening of the wings on the approach of the boat was only natural, for the bird was evidently wounded, as its feathers bear traces of the shot, and it was incapable of rising from the water, one tarsus being broken.

Different systematists have placed the genus *Chionis* in widely different families and orders. Gray ("Genera of Birds"), places the family *Chionididæ* in the order Gallinæ; Cuvier ("Règne Animal"), between the genera *Fulica* and *Glareola;* while Audouin & Co., in their "Dictionnaire d'Histoire Naturelle," rank it among the web-footed birds. The researches of Professor Blainville have, however, now set the matter at rest, as he has shown its structural and anatomical affinities to the Oyster-catchers (*Hæmatopus*); and Mivart ("Birds: the Elements of Ornithology"), places *Chionis* among the *Charadriidæ*, not even assigning to it a sub-family in common with *Thinocorus* and *Attagis*.

Of the genus *Chionis* there are two species,—*Chionis alba* and *C. minor;* the average dimensions are as follows:—

Chionis minor. Black-billed Sheathbill:		*Chionis alba.* Yellow-billed Sheathbill:	
Total length,	13 inches.	17 inches.	
Bill from point,	1.2 ,,	1.4 ,,	
Height at base,	.7 ,,	.8 ,,	
Breadth at gape,	.65 ,,	.75 ,,	
Wing,	9 ,,	10.5 ,,	
Tarsus,	1.10 ,,	1.11 ,,	
Middle toe,	1.8 ,,	2.1 ,,	
Bill black, sheath turned up in front like pommel of saddle.		Bill yellow, sheath flat like cere.[1]	

The bill is very strong and convex; on the cheek there is a bare spot, covered in the adults with yellowish papillæ; wing armed with a blunt knob at carpal joint; second primary longest; tail strong, nearly square; legs reddish-brown (colour seems to vary considerably according to age; and judging from the two specimens I have examined, becomes dull lead-colour after death); hind toe elevated from ground; claws black, short, channelled on under side; irides (? species) dull lead-colour; plumage all over pure white.

---

[1] For these dimensions, furnished by Professor Newton, I have again to thank Mr. Barrington.

The specimen taken at Carlingford was, doubtless, moulting, as the wing and tail feathers were uneven, but according to my friend, Mr. E. Williams, the old feathers, some of which were not yet cast, showed no signs of captivity. The young differ from the adults in having the papillæ on the face absent, or rudimentary. Not having had an opportunity of consulting a series of specimens, I am unable to say whether the Carlingford specimen had arrived at full maturity. Many voyagers have remarked on the extraordinary odour of the flesh and entrails of this bird, but the smell does not seem to be an essential attribute, as others have not noticed it; Mr. Williams did not think it different from that of other aquatic birds, whereas Mr. Tank declares that a specimen taken on board a ship during a storm, when seventy miles off the coast of Patagonia, and brought to him in a half-skinned condition, had a most remarkable stench, which he compared to that of a seal, and which was retained by the skin some time after mounting.

Both Mr. Williams and Mr. Tank affirm that there was a quantity of fat under the skin, a peculiarity shared by most birds inhabiting cold regions.

Voyagers differ as to the quality of the flesh; some comparing it with that of a duck, but others considering the odour sufficient to condemn it. Mr. Williams remarked that it was coarse and rank like that of an Oyster-catcher. The egg has been described by Prof. Newton in the *Proc. Zool. Soc. London*. I regret that I have not had an opportunity of consulting his paper.

Chionis alba lives like our Oyster-catcher, singly, or in small flocks, on the shores of antarctic islands; it feeds on mollusca, carrion, seaweed, and eggs. The mollusca in the stomach of one opened by Darwin, at Falkland, consisted chiefly of *Patellæ*. Can the odour exhaled by some specimens be due to their carrion-feeding propensities, like that of our Hooded Crow?

Chionis alba inhabits the coast of Patagonia, the Falkland Islands, and South Georgia; while eastward *C. minor* takes its place, inhabiting Kerguelen, the Crozettes, and Prince Edward Island. Darwin and other voyagers remark the great distances from land at which the bird is to be met with in the open ocean, and, according to Prof. Newton, the most northerly record is latitude 44° S., 260 miles off the coast of Patagonia, which is very remarkable for a wader; 44° S. lat. is also about the northern limit of drift ice, which the Sheathbill is said to frequent, and from which it takes one of its trivial names (Icebird). Is it altogether improbable that a bird which has been found occasionally so far from land, should wander still further from its usual limits? and once having reached the West Indies, it would be no more unlikely to fly over the Atlantic than any other of our American visitors, and the natural tendency would be to seek a climate similar to its own for breeding purposes. If the Sheathbill had escaped from any European aviary, the fact would probably have been published before now, and Mr. W. Cross, Liverpool, the well-known importer of wild animals, has not had one alive for several years.

Moreover, it is not a bird a sailor would bring home by choice, as it would require more liberty than the finches and parrots which are usually to be seen in the forecastle of a merchant ship, while if left at liberty to run about the decks it would probably soon escape, and if pinioned would be drowned in the first heavy sea, as happens to many Guillemots, Razorbills, and even occasionally Fulmars off our coast. The ships which visit antarctic islands are usually small vessels, such as sealers and whalers, from which a Sheathbill would have ample opportunities of escape. If on the other hand it flew on board a large merchant ship on a passage round Cape Horn, the majority of seamen would do their best to secure it for the pot. I write from experience, having seen the breast of an Albatross served up by the apprentices on a first-class London merchant ship. Of the many birds that came on board our ship during my voyage round the world, no attempt was made to tame any except a few finches captured in European waters.

I will not quote as similar instances the many petrels and terns, whose breeding limits are antarctic and circumtropical, as they are purely oceanic, some of them breeding in the extreme south, as Wilson's Petrel, the Sooty Shearwater, and the "Cape Pigeon," which is supposed to have occurred in Ireland, but which Mr. A. G. More and Mr. F. Williams inform me was too hastily accepted on faith of evidence, which at that time seemed sufficient, but which has since been discredited. Much interesting information on the antarctic and circumtropical species which visit the British shores, will be found in Mr. Henry Seebohm's "Geographical Distribution of British Birds."

Books containing information on *Chionis alba* :—
Darwin, "Naturalists' Voyage."
   „   "Zoology, Voyage H.M.S. *Beagle* (Birds)."
Dumeril, "Voyage de l'Uraine."
   „   "Voyage de la Bonité."
Gray, "Genera of Birds."
Shaw, "Naturalists' Miscellany."
   „   "General Zoology."
Pagenstecher, "Die Vögel süd Georgiens."

THE FLORA OF COUNTY ARMAGH.

BY R. LLOYD PRAEGER, B.E., M.R.I.A.

(*Continued from page* 134).

Verbascum thapsus, Linn. N. — —
   Near Armagh, but escaped; apparently not a native of the county, R. Ll. P.

Linaria repens, Ait. — — S.
   Sparingly on and beside the Greenore railway near the canal locks below Newry, R. Ll. P. Its only other station in Ulster lies six miles to the south-east, on the opposite (Co. Down) shore of Carlingford Lough.

(Scrophularia aquatica, Linn. [N.] — —
   "The water figwort or *Scrophularia aquatica* . . . grows on the banks of the Newry water."—*Coote's Armagh*. The determination may be correct, but I saw this species nowhere in the county.)

Melampyrum pratense, Linn. N. M. —
   Mullinure near Armagh, W. F. J. spec.! On bogs south of Annagariff lake, and between Lough Gullion and Lough Neagh; in a wood a mile S.E. of Tanderagee, and by the Cusher river near Clare Castle, R. Ll. P.

M. pratense, Linn., var. **montanum,** Johnst. — — S.
   Summit of a rocky hill a mile south of Fathom mountain, at about 800 feet elevation, R. Ll. P.

Veronica montana, Linn. N. M. —
   Copse within the park at Loughgall Manor! and banks of Lough Neagh, More *N.H.R.* Tynan Abbey, and upper and lower demesnes at Tanderagee, R. Ll. P.

V. agrestis, Linn. N. — —
   Grange, near Armagh, W. F. J. spec.!

*****V. buxbaumii,** Ten. N. — —
   A weed in the flower borders at Loughgall Manor, More *N.H.R.* I did not observe it in the county; it is now quite common in district 12.

*****Mentha rotundifolia,** Linn. N. M. S.
   Occasionally, but only as an escape, R. Ll. P.

‡**M. piperata,** Huds. N. — —
Near Tartaraghan and Killylea, but probably an escape from cultivation (form *M. officinalis,* Hull), R. Ll. P.

Origanum vulgare, Linn. N. — —
Loughgall (More), *Flor. Ulst.* and *Cyb. Hib.*! Abundant on a high grassy bank a little north of Loughgall; lanes at Derryhaw, east of Tynan, R. Ll. P.

Thymus serpyllum, Linn. — — S.
Apparently very rare in the county, and only once observed, R. Ll. P.

Scutellaria galericulata, Linn. N. — —
Lough near Killilea (Templeton), *Flor. Ulst.* Loughgall (More), *Flor. Ulst.*! Derrymacash in Seagoe parish, H. W. L. spec.! Near Armagh, S. A. S. Shores of Annagariff lake, R. Ll. P.

Lamium amplexicaule, Linn. N. — S.
Grange, near Armagh, W. F. J. spec.! Loughgall, Navan Fort, railway two miles south of Portadown, and on ruin at western base of Slieve Gullion, R. Ll. P.

L. intermedium, Fries. N. — —
Grange, near Armagh, W. F. J. spec.! Maghery, R. Ll. P.

(L. hybridum, Villars. [N.] — —
Loughgall (More), *Flor. Ulst.* Not in Mr. More's *N.H.R.* paper nor in *Cyb. Hib.*, and presumably omitted for a reason. I did not find it in the county, but noticed cut-leaved forms of *L. purpureum*, resembling this species, in the north.)

L. album, Linn. N. — S.
Common in the limestone district, whence there are numerous records and notes of it; its only occurrences beyond this limited area are Silverwood near Lurgan, H. W. L. spec.! and roadside south of Crossmaglen, R. Ll. P.

(Galeopsis speciosa, Miller. — [M.] —
Tanderagee (O'Meara), *Cyb. Hib.* Not seen since at Tanderagee or elsewhere in the county; many of the older records for this species are unreliable, large-flowered forms of *G. tetrahit* having been mistaken for it.)

Stachys betonica, Benth. N. — —
County Armagh (G. R.), *Flor. Ulst.* On an old fort near Tartaraghan (G. R.), *Cyb. Hib.* In considerable abundance at Crowhill, B. N. F. C., 1871. These notes all refer to one station, which is an old wooded rath near the road at the south side of Crowhill, where it was first found by Mr. Robinson. Seen here also by S. A. S. in 1877, but very sparingly. I visited the place both in July and August, 1892, and searched for it without success, but I can hardly believe it has died out, as the ground has been in no way disturbed or altered for many years.

S. palustris, Linn., var. **ambigua,** Smith. N. — —
Roadside at Silverwood near Lurgan, H. W. L. spec.! There are two hybrid forms in the North of Ireland; one, the *S. ambigua* of Smith, a coarse form with sub-cordate ovate-lanceolate leaves, tapering to a long point, and nearer to *S. sylvatica* than to *S. palustris*; the other, a smaller plant with narrower leaves, not cordate below, and with a shorter blunter point, and nearer to *S. palustris* than to *S. sylvatica*. To the former (*S. ambigua*) belong the Armagh plant, and a plant found by S. A. S. near Belfast; the latter is the commoner form, and to it all the records of *S. ambigua* in district 12 refer.

S. arvensis, Linn. — M. —
Extremely rare in Armagh: a few plants observed in one spot only, in a field near Clare, S.W. of Tanderagee, R. Ll. P.

Pinguicula lusitanica, Linn. — — S.
    On Camlough mountain, and west side of Slieve Gullion, R. Ll. P.

Utricularia vulgaris, Linn. N. — —
    Montiaghs bogs, H. W. L. spec.! Loughadian west of Armagh, Drummanmore Lough near Armagh, by Lough Neagh at Derryadd Bay, and drains on Derrywarragh Island at Maghery, R. Ll. P.

‡**Primula veris,** Linn. N. — —
    Park at Lurgan (Hyndman), and Loughgall (More), *Flor. Ulst.*; recently seen in the former station by H. W. L., and in the latter by W. F. J. Armagh Palace demesne and Castle Dillon demesne, W. F. J. spec.! Raughlan Point on Lough Neagh, H. W. L. spec.! Perhaps introduced in all these stations, but may be a native on the limestone.

Lysimachia nummularia, Linn. N. M. —
    In a limestone quarry at Grange, near Armagh, W. F. J. spec.! Lawn in Tanderagee upper demesne, R. Ll. P.

Glaux maritima, Linn.
    Abundant by estuary of Newry River, R. Ll. P.

Samolus valerandi, Linn. N. — —
    Shore of Lough Neagh by entrance of Lagan Canal, H. W. L. spec.!

Centunculus minimus, Linn. N. — —
    Shore of Lough Neagh south of Bird Island, and in a gravel-pit on west side of Derryadd Bay, R. Ll. P.

Statice bahusiensis, Fries. — — S.
    Estuary of Newry River, common, R. Ll. P.

Armeria maritima, Willd.
Plantago coronopus, Linn.
P. maritima, Linn.
Suæda maritima, Dum.
    } With the last, R. Ll. P. — — S.

Chenopodium bonus-henricus, Linn. N. — S.
    Benburb-bridge (Hyndman), *Flor. Ulst.* Roadside at east end of Lough Ross near Crossmaglen, R. Ll. P.

Beta maritima, Linn. — — S.
    By brackish streams in Newry, R. Ll. P.

Salicornia herbacea, Linn. — — S.
    Estuary of Newry River, R. Ll. P.

Atriplex deltoidea, Bab. — — S.
    Estuary of Newry River, R. Ll. P.

A. erecta, Huds. — — S.
    Field near Narrow-water, R. Ll. P.

A. babingtonii, Woods. — — S.
    Shore near Narrow-water, R. Ll. P.

Oblone portulacoides, Linn. — — S.
    One plant on shore at County bridge near Narrow-water, R. Ll. P. It is abundant on the opposite (Co. Down) shore of the estuary, which is its only station in district 12, and further southward on muddy shores at Dundalk, in district 5.

†**Polygonum bistorta,** Linn. N. — —
    Waste ground at Ardmore Glebe, H. W. L. spec.!

P. lapathifolium, Linn. N. — —
    Occasionally on the northern bogs; shore of Killybane Lough, near Crossmaglen, R. Ll. P.

P. minus, Huds. — M. —
By the canal between Scarva and Tanderagee, S. A. S. Shores of Clay Lake near Keady, and of Lough Neagh at Raughlan Point, R. Ll. P.

P. aviculare, Linn., var. N. — —
A form resembling *P. littorale*, Link, with long diffuse stems and thicker glaucous leaves, occurs on gravelly shores of Lough Neagh, R. Ll. P.

Mercurialis perennis, Linn. — M. —
County Armagh (G. R.), *Flor. Ulst.* A single locality near Tartaraghan (G. R.), *Cyb. Hib.*; "Tartaraghan" is here a slip or misprint, Tanderagee being the place intended. Several extensive patches by the Cusher river in Tanderagee lower demesne, and at a number of spots in Tanderagee upper demesne. R. Ll. P.

Callitriche autumnalis, Linn. N. M. —
In Ballylane lake south of Markethill, and dredged up in Lough Neagh at Derryadd Bay, R. Ll. P.

Parietaria officinalis, Linn. — — S.
Abundant on walls at Newry, R. Ll. P.

*****Humulus lupulus,** Linn. N. — —
In hedges near the Callan river west of Loughall, R. Ll. P.

*****Ulmus suberosa,** Sm. N. — —
Occasionally, but planted. R. Ll. P.

*****U. montana,** With. N. — —
Planted in Co. Armagh (More), *Cyb. Hib.*

Populus tremula, Linn. N. M. S.
Loughgall (More), *Flor. Ulst.* In hedges and copses throughout the county, in the N.W. especially—probably an original native. R. Ll. P.

*****P. alba,** Linn. N. — —
Occasionally, but only planted or escaped.

Hydrocharis morsus-ranæ, Linn. N. — —
Bog drains by roadside half a mile south of Derryadd bay, H. W. L.!
In its only present station in district 12 (Portmore, Co. Antrim) it has never been known to flower. On visiting the Co. Armagh station, I found the plant in abundance where described by Mr. Lett; the time of my visit (September) was too late for flower but Mr. Lett's specimen obtained here has a blossom on it, R. Ll. P.

Orchis pyramidalis, Linn. N. — —
Armagh (G. R.), *Flor. Ulst.* Near Loughgall, S. A. S. Castle Dillon, Loughgall, and Pavilion grounds at Armagh, W. F. J. spec.! Around the north end of Loughgall lake, and at quarries at the western extremity of the Manor demesne, R. Ll. P. Confined to the limestone district.

Gymnadenia conopsea, R. Br. N. — —
Between Armagh and Loughgall, B.N.F.C., 1877. Near Loughgall and at Mullinure, Grange, and Drummanmore, all near Armagh, W. F. J. spec.!

Listera cordata, R. Br. N. — S.
Montiaghs bogs, H. W. L. spec.! On Camlough mountain (1,300 feet), summit of Clermont (1,462), and north side of Slieve Gullion (1,500), R. Ll. P.

Neottia nidus-avis, Rich. — M. —
One plant in a copse at south end of Gosford Castle demesne, R. Ll. P.

Spiranthes romanzoviana, Cham.　　　　　　　　　　N. — —
　　On a wet worked-out bog in the northern portion of the county.
R. Ll. P. I have already (*Journal of Botany*, 1892, p. 272) published
the facts relating to the discovery of this extremely rare plant in
Co. Armagh. Previously known in the Old World only in the
widely separated stations of Co. Cork in Europe, and Kamtschatka
in Asia, a habitat in the north of Ireland has now been added, and
it is with perhaps pardonable pride that I am able to enumerate
it, and *Carex rhynchophysa* as the results of my exploration, made
on behalf of the "Irish Naturalist," of the flora of Co. Armagh.
I think it better not to publish the exact locality, lest the plant
should suffer, at the hands of over-enthusiastic collectors, the
penalty of its rarity.

Epipactis latifolia, All.　　　　　　　　　　　　　N. M. —
　　Castle Dillon, W. F. J. spec.! Ardmore glebe, H. W. L. spec.!
Abundant in Tanderagee upper and lower demesnes, and at Gosford
Castle; also seen at Clare, and Tynan Abbey, R. Ll. P. Mr. More's
doubtful note (N. H. R.), no doubt refers to *E. latifolia*.

Malaxis paludosa, Sw.　　　　　　　　　　　　N. — —
　　Moyntaghs bogs (Hyndman), *Flor. Ulst.* There is plenty of likely
ground on the northern bogs, where I looked for this little orchid,
but without success, R. Ll. P.

¡ Iris fœtidissima, Linn.　　　　　　　　　　　N. — —
　　County Armagh (G. R.), *Flor. Ulst.* Near Tartaraghan, S. A. S.
Hedgebank in Armagh Palace demesne, R. Ll. P.

Sagittaria sagittifolia, Linn.　　　　　　　　　　N. M.
　　In the Bann near Portadown, *Mackay Rar.*! Moyntaghs bog
(Hyndman), *Flor. Ulst.*! Maghery, W. F. J. spec.! Closet River
and Scarva, H. W. L.! Newry Canal, S. A. S.! Abundant in sheltered
places along the Lough Neagh shore, and in the Blackwater, Ulster
Canal, Bann, and Lagan Canal as far south as Goraghwood, R. Ll. P.

Butomus umbellatus, Linn.　　　　　　　　　　N. M. —
　　In the Blackwater near Maghery (G. R.), and in the canal
near Tanderagee, and upper Bann (Jones), *Cyb. Hib.* Ulster Canal
between Moy and Benburb, B. N. F. C., 1880. Maghery, W. F. J.
spec.! Montiaghs bogs, H. W. L. spec.! The distribution of this
plant is exactly the same as that of the last species. I found it
abundantly along the Lough Neagh shores and in the waterways
which connect with it; it is absent from the other lakes and
streams of the county, R. Ll. P.

Triglochin maritimum, Linn.　　　　　　　　　　— — S.
　　Estuary of Newry River, common, R. Ll. P.

(Colchicum autumnate, Linn.　　　　　　　　　　[N.] — —
　　"The Colchicum, or Meadow Saffron, grows on the borders of
the Blackwater and the Callan, and is highly ornamental . . .
the flowers are of a variety of shades, of red, yellow, white, and
purple; it grows in low meadows," *Coote's Armagh.* Probably an
escape from cultivation; not seen by R. Ll. P.

Juncus maritimus, Smith.　　　　　　　　　　— — S.
　　Brackish places below Newry, R. Ll. P.

J. glaucus, Sibth.　　　　　　　　　　　　　N. — —
　　Very abundant throughout the limestone area; quite absent from
the rest of the county, R. Ll. P. So sharply is its distribution
defined, that one could almost determine the boundaries of the
limestone district by observing the presence or absence of this rush.

J. gerardi, Lois.　　　　　　　　　　　　　　— — S.
　　Abundantly by the estuary of the Newry river, R. Ll. P.

(TO BE CONCLUDED.)　　　　　　c*

THE COLEOPTERIST IN IRELAND.
BY W. E. SHARP.
(*Concluded from page* 144.)

DUBLIN COUNTY—NORTH COAST.

There are, of course, the usual ubiquitous *Pterostichus madidus*, *Pt. niger*, and *Pt. melanarius*, and in wet places, *Pt. nigrita* and *Pt. diligens; Amara trivialis* is also very common, and among them appears a specimen of a larger *Amara*, which proves to be *A. ovata*. This is a species we have only taken in England among river shingle, and it is curious to meet it here in a grass field. It is not a very common species anywhere. Under another stone lurks a still larger *Amara*, *A. aulica*, or *A. spinipes*, as it used to be called. We also add to our list of *Amaræ*, *A. similata*, under a stone close down by the shingle. The only *Bembidium* we get besides the common *B. littorale* and *B. lampros*, is *B. femoratum*. Then there is that pretty little *Badister bipustulatus*, and a specimen or two of *Notiophilus aquaticus*. Among the *Staphylinidæ* nothing noteworthy occurs, and by this time we have reached and passed the little fishing hamlet of Loughshinney, and can see, not far beyond, the harbour and straggling cottages of Rush.

To avoid these we make a detour among the fields. The springing oats are just now turning to green the flattened brown tillage land, and we soon notice a dead scarecrow rook. The robber bird lies prone now, his gibbet having been overset, and in his half-dried body we find that handsome beetle, *Creophilus maxillosus*, with his great sickle-like jaws, two or three of the black *Necrophorus humator*, and quite a swarm of *Silpha rugosa*. The aforementioned *Silpha subrotundata*, although common under stones, etc., does not appear to share the generic love of carrion. We expected some *Choleva*, *Hister*, or *Saprinus*, but nothing of the kind appeared.

In the lane which led through these fields were moss-covered stones, and a little globular steel-blue beetle settled on them, basking in the sun, proved to be *Phædon tumidulum*. Beneath the stones was *Barynotus obscurus*, and shaken from the hedge above, an example of *Phytobius comari*. We regretted here that we had no net for beating or sweeping, our substitute for such necessary implement only succeeding in capturing a great number of *Meligethes aeneus*. On a dandelion-flower, however, we notice a speck, a touch as of an emerald, this is that beautiful little beetle, *Dolichosoma nobilis*, recently recorded from the Wicklow coast.

A few common *Telephori* and *Rhynchophora* complete our capture here, and we are soon crossing the town of Rush, towards a sandy tract, which we can descry beyond. A long, bare street, disproportionately wide; rows of low, whitewashed, thatched cottages, gardenless and naked. Against the walls lean nets, and the apparatus of the fishers' craft. The masts and spars of a few boats cut the sky at the end of the street, and beyond, the crisp blue sea, and the gentle cliffs and slopes of Lambay. Such was Rush. Beyond the town the coast bends round, and the point runs out in sandhills of no great size or elevation. We approached this ground with some expectancy, as we were somewhat intimate with other sandhills, which fringe the Cheshire sea-coast; and it would be, we thought, interesting to observe how far the inhabitants of these similar localities differed or agreed.

Unfortunately, just about this time, clouds, which had been gathering all the morning, drew together, and not only obscured the sun, but descended in a copious shower. Now, for collecting among sandhills of all places, bright sunshine, and absence of all wind, are essential elements of success. Hence, in the teeth of this blustering squall of wind and rain, we could not expect many captures, and, no doubt, the record of their coleopterous denizens is consequently very incomplete.

The most abundant beetle there seemed to be *Otiorrhynchus atroapterus*. There were also a few specimens of *O. sulcatus*, both crawling on the bare sand, and we also took one *Liosomus ovatulus*.

The Cheshire sandhills, to which we have referred, swarm on occasions with three species of *Hypera*, *H. nigrirostris*, *H. plantaginis*, and *H. variabilis*; also with *Cneorhinus geminatus*, and *Sitones griseus*. There is also to be taken there, more or less commonly, *Grypidius equiseti*, *Saprinus quadristriatus*, and *Sæneus*, *Anisotoma dubia*, *Notoxus monoceros*, and very profusely, *Heliopathes gibbus*, and *Microzoum tibiale*; a singularly large number of species of *Aphodii* have been taken there, and the Geodephaga are represented more especially by *Calathus mollis*. All of which insects are almost entirely limited in that district to the sandhill zone. Now, of these species, the only representatives which we took in these sandhills of Rush were *Hypera variabilis*, the *Cneorhinus*, *Heliopathes*, and *Microzoum*, and of these only two or three individuals. The two *Otiorrhynchi, sulcatus*, and *atroapterus*, which seemed to be the most plentiful beetles there, are almost unknown on the Cheshire dunes, while the only geodephagous beetles we took were *Dyschirius thoracicus* and *Harpalus tardus*, which latter we take in Cheshire on heaths, and not on the sandhills at all.

On the whole, the coleopterous fauna evident on these Rush sandhills was disappointingly small. This we attribute principally to the weather which then prevailed, but also, to some extent, to the fact that there appeared to be no herbiverous animals grazing among them, and consequently no *Aphodii, Staphylinidæ*, etc., and more especially to the low elevation of these hills compared with those on the Cheshire coast. These high summits are a great protection from the wind, and their enclosed hollows and deep rifts act as traps, and are the means whereby those beetles which inhabit them are retained in their recesses, instead of being blown out to sea or across to the unsuitable cultivated land on the other side. I believe that this is the true explanation of the vast number of individuals of such species as people these localities, and which are seen crawling all over the bare slopes on every sunny spring day.

The only other beetle we took here was a specimen of *Broscus cephalotes*, hidden, as usual, under a loose piece of driftwood. Just at this point, a narrow arm of sea cuts us off from a vast extent of desolate-looking sands, which appear to stretch almost to opposite Malahide. Turning round to the left, before striking up into the country, a low grassy bank claimed our attention, and here we took that fine *Chrysomela banksii*, and also a specimen of *Xantholinus tricolor*. That was our last capture. A tedious and uninteresting road lay between that point and Swords, whose ruined castle and ivy-clad tower we were anxious to reach that afternoon. The bag amounts to something like thirty-five species, none of them specially valuable, and none new to the Irish list. But we have had a pleasant morning's walk in a district to us quite new, and as we catch the outlines of the great Wicklow mountains, dim against the southern sky, we promise to ourselves some further exploration into their recesses, and console ourselves with the possibility of fine upland species to be discovered there.

NOTES ON IRISH CHARACEÆ.

BY H. AND J. GROVES, F.L.S.

HAVING received a good deal of promising material from Ireland, we have for some years past been anxious to see some of the plants in their native condition. During last summer we paid our first visit to Ireland with this object.

Before proceeding to the head-quarters of *Chara tomentosa*, the species we most wanted to study, on the kind invitation of Mr. Barrington we paid a short visit to Co. Wicklow, and under his guidance explored the pools and ditches of the Murrough of Wicklow, as well as some of the mountain lakes. In the former locality we collected *C. polyacantha*, unrecorded for the county, though we learn since that it had previously been found there by Mr. M'Ardle, and in Lough Luggala and Lough Dan we were fortunate enough to get a very fine form of *Nitella gracilis*, also new to the county, and one of the rarest British species.

We next went to Mullingar, and spent a day on Lough Ennell (Belvidere Lake) but were much hindered in dragging by the roughness of the water. We found a considerable quantity of *Chara tomentosa*, but most of it much incrusted and covered with Algæ, a nice little form of *C. aspera*, and in the deeper parts large patches of *Tolypella glomerata*, the last named being new to the county.

During the rest of our stay in Westmeath we were the guests of Mr. Levinge, of Knock Drin Castle, who was good enough to place his boats at our service, and himself guided us to the most likely spots for aquatics in Lough Deravaragh, Lough Owel, and the Knock Drin Lakes. In Lough Deravaragh the most important finds were *C. tomentosa* in plenty, and a few scraps of *T. glomerata*. In Brittas Lough, an artificial lake on the Knock Drin property, which was almost full of Charas, we found some interesting forms of *C. contraria*, a very long slender form of *C. hispida* var. *rudis*, and immense masses of a very fine form of *C. aspera*. In the Scraw bog near Lough Owel, to which Mr. Levinge took us to see some fine *C. polyacantha* and a number of interesting bog plants, we had the good fortune to find *Nitella tenuissima*, which had not previously been collected in Ireland. It appeared to be somewhat local, as we found it in only three out of a considerable number of peat-pits which we examined. In Lough Owel we found three forms of *C. tomentosa*—one the largest we have seen—*C. polyacantha*, and several forms of *C. aspera* and *C. contraria*.

We spent a few days in Galway, and in some peat-pits to the east of Lough Corrib, near Ballindo'oly, we found a very fine form of *N. tenuissima* growing with *C. polyacantha*. We also found the latter species in the western division of the county.

From Galway we went on to Killarney, but here unfortunately the weather was very unfavourable for dragging, and the water in the lakes was exceptionally high. We were not successful in finding the little *Nitella* discovered by Mr. Scully, which we formerly referred to *N. gracilis*. Mr. Scully was however kind enough to send us a quantity of fresh specimens, and an examination of these prove that the plant is not *N. gracilis* but a large form of *N. nordstedtiana*. The first Irish specimens of the plant which we received were collected by Mr. Scully in 1889 in Caragh Lake, and these much more resemble a small form of *N. gracilis* than any form of *N. nordstedtiana* with which we were then acquainted.

Since our return from Ireland Mr. Levinge has sent us a sterile specimen of a curious *Chara* collected by him in Brittas Lake, which seems to be closely related to the Swiss *C. dissoluta*. We hope to see fruiting specimens, which are necessary for a satisfactory determination.

We were much struck by the abundance of *Characeæ* in the Irish lakes. The great quantity and diversity of form of *Chara contraria* in the Westmeath lakes were very noticeable. *C. fragilis*, *C. aspera*, and *C. hispida* were common and generally distributed, while *C. vulgaris* and *N. opaca*, though noticed in several places, were not so general as in England. It is curious that the known localities for *N. tenuissima* in the British Isles—Cambridgeshire, Anglesea, Westmeath, and Galway, are nearly in a line from east to west. We think it probable, however, that it will be found to occur in the other peat districts of Ireland, and we hope that Irish botanists will search for this and for the other species likely to be found. *C. connivens*, *C. fragifera*, *C. baltica*, *C. canescens*, *L. alopecuroides*, and *L. stelliger*, which occurs in the south-west of England, should be looked for in pools near the sea in the southern counties. Lough Neagh should be searched for the *Tolypella* which Braun referred to *T. nidifica, forma intermedia*.

SOME NORTH OF IRELAND POLYZOA.

BY WILLIAM SWANSTON, F.G.S., AND J. E. DUERDEN, A.R.C.SC. (LOND.)

IN the summer of 1876 and 1877, W. Swanston and some friends had a few days' dredging off the entrance of Belfast lough, from Larne on the north to Donaghadee on the south, in depths varying from twenty to seventy-two fathoms. The Polyzoa obtained, which were chiefly on stones and dead shells, were sent, at the close of the dredging operations, to Dr. Thomas Hincks, F.R.S., who kindly named them, and duly returned the specimens, accompanied by a list of the species occurring. As this list, which has never been published, contains some very rare species, and gives additional stations for others which are less rare, it is thought desirable that it should be made public.

For the determinations alone Dr. Hincks is responsible: the notes on Irish distribution are the work of J. E. Duerden. Where the names in Dr. Hincks' original list are different from those now adopted, the former are printed in brackets after the modern appellation. The lists which follow contain forty-six species, four of which have not been previously recorded from the Irish coast.

TWENTY FATHOMS, OFF BLACKHEAD.

Bugula avicularia, Linn.—Not previously recorded from Ireland.
Cellepora (?) tubigera.—Busk.
Flustra securifrons, Pall.—(*F. truncata*, Linn.)—Found also from Dublin and Belfast bays.
Tubulipora flabellaris, Fab.—(*T. phalangea*, Couch.)—Mentioned for the first time from Ireland.
Idmonea serpens, Linn.—(*Tubulipora serpens*, Linn.)—Very common, and generally distributed.

TWENTY-TWO FATHOMS, OFF ENTRANCE TO LARNE HARBOUR.

Microporella ciliata, Pall.—(*Lepralia ciliata*, Pall.)—Very generally distributed.
Chorizopora brongniartii, Aud.—(*Lepralia brongniartii*, Aud.)—Also recorded from Dublin and Birterbuy bays.
Mucronella ventricosa, Flass.—(*Lepralia ventricosa*, Flass.)—Common. From Dublin and Belfast bays.
Schizoporella vulgaris, Moll.—(*Lepralia vulgaris*, Moll.)—Previously obtained from Birterbuy bay and Antrim coast.
Membranipora pilosa, var. **dentata,** Pall.
M. dumerilii, Aud.—Common on the Irish coasts, recorded by Hyndman from Antrim.

Membranipora catenularia, Jameson—(*Hippothoa catenularia,* Flem).
—Very common on old shells. Recorded by W. Thompson from off
the Gobbins, Co. Antrim.
Scrupocellaria scruposa, Linn.—Very common around the Irish
coasts.

THIRTY-TWO FATHOMS, DONAGHADEE.

Membraniporella nitida, Johnst.—Fairly common.
Mucronella variolosa, Johnst.—(*Lepralia variolosa,* Johnst.)—A common form.
M. peachii, Johnst.—(*Lepralia peachii,* Johnst.)—A very common species.
Schizotheca fissa, Busk—(*Lepralia fissa,* Busk.)—Not many recorded localities. Obtained from the coast of Antrim and from Birterbuy bay.
Membranipora flustroides, Hincks.—Recorded from Antrim and Birterbuy bay.
M. pilosa, Pall.—Common around all the coasts.
Flustra foliacea, Linn.—Very generally distributed.
Crisia aculeata, Hass.—(*Crisia eburnea,* with spines, Linn.)—*Crisia eburnea,* with spines, was made a distinct species (*Crisia aculeata*), by Hassall; but Hincks, Busk, and Smith, regard it only as a variety of the former. Harmer in his paper on the British species of *Crisia* in the *Quar. Jour. Micros. Sci.,* March, 1891, regards it as a distinct species from its particular form of ovicell, which never occurs in any other type of the colony.

FORTY-SEVEN FATHOMS.

Phylactella collaris, Norm.—(*Lepralia collaris,* Norm.)—Not previously recorded from Ireland.
Mucronella peachii, Johnst.—(*L. peachii,* Johnst.)—A very common form; var. *labiosa* recorded by W. Thompson from Belfast bay.
Microporella malusii, Aud.—(*L. malusii,* Aud.)—Widely distributed; previously obtained from Roundstone and the Antrim coast.
Schizoporella linearis, Hass. (*L. linearis,* Hass.)—A somewhat common species.
Smittia reticulata, J. Macgill. (*L. reticulata,* Macgill.)—Also recorded from Belfast bay by W. Thompson, and from Birterbuy bay by Norman.
Membranipora flemingii, Busk—A form often met with.
Hippothoa flagellum, Manz.—Found also from Mr. Hyndman's Antrim dredgings, and from Birterbuy bay.
Diastopora obelia, Flem.—Generally distributed.
Crisia aculeata, Hass.—(*C. eburnea,* with spines, Linn.).

SIXTY-TWO FATHOMS.

Schizoporella auriculata, Hass.—(*Lepralia auriculata,* Hass.).
Mastigopora hyndmanni, Johnst. (*L. hyndmanni,* Johnst.)—Recorded by Hyndman as abundant from the coast of Antrim; also by Thompson from Belfast bay.
Schizotheca fissa, Busk.—(*L. fissa,* Busk.).
Schizoporella linearis, Hass.—(*L. linearis,* Hass.).
Membranipora imbellis, Hincks—Obtained from the coast of Antrim by Hyndman.

Caberea ellisii, Flem.
Cellaria fistulosa, Ellis and Sol.—(*C. farciminoides*, Ellis and Sol.) Generally distributed. Recorded previously from Dublin and Belfast bays by W. Thompson.
Flustra foliacea, Linn.
Hippothoa flagellum, Manz.
Stomatopora granulata, M.-Edw.—(*Alecto granulata*, M.-Edw. Also recorded by Hyndman as abundant from the coast of Antrim.

BETWEEN SIXTY-TWO AND SEVENTY-TWO FATHOMS.

Phylactella collaris, Norm.—(*Leprallia collaris*, Norm.).
Schizoporella hyalina, Linn.—(*L. hyalina*, Linn.).
Microporella malusii, Aud.—(*L. malusii*, Aud.).
Mucronella peachii, Johnst.—(*L. peachii*, Johnst.).
M. coccinea, Busk.—(*L. coccinea*, Busk.)—Previously recorded by W. Thompson from Belfast bay; and the variety *mamillata* from the coast of Antrim by Hyndman.
Lepralia crystallina ?—Norm.
Membranipora pilosa, var. **dentata**, Pall.
M. Flemingii, Busk.
Hippothoa flagellum, Manz.
Membranipora catenularia, Jameson.—(*Hippothoa catenularia*. Jameson).
Palmicellaria skenei, Ellis and Sol.—(*Eschara skenei*, Ell. and Sol.)— Recorded from deep water on the east coast of Ireland by Miss Ball.
Cellepora dichotoma, Hincks—A rather common form, previously recorded from Ireland.
C. ramulosa, Linn.—Belfast bay, by Hyndman.
C. avicularis, Hincks—Also from the coast of Antrim, by Hyndman.
Cellaria sinuosa, Hass.—Recorded from Belfast and Dublin bays.
C. fistulosa, Linn.—(*C. farciminoides*, Ellis and Sol.).
Caberea ellisii, Flem.—This is a northern form, and the present is mentioned by Hincks as the most southern locality recorded on our coasts.
Flustra foliacea, Linn.
Gemellaria loricata, Linn.—Fine specimens occur around the Irish coasts.
Stomatopora diastoporides, Norm.—(*Alecto diastoporides*, Norm.)— A rare form, not mentioned previously from Ireland.
Diastopora patina, Lam.—Recorded from Strangford lough by W. Thompson.
Alecto sp.
Pustulopora sp.
Crisia eburnea, Linn.—Occurs plentifully on our coasts.

SEVENTY-TWO FATHOMS.

Phylactella collaris, Norm.—(*Lepralia collaris*, Norm.)
Mastigopora hyndmanni, Johnst.—(*Lepralia hyndmanni*, Johnst.)
Caberea ellisii, Flem.
Cellaria fistulosa, Linn.—(*C. farciminoides*, Ell. and Sol.)
Membranipora imbellis, Hincks.
Stomatopora granulata, M.-Edw.—(*Alecto granulata*, M.-Edw.)

With the exceptions of that for Co. Dublin, this is, as yet, the only important list of Polyzoa we possess for Ireland. The study of these minute, but interesting forms, has been much neglected in our country compared with England and Scotland. Especially have the north and west coasts suffered. Owing to the efforts of recent surveys, however, much is now being done in this group, and already some new and many rare forms have been obtained. Mr. Duerden, who is now working at the Irish Polyzoa and Hydrozoa, will be very glad to receive specimens from any part of the coast, but especially from the north and west, addressed to the Royal College of Science, Dublin.

THE BEAUTY AND USE OF IRISH BUILDING STONES.

BY PROF. GRENVILLE A. J. COLE, M.R.I.A., F.G.S.

(*Substance of a Lecture delivered in Dublin before the Irish Industrial League,* 13*th February,* 1893.)

From a decorative point of view the beauty of a stone depends on its effect upon the eye. In suitable surroundings, there is a rich beauty in the renowned black marbles of Galway and Kilkenny, or in the streaky grey limestones, passing into marble, common throughout the Carboniferous series. There is an inherent beauty in the variegated "Cork Red," which is now being largely used in London, and which has something firmer and more jaspery in its tone than the veined red marbles of South Devon. And, above all in this quality of obvious beauty, beyond all the ornamental stones yet quarried or detected in the British Isles, we have the serpentinous limestones of Co. Galway, the famous "Connemara Green."

But to the stonecutter and the builder, as well as to the geologist, there is a beauty in a good stone beyond that which appeals openly to the eye, a beauty more subtle, requiring a scientific as well as an artistic appreciation—the beauty of lastingness, of durability. An architect's work is not to be padded up with wool and protected for posterity in the glass-case of a museum. Despite its delicacies of form and moulding, it must, like the Forth Bridge or the steamers of the Irish Mail, earn its crown and glory by weathering out the worst of seasons. As Longfellow wrote in his *Michael Angelo*,

"Painting and sculpture are but images,
. . . . Architecture,
Existing in itself, and not in seeming
A something it is not, surpasses them
As substance shadow."

The old cathedral-builders of England, before the days of railways and long sea-carriage, were rather limited in their choice of materials, and, when once they had hit upon a good stone, they went on confidently using it. They were thus guided in most cases by experience; in others, as at Chester, their lack of geological knowledge led them into serious error. Now-a-days, when in our cities public and private bodies vie with one another in the costliness and handsomeness of their offices, a number of stones are being introduced, and a novelty is likely to be well received if its beauties—in all senses—can be demonstrated to the purchaser's satisfaction.

In books published for the guidance of architects and builders there is usually very scanty reference to the real mineral characters that determine the external beauty or the utility of a stone. Too few "practical" workers in the stone-trade have ever been shown how to determine the nature of the cementing material of a sandstone, with a view to learning something of its durability, or how to distinguish granite from dolerite, or even from rocks that are rich in olivine, and therefore liable to decay. The simple chemistry and the structural details of building-stones should be familiar to all who have an interest in their sale or in their purchase; old-fashioned analyses and inexact rock-names would not then be quoted, as they are too often now, to give a show of scientific respectability to circulars intended for the trade.

The constituent minerals of a rock, the materials that bind them together, and the extent to which they have been affected by decomposition, are best seen in a thin section viewed with a polarising microscope. Such sections are now commonly prepared and utilised by geologists; is it too much to hope that one person at least in every great builder's yard may some day be able to examine critically by such means the materials upon which his business-reputation may depend?

The specific gravity of a sample of a rock is often a test of its freedom from alteration. Mr. Walker of Dundee provided us twelve years ago with an instrument on the principle of the steelyard, by which the specific gravity of a rock can be accurately determined, to the second place of decimals, by two operations occupying together some four or five minutes.[1] This admirable instrument is as yet too little known outside scientific laboratories.

A knowledge of the use of the maps of the Geological Survey of Ireland, reference to the published memoirs of that body, and to such papers as Mr. G. H. Kinahan's "Economic Geology of Ireland,"[2] assist one largely in forming a judgment as to the extent of a stone at the surface, the trend of its outcrop, and its characters and utility as at present ascertained. The basis for most statements regarding the building-stones of this country is still, however, Wilkinson's remarkable work on the "Practical Geology and Ancient Architecture of Ireland," published in 1845.

The power of determining the fundamental nature of a stone, by the means hinted at above, must be applied also in the selection of individual blocks. The continuous export of such materials often depends upon their uniform excellence; and one badly selected mass or slab may bring discredit upon a whole quarry or even upon a county. In this matter every quarry-man has an interest as great as that of the quarry-owner or the builder; whether in blasting, excavating, or shaping, each man employed should possess an intelligent knowledge of the properties of the material beneath his hands.

When, with the absolute truthfulness of scientific method the qualities, the true beauties, of a stone have been ascertained, it should be brought into the market by well trained travellers or exhibitors, who should be able to discuss with an architect the difference between a marble and a granite, or a sandstone and an oolite, a state of things which is far from being realised at the present. Ireland may yet be able to mark a new era in the stone-market by sending out scientific descriptions of her materials, and by placing samples of them in some convenient place of reference in London, with details of their current price

[1] See Walker, *Geological Magazine*, 1883, p. 109; and Cole, "Aids in Practical Geology," p. 24.
[2] *Proc. Royal Dublin Society*, new series, vol. v., p. 372, etc.

and the customary rates of carriage. The antiquity of the descriptions in the usual works of reference makes it important that quarry-owners and agents should keep the outer world informed at first hand; for instance, the slates of Ashford, Co. Wicklow, are still quoted in the standard work on building materials published in 1892, while, on the other hand, new materials may easily escape insertion or adequate recognition.

Strange as it may appear, it is necessary to prove the advantages of Irish building-stones even in the country of their extraction. The competition, for instance, with the cheap labour of women and children in Belgium makes it difficult to force Irish marbles upon unsentimental and impecunious persons; but some of the success of foreign materials is due to technical methods of working, and especially to regularity of supply. Then, again, in a metropolis such as Dublin, a healthy variety of materials must be tolerated. No one can wish to replace the beautiful red brick of Merrion-square, one of the glories of the city on a sunny afternoon, by masses of grey Carboniferous limestone, however elegantly carved; and even the much-controverted introduction of terra-cotta, a material that will defy the smoke of Liverpool or London, may be best met, not by denying its advantages, but by a search for terra-cotta clays in Ireland.

The virtues of some Irish stones as road-metal call for more adequate recognition. Despite the lamentable absence of steam-rollers, and the usual absence, in consequence, of definite form in the surface of an Irish road, the materials in many counties have proved themselves magnificent, and great credit is generally due to the surveyors and to the workmen for the care with which patches of new metal are inserted during repairs. With the quartzites of Howth and Shankill, as one example, on the very sea-board, one may hope that enterprise and due representation of their qualities may lead to the adoption of Irish macadam in some of the west English cities. The success of Penmaenmawr in Wales gives one grounds for hope, at any rate. Quartzite and limestone in combination, well rolled in, seems an experiment worth trying, especially when we recollect the good dry surfaces produced by a mixture of Kentish Rag and Hythe Sandstone in the neighbourhood of Folkestone some years ago.

(TO BE CONCLUDED.)

PROCEEDINGS OF IRISH SOCIETIES.

ROYAL ZOOLOGICAL SOCIETY.

Recent donations include a monkey from Dr. A. G. Arthur; a gull from Rev. A. Tabuteau; a Badger from T. Hayden, Esq.; two white rats from Miss Topham; a Ring-tailed Coati from Right Hon. T. A. Dickson, and a pair of doves from W. J. Williams, Esq. A Brown Bear, a Chillingham Wild Heifer, a pair of Cheetahs, and a pair of Peafowl, have been purchased; a Gayal Cow has been acquired by exchange, and five Lion-cubs have been recently born.

17,060 persons visited the Gardens in April.

DUBLIN MICROSCOPICAL CLUB.

MARCH 16th.—The Club met at MR. W. ARCHER'S.

Section of Eurite containing Riebeckite (a blue soda-amphibole), found as pebbles at Killiney, Co. Dublin, was exhibited by PROF. COLE. This rock occurs similarly in the Glacial Drift of Caernarvonshire and the Isle of Man, and its probable source is the eurite with similar structure that forms the mass of Ailsa Craig at the mouth of the Clyde. Riebeckite is known in rocks of Socotra Island, near Aden, of Mynydd Mawr, near Snowdon, and of Ailsa Craig. The abundance of the pebbles at Killiney is of interest in connection with the distribution of the "drift" of the Irish Channel. Prof. Cole stated that he had found a pebble of the same rock in the raised beach of Greenore, Co. Down.

Preparations of a male shoot of Ephedra, showing the flowers in various stages of development, were shown by PROF. T. JOHNSON. The structure of the peculiar pollen-grains, the geographical distribution, and the relation of *Ephedra* to the other *Gnetaceæ*, and of this interesting group to the other Phanerogams, were briefly explained. *Ephedra* had not been previously found in flower by the exhibitor, who had examined, from time to time, for several years past, the specimens of the genus growing in the Royal Botanic Gardens at Kew and at Glasnevin. The particular plant from which the exhibit was taken, grows at Glasnevin, in the Nursery, close to the stone wall, with southern aspect.

Sections of a Human Kidney infected by micro-organisms, were shown by DR. SCOTT. The tubercles were seen blotched with micro-cocci, and large patches of leucocytes were to be found in the neighbourhood of the infected portion.

Section of a Cancerous Tumour prepared by M. Metschinkoff, and kindly forwarded by him, was shown by DR. E. J. M'WEENEY. The slide showed in a most typical manner the peculiar rounded bodies which are contained within the protoplasm of the cancer cells, and which are looked upon by an influential school of pathologists as parasitic protozoa, and connected in some way with the tendency to unbounded proliferation displayed by the cells in question.

Fertile specimen of Blepharostoma tricophylla was shown by MR. D. MCARDLE. This is a curious and pretty liverwort which is not like any other, except *B. setacea*, Web., which is more common. The leaves are deeply parted into three and often four setaceous-jointed segments, which give the plant the appearance of a species of Algæ. The specimen was collected in Co. Wicklow.

BELFAST NATURAL HISTORY AND PHILOSOPHICAL SOCIETY.

APRIL 18th.—The President (PROF. FITZGERALD, B.A., C.E.) read a paper entitled "Notes on Electric Power Supply for Tramways, at Paterson, N.J." DR. WILLIAM CALWELL read a paper on "The New Phrenology."

BELFAST NATURALISTS' FIELD CLUB.

APRIL 26th.—Annual Meeting. The President (MR. J. VINYCOMB, M.R.I.A.,) in the chair. The report and statement of accounts were submitted and adopted. The report showed a steady increase in all departments of the club's work. The membership, which last year was 323 now stands at 404; the statement of accounts showed an increased balance to the credit of the club. The announcement that in July members would have an opportunity of spending three days in the company of their fellow-members of the Dublin Naturalists' Field Club, was greeted with satisfaction. Mr. William Swanston, F.G.S., was elected President for the ensuing year, and Mr. F. W. Lockwood, Vice-President, and the other officers were, with some slight changes, re-elected. Club prizes were awarded to Miss Clara Patterson, Miss S. M. Thompson, Miss Jeanie Rea, and Mr. W. D. Donnan, for sets of microscopic slides, flowering plants, and beetles respectively.

DUBLIN NATURALISTS' FIELD CLUB.

APRIL 30th.—The first excursion of the season took place. Twenty-four members left town by the Blessington steam tram, and alighted at Balrothery, where the end of a fine Esker, two miles long, was examined under the direction of Rev. M. H. Close. The party then proceeded by tram to Tallaght, and walked to Friarstown Glen, where collecting was carried on, but the botanical specimens were not noteworthy. Among the Coleoptera, Mr. H. R. G. Cuthbert obtained with other common species:—*Benbidium punctulatum, B. tibiale, B. saxatile, B. decorum, Amara trivialis, Chlænius vestitus, Homalota currax, Stenus guttula, Hydroporus rufifrons, Laccobius alutaceus*, and *Otiorrhynchus ligneus*. Among Hymenoptera, *Vespa germanica*, and *Ammophila sabulosa* were noted, the latter being specially early.

CORK NATURALISTS' FIELD CLUB.

APRIL 17th.—DR. W. J. KNIGHT in the chair. The annual report of this club was read by the Secretary and showed a highly creditable condition. Officers for the ensuing year were elected, and some ordinary business transacted.

MISS H. MARTIN and MISS ABBOTT exhibited some fine specimens of plants obtained near Glengariff, Co. Cork. *Mitrula paludosa* Fries, a beautiful little saffron-coloured fungus, floating in bog pools—local; *Hymenophyllum tunbridgense* in fruit—abundant; *H. unilaterale*, Willd. (*H. wilsoni*, Hook.) also in fruit, local; *Ranunculus cœnosus*, Guss. (Floating Crow-foot), local; also *Gentiana verna*, L., received from Galway.

APRIL 26th.—The President, PROF. MARCUS M. HARTOG, F.L.S., in the chair. MR. R. A. PHILLIPS read a paper on "The Land and Fresh-water Shells of County Cork," illustrated by lantern slides, and a fine collection of shells collected in the district.

First explaining the life of snails and slugs in general, their different classes, and the formation and shapes of shells, Mr. Phillips gave a very full and exhaustive description of each species, its characteristics, haunts, and habits, pointing out the species most likely to be found in the county, and the best localities for research. The theories as to the original use of the love-darts of the snail were dwelt on.

Several members exhibited objects of interest.

MAY 10th.—The first excursion of the season to Rochestown took place, when *Cynoglossum officinale*, Tourn. (Hound's Tongue), so rare as an Irish plant, was found by Miss Harriett A. Martin.

NOTES.

BOTANY.

CLUB MOSSES.

Selaginella selaginoides, Gray, in Co. Dublin.—I found this interesting moss-like plant growing on a small shallow bog on the north side of Howth hill, last month. It is not included in Mr. Hart's "Flora of Howth," and I therefore note its occurrence there as interesting. It also grows abundantly amongst the sandhills to the north of Malahide, where Mr. R. W. Scully drew my attention to it a few years ago. This plant was formerly known as *Lycopodium selaginoides*. In Mr. Baker's "Handbook of the Fern Allies," p. 34, the name *Selaginella spinosa*, P.B. Aethog, 112 is given for this plant, and in the 8th edition of the London Catalogue that of *Selaginella selaginoides*, Gray.—DAVID M'ARDLE, Glasnevin.

PHANEROGAMS.

Colour-variation in Wild Flowers.—Mr. Colgan's note on this subject (p. 3) is decidedly interesting, and induces me to contribute the few notes I have on abnormal colours of wild flowers in our north-eastern district. It would appear that white and yellow may be classed together as the more fixed and constant colours, and blue, purple, and red, as the less constant. How invariable are the hues of the white cruciferous and umbelliferous plants, of the Stitchworts and Bedstraws, and of the yellow Buttercups, St. John's-worts, Potentillas, Ragworts, and plants of the Dandelion group; while among blue, purple, and red flowers, more variation is apparent, though some of these, too, are conspicuously constant in shade, such as the scarlet Poppies and blue Forget-me-nots. It may be remarked that the colour-changes affect not only the flowers, for in plants like the Purple Dead-nettle and Marjoram, that have a purplish tinge over the stem and leaves, this hue disappears if the flowers are white, and is replaced by a pure green; at any stage of growth, white Foxgloves or Canterbury Bells may be picked out from purple ones by the colour of the foliage and leaf-stems. The following notes explain themselves:—WHITE FLOWERS:—Burnet Rose (*R. spinosissima*), streaked with red (var. *ciphiana*) on roadside at Castlerock, Co. Derry; Cat's-foot (*Antennaria dioica*), rose-coloured, Mourne mountains, Co. Down, at about 1,500 feet, and on sand-dunes at Castlerock, Co. Derry. YELLOW FLOWERS:—Primrose (*P. vulgaris*), various shades of red not uncommon on the Holywood hills, Co. Down, where also I have found it quite white. BLUE FLOWERS:—Marsh Violet (*V. palustris*), white, marsh on Holywood hills, Co. Down; Devil's Bit (*Scabiosa succisa*), white, on heaths at Dunluce, Co. Antrim, and Castlerock, Co. Derry; pink, on heaths at Cultra, Holywood hills, and Scrabo, Co. Down, and Dunluce, Co. Antrim; Sea Starwort (*Aster tripolium*), white, in saltmarsh at Holywood, Co. Down; Sheep's Scabious (*Jasione montana*), pink, on the Antrim hills; Vernal Squill (*Scilla verna*), white, at Orlock Point, Co. Down, and on Rathlin Island, Co. Antrim; Wild Hyacinth (*Endymion nutans*), white, occasionally in various places. PURPLE FLOWERS:—Purple Vetch (*Vicia sepium*), white, at Marino, Co. Down (R. Ll. P.), and Lisburn, Co. Antrim (Mr. J. H. Davies, *fide* Mr. S. A. Stewart); Purple Clover (*Trifolium pratense*), occasionally white; Marsh Thistle (*Carduus palustris*), frequently white, from sea-level to 1,000 feet; Heather (*Erica cinerea*), white, near sea-level at Castlerock, Co. Derry, frequent among Mourne mountains at various elevations, and on Knockagh hill, Co. Antrim; pink, with the last; on Slieve Bingian (Mourne mountains), a beautiful rose-coloured form occurred, in some quantity; Marjoram (*Origanum vulgare*), white, on walls at

Clandeboye, Co. Down, and on bank at Loughgall, Co. Armagh; Thyme (*Thymus serpyllum*), white, on sand-dunes at Castlerock, Co. Derry, and Ballycastle, Co. Antrim, and on banks at Bray, Co. Wicklow; Purple Dead-nettle (*Lamium purpureum*), white, in field near Dundonald, Co. Down, and a large patch on roadside at Garron Tower, Co. Antrim; Hemp-nettle (*Galeopsis tetrahit*) as commonly white as purple; Early Purple Orchis (*O. mascula*), white and pale flesh-colour in field at Holywood Waterworks; Fragrant Orchis (*Gymademia conopsea*), white, on heath on Coulig hill, Co. Down; pale pink at Garron Point, Co. Antrim. RED AND PINK FLOWERS:—Ragged Robin (*Lychnis flos-cuculi*), white, in marsh at Holywood; Musk Mallow (*Malva moschata*), frequently white, as on stony shore at Ram's Island, in Lough Neagh, on bank near Newry, etc.; Smooth-leaved Willow-herb(*Epilobium montanum*), white, at Shane's Castle, Co. Antrim; Ling (*Calluna erica*), white, on bogs and mountains in Down and Armagh; Cross-leaved Heath (*Erica tetralix*), white, on Antrim and Mourne mountains, and on bogs in Armagh; Centaury (see p. 168, 1892); Red-rattle (*Pedicularis sylvatica*), white, on heath near Holywood; Spotted Persicaria (*Polygonum persicaria*), white as frequently as red. There are also, of course, some well-known examples, such as Milkwort (blue, purple, white), Downy Rose (red, white), Comfrey (purple, white), English Catchfly (red, white), and Timothy Grass (anthers purple or yellow), which affect two or more colours indifferently, and are as common in one shade as in another. Others, again, affect a gradation of colour, as *Orchis maculata*, which varies from white by degrees to deep purple. From the instances quoted above, it would appear that white flowers vary (very seldom) to red and purple (Mr. More found a deep purple form of the Wood Anemone in Armagh); of yellow flowers, the Primrose is the only example, varying to red and white; blue flowers generally turn to white, occasionally to purple or pink; purple flowers to pink or white; pink and red flowers to white. If other observers will contribute any notes they may have on the subject, we may gain more definite information. I cannot say I have noticed more blanching of colours at high than at low elevations, as mentioned by Mr. Colgan.—R. LLOYD PRAEGER.

ZOOLOGY.

INSECTS.

Lepidoptera of the Londonderry District.—I have been greatly interested in Mr. Campbell's list of Macro-lepidoptera from the Derry district. I was at Kilderry at Easter, and took a *Panolis piniperda* at sallow. This is an addition to his list. The only place I had taken it before was at Howth. I found *Pachnobia rubricosa* abundant, and *Lobophora carpinata* plentiful. I was surprised at the scarcity of *Tæniocampa stabilis*, but *T. gothica* and *T. incerta* were as common as usual. *Larentia multistrigaria* was still on the wing, and hibernated *Calocampa vetusta* and *C. exoleta* were at the sallows. I may mention that in March, 1891, I took *Eupithecia abbreviata* in the same locality.—GEORGE V. HART, Dublin.

Lepidoptera at Woodenbridge, Co. Wicklow.—Collecting at Woodenbridge last month was spoilt rather perfectly in two ways—firstly, by the catkins being nearly over; and, secondly, by cold, dry nights. The best insect taken was *Amphydasys strataria*, which I do not know of from Ireland before. I also took a *Tæniocampa munda*, which turned up for the first time, I believe, last year at this time in the same place, when Mr. Hart and I secured one each. Two *Lobophora carpinata*, some nice varieties of *Tæniocampa gothica*, and one or two other things, make up our catch.—MAURICE FITZGIBBON, Dublin.

[*A. strataria* was recorded from Wicklow by Birchall,—EDS.]

Early Spring Butterflies.—The small Tortoiseshell (*Vanessa urticæ*), is usually the first Butterfly observed in spring, as it comes out of its winter-quarters on the first warm days. This year, however, it has been anticipated here by the Small Cabbage White (*Pieris rapæ*), a specimen of which appeared in my garden on March 29th. *V. urticæ* did not appear till April 7th, when I captured a specimen in very fair order. The Orange Tip (*Euchloë cardamines*), was seen by Mrs. Johnson on April 19th. If the season goes on as it has begun, it should be a splendid insect year, and I hope the "brethren of the net" will keep their weather eyes open for rarities to swell Mr. Kane's Irish list.—W. F. JOHNSON, Armagh.

Two specimens of *Vanessa atalanta* were seen by me at Tullow, Co. Dublin, on April 22nd, and another in Rathmines on the following day. They were all in fine condition, and appeared quite fresh.—WM. STARKEY, Junr., Rathmines, Dublin.

MOLLUSCS.

Pleurophyllidia loveni, Bergh., in Ireland.—Among some specimens trawled in Bantry bay this spring by Mr. A. R. C. Newburgh, and sent up to the Science and Art Museum, Dublin, I lately discovered six specimens of *Pleurophyllidia loveni*, Bergh., the sole British representative of the family *Pleurophyllidiidæ* of the order Nudibranchiata (Sea Slugs). Dr. J. G. Jeffreys in "British Conchology," vol. v., gives only two British localities for this species,—viz., Shetland and Whitehaven, Co. Durham. In Leslie and Herdman's "Invertebrate Fauna of the Firth of Forth," a specimen is recorded as having been taken at Dunbar by Prof. F. M. Balfour. Prof. McIntosh records a specimen from off Aberdeen in 1884; Mr. Holt, two specimens from St. Andrews; Mr. Cunningham, one specimen from off the Eddystone; and Mr. Bles, six specimens from Loch Striven, Clyde area, but it has not hitherto been recorded as Irish. *T. loveni* is a north Atlantic form, occurring off the coasts of Denmark, Sweden, and Norway.—A. R. NICHOLS, Dublin.

FISHES.

A Fish New to Ireland, Motella cimbria, L.—Mr. A. R. C Newburgh last month secured the first Irish specimen of the "Four-beard Rockling," in Bantry bay. As its name denotes, this fish has four barbels on the snout, whilst the two common species of rockling have five and three barbels respectively. This species may also be recognized by the dark blotch on the posterior portion of the dorsal fin. It is a northern fish, ranging as far south as Cornwall, where it is extremely rare.—R. F. SCHARFF, Dublin.

AMPHIBIANS.

Arrested Development of the Frog's Tadpole.—Mr. Barton's remarks on some cases of arrested development of the Frog's tadpole are of very great theoretical interest, and I believe he is perfectly correct in attributing them to the fact of the tadpoles living in running water containing plenty of food. I am not aware of any experiments having been conducted with the view to prevent the larva or tadpole from relinquishing its fishy garb, but there are some instances on record that newts have had their transformation forcibly retarded for some seasons by similar methods to those adopted by Mr. Barton. But in these newts, transformation, although delayed, did finally occur. Perhaps the most interesting case known of arrested metamorphosis is that of the Mexican amphibian called Axolotl. In its own country the animal always remains in the fishy state, that is to say, breathing by means of gills, but in confinement it has been successfully transformed into a land animal

by gradually depriving it of the water in which it lived. Theoretically
t. s... ... . be as ...st..ting exper...ent. l... o. origin
o. species.— R. F. sc.. s... L....'n.

Frog Remains from Ballynamintra Cave.—In his paper on
the "Frog in ... ...," in your April number, Mr. Kane r... .. to the
bones of a Frog found by Prof. A. Leith Adams and mys... in the
deposits of this cave as a convincing proof of their antiquity. If the
stratum in which they were found was extremely ancient." It was not
so ... ..ng .he surface deposit, termed in the Report "No. 1." ... ...
... ... T A.. Iouin Society for April, 1881, while ... ...
t. ...... on B....amintra cave, we read,—" In No. 1 the p... ... of
r ... ...us birds, ...sibly of owls, contained fragments of bones o. ...g..."
W.. ..her these masses of frog-bones were accumulated by owls or flood-
mice, there was certainly nothing either in their position or condition to
denote their great antiquity.—R. J. USSHER, Cappagh, Co. Waterford.

BIRDS.

Spring Migrants at Armagh.—The Chiffchaff arrived on March
22nd. Sand Martins were seen on the Callan on March 29th, and the
first Swallow appeared on April 3rd; the main body of Swallows,
however, did not arrive till May. I heard the sweet song of the Willow
Wren for the first time on April 6th, and the harsh note of the Corncrake
saluted me as I strolled into Mullinure on April 20th. The Cuckoo
arrived on April 23rd, but I did not see either House Martins or Swifts
till May 5. Why the House Martin should have been so long after the
Swallow in its arrival I do not understand, and should be glad to know
if the same difference of time of arrival was observed elsewhere.—W. F.
JOHNSON, Armagh.

Early arrival of Migrants in Co. Cork.—Chiffchaff, 26th
March; Sand Martin, 1st April; Swallow, 9th April; Willow-warbler,
9th April; Cuckoo, 24th April; Swift, 2nd May; Landrail, 7th May;
Sedge-warbler, 7th May; Whitethroat, 7th May; Sandpiper, 9th May.
These dates are not extraordinary, but when compared with those of last
year tend to show that the general wave of migration has been decidedly
earlier this year here. Had I greater opportunities of being in the
country and of visiting likely haunts, I am sure I should have been able
to give a much earlier record, as on most of the dates which I give, I
either saw or heard the birds plentifully, and they appeared to have
arrived some time.—WM. B. BARRINGTON, Cork.

Hoopoe (Upupa epops) in Co. Wexford.—Mr. Wheelocke, the
birdstuffer, Wexford, has a Hoopoe in his shop, which, I am informed,
was shot at Drinagh, two miles south-east of Wexford, on Good Friday.—
G. E. H. BARRETT-HAMILTON, Cambridge.

Black Redstart (Ruticilla titys) in Co. Wexford.—A female
specimen of the Black Redstart was shot at Ballygeary, near Wexford, on
Feb. 22nd, and is now in my collection.—G. E. H. BARRETT-HAMILTON,
Cambridge.

**Occurrence of the King Duck (Somateria spectabilis) in
Achill Island.**—On December 12th, 1892, I fell in with a male specimen of this fine duck, and as it is of such rare occurrence in Ireland, I
thought an account of its capture in the west of Ireland might be of interest. I find Thompson only mentions four specimens having been
taken in Ireland. One shot at Kingstown, October, 1837. One shot at
D...... Co. Kerry, 1843. One shot in Tralee bay, Kerry, 1845-46. One
in B...st in 1850. And according to Mr. A. G. More, our great
a...o..., there is no record of any being taken in Ireland for the last
for..y-three years. The bird was not in full plumage, but judging from
the round white patch on the sides behind the legs, and the mottled
white on breast, and the black scapularies and flanks, the bird must

have been in the second year of plumage. It was tame and easy of approach, as I find all these northern stragglers, as was the case when I fell in with the Surf Scoter, and some of the white-winged gulls some time ago. I am now of opinion that if a good look-out were kept along our bold headlands in the autumn and winter, many rare stragglers could be found as they straggle down from the far north and mix up with the migratory birds which frequent our bays in winter, Barnacle, Brent, and many diving ducks. The bird is now in the possession of Edwin Bayles, Esq., of Birmingham, whose collection will be one of the finest in the kingdom. The bird in question was examined by Dr. Bowdler Sharp, of the British Museum, and by Messrs. Seebohm and Saunders.—J. R. SHERIDAN, Dugort, Achill Isle.

Iceland Gull (Larus leucopterus) at Londonderry.—On 11th April at 11.45 a.m., I saw an Iceland Gull hovering about the quay here along with some Herring Gulls. The birds were feeding on some garbage thrown from one of the vessels. I noticed the lighter colour of the Icelander and watched it until it circled above and below me, within ten yards. I noted the following particulars on the spot. About the size of large Herring Gull, but body heavier, back and wings very light grey, tips of wings for some inches quite white, bill pale yellow, legs and feet dull red. The bird had lost the second and fourth primaries and one or two of the secondaries of right wing, so that I was able to spot it among the other gulls one or two days afterwards.—D. C. CAMPBELL, Ballynagard, Londonderry

GEOLOGY.

Lough Neagh Petrifactions.—In connection with Mr. Swanston's valuable paper on the "Silicified Wood of Lough Neagh," the following very early and very circumstantial version of the popular fable may be read with interest. It is found on one of the descriptive scrolls of Fra Mauro's famous *Mappamondo*, a projection of the sphere executed in 1459 by a monk of Camaldoli, and preserved in the Archæological Museum at Venice. Having made a careful transcript from the original many years ago, I give a rendering here of so much of the passage as clearly relates to Lough Neagh, from which it will be seen that this version of the fable corresponds very closely with that quoted by Mr. Swanston from Boate:—

"In this island of Hibernia, which is passing fertile beyond measure *oltra modo è fertilissima*), 'tis said there is a water, in the which if a man putteth wood, the part thereof that sticketh i' the earth becometh in time iron, and that that is rounded with water becometh stone, and that that is above water remaineth wood . . . and they that desire to be made copious of these and other marvellous matters let them read in Albertus Magnus."

Albertus Magnus flourished about the middle of the thirteenth century, more than fifty years after Giraldus Cambrensis had written his "Topography of Ireland," and one would naturally expect to find that the fable had reached the Continent through Giraldus. But the petrifactive virtues of Lough Neagh are not amongst his Irish marvels, though he mentions a spring in the north of Ulster which by its excessive coldness turns wood into stone, after seven years' immersion. Perhaps Mr. Swanton, having so fully explored the archæology of this subject, could point us out the source whence Albertus drew his knowledge of what we may call the ferrifactive properties of Lough Neagh water.—N. COLGAN, Dublin.

The Irish Naturalist.

Vol. II.   JULY, 1893.   No. 7.

THE BEAUTY AND USE OF IRISH BUILDING STONES.

BY PROF. GRENVILLE A. J. COLE, M.R.I.A., F.G.S.

(*Substance of a Lecture delivered in Dublin before the Irish Industrial League,* 13*th February,* 1893.)

(*Concluded from page* 171.)

FOREIGN competition demands the cheapening of the carriage of some of the central and west Irish stones; perhaps more favourable terms might be made if a constant supply could be guaranteed.

So much, however, for generalities. When we consider particular stones, we see how Ireland, at any rate, has little need to import either her structural or ornamental materials. The homogeneous firm grey limestone, that of Ballinasloe for example, is capable of extensive use in our street architecture. Mr. Drew's handsome Ulster Bank in Dublin, with its rich Roman carving, shows how this stone may be used either massively or for elaborate ornament. Though by tradition we may respect the Portland stone of the Parliament House or Trinity College, there can be no question as to the possibilities of native limestone. As an easily worked structural material, the commoner limestones, both grey and "calpy," have been largely utilised, as in the railway-bridges, or in such massive blocks as Messrs. Boland's Flour Mills, on the Grand Canal. The latter building is an example of the simplest severity; practical stone-cutters will know how much or how little it would have cost to run one or two string-courses round it, with good hand-carving in them, just sufficient to remind Ringsend of the possibilities of commercial architecture, and

A

that after all, the souls of gas-workers and dock-hands are as worthy of artistic surroundings as the city-clerks of College-green. The chimney of the pumping-station at Grosvenor-road in London is an example of what may be done in this direction; and a love of the plain Irish limestone, arising from a scientific insight into its qualities, may yet end in beautifying many structures in our poorer districts, and in employing artistic labour in quarters where, at the present time, life seems invited to be ugly.

Where the colder grey seems undesirable, Ireland provides a superb pale-yellow building-stone for cities in the sandstones of Fermanagh and southern Donegal. The Mountcharles stone, as used by Sir Thomas Deane in the Museum in Kildare-street, Dublin, will serve as an example of the sharp edges that can be cut out of this hard material. No doubt it may be more costly to work than Portland stone, but any chemist or mineralogist will predict for it remarkable freedom from decay. London, in particular, is seeking for materials that will retain their form and colour despite the penetrating rain and fog. Though the smoke of such an atmosphere clings to almost everything but polished granite and terra-cotta, a fine-grained, pale-coloured, well-cemented sandstone should be able, by its durability, to drive limestones out of the field; and these Carboniferous sandstones of north-west Ireland seem to be more reliable than many English varieties, especially than the red, while they are, at the same time, not too difficult to work.

Granites require careful selection, as the Provost's wall at Trinity College shows; but the National Bank in College-green illustrates how even somewhat delicate caps of columns can be cut in this material. It will be interesting to note whether the light-coloured granites or the Mountcharles sandstones discolour more readily in a city atmosphere. For polished blocks, the grey granites of Newry are well known; and it is possible that, when people have enough of the ubiquitous Peterhead, the red and green granite of Galway, and the red of Donegal, may have a fair chance of public favour.

The brick-and-marble architecture of Italy suggests how two Irish industries might be pleasingly combined; but a white marble gives the most pleasing contrast when laid alternately with the courses of red brick. The real use of marble in the British Isles, as now in America, lies in internal decoration. There is a most satisfactory taste for marble panelling of walls, even in the palaces of nitrate-kings and the sober haunts of stockbrokers. A splendid exhibit of Irish marbles is formed by the entrance-hall of the new museum in Dublin; while the green "ophicalcite" of Connemara can be seen in perfection throughout the staircases of that building and the National Library. When we consider that the latter stone is practically unique, its nearest ally being the Eozoonal limestone of Canada, it may be hoped that in due time the quarry at Recess may be kept permanently active. The rock seems, like the olivine-bearing masses on Monte Somma, a product of contact-metamorphism; and the hydration of the olivine gives us the beautiful and varied green of the serpentinous streaks and patches. This stone requires to be cut up into slabs, from which suitable ones must be selected to be placed together; but its great charm is its infinite variety—one cannot grow tired of it as one can of Shap granite, or even of the beautiful Italian "Pavonazza." There are more rocks in Donegal also than have ever yet come out of it, and some of its marbles with silicates developed in them may in time prove attractive for ornamentation.

Though the foregoing notes have, in the nature of the subject, been somewhat utilitarian, I have endeavoured to show that the beauty and utility of a building-stone are in reality inseparable ideas. It is the business of practical men to demonstrate the utility of the materials in which they deal; and to do this they must thoroughly appreciate and understand them. This is, I take it, one of the aims of technical education—to teach a man to get the best and noblest out of the materials placed at his disposal. Such education should be within the reach of every man who handles a crowbar in a quarry; but with it comes a stimulus to better and firmer work, such as no considerations of pounds, shillings, and pence can ever give. The toiler among the rocks will learn to feel the beauty of them, and of the long processes by which they have finally come to be; his work will become daily more true, more thoughtful, less mechanical; and he will take care that his use and handling of the stone shall be always for the perfecting of its beauty.

THE FLORA OF COUNTY ARMAGH.

BY R. LLOYD PRAEGER, B.E., M.R.I.A.

(*Continued from page* 159).

Typha angustifolia, Linn. N. —
   Lough Gullion! and Closet river, H. W. L. Bann-mouth (Davies), S. A. S. Along the southern shore of Lough Gullion, and in some abundance at the mouth of the Lagan canal, R. Ll. P. "Among the ornamental aqueous plants (of Co. Armagh) are . . . the typha angustifolia, or narrow-leaved catstail, which produces a fine down, and certainly might be turned to some useful account, as stuffing cushions,"—*Coote's Armagh*; the cushion-stuffing suggestion rather points to *T. latifolia* as being the plant referred to.

Sparganium natans, Linn. N. M. S.
   Bog drains half-a-mile inland from Derryadd bay on Lough Neagh; Ballylane lake south of Markethill; abundant at Clay lake near Keady; Drummuckavall lake near Crossmaglen, R. Ll. P.

S. minimum, Fries. N. — —
   Loughnashade near Armagh, W. F. J.! Bog drains two miles south of Portadown, R. Ll. P.

Lemna gibba, Linn. N. — S.
   Brackish drains below Newry, and very abundant in the Closet river near its entrance to Lough Neagh, R. Ll. P.

Potamogeton alpinus, Balbis (*P. rufescens*, Schrad.) N. — —
   Abundant in stream in Tynan Abbey demesne, R. Ll. P.

P. alpinus x heterophyllus? N. — —
   In Lough Neagh at Maghery, R. Ll. P. ("A very interesting specimen,"—A. Bennett).

P. heterophyllus, Schreb. N. — S ?
   In Lough Neagh off Ardmore, H. W. L. spec.! Lough Ross near Crossmaglen, ("? A puzzling plant, off *heterophyllus* towards *nitens*,"—A. Bennett) R. Ll. P.

P. angustifolius, Presl. (*P. zizii*, Roth.) N. — —
   Lough Neagh off Derryadd bay, H. W. L. spec.! Lough Neagh near Kinnegoe, R. Ll. P.

P. lucens, Linn. N. — S.
   In the canal at Goraghwood (S. A. S.), Herb. N. H. P. S. spec.! Lough Neagh off Raughlan, H. W. L. spec.! Lakes at Tynan Abbey and Loughgall Manor, and in Lough Neagh at Kinnegoe, R. Ll. P.

P. obtusifolius, Koch. N. M. S.
   Ditches communicating with Lough Neagh near Lurgan (Moore), *Cyb. Hib.* (as *P. gramineus*). Drummuckavall lake, Mullaghmore lake, lake at Carnagh near Keady, and abundant at the mouth of the Closet river, R. Ll. P.

P. crispus, Linn. var.
   Of a curious pond-weed, without fruit, which I obtained in the canal between Caledon and Battleford Bridge, Mr. Bennett writes: —"This is *P. crispus*, L., *f.*, perhaps a modification of var. *serratus*. It might eventually prove a cross with one of the linear-leaved species, but the apex of the leaves, stem, and venation are *crispus*. It is an even more reduced form than that from Stirling."

P. pectinatus, Linn. N. — S.
   Lough Neagh at Derryadd bay, H. W. L. spec.! In Lough Neagh at east side of Ardmore Point, and in great abundance at the entrance to the canal at Maghery; brackish pools below Newry, R Ll. P.

Potamogeton filiformis, Pers. N. — —
In shallow water in Lough Neagh on east side of Ardmore Point, R. Ll. P. This rare pond-weed was long known in Ireland as confined to a limited area in Co. Mayo. More recently Mr. Barrington found it in Lough Erne, and Mr. Hart in Donegal; a station on the eastern side of Ireland is now added.

P. fluitans (auct.), Roth?
In Lough Neagh at Maghery, R. Ll. P. ("This is *P. fluitans* of English authors and of continental, but whether of Roth is difficult to say, as no one has ever seen a specimen named by him,"—A. Bennett).

Cladium mariscus, R. Br. N. — —
All around Loughgall lake, More *N. H. R.*! Grows now chiefly on the western and southern sides, R. Ll. P.

Rhynchospora alba, Vahl. N. — —
Bog at Annaghmore (G. R.), *Flor. Ulst.*! Maghery and Portadown, S. A. S. Montiaghs bogs, H. W. L.! Of frequent occurrence on the northern bogs, often in abundance, R. Ll. P.

Eleocharis multicaulis, Smith. N. — —
Frequent on the northern bogs, and noted from a number of stations there; Loughadian near Armagh; not seen on the southern mountains, R. Ll. P.

E. acicularis, Linn. N. — —
Banks of Lough Neagh, More *N. H. R.* Ardmore Glebe, H. W. L. spec.! Banks of Closet river, R. Ll. P.

Scirpus maritimus, Linn. — — S.
Estuary of Newry river, abundant, R. Ll. P.

S. sylvaticus, Linn. N. M. —
Damp meadows near Loughgall, More *N. H. R.* Riverside near Newry, H. W. L. spec.! By the Blackwater at Maghery, by Cusher river at Clare, at Tynan Abbey, and in several spots between Armagh and Castle Dillon, R. Ll. P.

S. tabernæmontani, Gmel. — — S.
Brackish drains below Newry, R. Ll. P.

S. pauciflorus, Lightf. N. — —
Occasionally on the northern bogs, but rare, R. Ll. P.

S. fluitans, Linn. N. M. —
Wet bog at Maghery (S. A. S.), Herb. N. H. P. S. spec.! Marsh by Lough Neagh south of Morrow's point, Derrywarragh island at Maghery, bog south of Portadown, and margins of Clay lake near Keady, R. Ll. P.

S. savii, S. and M. — — S.
Salt-marsh by the sea-wall below Newry, R. Ll. P.

Carex dioica, Linn. — — S.
Rare, only observed on Slieve Gullion, R. Ll. P.

C. disticha, Huds. N. — —
By the lake at Loughgall, More *N. H. R.* Loughnashade near Armagh, S. A. S.! Lowry's Lough near Armagh, W. F. J. spec.!

C. vulpina, Linn. N. — S.
Loughnashade near Armagh, and by the canal below Newry, R. Ll. P.

C. paniculata, Linn. N. — —
Near Maghery, B. N. F. C., 1871. Tartaraghan, S. A. S. Loughgall, Loughnashade, and Mullinure, all near Armagh, W. F. J. spec.! Croaghan island in Lough Neagh, H. W. L. spec.! Kinnegoe by Lough Neagh, R. Ll. P.

C. canescens, Linn. N. — —
"Near Tartaraghan, Rev. G. Robinson,!!" More *N. H. R.*; and

B

subsequently, S. A. S. Bog between Annaghmore and Maghery, B. N. F. C. 1871. Ardmore. H. W. L. spec.! Bog near Annagarriff lake, R. Ll. P.

Carex stricta, Good. N. M. —
By the lake at Loughgall abundantly, More *N. H. R.*! Mr. More believes that the variety mentioned in his paper was, as suggested, only a starved state of the plant. Ardmore, H. W. L. spec.! In some quantity by Lough Neagh at east side of Raughlan Point, and abundant on margins of Lough Gilly S. W. of Poyntzpass, R. Ll. P.

C. acuta, Linn. N. — —
By Lough Neagh at Raughlan, H. W. L. spec.!

C. pallescens, Linn. N. — —
Mullinure near Armagh, W. F. J. spec.! Ardmore, H. W. L. spec.!

C. strigosa, Huds. N. — —
Ardmore, H. W. L. spec.!

C. pendula, Huds. — M. —
By the Cusher river in Tanderagee lower demesne, H. W. L.!

C. œderi, Ehr. N. — —
Loughgall, and islet in Lough Neagh, More *N. H. R.* The latter station is possibly in Tyrone.

C. hornschuchiana, Hoppe. — — S.
On Slieve Gullion, R. Ll. P.; apparently rare.

C. xanthocarpa, Delg. N. — —
This supposed hybrid I obtained on the boggy shores of Derryadd lough in the N.W.; the determination was made by Mr. Bennett.

C. lævigata, Sm. N. — —
Near Armagh, W. F. J. spec.!

C. pseudo-cyperus, Linn. N. — —
Tartaraghan (G. R.), Herb. N. H. P. S.! On visiting the spot described by Mr. Robinson in answer to inquiries—the streamlet below the glebe house—I found about half-a-dozen fine plants, with abundant fruit stems three to four feet high; Mr. Robinson has also given me "near Lurgan" as a station; R. Ll. P.

C. rhynchophysa, C. A. Meyer. — M. —
Sparingly in a deep drain on the margin of Mullaghmore lough near Markethill, R. Ll. P. This fine sedge, which resembles *C. rostrata (ampullacea)* in general habit, is an addition to the British Flora. For full details of its synonomy, bibliography, and European distribution, the reader is referred to *Journal of Botany* for February, 1893. Suffice here to say that it is a native of northern Europe, inhabiting Scandinavia, Russia, etc. I succeeded in obtaining one specimen only, which, after a careful examination by Mr. Arthur Bennett, F.L.S., and comparison with continental examples in his own and the Kew herbarium, is referred unhesitatingly to *C. rhynchophysa*, C. A. Meyer. By the kindness of the editor and publishers of the *Journal of Botany* I am enabled to reproduce the figure of the Armagh plant which appeared in the Journal (Plate 5).
Since the above went to press I have visited the locality (June 9th) and obtained several specimens, but the plant appears to be very rare in its only station.

C. paludosa, Good. N. — —
Lakeside at Loughgall, More *N. H. R.*! Abundant and very luxuriant in the lake of Tynan Abbey demesne, B. N. F. C., 1873!; plentiful by streams and at the margin of the lake, *ibid.*, 1889; a specimen from this station is in Herb. N. H. P. S. In a marsh a mile N. E. of Loughall, R. Ll. P.

(TO BE CONCLUDED.)

THE BREEDING OF THE GARDEN WARBLER IN THE SHANNON VALLEY.

BY R. J. USSHER.

IT is an experience of high interest to the ornithologist when he first makes acquaintance with a species new to him, especially if he finds it in haunts previously unrecorded in his native country.

Thompson's correspondents found the Garden Warbler (*Sylvia hortensis*, Bechst.) in Antrim, at Ballybrado, in the south of Tipperary, and near Cork. The late Sir Victor Brooke observed several pairs frequenting the natural woods at Castle Caldwell on lower Lough Erne, where, as Mr. J. C. Bloomfield informs me, he is well acquainted with these birds, and observed them last spring.

I first heard the song of the Garden Warbler on one of the naturally wooded islands of Lough Erne, on 9th June, 1891. I again heard the song on 7th June, 1892, uttered from a thicket of blackthorn on Nun's Island in the centre of Lough Ree, and caught a glimpse of the bird, but failed to get a shot at it. My further acquaintance with it is due to Mr. Anthony Parker of Castle Lough, whose beautiful demesne, on the Tipperary side of Lough Derg near Killaloe, contains many vestiges of natural wood. He sent me, on the 10th May last, for determination, a fine male Garden Warbler shot there, which is now destined for the Science and Art Museum. He subsequently discovered the nest of another pair, which on the 26th May I had the pleasure of seeing. It was in a secluded corner of his grounds, but not far from the house and approach, and was placed in a mass of loose briars about two or three feet from the ground, a few trees, saplings, and elder bushes standing round. It was composed of dried stems of grasses and other plants, and lined with a few root-fibres and hairs. It contained five eggs in the first stage of incubation. I saw the female quit it, and soon discerned her threading her way through neighbouring bushes, uttering her warning note, which consists of the repetition of a sound not unlike the slow winding of a clock. To obtain full proof of the species, I shot this bird after seeing her leave the nest, and she also is in the hands of Messrs. Williams & Son. Before approaching the nest I heard in its vicinity the song of the male, which was continued in the same place the day after he had lost his mate. Another male sang habitually in a group of hazels between the flower-garden and the lake, and others in different parts of the demesne, but always about spots where there were masses of briars and a variety of shrubs and deciduous trees, not in a dense compact mass, but open between. Mr. Parker had noted eight or nine places where he had recently heard this species, and since my departure he has heard it elsewhere, but always in his demesne. The same bird might be heard throughout the day, and day after day, repeating his song at intervals about the same spot, where probably the nest was situated, as in the case of that which I took. If one approached, the song would stop, and soon recommence from a neighbouring tree or bush, but the bird secluded itself so carefully among the foliage as to be very rarely and briefly seen.

It was a powerful and sweet song that might be heard distinctly at a considerable distance, and contained some deep notes, recalling those of a Blackbird, but were not dwelt on with the emphasis of a Blackbird's song. This was uttered in a volley, high and deep notes struggling as it were to get out. In a few seconds it stopped, to recommence presently, after the manner of a warbler's. It is far sweeter and deeper than the brief chattering song of the Whitethroat, which I had opportunities of comparing with it, and it is uttered for a longer period at a time.

On 1st June I revisited Nun's Island, in Lough Ree, Co. Westmeath, and in the same bush where I heard it last year, a Garden Warbler was again singing, while another was rivalling his song on a different part of the island, which is encircled by a belt of tall Blackthorns.

Next day I visited the extensive woods of Castle Forbes, Co. Longford, which stretch for miles along Lough Forbes, an enlargement of the Shannon, and are evidently mainly of natural growth. Here I soon recognized the now familiar song, and as I wandered on came to a spot where a Garden Warbler was singing, close to a path, yet so closely did he seclude himself, that he sang again and again unseen, always changing his whereabouts, while I watched for nearly an hour. I then came to another place where I heard a similar song, and while moving about I was met by the alarm note of the female.

The male presently arrived, with a green-drake fly in his mouth, and both birds being excited about my proximity to their nest, gave me opportunities of seing them perfectly—the olive brown head and back, the slightly paler mark over the eye, the buff tinge on the throat and breast, and the white underparts. They used to come into a Wild Cherry when I withdrew, and I was convinced their nest was in the briars near, but I failed to find it until I had been absent for a while. On returning, I saw the bird in the cherry bush, and then alighting among the briars at a point where I believed these to be too low to hold the nest: but here it was, composed of grass stems exclusively, and containing four partially fledged young, which on my nearer approach quitted the nest, and it was with much difficulty that I secured one for the Museum by searching among the herbage on the ground. I heard the Garden Warbler's song in four places at Castle Forbes, evidently uttered by different birds, each of which keeps to his own haunt. I subsequently heard a bird of this species singing repeatedly for a long time from a neighbouring bush, while inspecting the picturesque ruins of the Seven Churches on Innishcleraun or Quaker Island, belonging to Co. Longford, in the northern part of Lough Ree, and in a different part of the same island, where great masses of Hawthorns and briars formed towering fences, I heard both the song and the warning note. After this I heard a Garden Warbler singing in a plantation near the house at Derrycarne, in the Co. Leitrim, on another of the lake expansions of the Shannon.

The farthest point I reached was Hollybrook, in Co. Sligo, on Lough Arrow. This beautiful demesne, lying between the mountain and the lake, contains the most picturesque and varied natural jungles, mingled in places with rhododendrons, and introduced species of trees. Here I heard the Garden Warbler's song in two places, in each of which it was as usual repeated, morning and afternoon, day after day, leaving no doubt that the birds were settled and breeding there. Mrs. Ffolliott writes on the 17th June:—"The Garden Warblers have been singing continuously the last few days, up near the house."

During my several observations of them I have seen the birds at different times, and they always agreed with the specimens shot at Castle Lough, and were not Blackcaps, which I could have easily distinguished had I seen them; but it has been remarked by Mr. Howard Saunders that the two species are not found commonly in the same resorts.

I have thus identified the Garden Warbler in five counties from Tipperary to Sligo, having met with it in large demesnes, or on islands where some remnants of the natural growth have been preserved   I have not found it in woods of Fir and Larch except where these were mixed with the indigenous wood. Its range is known to extend to Fermanagh, and it was formerly observed in Cork, and there is some reason to think it has been met with in Mayo. It should be looked for in all parts of Ireland where suitable haunts occur. Its song, however, uttered in May and June, is the chief means of recognizing it, and this is so little noticed that no one I met with, except Mr. Parker, had appeared to distinguish it or to know the bird. The warblers, from their skulking habits, and the brief period of the year that they sing, are among the least known of our land birds. The Wood Warbler should also be carefully looked for. Mr. R. E. Dillon has shown me a skin and egg of this species taken at Clonbrook in the Co. Galway, where he has heard the bird again this season, though I was not so fortunate.

THE EARTHWORMS OF IRELAND.
BY REV. HILDERIC FRIEND, F.L.S.

(*Continued from page* 122.)

I HAVE named the remaining group of *Allolobophora, Virgata*, because of the bands of colour which characterise the principal types (see page 42). Since that paper was written Dr. Rosa, of Turin, one of the best authorities on earthworms, has published a volume of great value and interest entitled *Revisione dei Lumbricidi*, in which he treats the whole subject from a wider standpoint, thus presenting the matter in a much truer light than it is possible to place it in when dealing only with a limited section. I must, however, adhere to my arrangement, and now deal with the species included under

GROUP IV. **Virgata.**

In the Irish worm-fauna there are at present only two species under this division. One of these is very widely distributed not only in Great

Britain, but also abroad. The other has hitherto been found only in a limited area in Ireland; it does not occur, so far as at present known, in England; but is identical with a species, or sub-species, found on the European Continent.

Allolobophora foetida, Savigny.—THE BRANDLING. This interesting species has been known to the angler for ages past as a most enticing bait for fish. So far as I have been able to glean, it was first recorded under this name of Brandling by the renowned author of "The Complete Angler." "For the trout, the Dew-worm, which some also call the Lob-worm, and the Brandling, are the chief." Thomas Moufet, whose "Insectorum Theatrum" appeared in 1634, speaks of it as Duggs, but I am unable to find any scientific term among the writings of Linnæus which indicates that he had learned to distinguish it from the common earthworm. Such writers of the present century on angling as Hofland, Stoddart, and Younger, call it the Brandling, or Brambleworm. The name has reference to the brand-marks, or alternate stripes of brown and yellow colour, by which the worm is at once recognised. It was first described as a distinct species in 1828 by Savigny, who named it *Enterion fœtidum*, the specific term being in allusion to the peculiar characteristic, and by no means attractive odour, which proceeds from the worm when handled.

The Brandling is from two to six inches in length, and has an average of about 100 segments. The girdle occupies the 26th to the 30th, the male pore being on the 15th. On the under surface of the 28th, 29th and 30th girdle-segments are the band or clitellar papillæ (*tubercula pubertatis*). The worm is not only brindled or striped, but exudes a large quantity of yellow fluid, which stains the fingers, and leaves a most unpleasant odour behind for a long time. It is probable that this, like the ink of the *Sepia*, is intended as a means of protection, and while the worm is greatly relished by certain fish, there can be no doubt but that its habit of throwing off a disagreeable fluid makes it very repugnant to some of its enemies. The 9th, 10th, and 11th segments are conspicuous by reason of their lighter colour and greater diameter, owing in part to the presence of important sexual organs in that region. The lip is tender and pallid, extending backwards into the 1st segment, or prostomium, to about one-half its diameter. The first dorsal pore is between segments 4 and 5.

This worm is peculiarly fond of old manure. It is still a problem how it finds its way to the heaps. If manure be deposited in a given place, where the worm appears to be unknown, a number of specimens will be almost certain to occur within a year, and the next season, when decomposition is complete, the worms may be counted by thousands. They probably have some acute sense of smell, by means of which they detect the whereabouts of a suitable nidus for their eggs and incubation.

DISTRIBUTION IN IRELAND. Ferns, Co. Wicklow (Dr. Greene); Blackrock, Co. Dublin (Miss Kelsall); Cork (Miss A. N. Abbott); Holywood, Co. Down (Miss Clara M. Patterson); Valencia, Co. Kerry (Miss Delap); Malahide, Co. Dublin (Dr. Trumbull); Portsalon, Co. Donegal (Mr. Hart); Glasnevin, Co. Dublin (Mr. Redding); Leeson-park, Dublin (Dr. Scharff), etc.

Through the courtesy of Dr. Scharff, I received in the middle of June, 1892, a consignment of earthworms collected in his garden at Dublin, which included, in addition to several species already well known to occur in Great Britain, one which has been taken in no other part of the United Kingdom. I submitted a detailed account of this interesting animal to the Royal Irish Academy last November, and must refer the reader to the *Proceedings* of that Institution (3rd ser., vol. ii., No. 3, pp. 402-410) for the statements then made. Since that time further light has been thrown upon the question of this worm's identity from an unexpected quarter. I wrote some months ago to Dr. Rosa, the Italian helminthologist, respecting the species under consideration, and learned in reply that there was undoubtedly a close affinity between it and a species or variety (*A. veneta*) which he had discovered at the same time on the Continent.

Dr Rosa has, within the past few days, favoured me with a copy of his newest work on the subject of Earthworms, and in this volume (*Revisione dei Lumbricidi*, 1893, p. 34) he does me the honour to print a full account of the Irish worm as a sub-species of *Allolobophora veneta*, Rosa.

Allolobophora hibernica, Friend.—IRISH WORM. When living, and extended in the act of crawling, the worm is about 50 mm. or two inches in length. In spirits it is from one to one and a-half inches, or 25 to 35 mm. long, and thus ranks in size with three or four of our British dendrobænic worms, such as the Tree-worm (*A. arborea*, Eisen), or the Celtic Worm (*A. celtica*, Rosa). Unlike those, however, its colour is fleeting, so that immediately upon being placed in alcohol the small quantity of colouring matter which is present in the living worm evanesces, leaving the preserved animal without the least indication of its pretty appearance in a state of nature. The anterior portion of the worm when alive is of a rosy hue, closely approaching flesh-colour; the girdle is of a dull yellow, while the rest of the body, excepting the caudal extremity, is a greyish hue, appearing brown along the line of the dorsal vessel. The last half-dozen segments are yellow, just as in the Gilt-tail or Cockspur of the angler (*A. subrubicunda*, Eisen). The presence of a pigment, which is exuded from the dorsal pores, accounts for this yellow tinge, which in the most adult specimens may be found pervading other portions of the body to a slight degree.

With a worm so short as this, it is rather unexpected to find so many segments, but the average is 90-100, so that they are very narrow, and closely arranged side by side. In this respect they come very near the Constricted Worm (*A. constricta*, Rosa). The position of the first dorsal pore has yet to be determined. In the Mucous Worm it can be readily seen, not so here.

The male pores are found on each side of the 15th segment, being easily recognised in adult specimens by the small papillæ upon which they are seated. In some worms bearing a close relationship to this species, the papillæ are so large as to affect the two adjoining segments (14-16), but, in this case, no such prominent position is held by them. The girdle is conspicuous, dense, and closely fused on the dorsal surface, but each segment is clearly defined beneath. It covers six to eight segments, two only of which bear the *tubercula pubertatis*. The general outline of the girdle ventrally closely resembles that of the nearly allied Mucous Worm (*A. mucosa*, Eisen), as it is truthfully pourtrayed by Eisen in the plate which accompanies his original description.

One rather striking peculiarity may here be emphasized. In several species of worms, such as the Brandling (*A. fœtida*, Sav.), the Long Worm (*A. longa*, Ude), and the Common Earthworm (*Lumbricus terrestris*, L.), we find a tendency on the part of those segments which contain the sexual organs to become tumid and pale on the ventral side. In this case, however, it is the dorsal surface which is so affected, especially in segments 10 and 11, and on the worm being dissected, the cause of this unusual appearance is at once discovered. Whereas in most species of worms the spermathecæ are ventrally or laterally placed, in the Irish Worm they are disposed on the back.

I was fortunate enough to find eight specimens of this worm in the batch consigned to me, and had recognised the novelty of the worm as soon as the first specimen or two had been transferred to alcohol, so that

I was able deliberately to study the whole series, first in a living state, and afterwards in spirits. I have since received two large series of the same worm from Dr. Scharff, by means of which I have been able to confirm and extend my earliest observations. The number of segments ranges between 86 and 108, so that the average is about 100. I find that whenever the number of segments in an adult worm falls below the average, there is a tendency for the segments to increase their longitudinal diameter. This inclines one to the opinion that there is a normal length which it is desirable for each worm to attain, if it is to discharge the functions of life in the fullest and best possible manner.

In the *Atti del R. Inst. Venet.*, iv. (1885-6), p. 674, Rosa gives an account of the earthworms of Venice, and, among others, makes mention of a new species, which he designated the Venice Worm (*A. veneta*, Rosa). As stated above, he is now inclined to regard my *A. hibernica* as a subspecies of this. In 1889, he published a note on a worm found in the Botanical Gardens of Coimbra, in Portugal, as well as in Liguria, the characters of which showed it also to be a variety of the foregoing. From what we learn respecting it we may judge that it approaches *A. hibernica* more nearly than the latter resembles *A. veneta*.

DISTRIBUTION IN IRELAND. Though the only locality from which I have received the typical worm is Leeson-park, Dublin, I have three specimens which closely resemble it from Miss Smith, Piperstown, Co. Louth. These specimens suggest the advisability of searching for others. Consignments may be addressed:—"The Grove," Idle, Bradford.

(TO BE CONTINUED).

A PLEA FOR THE ROTIFERA.

BY MISS L. S. GLASCOTT.

WHAT is a Rotifer? There are few people who have not some idea at least of what this name implies, for, small as it is, it has doubtless found its way into many of the journals, magazines, etc., of the day, whose editors recognise the growing love for natural history, by devoting a few pages to that delightful study; but as "the interests of the minority"—that burning question— may not be neglected with impunity, we will endeavour to describe "the nature o' the baste." There are those who would cut the Gordian knot with alacrity by stating that it is "a water insect," the name insect being often applied promiscuously to all animals under a certain size—very convenient, no doubt, if a trifle ambiguous. Our little friend has indeed been rather badly treated ; it has been shouldered about from pillar to post with scant ceremony, by some great people who ought to know better, but I believe, as in the case of the square man in the round hole, there were difficulties about accommodation. At present we find it quartered among that large and for the most part disagreeable group of animals, the "worms." Having thus placed our rotifer among its relations, we will next proceed to describe its appearance.

A denizen of the water, of microscopic size, it is barely to be seen by the naked eye, as a tiny white speck moving about against a dark background. The microscope reveals its typical form as that of a short cylinder, of which the upper end—the head—is furnished with a wreath of hairs, or *cilia*, which is kept in constant motion, having just the appearance of a revolving wheel (hence the name), and which serves a double purpose, that of an aid to locomotion, and that of creating a vortex to entrap the necessary pabulum. Besides this wreath of hairs, the head is also furnished, in the greater number of species, with lateral ear-like and ciliated appendages which can be everted or withdrawn at the will of the animal. The lower end terminates in a foot of one or several joints, which at its extremity is either developed into a suctorial disc, or bears one or more toes of a chitinous texture. The integument of the body is either soft and flexible, or hardened into a glassy coat, termed the "lorica," which is often developed into beautiful and fantastic patterns.

Tiny atom as it is, the creature possesses a comparatively high organization. A large brain occupies the interior of the head, and in connection with it are one or more eyes, sometimes of a most brilliant red or rose-colour, their position and number varying according to the species. It has jaws and teeth of quite formidable proportions, and knows how to use them too; in some families these are formed for biting and cutting only, in others they are modified into pounding and crushing machines. The digestive system is simple and easily discerned; it consists of a stomach, intestine, and gastric glands, which latter are usually in the form of two clear globate bodies seated on the fore-part of the stomach, at either side of the œsophagus. The excretory system is represented by loose, irregular, and sometimes branching tubes, which originate in the head, descend to and terminate in a clear bladder-like vesicle situated near the end of the body, which dilates and contracts at regular intervals, and is termed the contractile vesicle. There is a well-developed ovary, which lies along the ventral floor, and usually one or two ova are to be seen in an advanced stage of development. The muscles in some species are very conspicuous, notably in *Pleterodina*, in which they are seen stretching out in ribbon-like bundles from the viscera toward the margins of the glassy plates of the lorica. The variety of forms to be found among the Rotifera bids defiance to any description in a paper of such prescribed limits as this; suffice it to say that in each we find a beauty peculiar to itself. The prevailing colour is white, the tissues of many species being of such transparency that every detail of the internal structure is discerned with the greatest ease, and when to all this, enclosed in a little speck, measuring from $\frac{1}{30}$ to $\frac{1}{500}$ of an inch, is added the charm of an intelligent activity, of busy purpose, of graceful movements, of variety of character and temperament, of evidence of passions in common with our own, such as those of fear, of pleasure, of various desires, surely it is superfluous to say that in the study of the Rotifera we will find a keen and instructive pleasure.

But little is known of their habits and life-history, for though they have received some attention from naturalists of various nationalities, these have directed their observations more to the peculiarities of form, and to the internal structure, than to this department. Here then is a tempting field for our energies, surely it is time for us to be up and doing. Neither need we imagine it the only one remaining to us; numerous and varied as are the forms recorded belonging to the group which have been so ably described and portrayed in that splendid book "The Rotifera," the joint work of Dr. Hudson and the late Mr. P. H. Gosse, without which no library is now complete, the list is far from being exhausted; in the course of my own limited researches I have met with numbers of new and interesting members of almost every family among them, some of which I have endeavoured to sketch.

They are to be found in all waters, salt and fresh, but more especially in the latter. Pools, ponds, rivers, streams, tanks, water-butts, all afford good hunting-grounds. Many of them may be caught swimming in clear water, but the greater number delight to frequent small aquatic plants, algæ, moss, dead submerged leaves, sedimentous deposits, etc. Most of them are vegetarians in diet, but there is also a carnivorous class who fare sumptuously on dead animal substances, and are to be found within the skins of aquatic larvæ, the shells of tiny Entomostraca, dead flies which have met an untimely fate, and allied objects. There are parasites among them too, both internal and external, which feed upon their unwilling hosts; I have discovered lately two very formidable creatures which infest the eggs of water-snails and destroy whole clusters of them; and last but not least, there are cannibals, but this savage taste is restricted to some of the most innocent and guileless-looking of them all, the Floscules (a warning not to trust to appearances), and their name reminds me that I had almost forgotten to make mention of the group to which they belong, called the " Rhizota " (the rooted), which take first place, if not first rank, in the eyes of the authorities. As their name denotes, they remain fixed to one spot, within gelatinous tubes which are often strengthened with extraneous materials. Very beautiful indeed are their flower-like forms and "revolving wheels," but e'er the would-be admirer of their charms approach, let him take care first to arm himself with the patience of Job, for verily he will have need of it. Their coyness and timidity would well-nigh tempt that patriarch himself to make use of a few epithets more forcible than polite; after long watching perhaps, as the creature slowly and cautiously uprears itself beyond the sheltering walls of its dwelling-house, when every nerve is tightened with expectancy, as the extremities are upon the point of being unfurled—an inadvertant touch—a step upon the floor—a tremor in the table from some unlooked-for source, and behold! it has vanished, and the weary watch must begin again ; but courage ! I have noticed in them a marked appreciation of temperature, and on some auspicious occasions they seem to forget their fears, and exhibit a boldness and freedom of action which quite takes one by suprise. A drop of hot water applied to the edge of the cover-glass is often productive of very good results, and well worth the trial. But time presses, so having paid them this brief tribute of notice, I must bid them adieu, and trust that these few words may awaken an interest and invoke a desire for personal acquaintance with these fascinating little creatures in the minds of those to whom they are yet strangers.

In conclusion I would warn the Rotifer-hunter against choosing a day after heavy rains for his researches; the one quality of water a rotifer eschews is that fresh from the clouds, and testifies his disapproval by disappearing from his usual haunts.

PROCEEDINGS OF IRISH SOCIETIES.

ROYAL ZOOLOGICAL SOCIETY.

Recent donations comprise a Muscovy Duck from Miss Stubbs; three Belgian hares from H. Thynne, Esq.; four Golden Orioles from the Galway stall at the "Kosmos" bazaar; a White Pheasant from Mr. Hunt; a pair of Peafowl from the Governors of the Hospital for Incurables, Donnybrook; a Blue-breasted Lory from Miss McCausland; a pair of American Blue Robins from Mrs. O'Conor; three Ring-Doves from F. C. K. Cooper, Esq.; a Ring-necked Parrakeet from T. J. Lane, Esq.; and a pair of Kestrels from Constable B. Collins. A Yak has been born in the Gardens; an Ostrich, seventeen Prairie Marmots, and three monkeys have been acquired by purchase.

12,000 persons visited the Gardens in May.

DUBLIN MICROSCOPICAL CLUB.

APRIL 20th.—The Club met at DR. SCHARFF'S, who showed the shell of *Helix lamellata*—a terrestrial mollusc. Apart from its rarity, it is interesting chiefly from the fact that it is almost confined to the British islands, which seems to suggest the probability of its having originated there. The epidermis of the shell is thrown at regular intervals into most delicate folds, giving it the lamellar structure from which the species derives its name.

DR. MCWEENEY showed a simple form of moist chamber which he had found very efficient. It consists of a coffin-shaped glass vessel about half an inch deep, and covered with a glass lid which fits accurately. The micro-mount—in water or nährlösung—is simply placed in this vessel, a few drops of water having previously been introduced. The lid is put on, and the preparation remains unaltered for weeks, as evaporation is prevented by the saturation of the air contained in the vessel. It may be removed at any time for examination under the microscope, and the glass lid enables one to see with the naked eye whether any obvious development (or multiplication) of the enclosed objects has taken place. The whole apparatus can also be readily sterilised, but it is hardly adapted for repeated examination with the oil-immersion, owing to the difficulty of cleansing the upper surface of the cover-glass.

The same exhibitor showed a stick of *Acrospermum graminum*, Lib., a curious spheriaceous fungus, with a singly erect flesh-coloured perithecium, one-twentieth of an inch high. The cylindrical asci each contain eight filiform spores, which are of such tenuity, that it takes an extremely high power and good definition to distinguish them individually as they lie within the asci. The ascigerous condition of this fungus is stated by Mr. G. Massee, of the Royal Herbarium, Kew (to whom specimens had been forwarded by the exhibitor), to have been only recently recognized, and the species itself has not hitherto been met with in Ireland. He also showed the *Cordyceps* found on *Polietes lardaria*, already noted in the *I. Nat.* (p. 146).

PROF. G. A. J. COLE showed a section of silicified oolitic limestone of Middle Devonian age, from near Ilfracombe, exhibited on behalf of Mr. F. Chapman, F.R.M.S., and described by him in the *Geological Magazine*, 1893, p. 102. In this rock the first signs of shearing have been set up under earth pressure, and the oolitic grains show interesting elongations, deformations, and even truncations where they have been pressed against one another. A number of sinuous fissures have developed in the mass.

PROF. T. JOHNSON showed *Wildmania miniata*, f. *amplissima*, Foslie. At a recent meeting of the club he had shown herbarium specimens of this one-layered *Porphyra*-like red alga, but was not able to say whether the species was a native of Ireland or simply a drift weed. The material in the bottle now exhibited showed that the plant is not a drift weed. The slide preparation showed the thickenings of the stalk by the downgrowth of filaments from the lower cells of the thallus, a mode of thickening found in several sea-weeds.

MR. DUERDEN exhibited a new species of *Bourgainvillia* from Bantry Bay, obtained growing on the appendages of a *Stenorhynchus*. The form has not yet been fully described. It is regarded as intermediate between *B. muscus* and *B. ramosa*. The gonophores, which are well developed, grow in clusters. A peculiar feature is the presence of long fusiform bodies, which have been regarded as nests of parasitic larvæ, but are shown to be actual parts of the colony itself. In the gastric cavity of some of the polypites a small parasitic nematode was found.

MR. M'ARDLE exhibited a specimen of *Jubula hutchinsiæ* (Hook), var. β. *integrifolia*, s howing perianths and the amentæ, which bear the male flowers (*andrœcia*). This is the form described by Dr. Gottsche in "Synopsis Hepaticarum," p. 426, as having been found in Java by Blume. The specimen was collected by Mr. M'Ardle in the Maghanabo Glen, near Castlegregory, Co. Kerry, growing on the fronds of *Dumortiera hirsuta* (Swartz.), var. *irrigua* (Tayl. sp.), which is found in New Granada. Professor Lindberg, who also collected this rare plant in Co. Kerry, states in his paper on Hepaticæ collected in Ireland, that the plant is found in North America and in the island of Java.

MAY 18th.—The Club met at MR. GREENWOOD PIM'S, who showed leaves of the almond, of a brilliant crimson colour. The micro-section showed that the chlorophyll had almost entirely disappeared, and was replaced, especially in the vicinity of the fibro-vascular bundles, with red-coloured cell-contents, but no trace of fungoid-growth of any kind was discernible. Later on, however, these leaves lost somewhat of their bright colour, became bullate and thin; the characteristic asci and spores of *Ascomyces deformans* were then found in abundance.

MR. HEDLEY exhibited the head of *Cysticercus tenuicollis*, which is the bladder worm of *Tænia marginata* of the Dog. He remarked that although there was reason to believe this form of bladder worm was plentiful, yet he had failed to find any record of its occurring in Ireland. The specimen showed the crown with thirty-two hooklets, and four suckers, or bothria, and occurred, with several others, in the omentum, or caul of a lamb. The life-history of these interesting Cestoidæ is pretty much like those which infest the human subject. The cystic stage is found in sheep, in the liver and serous membranes of the abdominal cavity. These are eaten by the canine species, and after the bladder is digested, the young worm attaches itself to portions of the alimentary tract until mature. The eggs are voided in feculent matter, and carried into pools or other moist surfaces, where they undergo change, being protected by three membranes, between which an oily material exists. They eventually arrive in the abomasum, or fourth stomach of the sheep, and the membranes are digested, thus liberating the embryos, which at once penetrate the walls of the stomach, or if lower, in the tract of the intestines, finding their way to the liver, or serous abdominal membranes already referred to.

MR. G. H. CARPENTER showed the leg of a female pycnogon, *Phoxichilus lævis*, Grube. The muscles, nerves, intestinal diverticulum, and ovary, were well seen in the preparation.

MR. H. H. DIXON showed preparations of the leaf *Hakea victoria*, showing the peculiar structure of the stomata, and the inner tissues of the leaf.

MR. J. JOLY showed crystals of calcspar containing fluid-cavities, and exhibiting remarkable polarising effects.

BELFAST NATURALISTS' FIELD CLUB.

MAY 20th.—First excursion of the season to Antrim and Muckamore. A party of forty proceeded to Antrim by 10.15 train, where the shores of Lough Neagh, at the mouth of the Six-mile-water were first inspected.

Proceedings of Irish Societies.   197

It was still rather early for botanising, but *Draba verna, Ranunculus fluitans*, and *Cerastium arvense*, were noted. Road was then taken for Muckamore, a halt being made at Boghead to inspect a fine souterrain recently discovered there. On the route thither, *Carex strigosa, C. paniculata, Geum intermedium*, and *Ophioglossum vulgatum* were noted. After tea at Antrim, a business meeting was held, when a motion was passed congratulating the senior secretary (Mr. Praeger) on his appointment to the National Library of Ireland, Dublin, and expressing regret at his consequent resignation of the secretaryship of the Club. The party returned to Belfast by the 5.53 train.

DUBLIN NATURALISTS' FIELD CLUB.

MAY 27th.—The excursion to Skerries, attended by forty members, was not very productive botanically, but Mr. Cuthbert collected the following Hymenoptera on the low walls and sandbanks to the north of the village:—Terebrantia, *Tenthrenopsis scutellaris; Chrysis ignita* in great abundance, and various Ichneumons; Aculeata, *Odynerus pictus*, and *Pemphredon lethifer*. Thirty-six species of Coleoptera were taken by Mr. F. A. O'Brien. Two of these, *Otiorrhynchus maurus*, and *Rhynchites æneovirens*, are new to the Dublin list; whilst a third, *Tachinus intricatus*, has been once before recorded from Chapelizod.

CORK NATURALISTS' FIELD CLUB.

MAY 17th.—Excursion to Myshall, where a most interesting day was spent.

MAY 27th.—Excursion to Pota, where Mr. Osborne very kindly conducted the members through the grounds, and showed them the choice collection of trees and shrubs. About thirty-five availed of this excursion.

MAY 31st.—MR. J. H. BENNETT in the chair. MR. DILLON read a paper on "The Earthworms of Co. Cork" compiled from notes kindly lent by the Rev. Hilderic Friend, F.L.S. The structure of worms was first dealt with and the distinguishing characteristics of the two classes into which they are divided. The results of experiments made with light were given as showing the apparent absence of the organs of sight and hearing, and Mr. Dillon then gave some interesting facts as to the mode of life and habits, and a description of the different species to be found in the county and their haunts.

JUNE 14th.—Excursion to Glenbower Woods, where a most enjoyable evening was spent. Some specimens of *Hymenophyllum tunbridgense* were found, and a good number of entomological specimens.

ROYAL IRISH ACADEMY.

APRIL 10th.—Mr. F. W. Moore read a paper for MR. MCARDLE on "The Hepaticæ of the Hill of Howth." The list is important, and shows that the locality is rich in this class of plants; thirty-seven species are enumerated, many of which are very rare and interesting. Two are new to Ireland— *Cephalozia francisci*, Hook, and *Anthelia juratzkana*, Limpr. A third species, *Cephalozia denudata*, Nees, which grows abundantly on Howth hill, had previously only been known to grow in the Co. Mayo. Mr. McArdle claims the following fourteen species as being also new to the Co. Dublin, additions to the last list of that county published by the late Dr. D. Moore (*Sci. Proc. R. D. S.*, 1878):—*Cephalozia fluitans*, Nees; *C. divaricata*, Smith; *C. elachista*, Jack, (rare); *C. curvifolia*, Dicks; *C. multiflora*, Spruce; *C. catenulata*, Huben; *Blepharostoma setacea*, Web.; *Jungermania minuta*, Crantz (rare); *J. incisa*, Schrad.; *Pellia calycina*, Nees; *Metzgeria conjugata*, Ray, (Lindb.). The list is provisional only, and is the first attempt at a detailed account of these plants that has been made by any person for this locality so far as we are aware. From the number of species it will be obvious that Howth is by no means below the average of any other similar locality on the Irish coast.

MAY 8th.—PROF. W. J. SOLLAS read a paper on "The relative age of the Igneous Rocks at Barnavane, Carlingford." The intrusion of the granite into the gabbro at Barnavane was noted by Dr. Haughton and by Mr. Traill. There is no doubt whatever as to the accuracy of their conclusions; but we find in places the two rocks most intimately mingled, a fine plexus of granite veins, even on a microscopic scale, penetrating the gabbro, which becomes reduced to isolated flecks and fragments. Certain specimens, treated apart from the field evidence, would have been considered as gabbro containing mere segregation-veins. The independence of the two magmas is, in the surface-phenomena, at any rate, completely demonstrable, despite the actual fusion of portions of the gabbro by the invading granite. A good discussion followed, in which Dr. Haughton, Dr. V. Ball, Mr. G. H. Kinahan, Prof. Cole, and Mr. J. Nolan, took part.

MR. J. E. DUERDEN read a paper "On some new and rare Irish Polyzoa." The contribution dealt with the known British species of *Retepora, Crisia, Triticella,* and *Ascopodaria.* Examples of the finest British species of *Retepora, R. conchii,* Hincks, were exhibited. Prof. Allman's discovery of *Retepora beaniana,* King, from the west coast was confirmed. The six British species of *Crisia* were recorded from Dublin bay, including the newly-described *C. ramosa* of Harmer. The occurrence of three species of *Triticella* was described. Two, *T. horenii,* G. O. Sars, and *T. pedicellata,* Alder, have been only once recorded from English waters, and *T. boeckii,* G. O. Sars, is recorded for the first time from British waters. The abundance in which these rare forms occur on the west coast of Ireland has enabled the author to show the presence of a horny crest in all the three known species of this genus. The recently described species *Ascopodaria nodosa,* Lomas, was found by Mr. Duerden in material from Killiney bay.

ROYAL DUBLIN SOCIETY.

JUNE 21st.—PROF. G. A. J. COLE in the chair. MR. R. J. MOSS read a paper "On a Graphitic Schist from Donegal." An analysis showed that graphite was not present in sufficient quantity for the rock to be commercially valuable.

MR. G. H. CARPENTER read a paper "On some Pycnogonida from the Irish Coasts." The cruises of the "Fingal" and "Harlequin" and other collections, examined by the author, have yielded the following species:—*Nymphon gracile,* Leach, Dublin, Queenstown; *N. rubrum,* Hodge, Dublin; *N. gallicum,* Hoek, west coast; *Phoxichilidium femoratum,* Rathke, east and west coasts; *Anoplodactylus petiolatus,* Kr., west coast; *Phoxichilus spinosus,* Mont., west coast; *P. lævis,* Grube, Dublin and west coast; *Pycnogonum littorale,* Strom, east and west coasts. Only the first, fourth, and last of these are recorded in Thompson's list in the "Natural History of Ireland"; the other six species in that list must probably remain of doubtful identity, except *Chætonymphon spinosum,* Goods. The form now called *Phoxichilus lævis,* Grube, has been recorded in the *Irish Nat.* (vol. i., pp. 42, 168) as *P. spinosus.* The two forms are distinguishable, but it may be doubted if they can be regarded as distinct species.

MR. GILBERT C. BOURNE contributed a paper on "The Post-embryonic Development of Fungiæ." The budding and separation undergone by these corals is suggestive of an alternation of generations.

SELBORNE SOCIETY, FERNS BRANCH.

We are glad to learn that a branch of the Selborne Society has been formed at Ferns, Co. Wexford, under the presidency of Dr. G. E. J. Greene; Miss M. Kenny is the Honorary Secretary and Treasurer. The new society intends to devote itself especially to the study of Natural History; we heartily wish it success, and hope to record the results of its work.

NOTES.

BOTANY.

Earliness of the Season.—I found the Dingle mountains covered with *Pinguicula grandiflora*, on Whit Monday, May 22nd. I also found wild Strawberries ripe on the same day.—ERNEST H. BENNIS, Limerick.

On June 9th, *Meconopsis cambrica* was in splendid bloom on the Comeragh mountains. I also found *Hymenophyllum tunbridgense* in fruit. *Sedium rhodiola* was not in bloom.—J. ERNEST GRUBB, Carrick-on-Suir.

The Royal Forest of Glencree.—At a meeting of the Royal Society of Antiquaries, recently held in Kilkenny, Mr. Mills read a paper on this subject which had been prepared by Mr. T. P. Lefanue, B.A. From it we learn that as early as the 11th century Irish Oak was known, as would be seen by the request of William Rufus for Irish Oak for Westminster Hall.

As soon as the English had obtained a firm footing in the country a Royal forest was started, and the portion of the country more especially set apart was the valley of Glencree.

In 1244 eighty deer were sent over from the Royal Park at Chester, and the existence of some kind of enclosure was evident. That the deer were watched was plain from the fact that in 1291 a neighbouring abbot was attacked and accused of taking game with "nets and engines," and with "taking beasts and working his will with them to the injury of our Lord the King." From the foregoing springs the question: what kind of deer were introduced? the Fallow Deer seems not to have been introduced into England at the above date, so we must conclude that Red Deer were sent; that they were very numerous in this country at a very early date, is proved by the frequent "finds" of their bones in large quantities.—J. G. ROBERTSON, Dublin.

ZOOLOGY.

INSECTS.

Irish Wasps—Vespa arborea, Sm. at Bray.—Mr. R. M. Barrington kindly sent me during May and June a number of queen wasps taken near Bray. The vast majority proved to be *Vespa vulgaris;* there were also twelve specimens of *V. rufa*, seven of *V. norvegica*, one of *V. sylvestris*, and three of that very scarce form *V. arborea*, which has hitherto been recorded only from Yorkshire, Gloucestershire, Scotland, and Switzerland. My identification has been kindly confirmed by Mr. E. Saunders, who, however, informs me, that he considers it possible that this wasp may be merely an aberration from one of the other species; its male and worker are at present unknown.

Edgeworth in his paper on "Irish Vespidæ" (*Proc. N. H. S. Dub.* vol. iii. 1864), records *V. germanica*, so that we now know all the British species of the family in Ireland, except the Hornet (*V. crabro*), which in all probability will not be found here.—G. H. CARPENTER.

Timarcha tenebricosa, Fab. in Co. Waterford.—While on a visit to Mr. R. J. Ussher, I had the good fortune to secure a series of this interesting chrysomelid beetle, hitherto unrecorded from Ireland, though it has been taken by Mr. G. Garnett of the Newtown School, near Waterford. The specimens were taken on sea-cliffs near Stradbally. In Great Britain this species is, I believe, restricted to the southern counties. Irish coleopterists may expect some interesting discoveries when the south coast has been systematically worked.—H. LYSTER JAMESON, Killencoole, Co. Louth.

MOLLUSCA.

Additions to the Shell-fauna of Cork.—Judging from Dr. Scharff's useful and interesting list of Irish Land and Freshwater Mollusca (*I. N.* vol. i) the records of additional species from this district since the publication of Mr. Humphrey's list in 1843, must be few and far between. I, therefore, record the following species, taken by myself during the past year within a radius of twenty miles from Cork city, none of which were included by Mr. Humphrey's in his enumeration of fifty-nine species:—*Hyalinia draparnaudi* occurs in my own and other gardens. I had taken it to be a large form of *H. cellaria*, until, on my sending a specimen to Dr. Scharff, he identified it at once as *H. draparnaudi*. *H. pura, H. crystallina*, and *H. fulva*, are plentiful in the woods at Glanmire. *H. nitida* occurs in a marsh at Whitegate. *H. alliaria* var. *viridula* occurs in some plenty near Roche's Point, at which station the type seems to be absent. *Helix pygmæa* and *H. aculeata* are frequent in the neighbourhoods of Whitegate and Glanmire. *Vertigo pygmæa*. at Roche's Point, Cork Beg, and Ovens. *V. antivertigo*, in a marsh at Whitegate. (*V. angustior* and *Succinea oblonga* have both been recorded from the south of the county). *Carychium minimum* is abundant in woods and marshes. *Limnæa auricularia* was recorded doubtfully by Mr. Humphreys; my specimens, taken from the lough of Cork, have been verified by Dr. Scharff. *Planorbis crista* occurs in Bennett's lough, near Mayfield, and in streams in Cork Park, along with *Valvata cristata* already recorded (*I. N.*, vol. ii., p. 112). The variety *alba* of *Acme lineata* seems as plentiful in Lota wood, Glanmire, as the type. I hope, later on, when time permits me to study our slugs and bivalves, to make at least a few other additions to our local list.—R. A. PHILLIPS, Ashburton, Cork.

Testacella scutulum, Sow.—Mr. W. F. de V. Kane has recently discovered this rare species in his garden at Kingstown. This is the first record for the County Dublin, and the third for Ireland, it having previously been found in Louth and Waterford. Mr. Kane mentioned to me that he had also found specimens of a *Testacella* in Drumcaske demesne, Co. Monaghan, but he was not sure what species it belonged to.—R. F. SCHARFF, Dublin.

FISHES.

Basking-Shark (Selache maxima) on the Sligo Coast.— On the 5th inst. a splendid specimen of the Basking-Shark became entangled in the salmon-net of Mr. Kilgallan, at Aughriss, Co. Sligo, a short distance off the pier, and after a desperate struggle, in which it caused great damage to the net and ropes, was, by the united efforts of four boats, turned into shallow water on the sandy beach, where it was killed. The great fish was evidently full-grown, for it measured thirty feet in length.—ROBERT WARREN, Moyview, Ballina.

BIRDS.

Continental White Wagtail (Motacilla alba) in Co. Mayo.— On the 29th of April, when on the Island of Bartragh, Killala Bay, with Mr. H. Scroope, Junior, and his brother, we observed a Wagtail, having such a large patch of white on the sides of its neck and throat as to attract our attention, and on a nearer approach, the light grey back proved it to be the rare *Motacilla alba*. It flew off and joined another some yards distance, and having my gun, I secured one, which proved to be a fine adult male in perfect plumage.

Mr. H. Scroope, who visited Downpatrick Head a few days after, saw another bird near the ruins on the Head.— ROBERT WARREN. Moyview, Ballina.

Our Summer Migrants. —Rev. R. M. Miller kindly sends us a copy of an interesting and popular article, on our summer migrants, which he contributed to the *Clonmel Chronicle* for May 20th. Such attractive expositions of natural history should do good work, by increasing the number of those who know something of the feathered denizens of our woods and hedgerows, and therefore find pleasure in observing and protecting them.

Spring Migrants at Londonderry.—The very fine spring brought many of the migrants some days earlier than their usual dates. The earliest to reach us was the Chiffchaff, which was first heard on 26th March. Then the Willow-Wren appeared on 3rd April. The first Swallow was seen here on 5th April, although I did not notice them in any numbers until some ten days later. A few Sandmartins arrived on 4th April, and I noticed them in great numbers on the 6th, at one locality. The Wheatear was first seen at Inch on 9th April; I saw and heard the Whitethroat on 23rd April, and I heard the Sedgewarbler on same date. The Cuckoo appeared on 19th April, and I heard the Corncrake for the first time on the 20th April, but it was reported to have arrived here on 14th. The Swift arrived a week before its usual time. I saw a large flock of about thirty hawking over Derry quay on 5th May. Almost all these arrivals are earlier than last year's dates. The Cuckoo was very scarce here last year, not more than a quarter seemingly of the usual number reaching us. This season it is more than usually abundant.— D. C. CAMPBELL, Londonderry.

Arrival of Spring Migrants.—Seeing some notices in last month's *I. N.* of the early arrival of spring migrants, I wish to record that the Cuckoo was heard at Giants' Causeway on Easter Sunday, 2nd April, which seems to be exceptionally early for this bird. In Wm. Thompson's "Natural History of Ireland" the earliest mention of the arrival of the Cuckoo seems to be the 10th April. I saw the first Swallow this season on 5th April in Co. Derry.—ARTHUR J. COLLINS, Belfast.

On 24th April, the Night Jar (*Caprimulgus europæus*) was heard, *much earlier than usual;* it is abundant in this neighbourhood upon the hills, and can be heard before sunset simultaneously with the Thrush, Blackbird, Cuckoo, etc.—J. ERNEST GRUBB, Carrick-on-Suir.

Occurrence of the Osprey (Pandion haliæetus, L.) and the Quail (Coturnix communis, Bechst.) in Co. Cork.—Mr. Rohu, taxidermist, Cork, has now in his hands for preservation a fine immature female specimen of the Osprey, shot at Old Dromore, Co. Cork, on the 11th May; also an adult female specimen of the Quail, shot at Trabulgan, County Cork, on the 7th May.—W. B. BARRINGTON, Cork.

Quails in County Dublin.—On the 6th June my heart was gladdened by hearing the well-known note of a bird which I had not heard in a state of liberty for several years. I refer to the call of the Quail. In recording the arrival of this bird, I bear in mind the possibility that the birds which I heard may have been imported and liberated in the neighbourhood. Of course there must always be this element of doubt in recording the occurrence of a bird which is annually imported in large numbers by game-dealers. I have made careful inquiries in the neighbourhood, however, and have failed to obtain any evidence of birds having been liberated, and, having regard to the number of birds that may be heard calling in districts far apart, I have arrived at the conclusion that a true migration of Quail has occurred. It is well known that these birds were obtained in several parts of England last year, and I have good authority for stating that some were obtained in the County Wicklow at the same time. On looking up old shooting diaries, I find I shot my last Quail in the year 1876, which is probably the last year they were with us. I trust that after this long absence from our shores, they will be protected by both naturalists and sportsmen.—J. J. DOWLING, Foxrock.

Re-appearance of Quails near Londonderry.—After an absence of many years the Quails have visited us once more. They have been calling all over this district for the last ten days, and Mr. John McConnell reports them also from Inch. So far as I know, they have not been seen or heard for upwards of twelve years, except in July, 1892, when Mr. Milne heard the call-note once. I have not heard of their breeding in this neighbourhood since 1874. In that year we obtained eggs from two nests. I believe they are nesting with us this year.—D. C. CAMPBELL, Londonderry.

Stock Doves (Columba ænas) in Co. Wicklow.—Mr. E. C. Barrington writes (*Zoologist* for May) that he has observed a pair of Stock Doves among some rocks about six miles south of Powerscourt Waterfall, presumably nesting. We are glad to know than these birds are maintaining their ground in Co. Wicklow.

Supposed Iceland Gull at Londonderry.—From Mr. D. C. Campbell's description of the gull, seen by him on the 11th April, the bird was evidently a Glaucous Gull. He says "about the size of a large Herring Gull, but body heavier." The Iceland is altogether a larger-winged, *lighter-built* bird than the Herring Gull, and when seen together the difference of build is very obvious. The legs of the Glaucous and Iceland are the colour of those of the Herring Gulls.—ROBERT WARREN, Moyview, Ballina.

The Puffin (Fratercula arctica) in the Irish Midlands.—On Monday evening, the 22nd May, a lad brought me a living specimen of the Common Puffin, which he said had walked into a cottage beside a lake close to this demesne, called Quig lough, and though tame enough in its demeanour, it would not eat the food offered. They had kept it for some thirty hours before they decided to bring it to me; unfortunately before I could get any small fish it died. I have sent it up to the Dublin Museum, as it is a remarkable instance, I think, of a sea-bird so far inland. I presume it was making for its breeding haunts.—W. F. DE V. KANE, Drumreaske, Monaghan.

Chionis alba, Lath.—I am interested to see a paper in the June number of the *Irish Naturalist* on the occurrence of *Chionis alba* on the Irish coast, as I had an opportunity of witnessing the bird in its native haunts in the Straits of Magellan, between twenty and thirty years ago, and I published a short paper on some points in its anatomy in the "Journal of Anatomy and Physiology" for 1869. The flight of the bird, as I saw it, was not unlike that of a pigeon, and the Blue-jackets, the first time we encountered it, mistook it, not unnaturally, for a pigeon. Like some other observers who have handled specimens, I did not observe anything peculiar as regards its odour. The capture of a specimen on the coast of Ireland is certainly a very odd circumstance, and I cannot but think that the individual must have escaped from captivity somewhere.—ROBERT O. CUNNINGHAM, Belfast.

MAMMALS.

A Marten (Mustela martes) in Co. Antrim. A few days ago a fine specimen was trapped near Portglenone, Co. Antrim, by Mr. R. A. Alexander. The specimen is a male, and measures 2ft. 9in. in length. The "Marten Cat" as it is popularly called, is getting so rare in Ulster that the capture is worthy of record.—J. A. B. in *Land and Water*, April 22nd.

AMERICAN BIRD-VISITORS TO IRELAND AT HOME.

BY W. E. PRAEGER, OF KEOKUK, IOWA.

III. THE YELLOW-BILLED CUCKOO (*Goccyzus americanus*).

LONG will my first spring in America be the best remembered of springs to me. I had spent the winter in Iowa, an unusually severe and long-continued winter, and at last the hot sun had melted the snow, and the thick ice on pond and river had broken up, and rapidly the lately silent land was filled with sights and sounds, to me new and strange. And so, week after week it continued; daily new flowers, insects, and reptiles sprang into life again, while from the south the great stream of migration brought the birds in ever increasing number and variety. It can well be imagined what surfeit of surprise, wonder, and interest, the shortest country walk afforded under such circumstances.

Perhaps the most noticeable sound to me was a note heard in the woods and resembling the word "cow," often repeated, at first rather slowly, gradually getting quicker, but the last three or four notes suddenly becoming longer drawn out than any of the preceding ones. It sounded as if it might be the note of some gallinaceous bird, but it was no more like any bird's note that I had ever heard, than were those of many of the insects and frogs that made the woods resound with their extraordinary spring love-songs; and indeed I have since read that the note in question is very similar to that of the Burrowing Owl of the western prairies, and also of the Spade-footed Toad. After awhile I caught occasional glimpses of the mysterious originator of the sounds, and was told that they

A

were the notes of the "Raincrow," but this did not enlighten me much until I shot one of the birds from the upper branches of a tall hickory tree, and picked up what I easily recognised to be a Yellow-billed Cuckoo.

The right of the Yellow-billed Cuckoo to a place on the Irish list rests on the occurrence of two examples shot many years ago, in Co. Cork and Co. Dublin. The bird has also occurred four or five times in England, and also in Continental Europe, so that we have an unusual number of instances of this American bird crossing the Atlantic.

This bird's breeding range is the United States; it hardly passes north of the Canadian boundary line, and is found from ocean to ocean, though rather scarce west of the Rocky mountains. It probably leaves this country altogether in winter, and comes north in the spring after the trees are in full leaf, arriving in this latitude during the first week of May. Like the European Cuckoo, its presence is chiefly known by its note, for the bird is very shy, and manages to conceal itself among the densest foliage of the larger trees; but wherever there are trees, it is sure to be found, even round farm-houses, or in the city parks, or tree-lined streets. Looking at the stuffed skin in a cabinet, one can hardly believe how inconspicuous the bird is in its native haunts. The long slender build and brown colour make it look like one of the many branches with which it is surrounded, and seen from below, the white breast and spots on the tail feathers become mere glints of sunlight among the foliage. Not infrequently, after the observer has been peering into a tree in search of some noisy warbler in the upper branches, a slight movement will betray to him a "Raincrow" close at hand, and the bird will likely remain, with unusual composure for one that can boast of a stature of over twelve inches, and give plenty of time for mutual observation. It is always more secretive than shy; a proof that it knows its colours are protective.

The Yellow-billed Cuckoo builds its nest in a bush or low tree; it is a slight affair of sticks, not well made nor concealed with much art. The eggs are from four to six, rarely eight in number, and of a pale greenish-blue. They are usually laid in June, but oviposition is curiously irregular, eggs in all stages of incubation, and even young birds in various stages of development, being often found in the same nest. A satisfactory reason for this habit seems unknown as yet, as with the still more curious parasitic habits of many of the Old World Cuckoos, with which it has probably some connection. Though not parasites, there seem to be well authenticated instances of an egg of the American Cuckoo being slipped into the nest of some other bird. During the nesting season, both birds are very solicitous as to the safety of the nest, and in caring for the young.

The favourite food of this bird seems to be caterpillars, and most stomachs I have examined were well filled with them; it also eats other insects, and may sometimes be seen on the ground picking up grasshoppers; in the fall it occasionally indulges in fruit, and berries of various kinds. It has been accused of robbing other birds' nests, but whether with any more justice than in the case of *Cuculus canorus* I do not know.

The common name for both our species of Cuckoo is "Rain-crow" because their call is said to foretell rain; such widespread popular beliefs are apt to have a basis of truth, but the call is heard during dry weather as well as wet, and the mating season, when they are most noisy, is also the most showery time of year. From the call, the name "Cowbird," is sometimes given to them, but they must not be confused with the true Cowbird, a member of the American family *Icteridæ*, and which is, I believe, the only bird besides some of the cuckoos that is known to be parasitic in its habits.

Above, this bird is a bright olive-brown, with a peculiar satiny gloss showing a greenish tinge in some lights; below, pure white, excepting the two central feathers, which are like the back. The tail becomes almost black, with broad white tips; the wings have a patch of light chestnut, not very noticeable till the wing is opened; the bill is yellow at the base and below.

IV. THE BLACK-BILLED CUCKOO (*Coccyzus erythrophthalmus*).

THE Black-billed Cuckoo introduced himself to the fauna of Europe by turning up at Lucca, Italy, in 1858. On only one other occasion has his name appeared as a visitor to Europe, when he claimed for himself the right to an article in his honor in the *Irish Naturalist*, by appearing at Killead, Co. Antrim, on the 25th September, 1871.

After what has been said above on the Yellow-billed Cuckoo, our present subject can be dismissed with comparatively few words. The two species are so alike in appearance and habits that to point out some of the differences is all that will be necessary. The birds are commonly confused by unscientific observers, and cannot be distinguished except at very close quarters. The subject of the present sketch is rather the smaller of the two, he lacks the chestnut on the wings, and the black and white of the lateral tail feathers is restricted and obscure, with no bold contrasts between the colours; the bill is plumbeous and black, instead of yellow and black; the eyelids are red, hence the unwieldy specific name. Otherwise the plumage of the two birds is alike, so that when the wings and tail are closed one has to be near enough to distinguish the colour of the bill or eyelid to be certain as to the species.

In nesting habits the same close relationship is noticeable. The nest is similar, but the Black-billed more frequently builds in low situations, such as bushes. The eggs can usually, but not always, be distinguished with certainty; they are smaller, rounder, and deeper-coloured than the Yellow-billed's eggs. For comparison we give the measurements of eggs of the two species:—*C. americanus*, length 1.10 to 1.40, breadth .83 to .98, *C. erythrophthalmus*, length, 1.05 to 1.15, breadth .80 to .90. The same irregularity as to time of laying is noticed in both species.

The cry of this bird is said to be less harsh and not so often repeated as that of its near relative. Its habits, such as flight, movements, food, time, and rapidity of migration, and localities it most frequents, are very similar. There is, however, a decided difference in geographical distribution, the Black-billed being found only east of the Rocky mountains; but what it lacks in longitude it gains in latitude, as it ranges up into even Labrador, and is the only species found through most of the British possessions.

There is certainly a great absurdity in admitting a bird that has only once occurred in Ireland as a straggler, to the Irish list. While the occurrence is highly interesting, yet the inclusion of such names in a fauna are confusing and misleading. Two species of the genus *Coccyzus* are in the Irish list, and the same two in the Iowa list, and yet to say that the genus *does* occur in Iowa, and *does not* in Ireland is nearer the truth.

But absurd as the rule may be that entitles a bird once captured in a supposed wild state to a place in the fauna of the country, it seems to be the only rule that is workable. No two ornithologists would quite agree as to how often and under what circumstances a bird must occur to be admitted into the exclusive circle. And the probability of a bird being aided by resting on ships should not affect its standing, even if it could be proved that it did so. A favourite way of accounting for the present distribution of reptiles is that they or their eggs were carried to distant lands in hollow logs; and what is your Atlantic liner but a hollow log somewhat developed and specialized. It is useless for naturalists to make laws as to the means and methods which organisms are to use in spreading their species on the face of the earth, and we might speculate long and uselessly on what great results might spring from such accidental wanderings, and how they might affect the fauna or flora of a country, with all its sensitive interdependence. What small fortuitous occurrences often produce great results, and how little the means that brought them about matter. Is Ireland any less the land of saints because St. Patrick sailed over on a paving stone?

THE SHAMROCK: A FURTHER ATTEMPT TO FIX ITS SPECIES.

BY NATHANIEL COLGAN.

On the approach of last Saint Patrick's Day I was induced, chiefly by the kind offer of assistance made me by the editors of this Journal, to take in hands once more the inquiry into the species of our national badge, begun some years earlier, with the results detailed in the issue for last August. A notice to subscribers was accordingly inserted in the March number of this year, so framed as to ensure that all specimens sent in response should be certified as genuine by competent authorities, while, at the same time, as a provision against a not improbable lack of interest in the subject amongst the subscribers to the *Irish Naturalist*, some three dozens of circulars were prepared and sent by post to selected points in the Irish-speaking districts, chiefly along our western sea-board. These circulars, in almost all instances, were addressed to Roman Catholic parish clergymen; and, as I had fully expected, the percentage of replies they brought me was very much larger than in the case of the printed notice.[1] Of the circulars, twenty per cent. were answered, a proportion not far short of expectation. As for the printed notice distributed through the agency of the *Irish Naturalist*, I cannot presume to say exactly how small the percentage of answers may have been. Out of the whole body of subscribers, however, only eight forwarded specimens of Shamrocks; but, of these, one sent no less than five, another, four, and a third, three specimens, each certified as genuine by a distinct authority.

In addition to the plants thus secured, Mr. F. W. Burbidge, Director of Trinity College Botanic Garden, supplied me with a root, certified by one of his gardeners, a Tipperary man, as the real Shamrock, and part of the stock grown in the Gardens, and supplied as such to English inquirers; another specimen was bought from an advertiser in the Co. Louth, who offered the plant for sale, at a not unprofitable price, "as the true Irish variety," and, finally, three specimens were bought in Dublin on the 17th March as real Shamrock, from three different itinerant vendors, each of whom was required to exercise the most scrupulous care in the selection of the genuine plant from the obviously miscellaneous collection in her basket.[2]

Altogether, thirty-five Shamrocks were secured and carefully planted and labelled, after they had been provisionally

---

[1] I wish to express my thanks here to the following correspondents for their kindness in sending specimens from their respective districts:—Rev. T. O'Connor, Kilrosanty, Waterford (three plants); Rev. T. McGrath, Clogheen, Tipperary; Rev. P. MacPhilpin, Aranmore, Galway bay; Rev. P. Brennan, Corrigaholt, Clare; Rev. P. O'Keane, Easky, Sligo; Rev. P. Kelly, Ardara, Donegal (two plants); Mr. Michael Costello, Inisheer, Galway bay (two plants); Miss A. N. Abbott, Cork (three plants); Mrs. Delap, Valencia island, Kerry; Miss Garner, Dublin; Miss Kinahan, Dublin (plant from Ramelton, Donegal); Mrs. Leebody, Londonderry (four plants from counties Donegal, Derry, and Tyrone); Mr. A. J. Collins, Belfast; Mr. M. Comerford, Dundalk; Mr. T. Hunter, Ovoca, Wicklow (five plants); Mr. Owen Smith, Meath; and Mr. J. J. Wolfe, Skibbereen, Cork.

[2] These three plants matured into three distinct species, *Medicago lupulina*, *Trifolium repens*, and *T. minus*.

classified according to species. A study of the minuter distinctions of *Trifolium repens*, *T. minus* and *Medicago lupulina*, made it possible to carry out the classification with confidence even in the undeveloped stage in which most of the specimens reached me. In no single instance, indeed, in which the plant survived up to the flowering and fruiting season, (and only two out of the total of thirty-five succumbed to the extraordinary dryness of the remarkable spring and early summer of this year), was this provisional classification found in error; so that my Patrick's Day determination of these two as *T. repens* and *T. minus*, respectively, may be accepted as accurate.¹ Of the surviving thirty-three plants, all had flowered and many had fruited by the 23rd June, *T. minus* in all cases keeping well ahead of *T. repens*. By the end of June the entire crop of Shamrocks, or, at least, specimens of the thirty-three plants of which it was made up, was harvested and garnered, that is to say, dried, mounted, and labelled, for the satisfaction of obstinate adherents of *Trifolium repens*.

The results of this harvest may be most clearly shown in tabular form, thus :—

19 Shamrocks matured into *Trifolium repens*.
12   ,,   ,,   ,,   *T. minus*.
2   ,,   ,,   ,,   *T. pratense*.
2   ,,   ,,   ,,   *Medicago lupulina*.

It will be seen that the results of this year's inquiry shows, contrary to my expectation, a decided preponderance in favour of *T. repens*. But if we add in the results of the former inquiry, the balance between the two species is almost redressed. Out of a total of forty-nine certified Shamrocks grown on the two occasions, twenty-four proved to be *Trifolium repens*, and twenty-one *T. minus*, the remainder being equally divided between *T. pratense* and *Medicago lupulina*. Arranging the Shamrocks by counties so as to exhibit the area over which the use of the different species was found to prevail, we have the following table :—

¹ In the earlier stages of growth, the mucro to the leaflets of *Medicago lupulina* seems to me to afford the safest and readiest distinction between that species and *T. minus* and *T. repens*. There is little difficulty at any stage in separating *T. pratense* from the three other competitors.

C

TABLE SHOWING THE SPECIES OF SHAMROCK USED IN VARIOUS IRISH COUNTIES.

Trifolium repens is used in	*T. minus* is used in	*T. pratense* is used in	*Medicago lupulina* is used in
Armagh.	Armagh.		
Carlow.	Carlow.		Cork.
Cork.	Cork.		
Derry.	Derry.		Dublin.
Dublin.	Dublin.		
Galway.	Galway.		
Waterford.	Waterford.	Waterford.	
Wicklow.	Wicklow.	Wicklow.	
Antrim.	Clare.		
Tyrone.	Louth.		
Kerry.	Tipperary.		
Donegal.	Queen's Co.		
Meath.	Waterford.		
Sligo.			
Roscommon.			
Mayo.			

Here again the employment of *T. repens* as the national badge would appear to be more extended than that of *T. minus*, the former being used in sixteen, the latter only in thirteen of the Irish counties. But there is further evidence forthcoming on the side of *T. minus*; for Mr. James Britten, editor of the *Journal of Botany*, gives the following strong testimony in its favour, in a valuable note on the Shamrock in the *Dictionary of English Plant Names* (p. 425).[1]

"At the present day, *Trifolium minus* is the plant most in repute as the true Shamrock; it is this species which forms most of the Shamrock sold in Covent Garden on St. Patrick's Day, and in Ireland it is used as such in the counties of Antrim, Down, Meath, Fermanagh, Dublin, Wicklow, Carlow, Westmeath, Wexford, Limerick, Waterford, Cork, and Kerry."

When entering on this inquiry some five years ago, I was quite unaware of the existence of this interesting contribution to the subject, which only came under my notice so late as the April of this year. Had I known of these previous researches, by which the results recorded in these pages were so largely anticipated, I should probably have thought it unneces-

---

[1] Published by Trübner & Co. (for the English Dialect Society), London, 1886. All who are interested in the obscure history of the Shamrock are strongly recommended to read Mr. Britten's note, which gives, in condensed form, the fruit of much antiquarian research.

sary to make further investigation, so that my ignorance of Mr. Britten's paper has had the result of strengthening the case for *T. minus*, which, as I believe, he was the first to make out. Though Mr. Britten does not tell us that *T. minus* is exclusively used as the Shamrock in the thirteen counties covered by his inquiry, the evidence he has brought forward, coupled with that given in these pages, fully warrants, in my opinion, the conclusion that *T. repens* can no longer claim pre-eminence as the true Irish Shamrock.[1] It must hereafter be content to share the honour, at least evenly, with its rival *T. minus*. Future writers and editors of English and Irish Floras, if they aim at accuracy in their popular plant-names, must bracket these two species of *Trifolium* under the name Shamrock and must give, too, to Mr. Britten the credit of having been the first to clearly discern and boldly advocate the strong claims of *T. minus*.

While conceding that in the present day the neater *Trifolium minus* is equally in favour with *T. repens* as our national badge, some may be disposed to argue that the true Shamrock of earlier times, before modern culture had spread abroad a taste for the elegant and the delicate, was, nevertheless, the coarser *T. repens*. The fact that a decided majority of the specimens collected by me from the Irish-speaking districts of our island, where old national usages may be assumed to have the greatest tenacity of existence, belonged to this latter species, might be taken as lending a certain support to this view. But the discussion of such antiquarian aspects of the question, however fascinating it might be as opening up wide fields of speculation and inquiry, cannot properly find a place in the pages of a natural history Journal. I must content myself, then, with this endeavour to place clearly before those interested in the subject the available evidence as to the species of the modern Shamrock, leaving it to others, who may feel dissatisfied with the mass and tendency of this evidence, to pursue the inquiry still further on the lines laid down.[2]

[1] There is no reason why the name should not be written *shamroge*, as it is pronounced by Irishmen, and written by many of the earlier English writers.

[2] Taken together, Mr. Britten's inquiry and my own have covered twenty-five out of thirty-two Irish counties. The following counties still remain outside the inquiry:—Cavan, Kildare, Kilkenny, King's County, Leitrim, Longford, and Monaghan.

THE FLORA OF COUNTY ARMAGH.

BY R. LLOYD PRAEGER, B.E., M.R.I.A.

(*Concluded from page* 184.)

Milium effusum, Linn. N. — S.
Killooney near Armagh, W. F. J. spec.! Ivy Lodge near Newry, H. W. L. spec.!

Calamagrostis hookeri, Syme. N. — —
Abundant in a low meadow by the side of Lough Neagh, near the entrance of the Lagan canal, R. Ll. P. The plant grows plentifully here, over an area of perhaps a couple of acres, among *Lythrum, Lysimachia vulgaris,* and *Phragmites;* in a space of a few square yards I gathered 200 stems. Considering its very limited distribution, which in Great Britain is confined to Lough Neagh, its disappearance in some of its stations there, and its extreme rarity in the others, the discovery of a new locality in which it is abundant cannot but be highly satisfactory. More's note (*N. H. R.*) refers, as stated in *Recent Additions* (*Jour. Bot.,* 1873) to Scawdy island, in Tyrone; the plant has not been previously found in Armagh.

Agrostis vulgaris, With., var. **pumila,** Lightf. — — S.
Dry field at Cam Lough, and on G. N. railway south of Newry, R. Ll. P.

A. alba, Linn., var. **stolonifera.** — — S.
Muddy shores of Newry river, R. Ll. P.

Aira flexuosa, Linn. — — S.
Frequent on the southern hills; not observed elsewhere in the county, R. Ll. P.

Trisetum flavescens, Beauv. N. — —
A member of "the natural herbage of the soil," *Coote's Armagh.* Mullinure, W. F. J. spec.! Armagh, S. A. S. Lurgan, Portadown, Retreat, Navan Fort, and Eglish, being frequent in the limestone district, R. Ll. P.

Avena pubescens, Linn. N. — —
Quarries at Navan fort, R. Ll. P.

Poa compressa, Linn. N. — —
Bank by roadside, half a mile from Portadown towards Lurgan (McMillan), More's *Recent Additions* (*Jour. of Bot.,* 1873).

Schlerochloa maritima, Lindl. — — S.
Estuary of Newry river, R. Ll. P.

S. distans, Bab. — — S.
Shore near Narrow-water, R. Ll. P.

S. rigida, Linn. N. M. S.
Gravel-pit east of Grange near Armagh; on the Armagh and Goraghwood railway south of Drumnanmore lough, and near Loughgilly; abundant on the G.N. main line and walls adjoining at and north of Wellington cutting near Newry; wall of the platform at Goraghwood station, R. Ll. P. Frequent in Armagh, growing chiefly on railway tracks, where no doubt the dry gravelly material is the attraction. It is extremely rare in district 12, common in district 5.

Briza media, Linn. N. — —
Loughgall (More), *Flor. Ulst.*! and subsequently, B. N. F. C., S.A. S., etc. Mullinure, W. F. J. spec.! Navan fort, S. A. S.! Loughnashade, Eglish church, Killylea, Middletown, roadside south of Armagh, R. Ll. P. Frequent in the limestone district; not met with elsewhere.

Catabrosa aquatica, Beauv.   N. M. S.
 Tanderagee lower demesne, and by the canal near Newry! H.W.L.; by the railway between Lurgan and Portadown; Eglish crossroads; ditch near Clare Castle S.W. of Tanderagee; Straghan's lough near Keady, R. Ll. P.

Festuca sylvatica, Vill.   — M. —
 On steep banks by the Cusher river in Tanderagee lower demesne, R. Ll. P.

Bromus sterilis, Linn.   N — —
 Loughgall (More) *Flor. Ulst.*! Roadside near Navan Fort, R. Ll. P.

‡**B. commutatus,** Schrad.   N. — —
 Tartaraghan, probably introduced with grass-seed, More *N.II.R.* Mullinure meadows near Armagh, W. F. J. spec.!

Triticum caninum, Linn.   — M. —
 By Mullaghmore lake S. W. of Markethill; rare in the county, R. Ll. P.

Hordeum pratense, Hudson.   N. — —
 Mr. Stewart's herbarium contains specimens of this rare grass, collected by G. R. at Tartaraghan in 1880.

Lepturus filiformis, Trin.   — — S.
 By the canal locks below Newry, and on the shore abundantly at County bridge near Narrow-water, R. Ll. P.

Polypodium phegopteris, Linn.   — — S.
 Frequent on the N.E. slope of Slieve Gullion (Lett), *Ferns of Ulster* (B. N. F. C. 1885-6, App.) Mr. Lett informs me that it was in the woods near Killeavy church that he found the Beech Fern; I did not meet with it on the north or west slopes of Slieve Gullion.

Lastrea oreopteris, Presl.   — M. S.
 On Ferry Hill above Narrow-water (R. Ll. P.), *Ferns of Ulster;* I found it in the woods there in 1881, and saw it again in 1892. One fine plant in a wood in Tanderagee upper demesne, R. Ll. P.

L. æmula, Brack.   — — S.
 Plentiful on Ferry Hill above Narrow-water (R. Ll. P.), *Ferns of Ulster.*

Polystichum aculeatum, Roth.   N. M. S.
 Near Loughgall, but rare, More *N. II. R.*! On Ferry Hill above Narrow-water (R. Ll. P.), and near Tynan (Phillips), *Ferns of Ulster.* Near Armagh, W. F. J. spec.! Castlecrow near Loughgall, roadside at Beech Hill House near Armagh, Eglish cross-roads, lanes near Tartaraghan church, lanes east of Tynan, Marlacoo lough, and near Pointzpass, R. Ll. P.

Cystopteris fragilis, Bernh.   N. — —
 Bridge near Armagh (McCrum), *Ferns of Ulster.* Recently seen on the bridge in question, which is at Tassagh near Keady, by W. F. J.

Ceterach officinarum, Willd.   N. — S.
 Wall of Lurgan demesne, and near Bessbrook (Lett), *Ferns of Ulster.* Ballynahone House garden wall, and on the walls of Armagh observatory, courthouse, and gaol, W. F. J. spec.! Bridge over Ulster canal two miles north of Caledon, R. Ll. P.

Hymenophyllum tunbridgense, Sm.   — — S.
 In a glen on Ferry Hill above Narrow-water (R. Ll. P.), *Ferns of Ulster.* Found there in 1881, and refound in 1892. The stream on whose banks it grows forms the boundary of Armagh and Louth, and the record strictly belongs to districts 10 and 5.

Osmunda regalis, Linn. N. — —
"The Rev. G. Robinson showed me what might be called a small forest of this fine plant, not far from Maghery, where it forms large *tussacs*, like those of *Carex paniculata;* drainage is, however, gradually destroying it" (Dickie), *Flor. Ulst.* Bog at south end of Lough Neagh (Templeton), *Ferns of Ulster.* Near Maghery, B. N. F. C., 1871. "Near Tartaraghan, Rev. G. Robinson!!!" More *N.H.R.* Not now anywhere so abundant or luxuriant as described by Dr. Dickie, but still frequent on the northern bogs: I found it in a number of places on bogs from Maghery to Lurgan, and also thrown up by the waves on the shores of Annagarriff lake, where it evidently flourishes in security on the islands; also on a bog south of Portadown; often in some abundance, but generally rather stunted, R. Ll. P.

Botrychium lunaria, Sw. N. — —
One plant on top of Navan fort, W. F. J.: I have not seen Mr. Johnson's specimen, which was not preserved, but he is satisfied that it was right: I failed to refind it at Navan, R. Ll. P. Shore of Lough Neagh at Ardmore, H. W. L. spec.!

Ophioglossum vulgatum, Linn. N. — —
Loughgall near the lake, More *N. H. R.*! Armagh (Kinahan), *Flor. Ulst.* Ardmore near Lurgan; abundant in short grass on the shores of Lough Neagh, where it is under water for four winter months (Lett), *Ferns of Ulster.* Tartaraghan, B. N. F. C., 1877. Mullinure and Drumnanmore near Armagh, W. F. J. spec.! Bird island on Lough Neagh shore, R. Ll. P.

Isoetes lacustris, Linn. — M. S.
County Armagh, *Cyb. Hib.* In Cashel lake west of Slieve Gullion (444 feet elevation); and at the west end of Lough Ross near Crossmaglen (286 feet), and on east shore of Mullaghmore lough (200 feet elevation), June, 1893, R. Ll. P.

Lycopodium selago, Linn. N. M. S.
Very rare; one plant on bog north of Churchhill (under 100 feet); summit of Carrigatuke (1,200); and sparingly on Camlough mountain, R. Ll. P.

Selaginella spinosa, Beauv. — — S.
On Camlough mountain at about 700 to 1,000 feet, R. Ll. P.

(Pilularia globulifera, Linn. [N.] — —
Abundant in marshy ground two miles from the mouth of the Blackwater, near Lough Neagh (Campbell), *Flor. Hib.* and *Flor. Ulst.* This station may be in Armagh, or in Tyrone, but is not in district 12, as given in *Cyb. Hib.* I did not meet with the plant, and it is apparently one of these which the drainage of Lough Neagh has forced from its former habitats.)

Chara fragilis, Desv. N. — —
Lough Neagh at Ardmore Glebe (f. *delicatula*) and Bird island, H.W.L. spec! In Lough Neagh at Ardmore Point (form approaching *delicatula*), and at Maghery; pool beside Derrylileagh lake; lake at Tynan Abbey; and bog-holes south of Portadown (form with prominent primary cortical cells), R. Ll. P.

C. aspera, Willd. N. — —
In Lough Neagh at Derryadd Bay; Ardmore Point (f. *lacustris*), and Maghery (f. *subinermis*); quarries near Navan fort, R. Ll. P. *C. aspera* f. *lacustris* and *C. fragilis* f. *delicatula* grow abundantly in shallow water on the gravelly shores of Lough Neagh, where they may be observed covering the bottom with short bright green tufts. After storms they are cast ashore in large quantities, mixed with *Nitella opaca.*

Chara polyacantha, Braun.   N. — —
   Plentiful in Loughgall lake near the boat-house and elsewhere, and in quarry-holes at the eastern extremity of Loughgall manor demesne, R. Ll. P. This handsome plant has not been previously found in Ulster.

C. hispida, Linn.   N. — —
   Drains at Loughadian near Armagh, quarry-holes at Navan Fort (f. *rudis*), north of Loughgall (f. *rudis*), at Grange near Armagh, and at east end of Loughgall manor grounds (f. *rudis*); plentiful also in Loughgall lake (f. *rudis*).

C. vulgaris, Linn.   N. — S.
   Lough Neagh at Bird island, H. W. L. spec.! Pool at Mullinure near Armagh, quarries at Navan Fort (f. with prominent secondary cortical cells), quarry-hole at Drummanbeg near Armagh, shallow water by railway near Richhill, quarry-holes south of Armagh, lake at Tynan Abbey, quarry-holes north of Loughgall, and by the railway at Wellington cutting south of Newry, R. Ll. P. The commonest *Chara* in the county; it appears to be more amphibious than most of the species, frequently growing in water only a few inches deep, where it is never completely submerged.

C. contraria, Kuetz.   N. — —
   In Lough Neagh at Croaghan island, H. W. L. spec.!

Nitella translucens, Ag.   — — S.
   Abundantly in Cashel lake near Crossmaglen (447 feet elevation), R. Ll. P. *Isoetes lacustris* grows in the same lake.

N. flexilis, Ag.   — — S.
   Abundant in the Camlough river between the lake and the village, R. Ll. P. Not hitherto recorded from Ulster.

N. opaca, Ag.   N. M. —
   In Lough Neagh at Bird island! and Ardmore Glebe! H. W. L. Plentiful along the Lough Neagh shore; quarry-holes north of Loughgall, in a well near Markethill, and in Clay lake near Keady ("probably"), R. Ll. P.

ADDENDA ET CORRIGENDA.

Page 15. Mr. H. C. Hart writes (*J. N.* 1893, p. 84), that he considers the estimate of the flora of Donegal here given (about 720 species) to be too low.

„ 37. Line 20. For 104 read 106, and in the list which follows add *Elatine hexandra* after *Diplotaxis muralis* on p. 37, and *C. biennis* after *Crepis nicœensis* on p. 38.

„ 38. Line 31. After the words "Rev. G. Robinson," add "one by Mr. A. G. More."

„ 94. After *Elatine hydropiper* add
   E. hexandra, DC.   — M. —
   Eastern margin of Mullaghmore lake, R. Ll. P., June, 1893.

„ 159. Line 31. For "Lagan Canal" read "Newry Canal."

Note—Montiaghs or Moyntaghs, pronounced "Munches" (Celtic *Mointeach*, a boggy place), is the name of a parish bordering on Lough Neagh in the extreme N.E. of the county, but the name appears to be locally applied to the whole of the northern bog district.

THE EARTHWORMS OF IRELAND.

BY REV. HILDERIC FRIEND, F.L.S.

(Continued from page 191.)

HITHERTO no attention whatever seems to have been paid by British naturalists to that group of worms whose principal habitat is the old and decaying stumps or trunks of fallen trees, and whose chief service consists in the breaking up of useless timber, and reducing it to a vegetable mould. When I commenced the study of these animals two years ago nothing was known of the subject in this country, and I was therefore compelled to examine the works of such continental naturalists as Eisen, Rosa, and Levinsen, in order to ascertain the character of those tree-worms which had already been made known to the scientific world. Thanks to their industry, it has been possible for me to identify every species hitherto discovered in Great Britain. So far as present research enables us to speak definitely on the subject, we have no tree-worms peculiar to this island. Every species hitherto examined is known to occur in one or other of the countries of Europe, from Russia and Scandinavia to Brittany and the Italian peninsula.

But though it has not fallen to the lot of our countrymen to add any species of arboreal worm to the list of new discoveries, it must be admitted that foreign writers on the subject have, so far, almost without exception, failed to recognize the affinities of the group, and present us with any satisfactory system of classification. I purpose therefore, in the present paper, giving the whole subject a careful revision in the light of our indigenous species, with this proviso, however, that when our boreal and Irish species have been as carefully worked as I have worked those found south of the Clyde, it may be necessary to somewhat modify the characters of the group.

Eisen was the first naturalist to show that the worms which were formerly included in the genus *Lumbricus* were marked by such differences as would justify the creation of new genera. He accordingly, in 1873, took the family *Lumbricidæ* and split it up into four genera—*Lumbricus, Allolobophora, Dendrobæna,* and *Allurus*. He has since added *Tetragonurus*. The curious point to be noticed is, that though Eisen created the genus *Dendrobæna*, he did not recognize the species which would naturally fall under that generic designation, and hence his perfectly natural and appropriate term has been quietly ignored. It is my purpose, therefore, to revive the term first introduced by Eisen, and to show which of the species hitherto placed under *Lumbricus* and *Allolobophora* must be transferred to the subgenus *Dendrobæna*.

In revising Eisen's genus, however, it will be necessary to extend the characters considerably, since he included therein only one species, and that, till now, a very badly described and little understood worm. His diagnosis is as follows:—

Dendrobæna, n. gen.

Tubercula ventralia in segmento 14 [= 15 Eng. method].

Setæ ubique æquo intervallo distantes, exceptis duabus summis, quarum intervallum aliquanto majus est.

Lobus cephalicus tres partes segmenti buccalis occupans.

Referring to this subject, Dr. Benham says:—"Eisen was the first to subdivide the genus *Lumbricus* into subgenera, according to the relative amount of dovetailing of the prostomium into the peristomium. This is accompanied by certain other characters, which have been held sufficient to characterize genera in other cases. So that I have retained his subdivisions *Lumbricus* and *Allolobophora*; but as his genus *Dendrobæna* is only distinguished from the latter genus in having all the setæ equidistant, and as all stages occurring in the separation are found in *Allolobophora*, I agree with Rosa that we ought not to recognize it."

Consequently the name has been dropped, and in Beddard's " Classification and Distribution of Earthworms," 1891, and Rosa's " Revisione dei Lumb.," 1893, is omitted from notice altogether. The statement of Benham to the effect that every degree of separation of the setæ is found in *Allolobophora* is true till we remove the species which properly fall under the genus *Dendrobæna*. Almost without exception do we find that the species of *Allolobophora*, as classified by Eisen, which have the setæ widely separated, are dendrobænic in character. It is true that I shall have to deal with one exception, but this is due to the fact that we are not yet acquainted with all the species that exist, and cannot therefore assign those with which we are familiar their exact position. The characters of the group will be better understood when the different species have been discussed. Generally speaking, however, we may say that the worms are rose-red or flesh-coloured, small, with setæ more or less widely separated, arboreal in character, or found usually in and about decaying timber or tree refuse.

We may take *Allolobophora celtica*, Rosa, as a type. Rosa's original description was based upon three living specimens received from Brest, in

Brittany, during the month of March, 1886. It may be here remarked that in England March is an excellent month for collecting earthworms, as the sexual organs are then becoming active and fully developed. Rosa states that the worms are about equal in dimensions to *Lumbricus purpureus*, Eisen; being from 2 to 2½ millim. in diameter, and 35 to 40 in length. The form is cylindrical, with the posterior part somewhat attenuated. Colour violaceo-pallid dorsally, carneo-livid ventrally. Segments about 100 in number. Cephalic lobe or prostomium with a large backward prolongation which cuts or dovetails into the peristomium to about one-half its longitudinal diameter, the lobe being destitute of an inferior longitudinal groove. The male pore situated on segment 15, and extending from the second to the third seta, the two adjoining (14 and 16) being affected. Rosa terms these papillæ carrying the male pore the atria, but Beddard disputes the strict accuracy of this designation. I prefer for the present to state, when these glandular processes occur, that the male pore is carried by or borne on papillæ. The female pore is well seen, says Rosa, as a small fissure on each side of segment 14 against the second setæ, but on the side external to that occupied by the male pore. The girdle occupies six segments, extending over 31 36, slightly raised and not very closely fused. The *tubercula pubertatis* occur ventrally on segments 33, 34, in the form of a continuous ridge (not on papillæ as in *Allolobophora chlorotica*, for example). Setæ distant, the lateral increasing from below upwards, that is, the interval between 2-3 is greater than between 1-2, and less than that between 3-4; the ventral inferior (1-1) not greater than the lateral inferior (1-2); the dorsal interval (4-4) being about twice that of the lateral superior (3-4.) The setæ on the ventral surface of segments 31, 32, 35 (before and behind the *tubercula pubertatis*) borne on relieved papillæ. An interesting note on the nephridiopores, which need not be reproduced in this connection, brings Rosa's account to a close.

In 1890 I found three specimens of this worm a few miles north of Langholm, N.B., and the same year three others were discovered in an immature condition near Carlisle, when they were at first mistaken for the young of *Lumbricus purpureus*, Eisen. More recently I have received specimens from, or collected them myself, in Devonshire, Gloucestershire, Yorkshire, Northants, Lancashire, Lanark, Sussex, and several Irish localities. It is therefore evident that the species is widely distributed in Britain.

It only needs that this species should be studied by the side of *Allolobophora Boeckii*, the type upon which Eisen founded the subgenus *Dendrobæna*, to show that they are very closely allied. I will not at this point inquire what relationship exists between *A. Boeckii* and *Lumbricus puter*, Hoffmeister. Eisen says the girdle is usually composed of five segments (29-33), over three of which (31-33) the *tubercula pubertatis* extend. I give the figures according to the English notation, which makes the peristomium the first segment, and places the male pore on the 15th. Eisen's description, published in 1870, is faulty, owing to the inclusion of two or three species under one name. The generic title adopted in 1873 was based upon the fact that the worm was found under the bark of decaying trees. It has often been confused with another closely allied species which Eisen first differentiated under the title of *Allolobophora subrubicunda*. This worm is very widely distributed, and when once seen is not easily mistaken for any other, notwithstanding the fact that its girdle or clitellum occupies almost exactly the same position as that of one or two other species. It is true that the Gilt-tail (*Allolobophora subrubicunda*, Eisen) is by no means confined to woodlands, but its affinities are entirely with the *Dendrobænæ*, and it specially delights to live among fallen and decaying leaves, dead branches of trees, and similar vegetable debris. I have found it depositing its egg-capsules quite under the bark of decaying trees.

When Eisen established the genus *Dendrobæna*, it is remarkable that he did not place therein his new species *Allolobophora arborea*. It is described as an arboreal or dendrobænic species, and its characters were in many respects so similar to those of his type of the new genus that at first we are astonished to find the two placed under different genera. The fault lay in the fact that Eisen placed too much stress upon one character, to the exclusion of the rest. With him, any worm whose prostomium cut the peristomium in two was a *Lumbricus*, whatever other characters it possessed. In *Dendrobæna* the prostomium occupied about three parts of the peristomium, while in *Allolobophora* the prostomium only slightly cut into or divided the buccal segment. It is now found that this is far too arbitrary and unnatural an arrangement, and that while undoubtedly every true *Lumbricus* has the peristomium completely divided by the hinder process of the prostomium, yet not every worm with this feature is a true *Lumbricus*. Want of attention to this fact has led to further confusion in the case of a recently discovered worm which Levinsen has described as *Lumbricus eiseni*. This worm, which was first described from specimens found at Copenhagen, has been obtained by Rosa in Italy, and by myself in various parts of Great Britain; and is a true *Dendrobæna*, notwithstanding the fact that it has the buccal arrangements of a typical *Lumbricus*. In colour and in the disposition of the setæ it somewhat closely resembles *Lumbricus purpureus*, Eisen, but there the resemblances end. The true *Lumbricus* has five or six girdle segments, in this worm there are eight or nine. In *Lumbricus* the *tubercula pubertatis* stretch across the four inner segments of the girdle; here they are absent, or if present their position is abnormal. In *Lumbricus* there are two pairs of spermathecæ, in this worm they are entirely wanting. *Lumbricus* emits no yellow fluid; this species does, though not always. *Lumbricus* is a true earthworm, this is as truly dendrobænic. Surely these are characters which cannot be ignored, and show conclusively that the mere shape of the prostomium is an insufficient generic character unless accompanied by others which are permanent.

We are now in a position to consider the several British species of the subgenus *Dendrobæna* which have so far been observed and described.

Genus **Allolobophora**, § **Dendrobæna** = Group No. 3 of Rosa's Classification.

1. **A. (Dendrobæna) celtica**, Rosa.—Prostomium only partially dovetailed into the peristomium. Individual setæ somewhat widely

separated. Length 1 to 1½ inches, of a dark brown or violaceous colour dorsally, tending to iridescence; lighter on the ventral side. Clitellum flesh-coloured, dirty yellow or grey, and depending considerably on the habitat, occupying 6 segments (31-36); *tubercula pubertatis* on 33-34. Male pore on segment 15, borne on papillæ which extend to segments 14 and 16. In adult specimens segments 9, 25, and 26, also have glandular tumidities or papillæ. First dorsal pore between 5 and 6. Copulatory setæ on segments 31, 32, 35. About 100 segments.

Synonym: *Allolobophora celtica*, Rosa, Boll. Mus. Zool. Torino, 1886; *A. mammalis*, Rosa, 1893, see Rev. dei Lumb. p. 39.

DISTRIBUTION IN IRELAND.—Loughlinstown, Co. Dublin (Dr. Scharff); Woodenbridge, Co. Wicklow (Dr. Scharff); Aghaderg, Co. Down (Rev. H. W. Lett); Holywood, Co. Down (Miss C. M. Patterson); Valencia, Co. Kerry, (Miss Delap); Carrablagh, Lough Swilly (Mr. Hart), etc.

I have received some very suggestive varieties from Counties Down and Dublin, one of which I have in some of my papers called var. *rosea*, Friend. I find that this variety is in reality the tree-haunter, while the type is a terrestrial form. Here we have room for fuller investigation, that it may be ascertained to what extent the habitat affects the species. It would be profitable also to endeavour to ascertain something more respecting the question whether these species have adopted the dendrobænic mode of life from the terrestrial, or *vice versa*.

[2. **A. (Dendrobæna) boeckii,** Eisen.—This worm has rarely been taken in Great Britain. I have, in fact, up till the present only three absolutely reliable records. The species is well-defined, but there has been in the past endless confusion owing to the supposed connection between it and *Lumbricus puter*, Hoffmeister. Eisen's description is very brief, and I, therefore, describe the species from my own material.

Prostomium more deeply imbedded in the peristomium than in the last species. Male pore on segment 15, on somewhat prominent papillæ. First dorsal pore large, between segments 5 and 6. Girdle of 5 segments normally, covering 29-33, with *tubercula pubertatis* on 31, 32, 33. Anal segment somewhat pear-shaped. Length about 1¼ inches (Rosa gives 25-35 millim. for specimens in spirits). Total number of segments 80-100. Colour reddish-brown, with red clitellum and light, flesh-coloured ventral surface. Setæ in 8 almost equidistant rows. Although Eisen and many others have regarded *Lumbricus puter*, Hoffm., as corresponding with this species, my examination of the subject negatives the idea,[1] and I have no hesitation in referring Hoffmeister's worm to Eisen's *Allolobophora subrubicunda*—a worm which is far more widely distributed than *D. boeckii*, and one which has been mistaken for the latter by many authors. I regard this synonymy as being without foundation, and take Eisen's description as the original account of a new species as well as a new genus. This worm is so much like *Lumbricus purpureus*, Eisen, that it might easily pass as a true *Lumbricus*. We may compare also *L. melibœus*, Rosa.

Found in similar haunts to those chosen by the last species, but not yet on record for Ireland, where it ought to occur in the upland districts.]

---

[1] I am glad to find myself supported in this view by so reliable an authority as Dr. Rosa, of Turin.

(TO BE CONTINUED.)

MAGNESIAN LIMESTONE
IN THE NEIGHBOURHOOD OF CORK.
BY JAMES PORTER, B.E.

[At the Meeting of the Cork Naturalists' Field Club, before which Mr. Farrington read his paper on the above, Professor Hartog suggested that the criticisms of the writer should be embodied in the present communication.]

THOSE who are acquainted with the state of geological science will not consider it remarkable that the revolutionary views put forward by Mr. Farrington in the May number of the *Irish Naturalist* should be promptly challenged. If geological problems could be solved independently, without taking into account their mutual bearings, his theory might be accepted ; but as things are, I believe we must continue to regard our Cork dolomite as simply altered Carboniferous limestone.

Of the seven propositions which Mr. Farrington lays down as inconsistent with the theory of Harkness, I cannot see the adverse bearing of more than one, which refers to the abruptness of the change from limestone to dolomite. But the Cork examples cannot be looked at by themselves in this way. There are numerous instances of transitions as abrupt as any to be found in Cork, in districts where the evidence of pseudomorphic origin in the case of the dolomite, is too complete to leave any room for doubt. Professor Cole informs me that such instances are frequent in Co. Dublin ; and the expression "vertical dyke-like masses," used in the Geological Survey memoir to describe some portions of the pseudomorphic limestone near Mallow, would apply equally well to the aspect of those magnesian deposits whose origin is under discussion.

Most geologists will regard the fact stated by Mr. Farrington that "the dolomite is generally less pure than the limestone," as a pretty clear indication that the magnesian bands mark the course formerly taken by underground water, which carried with it the products of its action on the overlying rocks, including ferruginous and other impurities as well as magnesia itself. If, instead of the expression of Mr. Farrington, "nearly fifty per cent. more foreign matter," we use his figures of 2.5 for the dolomite and 1.7 for the limestone as the percentage of foreign matter in each, they would suggest to our minds, not an utter want of connexion between the two as regards origin, but rather some such relation as that which I have just referred to.

The sketches given by Mr. Farrington in the May number do not exaggerate the steepness of the walls of our local magnesian deposits. He supposes that the spaces now occupied by these were either carved out by the action of rapid streams, or opened by terrestrial disturbances. As regards the first supposition, we are met with the difficulty that there is no instance known of a natural open water-channel which could form the counterpart of these hollows in point of steepness of sides; while their abrupt termination at both ends introduces a fatal objection to the cañon theory of their origin. On the other hand, the idea of earth-movements giving rise to widely-gaping fissures which remained open long enough to be filled by the necessarily slow process of chemical precipitation, will hardly appear a plausible one to any observer of actual rock-forms.

On Mr. Farrington's view of their origin, the magnesian deposits ought to show distinct traces of bedding other than that of the limestone around. It was perhaps his desire to account for the absence of anything of the kind, which led him to conclude, on what seems very slender evidence, that the dolomite had been always subjected to the action of heat. It would indeed be remarkable if the heat had rendered it crystalline without seriously affecting the limestone in immediate contact with it. But the mere fact of dolomite resembling saccharine marble does not tend to prove the action of heat at all. The structure of dolomite is usually distinctly crystalline; and the difference between it and limestone in this respect is occasionally relied upon as a rough means of discrimination. The presence of iron pyrites in the dolomite suggests rather the reducing action of percolating water charged with organic matter than the action of heat.

When we come to the history of our southern land-surface we reach he climax of difficulty. The Permian theory requires that denudation should have been so rapid during the early part of the Permian period as to strip off the Coal-measures and much of the Carboniferous limestone, leaving ample time for a series of crust-movements which extended over hundreds of square miles and squeezed the rocks of Cork and Kerry into numerous folds. All this geological work would have had to be accomplished before the close of the Permian period, for time must of course be allowed for the newly-opened fissures to be filled with their magnesian contents. As regards the denudation, the most rapidly-working agencies with which we are acquainted could not possibly have done this; and we have no particular reason to think that the monitors of the Californian gold-miners were anticipated and dwarfed by any corresponding machinery guided by armies of Labyrinthodonts. The view generally held by geologists regarding the history of the Irish land-surface, assigns almost the entire interval between the Carboniferous and the present time for this denudation. Mr. Farrington's theory, however, further requires that the fissured limestone surface which formed the bottom of the Permian lake, should have been preserved from complete removal during the long Secondary and Tertiary revolutions, with only a thin layer of "soft Permian strata" to protect it; a layer which when the time came was cleared away without difficulty by the glacial action which has been known to spare many softer deposits. The acceptance of all this is really impossible.

The chemical part of the original theory of Harkness is certainly open to modification. It would seem that the alteration of the Carboniferous limestone into dolomite was effected, not by the magnesian salts in sea-water, but by magnesia held in solution by carbonic or humus acids in the water which penetrated downwards through the surface rocks. I am inclined to think that in some cases a line of fault-rock furnished a readier passage for the water percolating through the limestone than its joints afforded, as the soft fissile layer between the dolomite and the limestone which Mr. Farrington has described looks very like a slickenside at times; but this is a point which is better left to those who can examine a great development of the rock. I am quite convinced that nothing is likely to be adduced regarding the Cork dolomites which can seriously affect the main conclusion of Harkness, that they are products of alteration.

REVIEW.

Guy's South of Ireland Pictorial Guide. Cork: Guy & Co., 1893.

We have received a copy of "Guy's South of Ireland Pictorial Guide," which will supply visitors with an excellent and profusely-illustrated guide to the southern counties, and to Cork city and Killarney in particular. The most novel feature of the hand-book, and the one to which we wish to draw attention, is the series of short articles on local vertebrate zoology, phanerogamic botany, and mineralogy, specially contributed by such well-know Irish naturalists as Messrs. A. G. More, F.L.S., R. J. Ussher, J.P., G. H. Kinahan, M.R.I.A., and R. A. Phillips. This is a department in which local guide-books are usually lamentably deficient, natural history being frequently altogether ignored, or if mentioned at all, being treated in a manner at once incompetent and inaccurate. In Messrs. Guy's production, however, the botany is from the pen of Mr. More, the recognised authority on the subject in Ireland, and his remarks take the form of a short and interesting essay on the peculiar and characteristic plants of the south and west of Ireland, and their origin and distribution. Mr. Ussher supplies excellent notes on the birds of the district, and Mr. More on the fresh-water fishes; Mr. Phillips contributes pleasantly-written articles on the orchids and ferns, and Mr. Kinahan discusses the mineralogy of the southern counties. Messrs. Guy are certainly to be congratulated on having produced the first Irish guide-book in which at least a portion of the natural history of the district treated of is given the prominence which it deserves, and is described with accuracy by competent naturalists.

OBITUARY.

ROBERT J. BURKITT.

On the 3rd July, passed away at Carne Prospect, Belmullet, at the advanced age of eighty-six, Dr. Robert J. Burkitt, whose life-long devotion to ornithology may be inferred from the many references to him in Thompson's work, as well as from the specimens of unexampled rarity he preserved, and contributed to our museums from time to time. Resident as a physician in Waterford, he there collected and preserved birds with his own hands from 1830 until he left it about ten years ago, all of which he obtained in the flesh from that part of Ireland, and since he went to Belmullet he added to the Irish list the only recorded example of the Barred Warbler. During that long period he appears to have had no neighbours who sympathized in his pursuits. His generosity of disposition, so well known in Waterford by his gratuitous attendance on the poor, led him to bestow his Great Auk and other rarities on Trinity College Museum, and it is gratifying to know that his services as a naturalist, and his valuable gifts to the Museum, though long unacknowledged, were recognized by the present Board of Trinity College, who, a few months since, did a graceful act towards Dr. Burkitt.

Among the proofs of his friendship I have received, I may instance the gifts of his South African Eagle Owl and Baillon's Crake, both shot near Waterford, and now in the Science and Art Museum; also his set of Thompson's works, rendered doubly precious by being interleaved with letters written to him by Yarrell and Thompson. In Dr. Burkitt we have lost an Irish ornithologist who was a contemporary and friend of those men. Of a singular sincerity and simplicity of character, he abhorred shams of every description, and could not endure to owe money. Looking back on his long life, those closely related to him can remember no variance with him. He was ever the same true-hearted man. His intellect remained as clear as his handwriting to the last, a notice of his on Wild Swans having appeared in the May number of *The Irish Naturalist*.

R. J. USSHER.

PROCEEDINGS OF IRISH SOCIETIES.

ROYAL ZOOLOGICAL SOCIETY.

A Seal, captured at Moy, Ballina, has been presented to the Gardens by George Shannon, Esq. Three Lion cubs, and three Puma cubs, have been born in the Gardens.

9,460 persons visited the Gardens in June.

ARMAGH NATURAL HISTORY AND PHILOSOPHICAL SOCIETY.

JUNE 6th.—Field excursion to Ballybrawley stone circle and Navan Fort. In spite of the great heat, the few members that assembled determined to carry out the programme. On arriving at Ballybrawley it was observed with regret that one of the large boulders forming the circle was being broken up. If this course be persevered in there will soon be no stone circle left. Proceeding from Ballybrawley to Navan Fort, the party took a line across the country. Arrived at Navan Fort, much speculation was indulged in as to the disposition of the ancient town, if such it can be called. On the way home specimens were met with, on the old road to Armagh, of *Geranium pratense*, and its handsome purple flowers were much admired. On the railway bridge at Ballybrawley, a quantity of the pretty little Wall-rue (*Asplenium ruta-muraria*) was observed. Various insects were captured, the most noteworthy being the Hemipteron, *Calocoris roseomaculatus* and the Orthopteron, *Labia minor*.

JUNE 24th.—Field excursion to the souterrain at Drummanmore. This interesting relic of the early habitations lies about one and a-half miles north-east from Armagh. It does not seem to be well known to the inhabitants, and, consequently, it was hoped that a number would be attracted to the excursion. However, but few assembled, but these reaped the reward of their efforts. MR. R. PILLOW gave an account of this interesting structure. The souterrain now opens towards the west, and there is a passage running from the side opposite the present entrance in a south-eastern direction. This passage, Mr. Pillow informed the party, was twenty-one feet in length, and opened into another chamber which is now blocked up. The floor is covered with mud and earth, but appears to have been considerably lower than at present. Mr. Pillow gave the actual height as about seven feet, breadth about ten feet. It is hoped that the Society will undertake the clearing out of the chamber and passage, and no doubt leave could be obtained to excavate the second chamber. Mr. Pillow read a passage from the "Tripartite Life of St. Patrick," from which it appeared that a religious cell was established east of Armagh by Crumtheris, one of a party of virgins who came to visit St. Patrick. It was conjectured that this souterrain might have had some connection with this lady's settlement. It is much to be regretted that more of the members did not attend these excursions, and it seems strange that none of the officers of the society were present on either occasion, with the exception of the President.

BELFAST NATURALISTS' FIELD CLUB.

JUNE 24th.—Half-day excursion to Blackhead, which was attended by a party of over sixty. The basaltic rocks of the promontory claimed attention, and a short lecture on the geology of the neighbourhood was delivered by the President (MR. WM. SWANSTON, F.G.S.). A compliment was paid to Mr. B. D. Wise, C.E., Engineer of the Northern Counties railway, for the skill and good taste which he has displayed in the construction of a path along the hitherto inaccessible base of the cliffs.

BELFAST AND DUBLIN NATURALISTS' FIELD CLUBS.

JULY 4th, 5th, and 6th.—The joint three-day excursion of the two Clubs to Dundalk, Newry, and Carlingford, proved an unqualified success, and we are glad to learn that a determination was expressed by members on both sides that such meetings should be made periodic, and that the southern Field Clubs also should be given an opportunity of meeting their fellow-societies. On the first day, the combined party, numbering five-and-twenty, assembled at Dundalk, and drove first to Ballymascanlan, where one of the finest cromlechs in Ireland was inspected, and also a kistvaen. Proceeding northward, a halt was called at the interesting carved pillar-stone of Kilnasoggarth, which received due attention. The next item on the programme was the ascent of Slieve Gullion (1,893 feet), which was accomplished by a large section of the party, the others proceeding in wagonettes to the ancient and interesting church of Killeavy, where they were subsequently joined by the mountaineers. On Slieve Gullion some good plants were obtained, and some interesting insects. On the way to Newry a halt was called at the Bessbrook granite quarries, where Mr. Flynn, the proprietor, had a number of blasts ready, which were fired, and several hundred tons of rock brought down. Dinner was served at the Victoria Hotel, Newry, at 9.30, and, subsequently, a presentation, consisting of a beautiful morocco album filled with photographs taken on the B.N.F.C. excursions, was made to Mr. R. Lloyd Praeger, by the members of the Belfast Club.

On the second day an early start was made, and the party drove to Carlingford mountain, picking up some good plants on the route. While the greater portion of the members ascended the mountain, a few proceeded by road to Carlingford town. Several hours were spent on the mountain, and a large amount of collecting was done; the fungi and flowering plants proved to be the groups which yielded the best results. On the highest point of the mountain, Prof. Cole, F.G.S., briefly drew attention to the geological formation of the surrounding country, which lay spread out like a map on every hand. Lunch was partaken of at Carlingford, among the picturesque ruins of King John's Castle, and the party proceeded by rail to Greenore, where a couple of hours' examination yielded good results to zoologists, botanists, and geologists alike. After dinner at Newry, an evening meeting was held, under the chairmanship of Dr. McWeeney, President D.N.F.C., when the following communications were brought forward:—"Mosses and Hepatics of the district," D. M'Ardle; "Flowering Plants of the district," R. Lloyd Praeger, M.R.I.A.; "Local Geology," illustrated by limelight views, Prof. Cole (in the regretted absence of Prof. Sollas, F.R.S., who had met with an accident on Lambay island); "Antiquities of the district," F. J. Bigger, Hon. Sec., B.N.F.C.; "Vertebrates of the district," H. Lyster Jameson; "Fungi collected on the excursion," Dr. McWeeney.

On the third day members turned out at seven a.m., and paid an early visit to the nursery garden of Mr. Thomas Smith, well known for its botanical rarities. After breakfast, the party drove by the picturesque upper road to the woods of Ferry-hill, where a profitable hour was spent. Crossing Narrow-water ferry, Major Hall's beautiful grounds were entered, and the artificial and natural beauties of the place were much appreciated. Returning to Newry, early dinner occupied attention, after which the business meetings of the respective Clubs were held, and a number of new members elected, and after mutual congratulations on the success of the trip, and a most kind invitation from the Dublin members to their Belfast brethren to spend three days with them in Dublin at the end of the month, the party adjourned to "The Glen," where they were most hospitably entertained by Mr. Barcroft. Subsequently members proceeded to the railway station, taking their respective trains to Belfast and Dublin.

Among the more interesting species taken on the excursion are the following:—Flowering plants:—*Carduus crispus* and *Lychnis vespertina*, near

Dundalk; *Torilis nodosa*, at Dromantee; *Vaccinium vitis-idæa*, *Melampyrum pratense* var. *montanum*, and *Pinguicula lusitanica*, on Slieve Gullion; *Circæa alpina* and *Trifolium medium*, base of Carlingford mountain; *Polypodium phegopteris*, *Hymenophyllum wilsoni*, and *Sedum rhodiola*, near summit of Carlingford mountain; *Chenopodium bonus-henricus* and *Malva rotundifolia*, Carlingford town; *Eryngium maritimum*, *Glaucium flavum*, *Torilis nodosa*, *Polygonum raii*, *Atriplex arenaria*, *Silene anglica*, *Sinapis alba*, *Cynoglossum officinale*, *Linaria minor*, *Euphorbia exigua*, *Papaver argemone* and *Carduus crispus*, at Greenore; *Lastræa æmula*, *L. oreopteris*, and *Hymenophyllum tunbridgense*, on Ferry-hill; *Statice bahusiensis*, and *Obione portulacoides*, Narrowwater ferry; and *Thrincia hirta*, on lawn at Narrow-water castle. The mosses, hepatics, and fungi are in the hands of Dr. McWeeney and Mr. M'Ardle, who will report on them later, when the material collected is worked out. In the department of zoology, the beetles taken include:— *Notiophilus biguttatus*, *Eluphrus cupreus*, *Phædon tumidulus*, *Erirrhinus æridulus*, Dundalk; *Silpha subrotundata*, *Lochmæa suturalis*, Fathom mountain; *Cafius xantholoma*, *Gastroidea polygoni*, *Hypera polygoni*, at Greenore; *Serica brunnea*, *Otiorrhynchus maurus*, Carlingford; *Barynotus schonhetri*, Slieve Gullion; while among the rarer *Hemiptera* are:—*Gerris costæ*, in small pool near top of Slieve Gullion; *Salda orthochila*, Slieve Gullion; *Pithanus maerkeli*, Dundalk; *Calocoris roseomaculatus*, Carlingford; *Lygus lucorum*, Dundalk and Fathom; *Notonecta glauca*, in lake at 1,800 feet on Slieve Gullion. Lepidoptera were very few in number, and of no special interest.

NOTES.

BOTANY.

FUNGI.

Fungi from the South-West.—On the Royal Irish Academy excursion to the neighbourhood of Castletown Bere, Co. Cork, I collected the following as well as other species:—*Tremella indurata*, Sommerf., Dunboy Castle ; *Coniophora*, sp. indet., ibid. ; *Marasmius*, sp. indet., ibid. ; *Ceratium hydnoides*, A. and S., abundant in Dunboy wood ; *Dactylium roseum*, Bk. ; *Stachybotrys atra*, Ca., growing in conjunction with *Chætomium chartarum*, Ehrb. ; *Puccinia saxifragæ*, Schlecht, on *S. umbrosa*, Hungry Hill ; *Melampsora helioscopiæ*, Pers., on *Euphorbia hiberna*, everywhere; *Sphærotheca castagnei*, Lev., abundantly on *Euphorbia hiberna*. (As the conceptacles were not perfectly ripe, some doubt remains as to the identity of the species.) *Nibrissea margarita*, White, on dead heather stems in boggy places, at altitudes above 1,000 feet on Hungry-hill, Co. Cork ; *Lachnea scutellata*, Linn., Dunboy ; *Arcyrea incarnata*, P., ibid. In conclusion, it should be stated that two circumstances were especially unfavourable to the collection of large numbers of fungi—the dryness of the weather, and the rapidity with which it was necessary to proceed. I have no doubt that had I been able to devote several days to Dunboy wood, I should have been able to record a much greater number of interesting species.—ED. J. M'WEENEY, Dublin.

Fungi from Altadore, Co. Wicklow.—Towards the end of June I paid a visit to this beautiful little glen along with Dr. Scharff and Mr. Praeger, and found the following species :—*A. (Pluteus) cervinus*, Scharff ; *A. (Mycena) epipterygius*, Scop. ; *Calocera cornea*, Fr. ; *Hydnum alutaceum*, Fr. ; *Mollesia discolor*, Mont. ; *Lachnella schumacheri*, Fr., var.

plumbea, Grev.; *Lachnella cerina*, Pers.; *Calloria xanthostigma*, Fr.; *Calloria vinosa*, A. and S.; *Vibrissea guernisaci*, Cronan; *Ceratium hydnoides*, A. and S.; a very curious sp., probably an *Achlya*, on dead flies lying on dripping *Fontinalis antipyretica* that had been exposed by the shrinkage of the stream. *Trichia fallax*, Pers.; *Arcyrea punicea*, Pers. For the identification of some of the Discomycetes I am indebted to the kindness of Mr. W. Phillips, of Shrewsbury.—ED. J. M'WEENEY, Dublin.

PHANEROGAMS.

Spiranthes romanzoviana in Co. Londonderry.—On July 15th, while collecting plants on the Derry banks of the Bann, near Kilrea, I was struck by the appearance of an orchid, which seemed to be one of the *Habenariæ*. A second glance, however, showed me that it was something with which I was unfamiliar, and I gathered the plants which I saw, six in flower, but only taking one root. I put them into my vasculum, and continued my walk down the river, meeting with several other plants new to me. After getting back in the evening, I compared my specimens with the descriptions given in Hooker and Bentham, and came to the conclusion that I had been so fortunate as to find one of the very rare *Spiranthes*, probably *S. romanzoviana*. I had read Mr. Praeger's description of it in the September number of *Journal of Botany* for 1892, but had not it at hand to help me. The flowers were most fragrant. I forwarded specimens to Mr. S. A. Stewart and Mr. Lloyd Praeger, and to my great delight they have confirmed my conjecture. The land in the vicinity of the place where I found the plant consists of worn-out and long-disused bog, as is proved by the portions of bog-oak projecting into the river. It apparently has been little cultivated, but kept for pasture or meadow. While writing I may add to this note that I refound *Stachys betonica* growing plentifully in the station given by Dr. Moore, not very far from the bridge at Kilrea. The field in which it grows has been long used for pasture, and the plants, owing, I presume, to their having been often cropped by cattle, are smaller and more stunted than those I gathered in Co. Donegal some years ago.—MRS. LEEBODY, Londonderry.

Helianthemum vulgare in Ireland.—In the *Journal of Botany* for July, Mr. H. Chicester Hart records his finding of *Helianthemum vulgare* on the limestone between Donegal and Ballyshannon. This very pretty plant, though abundant in many parts of England and Scotland, has not been previously found in Ireland. While congratulating Mr. Hart on his discovery, might we suggest to him the desirability of placing a specimen in the herbarium of our National Museum, where the Irish flora is receiving careful attention at the hands of Prof. Johnson.

Malva moschata.—Rev. H. W. Lett writes us from Loughbrickland, Co. Down :—"I enclose a specimen of *Malva moschata* from the seven-acre meadow lying between the glebe house and the lough. The field has been under my notice for the last seven and a-half years, and I never observed the plant until this summer, when it was very conspicuous among the short grass. The field where it grows has not been broken up within the last ten years, and there are no plants of this *Malva* in my garden, or anywhere else that I know of in the neighbourhood, nor have I had seed or plant of the same for seven and a-half years. At Ardmore [Co. Armagh] I found *M. moschata* in old pastures similar to the one here." This appears to be an interesting case of colonization : can any of our readers quote similar instances ?

Flora of Co. Armagh.—To my enumeration of the flora, I may add the names of three additional species, all of which, however, must rank as casuals or escapes. *Silene armeria* I found on the G. N. railway at Wellington cutting, along with *Diplotaxis muralis* and *Carum carui*;

Melilotus officinalis, Willd., on the railway at Bessbrook; while *Geranium pratense* grows in some abundance by the old road from Armagh to Killylea, where it was observed last year by myself, and the present year by Rev. W. F. Johnson; it is no doubt an escape from a cottage-garden. The recent Field Club trip to Slieve Gullion added another station for *Melampyrum pratense*, var. *montanum*; several members obtained good specimens on the southern side of the mountain at 1,000–1,500 feet.—R. LLOYD PRAEGER.

Azolla carolineana in fruit.—It may be interesting to some to note that this curious little aquatic—albeit not a native of Ireland—is now producing its fruit abundantly in a shallow pond in Mount Usher garden, Co. Wicklow. I understand it has rarely been known to fruit in the open air in Great Britain or Ireland, although it does so on the Continent of Europe.—GREENWOOD PIM.

Colour-variation in Wild Flowers.—In reference to Mr. Praeger's remarks on this subject in the *I. N.* for June, I may add a species to his list—*Silene acaulis*, of which I found patches with pure white flowers among others of the normal colour on Binevenagh, Co. Derry, a few years ago.—MRS. LEEBODY, Londonderry.

Obione portulacoides, L. at Dundalk.—I mentioned in "Flora of Armagh" on p. 157, the occurrence of this local plant at Dundalk, but it may be well to make a separate note of it, as it is rare in Ireland, and apparently not on record from this locality. It grows in great abundance over the immense stretch of salt-marsh that fringes the sea south of Dundalk harbour, along with *Statice bahusiensis*. I first observed it there in January, 1889.—R. LLOYD PRAEGER.

ZOOLOGY.

INSECTS.

Sirex gigas and Macroglossa stellatarum in Co. Louth.—On July 9th I received from Rev. R. M. P. Freeman a female *Sirex*, taken at his rectory (Collon, Co. Louth.) In the same consignment was a specimen of *Macroglossa stellatarum* also taken at Collon, where it attracted Mr. Freeman's attention by its humming, while it hovered over some flowers outside his house. *Sirex gigas* is apparently not unknown to the country people at Cotton, who, according to Mr. Freeman, accuse it of stinging their cattle!—H. LYSTER JAMESON, Killencoole, Co. Louth.

Coleoptera in Co. Dublin.—The following Coleoptera, taken by me, and identified through the kind assistance of the Rev. W. F. Johnson, have apparently not been previously recorded from Ireland. *Anisotoma parvula*, Sahl., one specimen, Santry, by sweeping; *Malthodes mysticus*, Kies., occurred near Santry (in company with *M. marginatus*, Latr.); *Dasytes ærosus*, Kies., Santry, one specimen, sweeping; *Cis alni*. Gyll., found one specimen last January in a fungus on an elm in Phœnix Park (with great numbers of *C. nitidus*, Herbst.); *Anaspis garneysi*, Fowler, rare, sweeping nettles, Royal Canal bank; *Apion ulicis*, Forst., Friarstown Glen, near Tallaght, by beating furze; *Hypera meles*, F., I was fortunate enough to capture this rare species among the long grass on the railway bank near Sutton, by sweeping; *Magdalis carbonaria*, L., one specimen off birch, Santry; *Hylesinus fraxini*, Panz., Lucan demesne. With the exception of *Cis alni*, Gyll., all the above were taken during the months of April and May.—J. N. HALBERT, Dublin.

MOLLUSCA.

Donegal Mollusca.—The July number of the *Journal of Conchology* (vol. vii., No. 7, 1893,) contains an interesting article by Mr. R. Standen on the land and fresh-water Mollusca collected by him around Portsalon, Co. Donegal. The rejectamenta on the golf-links proved to be very productive. Large quantities of shells had accumulated in a sheltered hollow, and with painstaking industry Mr. Standen picked out a number of rarities. Although these were dead shells, he found them in remarkably good condition, and as fresh-looking as living specimens. The following deserve special mention :—*Hyalinia draparnaldi* :—this had never previously been taken in the north of Ireland; Portsalon is probably the most northern station of the species in Europe. *Helix arbustorum* :—one dead shell was found; although it does not place the occurrence of this species at Portsalon beyond a doubt, it is extremely probable that it will be found living in the neighbourhood. *Helix hortensis* is mentioned as being more plentiful at Portsalon than *Helix nemoralis*. *Vertigo alpestris* :—this arctic species, of which only a single specimen had hitherto been found in Ireland, is no doubt the most important discovery Mr. Standen made. Sixty-four species in all are recorded. A number of these are new records for the Co. of Donegal, but some of them had been previously found by Mr. Milne without having been recorded.

FISHES.

Ray's Bream (Brama raii) in Co. Waterford.—A specimen of this rare fish, caught about 3rd June last at Dungannon, was seen by me at Street's establishment, in the city of Waterford, on 6th June. I at once made a water-colour sketch of the fish, and forwarded it through a friend to Dr. Scharff, of the Science and Art Museum, Dublin. He identified the specimen from the sketch, as did also Mr. A. G. More, to whom it was shown. Unfortunately the eyes of this specimen were missing when it arrived in Waterford.—C. P. CRANE, Waterford.

BIRDS.

Quails (Coturnix communis) in Co. Wicklow.—On 10th June, while walking through a meadow in the vicinity of Enniskerry, I flushed a Quail, and some hours later on the same evening, I heard its well-known note in the same place. On the 2nd July I visited the spot again, and found the meadow had been cut, and the Quail had located itself in the adjoining corn-field. A friend of mine, in Greystones, informed me that he heard the Quail frequently in June last among some corn outside Delgany.—E. C. BARRINGTON, Dublin.

MAMMALS.

The Reddish-grey Bat (Vespertilio nattereri) in Co. Louth.—A male of this species flew into a house in Dundalk, on June 16th, and was captured by Mr. T. Kerr, who brought it to me alive. I am indebted to Dr. R. F. Scharff for the identification of my specimen.— H. LYSTER JAMESON, Killencoole, Co. Louth.

The Irish Naturalist.

Vol. II.   SEPTEMBER, 1893.   No. 9.

THE BIRDS OF THE MIDLAND LAKES AND BOGS,
CHIEFLY AS OBSERVED IN THE BREEDING-SEASON.
BY R. J. USSHER.

BEFORE I had visited those parts of Ireland herein referred to, when I looked at the map of counties seamed with lakes and their ramifications, I imagined vast swamps must exist, where the waters lost themselves among extensive reed-beds. In reality, however, Ireland being an undulating, not a flat country, vast swampy solitudes are hardly to be found anywhere in summer. The shores of Irish lakes usually rise rapidly into dry inhabited ground, often swelling into heights, so that, except in certain bays, and at the tail-ends of lakes, large reed-beds seldom occur. The humid boggy soil, however, even on sloping ground yields abundance of rushes, Iris, Meadow-sweet, and other rank vegetation which affords to ducks, Redshanks, Lapwings, and Snipe, cover to nest in, and the numerous islands often contain scrub or natural wood. The open islands are, unfortunately for the feathered race, invaded habitually in the breeding season by persons fishing on the lakes, who, in pursuit of green-drake flies for bait, trample the whole surface. Elsewhere turkeys are fed on eggs of gulls and terns, until the latter are driven from their breeding-grounds. In certain shooting-preserves, however, as the marshes of the Erken on Lord Castletown's property in Queen's Co., at Barronston on Lough Iron in Westmeath, on Killeenmore bog near Geashill, the property of Lord Digby, and Lough Key in Roscommon, which adjoins the demesne of Rockingham, great assemblages of birds of many species, breeding in peace, attest the benefits of protection.

The "red bogs" are tracts of country overlaid by level beds of peat, often covering thousands of acres, which from their barren nature, and the dangers of their swampy portions, are seldom invaded by men or cattle. Here the Curlews lay among the heather, and Black-headed Gulls breed in the wetter and more lonely parts. Such bogs skirt much of the Shannon, as between Athlone and Banagher, the flats along the river being the only green surface visible. These flats, called "callows," overflowed in winter, yield in summer a rank crop, chiefly of Meadow-sweet, which is annually meadowed, but before it is cut, affords unlimited breeding-grounds to the numerous Redshanks that frequent it.

Some of the larger lakes, especially Lower Lough Erne, are exceedingly beautiful, where adjoining proprietors have preserved along the shores remnants of the natural woods, which clothe the islands with a growth of Oak, Rowan, Ash, Birch, and willows. Here every island is tenanted by its pair of Mergansers, which display their chequered plumage as they dart past, while light terns flit over on their dainty wings, and Tufted Ducks breed in the flags among colonies of gulls, or among the dense rushes on the slopes of the islands.

Taking the valley of the Shannon, with its chain of lakes, I include the adjoining counties of Connaught, or the eastern portions of them, and the lakes and bogs of Sligo, Leitrim, Fermanagh, Cavan, Longford, Westmeath, King's and Queen's Counties, and Tipperary, but I do not refer to Lough Neagh, to the western lakes of Conn, Mask, and Corrib, nor to the lower Shannon, west of Lough Derg.

I have made excursions in the end of May and beginning of June for the past three seasons through the above lake-districts. Where I give a list of localities, I refer chiefly to my own observation of the bird at these times, prefixing an asterisk where I obtained proof of its having eggs or young.

My selection of species depends on my having something special to say about them in connection with the above parts of Ireland. I do not enumerate birds which, though found about the lakes, are not characteristic of them, being found commonly in counties of a different character; as the Heron, Moor-hen, Water-rail, and Snipe, but I have given special attention to certain waders, grebes and gulls, as these chiefly breed in the region of the lakes. The Ducks, except the marine species, are given at greater length, as being frequenters of the lakes, whether in summer or winter, and among them we may chiefly add to our list of the breeding birds of this region. The Geese and Swans also deserve a mention.

I am largely indebted to the help and hospitality of those gentlemen who have promoted my researches, and contributed their own information.

The MERLIN, not confined to the mountains, is resident in small numbers on the great red bogs of the central plain. Its eggs have been obtained in Westmeath, King's Co., and Queen's Co. in such situations, and it is reported to breed in eastern Galway.

The MARSH HARRIER, previous to about 1840, was a common resident on Lough Erne. Its nests were found on waste ground about the lake. Since then it has been practically exterminated by game-keepers, and so reduced in its haunts in Westmeath and King's Co., as to be quite a rare, or at least, a scarce bird there now. The only occasion in which I met with it was on the 14th April, 1893, when I visited the extensive marshes of Lord Castletown, near Granston Manor, in Queen's Co. These cover more than eight hundred statute acres, and are a paradise for ducks, Lapwings, Redshanks, Coots, and Gulls. High over these marshes I saw sweeping in curves, three Marsh Harriers, two together, and a third apart. After two or three flaps, they would sail round, holding the wings slanting upwards. In wind, however, they are seen flying low, almost beating the tops of the flags with their wings in quest of their prey. As they are seen there at all seasons, they must breed. On the extensive red bogs in the east of King's Co., Mr. Digby used to see Marsh Harriers at all seasons until 1889, and has heard of the nest being found, and some have since been seen by keepers. Lough Iron, in Westmeath, was a favourite resort, where many have been shot, from time to time. A pair usually appear there about August, but they do not remain. Co. Galway was another stronghold of the Marsh Harrier. It has been reported to me, apparently as a straggler, from Derrycarne, Co. Leitrim, on the Shannon; from bogs near Lough Annagh, King's and Queen's Counties; from Co. Tipperary; and from the Shannon near Banagher, where my informant has observed it hover over a Coot, which dived until it could dive no longer, and was then taken for a prey.

The SEDGE WARBLER struck me not by its presence in the lake-districts so much as by its scarcity. It is reported to me as breeding in every Irish county, except Longford, where I have met with it, and in Cavan, Clare, and Leitrim, where my informants have probably overlooked it. I have observed it near Castle Irvine, Fermanagh; on Lough Oughter, Cavan; Lough Iron, Lough Owel, and Lough Drin, in Westmeath; and on the Shannon near Banagher. Still these instances are few, and I was greatly surprised when I listened for it in vain about Lough Derg, Lough Ree, and a host of other lakes and marshy spots. It is stated to be local and uncommon in Westmeath and King's Co.

The GARDEN WARBLER, though not confined to the lake-districts, has only been observed by me there, and as yet my knowledge of it points to the valleys of the Shannon, to Lough Erne and Lough Arrow, as some of its chief resorts in Ireland, but I have reason to think that it is to be found in Queen's Co., and probably in many other districts. I have recently treated of it at greater length (see *Irish Naturalist*, July, 1893).

The WILLOW WARBLER is very abundant about the lakes and among the willows, even on the lonely parts of the Shannon.

The REED BUNTING is the most characteristic passerine bird of the lakes. It is to be found where no other small bird is to be seen. On every islet one may find nests of this species among the coarse sedgy grass. It is usually hatching, but sometimes rearing young, the first week in June. It is reported to breed in every Irish county, except Carlow, where it must have been overlooked.

The SPOTTED CRAKE, though uncommon, probably breeds in many instances. Its eggs, taken by Col. Irwin, in Roscommon, about 1856, are now in the Science and Art Museum. Two were shot, and two others seen on Upper Lough Erne in late summer or early autumn, 1890, by Mr. George Husbands, of Enniskillen; one was shot at Colebrooke, also in Fermanagh, on 27th September, 1890; two were shot in August, 1880, in Queen's Co., by Mr. T. Trench; and two were shot in Westmeath, in October, 1892 (*Irish Sportsman*, 29th October, 1892).

The COOT has its great strongholds in the lakes. Though

breeding all over Ireland, in some counties locally, it is exceedingly numerous where the shallower parts of lakes and the Shannon are margined with large beds of flags and tall rushes. Among these one finds its nests everywhere. On the larger lakes Coots do not seem to lay until the end of May or beginning of June, as their clutches are then usually incomplete. Where a rise had taken place in the waters of Lough Ree, I found a nest containing a flooded egg built upon, and another laid over it.

The RINGED PLOVER breeds in small numbers on most of the lakes. I have observed it in the breeding season, or found its eggs on *Lough Arrow, Lough Boderg (an expansion of the Shannon in Leitrim), Lough Forbes (another expansion in Longford), *Lough Sheelin, Lough Gowna, *Currygrane Lake, Lough Ree, *Glen Lough, Lough Iron, *Lough Derg, and Lough Annagh; and it is reported to breed in the Queen's Co. by Mrs. Croasdaile. In these localities the Ringed Plover lays in the end of May or beginning of June, and will sit on three eggs, as I have found more than once. On the 9th June I found young in down on the stony shore of Currygrane Lake. The nests are hollows in the gravelly or pebbly shores. On an island in Lough Sheelin I found a Ringed Plover's nest, with eggs, at the foot of a willow bush, and overshadowed by it; but it was a characteristic hollow in the gravel without lining, a nest of Common Sandpiper close by being comfortably lined. The Ringed Plover is a spring and summer visitant to the lakes, arriving on Lough Derg in February or March.

The LAPWING is a very common breeding bird throughout the region we are treating of. Though reported to breed in every Irish county, and numerously in most of them, one sees a great increase when passing into these lake counties. I have observed Lapwings in May and June on Lough Erne, Castle Irwin dam, Lough Arrow, Lough Allen, Lough Boderg, Lough Forbes, Lough Gowna, Currygrane Lake, Lough Ree, Glen Lough, Lough Iron, the Shannon "callows" near Banagher, Lough Derg, Lough Annagh, and Granston marshes. On the latter vast numbers of Lapwings were laying in the middle of April. They usually have young able to fly the first week in June. These, when squatting on the grass, lie with flattened back and wings, their brown plumage making them look like cow-dung. I have more than once seen a Lapwing fly screaming at a Heron, which was evidently in dangerous proximity to its young, no doubt an acceptable meal to a Heron.

The DUNLIN is a bird that I have met with in breeding plumage, in which it is recognisable by its black breast-spot, on Lough Arrow, Lough Sheelin, Lough Gowna, Lough Ree, *Glen Lough, *Lough Iron, the Shannon near Banagher and again near Athlone, Lough Derg, and Lough Annagh. Mrs. Croasdaile has seen one on 11th May, on a lough near Rhynn, Queen's Co. I found the nest with eggs, incubation just commenced, on the 14th June, 1891. It was among coarse grass, where the Inny flows into Lough Iron. I identified the bird fully. Mrs. Battersby has in her collection a series of Dunlin's eggs, taken on the shores of Glen Lough, on the borders of Westmeath and Longford. She says the bird is a spring visitor there. On Lough Annagh, King's Co., I saw a party of fourteen in breeding plumage, on 30th April, 1892. On 1st June, 1893, I saw a party of four on an island in Lough Ree, which let me approach within ten yards. These could hardly have been breeding, but those that I saw on the "callows" of the Shannon, on Lough Gowna and Lough Sheelin, and elsewhere, were feeding busily, and I took them to be males foraging for hatching females, the localities being suitable, as well as the season—the end of May and beginning of June. The Dunlin does not seem to have been previously recorded as breeding in the midland counties.

The COMMON SANDPIPER is reported to breed in every Irish county, except Kilkenny, Wexford, and Waterford. I have observed it commonly on the various lakes I visited, as well as on the Shannon. There is no more noticeable bird on the lake-shores, which are enlivened by its musical, sustained cry as it skims over the water. On Lough Derg, Sandpipers' nests contained hard-set eggs by the end of May. On Lough Sheelin they were not so far advanced by the 11th June. In Hollybrook demesne is a promontory running into Lough Arrow, covered with tall Beech, beneath which I saw a Sandpiper hatching, while another had been known to nest on a high mossy bank, beside a shrubbery walk, beneath a large Beech.

The REDSHANK breeds commonly throughout the parts of Ireland we have noticed. Along the "callows" of the Shannon these birds are exceedingly numerous, and some were apparently still laying on the 4th June, though this must be exceptionally late, as I saw a young Redshank, of about ten days old, on Lough Gowna on 11th June. During my visit to Lord Castletown's marshes, in Queen's Co., on the 14th April, Redshanks, which were exceedingly numerous, were laying, or beginning to hatch. We saw there as many as nine or ten on the wing at a time, and their chorus of piping was in our ears all day. They were similarly numerous along the preserved shores of Lough Iron at Barronston. These birds, when excited by the invasion of their breeding-ground, perform a singular antic, rising in the air with violent cries and vibrating wings, and then slanting downwards, with rigid depressed wings, they reach the ground like a parachute. I have observed them in May or June on Lough Erne, Lough Arrow, Lough Key, Lough Oughter, Lough Sheelin, *Lough Gowna, Currygrane Lake, Lough Ree, *Glen Lough, Lough Iron, the Shannon, *Lough Derg, Lough Annagh, and at *Granston. They are reported to breed in Fermanagh, Roscommon, Leitrim, Cavan, Longford, Westmeath, Meath, Queen's Co., King's Co., and Tipperary, being, for the most part, summer visitors to the lakes; though Mr. Parker has observed them on Lough Derg in winter.

The CURLEW breeds extensively on the great red bogs, on which I have observed it near *Clonbrock, in Galway, and in Galway and Roscommon along the Shannon, Longford, *Westmeath, and King's Co. It is also reported to breed in Monaghan, Fermanagh, Cavan, Longford, Meath, King's Co., Queen's Co., and Tipperary. Between Banagher and Athlone, as I sailed up the Shannon on 4th June, it was the most noticeable bird feeding on the banks, and flying to and from the red bogs on the western side, where, as I was informed, young Curlews had been found on the 20th May. On Crit Bog, near Clonbrock, Co. Galway, on 30th May, Curlews, which evidently had young, came flying up one by one as we advanced, uttering a quavering whistle, quite different from their call-note, and skimming on before, alighted in full view to lure us away. I found a Curlew's nest among the taller heather, with remains of egg-shells. At Athlone I was informed that Curlew's eggs were often found on the bogs in May. Unlike the above waders, the Curlew, so far from forsaking its breeding-haunts in winter, is at that season seen on the bogs in flocks.

The WHIMBREL was only once met with by me on the Shannon, near Banagher, on 3rd June, 1892, but my visits to the lakes were too late for it. In King's Co., Mr. Digby states that it is "fairly common in early summer," and Mr. F. Dunne, that it is "common in May." In Queen's Co., Mrs. Croasdaile says that it is a "spring migrant," and Lord Castletown, that it is a "spring visitor in May," while on Lough Derg, Mr. Parker records it in a similar way. Thus it appears that the Whimbrel visits the central counties as well as the sea-shores.

BITTERNS. I am informed by Lord Clonbrock, that when he was a youth, about 1820 to 1830, he used every season, when grouse-shooting on his property, to meet with Bitterns, usually in pairs, which used to annoy him by running before the dogs a long distance before getting up.

(TO BE CONCLUDED.)

THE EARTHWORMS OF IRELAND.
BY REV. HILDERIC FRIEND, F.L.S.

(*Continued from page* 220.)

3. **A. (Dendrobæna) subrubicunda,** Eisen.—A well-defined species, and more widely distributed than any of the other dendrobænic forms. It often occurs by scores and hundreds in the midst of vegetable debris on the banks of rivers and streams, and is easily recognized. It is the largest, and in point of size, the most variable species of the group, and is more frequently found away from trees than the others.

Eisen described it in 1873 as a new species, but I am convinced that this is the *Lumbricus puter* of Hoffmeister, and must be identical with many of the worms which are now reckoned as synonymous with this. Eisen's description is clear and full, so far as external characters are concerned, and a slightly modified translation, to meet our methods of notation, will exactly suit our indigenous species.

Body cylindrical, somewhat depressed anteriorly and attenuated posteriorly, flattened on the under surface. Prostomium large and pallid, dividing the peristomium to about one-half its diameter. Girdle large and conspicuous, of a dull grey colour, and usually covering six or seven segments, 25, 26-31. On each side of the girdle ventrally, and covering segments 28, 29, 30, is a band which constitutes the *tubercula pubertatis*. Setæ in distant couples, not close together as in *Lumbricus*, or slightly separated as in the Brandling. Total number of segments about 90 or 100, length averaging 90 millimetres.

I may add that the colour is rosy red, with somewhat lighter undersurface. Setæ on pale glands, which arrangement makes them conspicuous. Spermathecæ opening in the line of the dorsal setæ (Rosa).

A tender delicate worm, well adapted for bait. It is largely employed by anglers in England, under the name of the Cockspur or Gilt-tail, the latter name being derived from the colour of the anal extremity. When a drop of methylated spirit is placed upon the living worm it exudes a yellow fluid, and this may be readily observed flowing from the dorsal pores, the first of which occurs, as Ude has correctly pointed out, between segments 5 and 6. Spermathecæ are found in the 10th segment, which open in intersegment 9/10 in the direction of the superior pair of setæ. Eisen gives full directions for distinguishing between this species and the Branding (*Allolobophora fœtida*, Sav.); but if examined in a living condition, these instructions are absolutely unnecessary. Dr. Greene informs me the Gilt-tail is called the Small Brambling [=Brandling] at Ferns. Benham is in error[1] when he says *A. subrubicunda* is destitute of spermathecæ and *tubercula pubertatis*.

Synonyms: *Allolobophora subrubicunda*, Eisen (*op. cit.*, p. 51). *A. putris*, Rosa, 1893. *Lumbricus puter*, Hoffmeister, 1845; *Dendrobæna puter*, Œrley, "A Mag. Olig. Faunája," 1880, p. 586. Œrley has rightly identified the worm, but did not recognize that it was the same as Eisen's *subrubicunda*. He, however, doubted the accuracy of assigning *L. puter*, Hoffm., to *D. boeckii*, Eisen. To this species, and not to *D. boeckii*, Eisen, as Rosa suggests, we must, I think, relegate the *Enterion octaedrum*, Savigny, and perhaps also *A. fraissei*, Œrley.

DISTRIBUTION IN IRELAND.—Loughlinstown, Co. Dublin (Dr. Scharff); Leeson-park (do.); Blackrock, Co. Dublin (Miss Kelsall); Woodenbridge, Co. Wicklow (Dr. Scharff); Cashel, Co. Tipperary (Lieut.-Colonel R. E. Kelsall); Ferns, Co. Wexford (Dr. Greene); Aghaderg, Co. Down (Rev. H. W. Lett); Cork (Miss A. N. Abbott); Holywood, Co. Down (Miss C. M. Patterson); Valencia, Co. Kerry (Miss Delap); Kilmartin, Co. Dublin (Dr. Trumbull); Malahide (do); Carrablagh, Lough Swilly (Mr. Hart); Glasnevin, Co. Dublin (Mr. Redding).

4. **A. (Dendrobæna) arborea**, Eisen. This diminutive worm was first described by Eisen in 1873. It appears to have been as entirely overlooked up till that date, as the last-named species was till eight years ago; and I have little doubt but that in future years, when the decaying forest trees of other lands come to be explored, we shall find several other species which up till the present time have passed altogether unobserved. The description of Eisen is true of our native species. Body cylindrical, prostomium large and pale, occupying about one-half of the first segment. Male pores on segment 15, tumid and conspicuous. Girdle for the most part composed of six segments, extending over 26–31. *Tubercula pubertatis* on the 14th and 15th segments behind the male pore, *i.e.*, on segments 29, 30. The anal segment somewhat exceeds in length that which precedes it. The setæ are everywhere in distant pairs. Segment 50-60 (sometimes more in British specimens); length about 50 millimetres (not so great in my British specimens). First dorsal pore between 5 and 6. Like *Dendrobæna boeckii* (says Eisen), this species is found in old stumps of trees, into which, however, it penetrates further than the latter species. The specimens which I have examined were found deep in the wood, while the two other species (*A. celtica* and *A. eiseni*) were found, as a rule, less deeply imbedded. Eisen examined one specimen in which the *tubercula pubertatis* extended over segments 28, 31. At first sight the species resembles *D. boeckii*, remarks Eisen; and it is marvellous that he should found a genus for tree-haunting worms, and exclude from it his own *arborea*.

Synonym: *Allolobophora arborea*, Eisen, Om Skand. Lumb. 1873. Sub-species of *A. putris*, Rosa, Rev. dei Lumb. 1893.

DISTRIBUTION IN IRELAND.—Malahide, Co. Dublin (Dr. Trumbull); Leeson-park, Dublin (Dr. Scharff).

5. **A. (Dendrobæna) eiseni**, Levinsen. Up to the present time this

---

[1] "Attempt to Classify Earthworms," Q.J.M.S., xxxi., p. 260.

worm has happily passed through the hands of systematists invariably as *Lumbricus eiseni*, Levinsen; but the time has come when it must be removed from the false position it has occupied undisturbed till the present. It must, however, be admitted that it does not fit in with the genus *Allolobophora*, though it belongs to this place as a true tree-worm.

The worm is small, cylindrical, slightly attenuated, usually about an inch, or at most an inch and a half, in length, *i.e.*, 30 to 40 millimetres. Its prostomium, like that of the true *Lumbricus*, forms with the peristomium a perfect mortise and tenon. It often closely resembles the typical *Lumbricus* in colour, being a warm brown, frequently with iridescence, and has the setæ in couples somewhat closer together. These are its only affinities in that direction. It lives in old trunks of trees and among decaying timber or woodland debris, is small, destitute of the two pairs of spermathecæ which every true *Lumbricus* possesses, and in the matter of clitellum and its accessories is separated very widely from that genus.

The girdle covers eight segments, extending from 24 to 31; total number of segments, 90-110. There are no *tubercula pubertatis*; the male pore on segment 15 is on papillæ slightly developed, and the first dorsal pore is between 5 and 6. The constancy of this feature in the dendrobænic group is striking. Rosa submitted specimens exactly answering this descriptions to Levinsen, who stated that they were identical with his *Lumbricus eiseni*.[1] The original specimens from Copenhagen were taken, according to Rosa's translation of Levinsen's account, from old trees, and my British specimens have been obtained from similar habitats.

Synonym: *Lumbricus eiseni*, Levinsen (Syst. geogr. Oversigt over de nord. Ann. &c., Copenhagen, 1883). *A. eiseni*, Rosa, 1893. Dr. Rosa has done me the honour to place on record the fact that I was the first to assign this curious worm to its rightful place.

DISTRIBUTION IN IRELAND.—Woodenbridge, Co. Wicklow (Dr. Scharff); Valencia, Co. Kerry (Miss Delap); Malahide, Co. Dublin (Dr. Trumbull); Carrablagh, Lough Swilly (Mr. Hart); Leeson-park, Dublin (Dr. Scharff).

We are now prepared for a survey of the principal characteristics. of the group.

§ DENDROBÆNA, Eisen.

Small tender worms, from 1 to 2½ inches in length, found in decaying trees, among dead leaves, and rotten vegetable matter; sometimes wandering to other habitats. Colour usually brown, rose-red or flesh, with dull clitellum and lighter-under-surface. Prostomium more or less deeply imbedded in the peristomium, which is without setæ. Setæ always in eight rows or in four couples, more or less distant, making the body appear octangular.

Girdle occuping five to eight segments, commencing somewhere between the 24th and 31st.

Male or spermiducal pores on segment 15, usually with prominent papillæ, which sometimes extend over the two adjoining segments.

Tubercula pubertatis in two or three pairs on consecutive segments; not observed in one species.

First dorsal pore usually between segments 5 and 6. Spermatophores between the male pore and the clitellum.

The internal characters have not yet been made out with sufficient accuracy by any investigator to allow of classification. Spermathecæ are present in some species, but absent from others. When present they are open in the direction of the superior pair of setæ (Rosa).

Usually secreting a small quantity of yellow fluid from the dorsal pores.

The accompanying table supplies in concise form the principal distinguishing features of this interesting group of worms.

---

[1] Bolletino Mus. Zool. ed Anat. 1887, 1889.

TABULAR VIEW OF BRITISH ALLOLOBOPHORÆ.
§ Dendrobæna.

Name.	Clitellum occupies.	Tubercula pubertatis.	First Dorsal Pore.	Total segments.	Length.	Colour.	Prostomium imbedded	Setæ.
1. *celtica*, Rosa ...	31-36	33-34	5/6?	90-110	1-1½ in.	Brown or Rose-red.	Partially.	4 pairs wide.
2. *boeckii*, Eisen	29-33	31, 32, 33	5/6	90-100	1-1½ in.	Red-brown.	Two-thirds.	8 rows.
3. *subrubicunda*, Eisen ...	25-31	28, 29, 30	5/6	100-120	1½-2½ in.	Rose-red.	Partially.	4 pairs separated
4. *arborea*, Eisen	26-31	29, 30	5/6	50-80	1 in.	Rose-red.	Slightly.	4 pairs wide.
5. *eiseni*, Levinsen	24-31	0	5/6	90-110	1½ in.	Red-brown iridescent	Completely.	4 pairs close.

I beg to thank my numerous correspondents for their favours, and to inform them that my address in future will be "Fernbank, Cockermouth, Cumberland." As I must conclude my Irish researches this year, I shall be thankful to receive specimens from collectors at an early date, and should be specially glad to have typical series from those parts of the island which have not yet been worked. Living worms may be sent in tin boxes with soft moss, and should be marked "NATURAL HISTORY SPECIMENS."

(TO BE CONTINUED.)

THE SCALP, COUNTY DUBLIN.
BY G. H. KINAHAN, M.R.I.A.

SHOTOVER Hill is a godsend to the geological professors of Oxford, as no one will ever be able to determine the exact ages of its rocks; and similarly the Scalp is a godsend to the professors of geology in the Dublin schools, because, as to its age and the process of its formation, there have been numerous theories; and there will be, as long as there are successive generations of geologists in Dublin.

Jukes, to account for the transverse nearly N. and S. gashes across the S.W. Cork ridges, suggested that at one time there was high land to the northward, the drainage from which cut N. and S. transverse valleys. This theory he seems, however, to have afterwards abandoned; as, on more matured examination and consideration, he found that the transverse valleys must have had a much more recent origin than the longitudinal ones.

A similar theory to that abandoned by Jukes was adopted by Prof. Hull to account for the Scalp. He considered that in the Co. Dublin there was high land to the northward, the drainage from which excavated the Scalp. He said nothing of the parallel valleys, such as those of the Slaney, etc., but, presumably, they ought also to be included. His view as to the Scalp seems now to be also adopted by Professors Sollas and Cole.

It seems to me indisputable, that the plain of Dublin was at one time much higher than at present, as a vast thickness of the Carboniferous limestone has been denuded away, and also of the Coal-measures, the latter alone being more than 4,000 feet thick. But at what time did this great denudation take place? And during this period of denudation, at what time was the granite ridge exposed? It is self-evident that the Granite, and its adjuncts, the Ordovicians, and the other older rocks, were protrudes prior to the accumulation of the Carboniferous rocks; but, at the same time, it appears highly improbable, that at the time when there were high Coal-measure hills in the Co. Dublin, an iota of the old rocks came to the surface, the granitic and associated rocks never having appeared until after the envelope was removed; that is, not till after the Coal-measure hills of the Co. Dublin had disappeared. It cannot be denied that the granite ridge was a margin of a basin in the Carboniferous sea, as we find the littoral conglomerates of the Carboniferous high up on it; but was it always land during the Carboniferous epoch? or was it so near the surface as to be susceptible of denudation? that is, while the Carboniferous hills were high enough to send their drainage southward.[1]

It has been suggested, I think, by more than one authority, that the Irish Coal-measures were denuded to form the Lias

---

[1] It is not only possible, but to me it seems probable, that old rocks, pre-Cambrian, Ordovician, and granite, formed hills margining the plain of Dublin to the south, and that of Kildare, Carlow, and Kilkenny to the east. This is proved by the blocks of granite found in the Kimmage limestones; but that the Carboniferous rocks extended over these hills seem to be problematical, as the Carboniferous rocks in Co. Wexford and

accumulations elsewhere; and if this is correct, the Carboniferous hills of the Dublin plain must have disappeared thousands and thousands of years before the Scalp existed.

But had the denudants anything to do with the Scalp? To me it would seem that they had not. Ireland was under water or ice, or some such envelope, and when "the dry land appeared," it contracted during the drying process, and shrinkage-fissures formed. This subject has been very exhaustively entered into in my work on "Valleys and their relation to Faults, Fissures, etc.,"[1] and especially in chapter ii.

In 1878, I suggested in the "Geology of Ireland" that the Scalp was "probably excavated by marine action aided by ice along dykes of fault-rock." Since then, however, I have had opportunities of more carefully studying it and similar valleys, and would be inclined to suggest that it is nearly solely due to simple shrinkage-fissures, and that, since its formation, it has not been subjected to the effects of any denudants.

A study of the ravines, the adjuncts of the granite range of Leinster, shows that these are of different ages, some being comparatively recent. The ravine of the Liffey at Poulaphuca must be very modern, as the river-bed in which it formerly flowed southward is still very conspicuous and unchanged. The valley of the Slaney must have opened before or during the Esker sea period, as in it is found the marine drift. The valley of Tinnahely is probably older, as it is in parts occupied by moraine detritus; while the Devil's Glen, like the Scalp, is due to a movement that took place at quite a recent date. It may be allowable to suggest that the ravines at Poulaphuca, the Devil's Glen, and the Scalp, were formed at about one and the same time; that is, after the ice-cap had disappeared, and the Esker sea had retreated, so that now, in none of these, is there found drift of any kind, except meteoric accumulations, still daily forming.[2]

Waterford suggest estuarine accumulations; at the same time it must be allowed that these small areas may be the remains or roots of the formed Carboniferous sheet. Low down in the Queen's Co. and Tipperary fields there is a continuous massive sandstone made up almost solely of granite detritus.

[1] Trübner and Co., London, 1875.

[2] In the Scalp there are said to be foreign blocks; these, however, may have come down from the drift.

Let us suppose that the Scalp was excavated by a stream flowing south. If so, where is now the granite detritus that was excavated? The nearly total absence of all granite detritus in the drift of the Bray and Enniskerry valley is remarkable; in fact, you find nearly as many blocks of conglomerate (from Portraine and Rush) as of granite. It has been suggested that possibly the numerous pieces of limestone in the drift of the country south of the Scalp range came from the "Dublin Carboniferous hills" through the Scalp gorge. As, however, this drift in which the limestone is found is glacial, it would necessitate that the drift was carried by ice, not normal water; but in the Scalp there is not a trace of glacial or any other drifts, except æolian and meteoric. Compare the Scalp with the nearest valley, Glencullen. The latter must be much more ancient, as in it are different phases of the accumulation of drift—first, moraine matter that was subsequently denuded by the force that excavated the stream-ravine; then, still more subsequently, there were modifications due to meteoric abrasion and its adjuncts; the latter still taking place. In fact, this longitudinal valley must be more ancient than the transverse one.

In favour of the formation of the Scalp being due to a shrinkage-fissure, the enquirer's attention may be directed to the numerous facts recorded in the book already referred to ("Valleys and their relation to Faults, Fissures etc."). Numerous examples might be given of shrinkage-gorges, but we will only refer to one; as this valley, in its general characters, is very similar to the Scalp. The example to which I refer is Barnesbeg, Co. Donegal, through which the road from Kilmacrenan to the country on the northward has been made. To me it would appear evident that this valley owes its origin to a combination of shrinkage-fissures, one of which at least, as in the Scalp, caused a lateral displacement, but associated with them there is no record of any drift-forming agent. The fissures formed, while subsequently atmospheric abrasion and disintegration came into force, blocks falling from the different marginal cliffs to form rocky tali, the blocks being slightly modified by meteoric action, while the detritus thus formed was carried away by the winter and summer floods. Thus here, as in connection with the Scalp, there is no accumulation, that can legitimately be called drift, which has been carried out of the valley, the sole drift being gravel, a mere bagatelle, due to runlets and streams during summer and winter storms. I purposely put summer before winter, as a summer downpour, acting on sun-baked rocks, carries down more detritus than winter rain.

NOTES ON THE FUNGI OF THE DUBLIN DISTRICT (COUNTIES OF DUBLIN AND WICKLOW).

BY GREENWOOD PIM, M.A., F.L.S., AND E. J. M'WEENEY, M.A, M.D.

[Read before the Dublin Naturalists' Field Club, 14th February, 1893.]

INTRODUCTION.—BY GREENWOOD PIM.

THE first attempt at a mycologic flora of the Dublin district appeared in the handbook compiled for the British Association meeting in 1878, and was published simultaneously in the *Scientific Proceedings of the Royal Dublin Society* for that year. It included about 470 species. In 1883 a short supplemental list of some sixty species was published by the Royal Irish Academy. Since then, with the exception of a few stray notes in the proceedings of the Dublin Microscopical Club in the *Irish Naturalist*, nothing bearing on this subject, so far as I am aware, has appeared.

During the ten years that have since elapsed, a considerable number of new species have come under my notice, notwithstanding that I have been able to devote but little time to the subject of mycology, and my colleague in this paper has also added a large number to the record. It seemed, therefore, desirable to gather together what has been done, and put it into a form available for future reference. It was, indeed, suggested that the former lists should be incorporated in the present one, so as to give a complete catalogue of the species hitherto met with in the district, but it was found that this would occupy too much space; moreover, it is very certain that there are many more forms still to record before anything like a complete mycologic flora of Dublin and Wicklow is possible. Hence only those not previously recorded appear in the annexed catalogue. The groups of Uredinei, Ustilaginei, and Alluviacei, form, however, an exception to this rule. Recent investigations have so completely revolutionized their nomenclature and arrangement that it has been thought necessary to give a complete list of all the species hitherto met with in the district. The extremely evanescent nature of many fungi causes a twofold difficulty in their study. Firstly, in a given district, at a given period, a species may occur abundantly of which no trace was visible a week before, or would be a week after. Secondly, they decay very rapidly, and hence when necessity arises—as it constantly does—of obtaining the opinion of another worker, by the time the specimen reaches him, it may be unrecognizable.

The list appended hereto contains about 245 species not included in previous lists, bringing the total number up to nearly 780. Of the aforesaid 245, eighty belong to the Agaricini, twenty-six to eighteen other orders of Hymenomycetes. Gasteromycetes (including Myxomycetes) number thirteen. Coniomycetes, amongst which are the Uredinei and Ustalaginei, forty-two. Hyphomycetes (including Peronosporeæ) twenty-four. Discomycetes, thirty-six. Pyrenomycetes, twenty. The Agaricini generally are fairly well represented in the district, but the genus *Cortinarius* is conspicuous by its comparative absence, and the same may be said of the pink-spored division of the agarics, and of the woody or coriaceous genera. Two species of *Panus* are, however, recorded for the first time. Several new Polyporei are added to the list, and a few of other orders of the Hymenomycetes.

Amongst the Gasteromycetes, the occurrence in Powerscourt of *Cynophallus caninus* may be noted. Several additions are made to the Myxogastres, which are fairly represented, though perhaps not so numerously as might be expected, considering the dampness of the climate. Not a single new subterraneous gasteromycete is recorded, nor is there anything to add in the corresponding group of Tuberacei, or Truffles.

The Uredinei and Ustilaginei (Rusts, Brands, and Smuts), are, perhaps, the most numerous, relatively, of any of the groups, no fewer than seventy-seven species being recorded, and it can scarcely be doubted that careful searching would reveal many more. Amongst the Hyphomycetes, a very curious minute form occurred on decaying passion-flower leaves, parasitic on a larger mould. Mr. Grove considered it a new genus, which he honoured me with calling *Pimia*. Two remarkable forms occurred a few years ago on Silo grass at the Model Farm, Glasnevin, which are fully described in Mr. W. G. Smith's "Diseases of Field and Garden Crops," under the names of *Isaria fuciformis* and *Saprolegnia philomukes*. The peculiar and beautiful mould, *Myxotrichum deflexum*, occurred on a whitened wall at Royal College of Surgeons, along with the minute *Peziza domestica*, while Dr. McWeeney adds no less than six species of *Peronospora*.

Turning to the Discomycetes, some thirty-eight new species are noted, among which are the rare forms, *Vibrissea truncorum*, which recurs regularly every spring in the same spot in Powerscourt demesne, and also found by Dr. M'Weeney in the Slade Brook, and *V. guernisaci* at Altadore. Even with these additions our list of Discomycetes is far from large. This seems strange, as though frequently not very prominent, they are not usually so small as to be very readily overlooked, and our climate and conditions seem admirably adapted to their production.

Of the Pyrenomycetes, the same remarks hold good, except as regards their size, which is generally very minute, which may possibly account for the exceedingly small number recorded. Amongst the additions is *Torrubia militaris*, a most remarkable object always found on dead pupæ, or caterpillars.

The large extent to which the following list is indebted to Dr. M'Weeney, the initial letters in brackets (M'W.) will indicate, as representing the species found by him, (P.) is similarly appended to those for which I am responsible. There can, I think, be little doubt that careful investigation will be rewarded with many discoveries even in our best-worked localities, while almost the whole of the rest of Ireland is a *terra incognita* as regards Fungi. An exception must, howbe made as regards the north-east, which has been well explored by Rev. H. W. Lett, while a few species from Killarney and Glengariff may be found in my report in *Proceedings Royal Irish Academy* (Science) for 1885.

The following list has for convenience been arranged generally on the lines of that in Cooke's "Handbook," as being the book in most general use, although not quite up to modern ideas:—

LIST OF SPECIES.
HYMENOMYCETES.
AGARICINI.

Agaricus (Amanita)
phalloides, Fr.—Knocksink (P.), Powerscourt (P.)
excelsus, Fr.—Kilruddery (P.)
strobiliformis, Fr.—Glenarty (P.)
spissus, Fr.—Ovoca (P.)
lenticularis, Lasch.—Powerscourt (P.)

A. (Lepiota)
granulosus, Batsch—Powerscourt (P.)
var. **broadwoodiæ** (?)—Montpelier (M'W.); Glencullen (M'W.)
cepæstipes, Sow.—Monkstown (P.)

A. (Tricholoma)
nictitans, Fr.—Ovoca (P.)
cælatus,—Ovoca (P.)
columbetta, Fr.—Glencullen (McW.)
vaccinus, P.—Whitechurch (McW.)

A. (Clitocybe)
inversus, Scop.—Powerscourt (P.)
difformis, P.— do. (P.)
bellus, Fr.—Glencullen (M'W.)

A. (Pleurotus)
septicus, Fr.—Friarstown (M'W.)
subpalmatus, Fr.—Hollybrook (P.)
acerosus, Fr.—W. Pier, Kingstown (P.)

A. (Collybia)
atratus, Fr.—Glenart (P.)
protractus, Fr.—Glencullen (M'W.)
plexipes, Fr.— do. (M'W.)

A. (Mycena)
hiemalis, Obs.—Powerscourt (P.)
capillaris, Schum.—do. (P.) Friarstown (M'W.)
filopes, Bull.—Glencullen (M'W.)
elegans, P.—Whitechurch (M'W.)
vitilis, F.—Glencullen (M'W.)
galopus, Schrad.—do. (M'W.)
stylobates, P.—Whitechurch (M'W.)
corticola, Schum.—Altadore (M'W.)

A. (Omphalia)
affricatus, Fr.—Glencullen (M'W.)

A. (Entoloma)
jubatus, Fr.—Glencullen, Mountpellier (M'W.)

A. (Leptonia)
æthiops, Fr.—Celbridge, Powerscourt (P.).

A. (Pholiota)
durus, Bolt.—Ovoca (P.)
præcox, P.—Rocky Valley (P.) Rush (M'W.)
levelllianus, D. & M.—Tullow (P.)
capistratus, Cks.—Near Lucan (M'W.)
marginatus, Blach.—do. and Mountpelier (M'W.)

A. (Hebeloma)
longicaudus, P.—Monkstown (P.)
eutheles, B. & Br.,—Knocksink (P.)

A. (Crepidotus)
alveolus, Lasch.—Enniskerry (P.)
mollis, Schaeff.—Loughlinstown (P.); Glencullen, Altadore (M'W.)

A. (Naucoria).
conspersus, Fr.—In store, Monkstown (P.)

A. (Galera)
ovalis, Fr.—In store, Dundrum (P.)
mniophilus Lasch.—On *Pellia*, Glencullen (M'W.)

A. (Stropharia)
melaspermus, Bull.—Kilruddery (P.)
stercorarius, Fr.—Seven Churhes (P.), Glencullen (M'W.)

A. (Hypholoma)
epixanthus, Fr.—Powerscourt (P.), Whitechurch (M'W.)
velutinus, P.—Kilruddery (P.)

A. (Psilocybe)
ericaceus, Pers.—Glasamuck (M'W.)
clivensis, Bk.—Whitechurch (M'W.)

A. (Psathyra)
  spadiceo-griseus, Schaeff.—Glencullen, Powerscourt(M'W.)
A. (Panæolus)
  phalænarum, Fr.—(M'W.)
A. (Psathyrella)
  disseminatus, Fr.—Monkstown (P.); Lough Bray (M'W.)
Coprinus
  extinctorius, Fr.—Knocksink (P.)
  tomentosus, Fr.—Rathgar (M'W.)
Cortinarius (Inoloma)
  violaceus, Fr.—Glencullen (M'W.)
  subianatus, Fr.—do. (M'W.) Rathgar (M'W.)
C. (Myxacium)
  collinitus, Fr.—Mountpelier, (M'W.)
C. (Dermocybe)
  anomalus, Fr.—Enniskerry(P.)
  miltinus, Fr.—Glencullen (M'W.)
  uliginosus, Bk.—Glencree (M'W.)
Lepista
  cineraneus, Bull.—Enniskerry (M'W.)
Hygrophorus
  nemoreus, Fr.—Hollybrook (P.)
Lactarius
  tormenosus, Fr.— Monkstown, Altadore (P.)
  pallidus, Fr.—Ovoca (P.)
  rufus, Fr.—Scalp (P.); Glencullen (M'W.)
  quietus, Fr.—Glencullen(M'W.)
  zonarius, Fr.—Glencullen (M'W.)
Russula
  adusta, Fr.—Powerscourt (P.)
  heterophylla, Fr.—Ovoca (P.)
  decolorans, Fr.— do. (P.)
  rubra, Fr.—Glencullen (M'W.)
  ochroleuca, Fr.—do. (M'W.)
  depallens, Fr.—do. and Whitechurch (M'W.)
  sardonia, Fr.—do. (M'W.)
Cantharellus
  lobatus, Fr.—Glencullen (P.)
  tubæformis, Fr.—do. (M'W.)

Marasmus
  epiphyllus, Fr.—Enniskerry (M'W.)
Panus
  torulosus, Fr.—Near Lucan (M'W.); Powerscourt (P.)
  stypticus, Fr.—Enniskerry (M'W.)
Boletus
  granulatus, L.—Enniskerry (P.); Bray Head (M'W.)
  cyanescens, Bull.—Ovoca (P.)
Polyporus
  bombycinus, Fr.—Whitechurch (M'W.)
  melanopus, Fr.—Powerscourt and Kilruddery (P.)
  rufescens, Fr.—Kilruddery(P.)
  varius, Fr.—Powerscourt (P.)
  elegans, Fr.—Powerscourt and Kilruddery (P.)
  salicinus, Fr.—Monkstown (P.)
  ulmarius, Fr.—Kilruddery (P.)
  fraxinus, Fr.—Monkstown (P.)
  obducens, Fr.,—Near Lucan (M'W.)
Daedalea
  unicolor, Fr.—Near Lucan (M'W.)
Hydnum
  ferruginosum, Fr.—Kilruddery (P.)
Craterellus
  crispus, Fr.—Ovoca (P.)
Thelephora
  anthocephala, Fr.—Kilruddery (P.)
  laciniata, Per.—Killakee (M'W.)
  sebacea, Fr.—Altadore (M'W.)
  puteana, Schum.—Altadore (M'W.)
Hymenochæte
  corrugata, B.—Powerscourt (P.)
Cyphella
  pimii, Phill.—On stem in water, Monkstown (P.)
Solenia
  ochracea, Hoffm.—Kilruddery (P.)

(TO BE CONCLUDED.)

NOTES.

BOTANY.

LIVERWORTS.

Ricciocarpus natans, Corda [Riccia natans, Linn.] in Co. Dublin.—While botanizing along the Grand Canal early last month (7th August), I discovered this interesting species growing in great abundance in a sluggish ditch, evidently long undisturbed, beside an old grass-grown road near Ballyfermott. The plant, mingled with *Lemna minor*, extends along the ditch here, at intervals, for more than a hundred yards, spreading its starry root-like processes over the surface of the water in a dark-brown sheet which at once arrests attention. Mr. David McArdle, of the Glasnevin Botanic Gardens, who has kindly examined my specimens and determined the species, assures me that he can find no record of its having been previously noted in the Co. Dublin, and supplies me with the following details as to its distribution in Ireland, so far as hitherto made out, the known stations for the species being (1) boggy pool between Navan and Drogheda; (2) ditch by the side of the Shannon, near Portumna, Co. Galway; (3) near Passy, Co. Limerick (Dr. Harvey); (4) ditch by the River Barrow, three miles below Athy, Co Kildare (Mr. R. W. Scully).—NATHANIEL COLGAN, Dublin.

CLUB-MOSSES.

Lycopodium clavatum L. in Co. Armagh.—On August 10th I received from Rev. H. W. Lett a specimen of this plant, collected two days previously, on Brackagh Bog, south of Portadown, Co. Armagh; Mr. Lett describes the plant as plentiful in one spot. This is an interesting addition to the county flora, especially since the elevation of the bog in question is only fifty feet above sea-level; in the north of Ireland at least this Club-moss usually occurs on mountain heaths.—R. LLOYD PRAEGER.

PHANEROGAMS.

Euphorbia cyparissias L. in King's County.—In the early part of this year I received from Miss Margaret Goodbody, of Charlestown House, Clara, King's Co., some imperfect specimens of a plant unknown to her. They were a puzzle to me at the time, but subsequently proved to be the rare and peculiar *Euphorbia cyparissias* L. On the 23rd May last, I was taken to the spot, and found it profusely in flower and in considerable quantity, extending along a dry hedge-bank with one or two intervals for about twenty yards. It grows in a lane near Horseleap, about two and a-half miles from Clara, and the only house near it is a cottage, from the garden of which it does not seem likely to have escaped. In the "English Flora" it is looked upon as having been introduced, and no doubt the same applies to the specimen we are now considering, which is however remarkable from its remote situation, and the extent to which it has been established. On finding it, I immediately sent fresh specimens to Mr. A. G. More, and to Mr. Stewart, of Belfast, and have since placed dried specimens in the Herbarium of the Science and Art Museum, Dublin. —THOMAS CHANDLEE, Athy.

The Shamrock.—A Postscript.—In the paper on this subject, published in last month's number of the *Irish Naturalist*, I omitted through oversight to mention that the plant supplied to me by Mr. Bur-

bidge, from the stock grown in the College Botanic Garden, to meet the
demands of English inquirers for the real Shamrock, was *Trifolium
minus*, as were also the plants purchased from an advertiser in the Co.
Louth, as the "true Irish variety."—NATHANIEL COLGAN, Dublin.

The Shamrock.—As Mr. Colgan, in his interesting paper of last
month, was unable to include Kerry in his list of the counties using *T.
minus* as the Shamrock, it may be of interest to mention that as I passed
through the Gap of Dunloe, Killarney, in the month of July, I noticed
that this was the plant (then in flower) offered to tourists by the mountain
guides. It may also be here stated that so far as Cork is concerned, notwithstanding the fact that Mr. Colgan was sent two other species from this
district, *T. minus* is the true Shamrock; it is this is selected for St.
Patrick's Day by everybody who is sufficiently observant to notice that
there are more species of trefoil than one, and it is this that is sold in the
shops and in the streets, being distinguished by its small leaves and by
the absence of the white and black markings which usually occur on the
foliage of *T. repens* and *T. pratense*. I have seen people wearing *T. repens*
ridiculed for decorating themselves with "clover." I was rather disappointed to find that the results of Mr. Colgan's painstaking investigation
were not much more in favour of *T. minus*, as I have always looked upon
that species as the Shamrock, even though many botanical works give
the honour to *T. repens*. A fact which tends to show that *T. minus* is
regarded throughout Ireland as the national badge is, that the manu-
facturers of Christmas and St. Patrick's Day cards on which sprays of
real Shamrock are mounted, so far as I have observed on cards made in
Belfast and Cork, invariably use this species.—R. A. PHILLIPS, Cork.

Clare Plants.—We have received from Mr. Patrick B. O'Kelly, of
Ballyvaughan, Co. Clare, a "Complete List of the Rare Perennial Plants
and Shrubs of the Burren Mountains of Ballyvaughan," which has been
compiled by its industrious author, not merely to assist the cause of
science, but with ulterior motives of a pecuniary nature. Indeed, a
pretty smart price is affixed to many of the "rare perennial plants," and
notwithstanding Mr. O'Kelly's assurance that they are all "real gems of
the first water," few of us would care to pay the sum of 1s. for specimens
of such plants as *Asperula odorata*, *Carex stellulata*, *C. sylvatica*, or *Nardus
stricta*; or even a modest 6d. for *Reseda luteola*, *Juncus maritimus*, or *J.
squarrosus*. In passing, we may mention that it is with some surprise that
we learn that *Arabis thaliana*, *Chlora perfoliata*, *Erodium cicutarium*, *Gentiana
campestris*, *Jasione montana*, *Linum catharticum*, and many similar plants are
perennials! It is of interest also to find enumerated in the flora of the
Burren mountains, *Lathyrus maritimus*, *Lysimachia punctata*, *Œnothera odorata*, *Narcissus major*, and "*Primula veris elatior*"—the editor of the new
edition of "Cybele Hibernica" will please note. The names of some of
the Ballyvaughan plants strike us as infamiliar, such as *Chlora aureum*,
Melampyrum aquaticum, *Rubia tinctoria*, and *Adiantum incisum*. Are these
additions to the British flora which Mr. O'Kelly has made, or are they
new to science? if the latter, they should be duly described. With the
praiseworthy object of assisting in bringing our native plants more into
cultivation in gardens, Mr. O'Kelly kindly volunteers to name any such
plants which may be sent to him (return postage prepaid); but if the
plants are returned labelled with such apellations as "*Anemone nemorosa
purpurea Livingrii*," "*Berberis vulgaris superbum*," or "*Trifolium repens purpurea
foliis*," we fear that serious injury may be caused to the enquirer's nervous
system. Space does not permit of our availing ourselves of Mr. O'Kelly's
kind permission to publish his price-list *in extenso* in the pages of the
Irish Naturalist; but those who are interested in native plants should
certainly write for it, as they will find in it much novel information
respecting the local flora.

ZOOLOGY.

INSECTS.

Lemaerichsoni, Suffr., at Santry, Co. Dublin.—Examining some specimens of *Lema* collected by me last May, I noticed one which was very distinct from *L. lichenis*, and greatly resembled the rare *Lema erichsoni*. On sending it to Canon Fowler, the identification was confirmed. I succeeded in taking several more specimens on subsequent collecting excursions to the same locality. Dr. Power's capture of *L. erichsoni*, near Waterford, in the autumn of 1857, seems the only record from Ireland. The coleopterist in whose district *L. melanopa* is known to occur, should make a good search for *L. erichsoni*, as the British examples are considered by some authorities referrable to an unnamed concolorous variety of *L. melanopa*, and Canon Fowler has described the last-mentioned insect as probably widely distributed in Ireland. The specimens of *L. erichsoni* were taken by sweeping.—J. N. HALBERT, Dublin.

Wasps in Co. Antrim.—In the July issue of the *Irish Naturalist* there is a note on Irish Wasps from Mr. G. H. Carpenter.—I beg to send a list of Wasps collected by me in 1887 at Cushendun, Co. Antrim, and verified by Mr. F. W. Elliott, of Buckhurst-hill, Essex:—*Vespa norvegica, V. sylvestris, V. vulgaris, V. rufa,* and *V. germanica.*—SL. ARTHUR BRENAN, Knocknacarry, Co. Antrim.

Sirex gigas and Acherontia atropos in Co. Antrim.—These two insects were taken in August, 1892, at the Cushendun coastguard station, and are both new to this locality.—SL. ARTHUR BRENAN, Knocknacarry.

Gonopteryx rhamni and Nonagria arundinis, near Limerick. I captured the "Brimstone" butterfly in Cratloe Wood, Co. Clare, on the 12th and 18th August, 1893. Two specimens (both males) in beautiful condition, were taken. The record is of considerable interest, as the insect has so far been taken in Ireland only at Killarney, and near Kylemore, Co. Galway. It is a common butterfly in England, appearing early in the spring after hybernating, when it is very often observed. In August, 1892, whilst gathering Reed-maces (*Typha latifolia*), usually designated "Bullrushes," to my surprise I observed several of the stems contained the living pupæ of a fair-sized moth. I took examples so affected, near Coonagh, Co. Clare, and also at Mungret, Co. Limerick, but unfortunately failed to secure any imagos of the insect, those which emerged making good their escape, owing to the difficulty of keeping the pupæ moist in the long stems of the plants. This season I have been more fortunate, and have bred some sixteen good specimens from plants gathered near Mungret and Castleconnell, thus satisfactorily proving the identity of the insect as the "Bullrush" Moth (*Nonagria arundinis*), hitherto recorded only in Ireland from counties Down, Cork, and Wicklow.—FRANCIS NEALE, Limerick.

MOLLUSCS.

Trochus duminyi and Odostomia delicata on the Irish Coast.—I spent the last week in June at Bundoran, but owing to a most adverse change of weather, a gale from the north-west with rain, I was not able to work on the shore as I wished, and it was only the day before I returned home, that I was able to procure some promising drift. My great hope was to obtain *Trochus duminyi*, and I am happy to say that three specimens were found in the portion searched. I got one, and Mr. Marshall, of Seven Oaks, Torquay (with whom I shared the drift), secured two. He also records the occurrence in the same drift, of the new shell *Odostomia delicata;* he states "this shell was described by the Marquis de Monterosata in the *Journal de Conchyliologie* (1874, p. 267) as Mediterranean, and it is figured in Sowerby's 'Index of British Shells,' as *Chemnitzia similima*, Montagu, dredged in the 'Porcupine' Expedition off Donegal bay." It is a curious coincidence that I have to record these two rare shells from Killala bay also. Early in July, I was fortunate enough to procure some shell-drift from the sandy shore of Bartra Island, a portion of which I sent to Mr. Marshall, and he got one specimen of each of these shells; this is the second *T. duminyi* found in Bartra drift, and Mr. Marshall has one from near Portrush; he thinks it probable that it may be scattered along the coast, though rarely.—AMY WARREN, Ballina.

Testacella scutulum, Sow.—In my record of this species in the July number, I omitted to mention that its discovery in the Co. Dublin is really due to Mr. W. F. Burbidge, who found it some years ago in the Botanic Gardens of Trinity College, Dublin.—R. F. SCHARFF, Dublin.

FISHES.

Ray's Bream—A Correction.—On page 230 of our last issue "Dungannon" should read "Dungarvan."

BIRDS.

Montague's Harrier (Circus cineraceus) in Ireland.—A specimen of this rare Irish bird was shot by Mr. Power's gamekeeper at Glenasmole, on the 3rd of July, where, according to his account, it had been feeding on young Grouse for some time previously. The bird is a male, in second year's plumage. A rather curious fact about the occurrence of this species in Ireland is that, out of five recorded occurrences, four were either on the Dublin mountains, or in their immediate vicinity.—E. WILLIAMS, Dublin.

White-winged Black Tern (Sterna leucoptera) in Ireland.—A specimen of this beautiful bird has been obtained in the immediate vicinity of Newmarket-on-Fergus, Co. Leitrim, where it was engaged in hawking for flies over a small lake. This is, I believe, the fifth recorded occurrence of this bird in Ireland.—E. WILLIAMS, Dublin.

Stock-Doves (Columba ænas) at Rostrevor.—Dr. V. Ball F.R.S., hands us the following letter from Mr. A. S. G. Canning, of The Lodge, Rostrevor, Co. Down:—

"I write to mention a fact which may interest all lovers of natural history in this country. It is the appearance at this place of what seems to be the Stock-Dove (*Columba ænas*). Two pair or more have nested here this summer, and there are two young ones now not yet fledged. They make their nests on the ground near or in rabbit holes, and under whin bushes. They are smaller than the Cushat, and have no white on them. Perhaps you would like to communicate what I have written to any naturalists of your acquaintance."

GEOLOGY.

Visit of the Geologists' Association to Dublin.—During the last week of July an event of much interest to local geologists took place—the visit of the Geologists' Association of London to Dublin. Our English fellow-scientists turned out in good numbers, and, when joined by the local recruits, made a party of quite formidable dimensions. An excellent week's programme had been drawn out by Professors Sollas and Cole, and under guidance of these and other local experts, Portraine, Howth, Killiney, Bray, and other spots of geological interest in the neighbourhood were seen to full advantage, especially since the visitors were favoured with magnificent weather throughout their stay. We were not surprised to hear that the English visitors were charmed with their visit to the Irish capital, and with its geological surroundings, and we learn with pleasure that another Irish excursion is already spoken of—this time to Belfast and its beautiful district.

PROCEEDINGS OF IRISH SOCIETIES.

ROYAL ZOOLOGICAL SOCIETY.

Recent donations comprise Fish from Mr. Godden, a pair of White Rats from Mrs. Elliott, a pair of Badgers from the Earl of Clonmel, a Nightjar from J. Bates, Esq., and a pair of Barn Owls from N. McLean, Esq. 14,489 persons visited the Gardens in July.

BELFAST NATURAL HISTORY AND PHILOSOPHICAL SOCIETY.

JULY 21st.—Annual Meeting, the President (PROF. FITZGERALD, B.A.) in the chair. The Secretary (MR. R. M. YOUNG, M.R.I.A.) submitted the annual report, and the Treasurer (MR. J. BROWN) the statement of accounts, which were adopted, on the motion of Rev. Mr. Kinghan, seconded by Dr. McCormac. The report of the Ulster Fauna Committee, which was next submitted, showed that information respecting the local fauna was being steadily collected. A list of donations to the Museum was read, and a vote of thanks passed to the donors. The existing officebearers were re-elected for the coming year; and a motion authorising the council to exchange duplicate specimens of Irish antiquities for geological specimens with Mr. W. E. Praeger, Keokuk, U.S.A., concluded the business.

BELFAST NATURALISTS' FIELD CLUB.

JULY 29th.—Excursion to Ballynahinch. A large party proceeded by rail to Ballynahinch, and visited the ancient graveyard of Killgoney, where are the remains of a cromlech. After a halt at Magherahamlet the well-known spa claimed attention. Subsequently Montalto demesne was entered, where the lake-margins were found to be fringed with the Sweet Flag (*Acorus calamus*). Among the Lepidoptera taken during the day were *Vanessa atalanta*, *Charæas graminis*, *Crambus tristellus*, *Argyrothecia mendica*, and *Dictyopteryx contaminata*. At the business meeting held after the tea-hour the best thanks of the members were returned to Rev. Father Quail, P.P., for his unremitting kindness and attention to the party during the day.

DUBLIN NATURALISTS' FIELD CLUB.

JULY 29th.—Excursion to Lough Bray and Luggala in conjunction with the London Geologists' Association; a number of members of the Belfast Naturalists' Field Club were also present. The combined party, numbering between seventy and eighty, proceeded by 9 a.m. train to Bray, and drove via Enniskerry to Lough Bray, where an hour was spent. Thence the route lay through Sally Gap to Lough Tay, where the party descended on foot to the lake and walked through the grounds of Luggala Lodge, subsequently returning by car to Bray. On account of the large extent of ground covered, time did not permit of much collecting. The local *Andromeda polifolia* was observed in some quantity on bogs by the military road to the eastward of Lough Bray, at 1,650 feet elevation. *Listera cordata*, *Lastrea æmula*, and *L. montana* were gathered about Lough Bray, and *Wahlenbergia hederacea* on the way thither.

Fig. 1.

The track starts at **A**, and ends in a pit just beneath the handle of the walking-stick. Piece of seaweed, attached to stone, at **B**.

Fig. 2

The track starts at **A**, and ends in the pit below the centre of the figure. The stone to which the seaweed is attached lies in the pit.

SEAWEED TRACKS IN SAND.

SEAWEED TRACKS IN SAND.

BY PROF. W. J. SOLLAS, LL.D., F.R.S.

The shining, level, sandy flats of the seashore, spreading like a satiny quilted margin to the land, possess a charm to which we all succumb. The youngsters with their toy spades, the artist, and scientific wanderers of many kinds, open their ears to the enticement "Come unto these yellow sands," and though with various aims they go, their pleasure is the same.

Our coast is rich in wide expanses of rippled sand, but rarely will the geologist find one more full of interest than that which occurs at Sutton, on the coast of Howth. The ripple-marks, in their diverse character, afford an interesting study in connection with those so commonly met with on the sandy surface of ancient bedded rocks; the pits and hillocks which mark the home of the lobworm underground, will call to mind the trumpet-mouthed burrows which penetrate the Cambrian quartzite at Bray; and the crabs, sidling speedily to some lurk-hole, leave impressions on the sand that we may take careful note of, hoping some day to parallel them with problematic markings on the sands of ancient buried seashores. Less familiar than these common seashore sights are the long tracks to which we now call attention. Varying in width, frequently about an inch across, with raised margins, and a central groove which is minutely ridged and furrowed transversely, they run for long distances, undulating in wide curves (plate 6, fig. 1) to end in a little well-marked pit. To the question, "What made them?" everyone I have asked has immediately replied to the effect: "Evidently a wandering worm, or perhaps some kind of mollusc, say, a periwinkle for instance." Clearly: and there is the pit at the end, where he has gone underground! If we had a spade we would dig him out! As we have not, let us trace quickly a few of these grooves to the end, and see if we can catch sight of the creature in the act of making tracks.

In doing this we find that some of them extend for a long distance, one is measured twenty-three feet in length, but we never catch the culprit; and curiously enough, many of the tracks end beneath a piece of seaweed. It seems to be a very intelligent kind of animal that finds its path always to the same kind of shelter. Let us turn the seaweed over and see if it is underneath. No success; but in doing so we come across a curious find; attached to the seaweed is a little stone which lies in the terminal pit, and is just as broad as the furrow is wide (fig. 2). If we return to fig. 1 we shall see there also is a piece of seaweed sticking to a stone, and lying quite close to the end of the furrow. The murder is out; after all no animal was responsible, neither worm nor mollusc, simply a tuft of seaweed, dragging a stone after it as it was drifted seaward by the ebbing tide. The stone scores the furrow, driving out the sand to make a ridge on each side of its trail, and since, like every movement in nature, its progress is not continuous but interrupted, so the bottom of the furrow is not even, but ridged across at frequent intervals, and, as it were, rhythmically.

The story is instructive to the student of fossil markings, but it would be rash to conclude that every long ridge and furrow which has been attributed to annelids is a mere mare's nest. Both worms and molluscs do make tracks in the sand, and fossil examples of these are well known to exist, which, though not altogether dissimilar to those we have described, can be clearly distinguished by characters of their own.

The Earthworms of Ireland.—REV. H. FRIEND, whose new address is " Fernbank, Cockermouth, Cumberland," desires live specimens of Earthworms in damp moss, to enable him to make his lists of Irish localities as complete as possible.

NOTES ON THE FUNGI OF THE DUBLIN DISTRICT (COUNTIES OF DUBLIN AND WICKLOW).

BY GREENWOOD PIM, M.A., F.L.S., AND E. J. M'WEENEY, M.A., M.D.

(Concluded from page 249.)

HYMENOMYCETES.

Typhula grevillei, Fr.—Glencullen (M'W.)
Pistillaria culmigena, Mont.—Foxrock (M'W.)
Tremella indecorata, Schum.—Altadore (M'W.)
Tremella viscosa, P.—near Whitechurch (M'W.)
Apyrenium lignatile, Fr. Bray Head (M'W.)

GASTEROMYCETES.

Cynophallus caninus, Fr.—Powerscourt (P.)
Bovista plumbea, P.—Whitechurch (M'W)

UREDINEÆ.

[The arrangement of this order and of the Ustilagineæ has been so entirely revolutionized by recent investigations that it has been thought advisable to give a complete list of all the forms found in the district, arranged as in Dr. Plowright's book.]

Uromyces
 fabæ, Pers.—Monkstown (P.)
 geranii, DC.—Lucan, Dunran (M'W.)
 dactylidis, Otth.—Ballybrack (P.); Lucan (M'W.)
 poæ, Rabh.—Common (M'W.)
 rumicis, Schum.—Killiney (P.); Bray Head (M'W.)
 anthyllidis, Grev.—Bray Head (M'W.)
 alchemillæ, Pers.—Friarstown and Glenasmole (M'W.)
 ficariæ, Schum.—Rathfarnham (M'W.)

Puccinia
 galii, Pers.—Lucan (M'W.)
 calthæ, Lk.—Ballybrack (P.); Glenasmole (M'W.)
 silenes, Schrst.—Skerries (M'W.)
 variabilis, Grev.—Bray Head (M'W.); Ballybrack, Rocky Valley (P.)
 lapsanæ, Schltz.—Monkstown (P.)
 violæ, Schum.—Common (P.) (M'W.)
 pimpinellæ, Strauss.—Common (M'W.)
 apii, Ca.—Per Mr. F. Moore (P.)
 menthæ, Pers.—Common (P.) (M'W.)
 primulæ, DC.—Monkstown and Devil's Glen (P.)
 pulverulenta, Grev.—Bray Head (M'W.); Ballybrack (P.)
 saniculæ, Grev.—Common (P); Friarstown (M'W.)
 Puccinia vincæ, DC.—Monkstown (P.) (M'W.)
 graminis, Pers.—Common.
 phalaridis, Plow.—Lucan, Wicklow (M'W.)
 rubigo-vera, DC.—Not uncommon (P.) (M'W.)
 poarum, Niels.—Common (P.) (M'W.)
 caricis, Schum.—Common (P.) (M'W.)
 obscura, Schröt.—Ovoca (P.)
 arundinacea, Hed.—Ballybrack (P.)
 moliniæ, Tul.—Leixlip (M'W.)
 suaveolens, Pers.—Common (P.) (M'W.)
 bullata, Pers.—Common (P.); Murrough (M'W.)
 hieracii, Schum.—Kilmacanoge, Ovoca (P.); common (M'W.)
 taraxaci, Plow.—Bray Head (M'W.)
 oblongata, Lk.—Glendruid(P.)
 centaureæ, Mart.—Common (M'W.)
 pruni, Lk.—Rathgar (M'W.); Dalkey (P.)
 smyrnii, Ca.—Common (P.); Dodder Bank (M'W.)
 epilobii, DC.—Common (P.)
 umbilici, Grev.—Scalp(M'W.); common (P.)
 fergussoni, B. & Br.—Monkstown (P.)
 fusca, Relh.—Lucan (M'W.)
 bunii, DC.—Friarstown (M'W.)

Puccinia glomerata, Grev.— Lucan, Bray Head (P.) (M'W.); Ballybrack (P.)
malvacearum, Mont.—Common (P.) (M'W.)
circææ, Pers.—Not uncommon (M'W.)
veronicarum, DC.—Dray (P.)
glechomatis, DC.—Enniskerry (P.)
buxi, DC.—Mount Merrion (P.)
annularis, Strauss.—Devil's Glen (P.); Bray Head (M'W.)
Triphragmium ulmariæ, Schum.—Ballybrack(P.); Rathfarnham (M'W.)
Phragmidium fragariastri, DC.—Common (M'W.) (P.)
violaceum, Schltz.—Glencullen (M'W.)
rubi, Pers.—Very common (P.)
subcorticatum, Schrank.—Common (P.) (M'W.)

Gymnosporangium juniperinum, Lev.—Powerscourt, Ashford (P.)
sabinæ, Fr.—Blackrock, per Rev. M. H. Close (P.)
Melampsora helioscopiæ, Pers.—Common (P.) (M'W.)
lini, Pers.—Bray Head (M'W.)
farinosa, Pers.—Common (P.)
populina, Lev.—Fassaroe (P.)
hypericorum, DC.—Friarstown (M'W.); Dargle (P.)
betulina, Pers.—Glencree (M'W.)
Coleosporium senecionis, Pers.—Common (P.) (M'W.)
sonchi, Pers.—do. (P.) (M'W.)
euphrasiæ, Schm.—Common (P.) (M'W.)
Æcidium grossulariæ, Gmelin.—Common (P.)
periclymeni, Schm.—Bray Head (M'W.)

USTILAGINEÆ.

Ustilago segetum, Bull.—Common (P.) (M'W.)
flosculorum, DC.—Greystones, per A. F. Dixon (P.)
Tilletia tritici, Bjerk.—Fassaroe (P.); probably not uncommon, easily overlooked.

Urocystis anemones, Pers.—Dalkey, Powerscourt, (P); not uncommon (M'W.)
violæ, Sow.—Rathfarnham, (M'W.)
Entyloma ranunculi, Bon.—Rathfarnham (M'W.)

[The remainder of the list is arranged according to the nomenclature of Succardo in his "Sylloge Fungorum."]

MYXOMYCETES.

Fuligo septica, Fr.—Glencullen (M'W.)
Spumaria alba, DC.—Fassaroe, Bray (P.)
Didymium squamulosum, A. & S.—Mount Merrion (P.)
Tilmadoche nutans, Pers.—Powerscourt (P.)
Stemonitis ferruginosa, Ehrb.—Monkstown (P.); Lucan (M'W.)

Dictydium cernuum, Pers.—Glendalough House (P.)
Cribraia intermedia, Rost.—Dargle (P.)
Trichia varia, Pers.—Glasnevin (P.) (M'W.)
chrysosperma, DC.—Common (P.) (M'W.)
Prototrichia flagellifer, B. & Br.—(P.)

CHYTRIDIACEÆ.

Protomyces menyanthis, De By.—On plants received from Annamoe (P.); Murrough of Wicklow (M'W.)

Protomyces macrosporus, Ung.—Goatstown and Rathfarnham (M'W.)
Synchytrium taraxaci, De By.—Dalkey (M'W.)

HYPHOMYCETES.

Stilbum tomentosum, Schrad.—Powerscourt (P.); Altadore (M'W.)
fimetarium, B. & Br.—Clonsilla (M'W.)

Stilbum vulgare, Tode.—Glencullen (M'W.)
Isaria fuciformis, Bk.—Glasnevin (P.)

Septosporium bulbotrichum, Ca.—Terenure (M'W.)

Pimia parasitica, Grove.—In Passion-flower leaves, Monkstown (P.)

Stachybotrys atra, Ca.—Monkstown (P.)
lobulata, D.— do.

Cephalosporium macrocarpum, Corda—Monkstown (P.)

Oidium fasciculatum, B.—On orange, D. Frazer (P.)

Stysanus putredinis, Ca.—On decaying seaweed, per Mr. W. N. Allen (P.)

Monilia racemosa, Pers.— Monkstown (P.)

Zygodesmus sp.—Kilruddery (P.)

Menispora ciliata, Ca.—Friarstown (M'W.); Powerscourt (P.)

Verticillium nanum, B. & Br.— A form agreeing closely with this on *Marasmius,* Dalkey Island (M'W.)

Myxotrichum deflexum, Br.— On wall, R. Coll. Surgeons (P.)

Fusidium griseum, Lk.— Friarstown (M'W.)

PHYCOMYCETES.

Plasmopara nivea, Ung.— Common (P.) (M'W.)
pygmæa, Ung.—Clonsilla (M'W.)
urticæ, Casp.—Common (M'W.)

Peronospora trifoliorum, De By.—Bray Head (M'W.)
schleideni, De By.—Lucan (M'W.)
lamii, De By.—Lucan (M'W.)

Pythium de-baryanum, Hesse —On cress (P.)

Fœnaria, Pim.[1]
philomukes (*Saprolegnia philomukes,* Smith).—On silo, Glasnevin. A fine description, with cut, of this curious species will be found in "Diseases of Field and Garden Crops," by W. G. Smith.

Septocylindrium elongatisporum, B. & Br.—Glencullen (M'W.)

Torula parasitica, nov. sp.[2]—Monkstown (P.)
pulvillus, B. & Br.—Powerscourt (P.)

Bispora monilioides, Ca.— (P.)

Spinellus fusiger, Lk.—On Agarics (M'W.)

Thamnidium elegans, Ca.— On fungi (P.)

Mortierella sp.—On fish manure (P.)

Pilobolus crystallinus, Tode. —Frequent (P.) (M'W.)

Chætocladium brefeldii, Van Tiegh & Lemon—Monkstown (P.)

DISCOMYCETES.

Helvella lacunosa, Afz.—Glencullen (M'W.)

Vibrissea truncorum, Fr.—Powerscourt, recurring in the same place every spring (P.); Sladebrook (M'W.)
guernisaci, Crouan—Altadore (M'W.)

Geoglossum hirsutum, Pers.—Rocky Valley (P.)
difforme, Fr.—Glencullen (P.)

Peziza (Cochlearia) cochleata, Bull.—Per Mr. D. M'Ardle (M'W.)
aurantia, Pers.—Kilruddery (P.)
P. (Geoscypha) violacea, Pers. --Monkstown (P.)
exidiiformis, B. & Br.—Enniskerry (P.)
P. (Pyronema) domestica, Sow.—R. Coll. Surgeons, on wall (P.)

---

[1] Gen. nov. Described in *Gardener's Chronicle,* 22nd December, 1883, as "Mould on Ensilage."

[2] Extremely minute. Hyphasma well developed, creeping, giving off delicate spherical spores in strings. Parasitic on Dematiei, damp paper, and leaves.

P. (Phialea)
virgultorum, Vohl.—Glen of the Downs (P.); Enniskerry (M'W.)
cyathoidea, Bull.—Lucan (M'W.)
urticæ, Pers.—Lucan (M'W.)
tuba, Bolt.—Enniskerry (M'W.)

Lachnea
bulbocrinita, Phill.—Lucan (M'W.)
coccinea, Jacq.—Powerscourt (P.)

Dasyscypha
bicolor, Bull.—Whitechurch (M'W.)
calyculaeformis, Schum.—Bray (P.)
canescens, Ck.—Altadore (M'W.)
sulphurea (Pers.)—Glencullen (M'W.)
aspidicola, B. & Br.—Kilmashogue (M'W.)

Pyrenopeziza
atrata, Pers.—Powerscourt (P.)

Pyrenopeziza
sarcoides, (Jacq.)—Kilruddery (M'W.)

Coryne clavus, A. & S.—Sladebrook (M'W.)

Calloria fusarioides, (Bk.)—Ballyowen, etc., (M'W.); Mt. Merrion (P.)

Ascobolus glaber, Pers.—Altadore (M'W.)

Ascophanus argenteus, Cur.—(M'W.)

Lasiobolus ciliatus, B. & Br.—Glencullen (M'W.)

Saccobolus violascens, Boud.—Glencullen (M'W.)

Ascomyces deformans, Bk.—Stradbrook (P.)

Pseudopeziza trifolii, Fuckel.—Bray Head (M'W.)

Stegia ilicis, Fr.—Common (P.) (M'W.)

PYRENOMYCETES.

Erysiphe lamprocarpa, Lev.—Monkstown (P.); Wicklow (M'W.)
montagnei, Lev.—Rathfarnham (M'W.)

Podosphaera myrtillina, Kze.—On *Vaccinium*, Glencree, Altadore, Dunran, (M'W.)

Microsphaera
dubyi, Lev.—Near Bray (P.)
berberidis, Lev.—Monkstown (P.)

Cordyceps militaris, Fr.—Powerscourt (P.)

Claviceps purpurea, Tul.—Ballybrack, Glendruid, Blackrock (P.)

Chaetomium comatum, Fr.—Monkstown (P.)

Nectria pulicaris, Tul.—Terenure (M'W.)

Xylaria
corniformis, Fr.—Bray (P.)
carpophila, Fr.—Mt. Merrion (P.); common (M'W.)

Phyllachora graminis, Fuckel.—Bray Head (M'W.)

Ustuli navulgaris, Tul.—Dunran (P.)

Hypoxylon rubiginosum, Fr.—Dargle (P.)

Polystigma rubrum, P.—Ovoca (P.)

Cucurbitaria berberidis, Gray.—Monkstown (P.)

Rosellinia
thilina, Fr.—Monkstown (P.)
mammiformis, Pers.—Dargle (P).

Lasiosphaeria hirsuta, Fr.—Glencullen (P.)

Trichosphaeria pilosa, Pers.—Powerscourt (P.) (M'W.)

Stigmatia
ostruthii, Fr.—Dodder (M'W.)
ranunculi, Fr.—Dodder and Mt. Merrion (M'W.)

Venturia ilicifolia, Cke.—Mt. Merrion (P.)

Hysterium commune, Fr.—Rathgar (M'W.)

SPHÆRIOIDEÆ.

Piggotia astroidea, B. & Br.—Passaroe (P.)

Septoria aceris, B. & Br.—Powerscourt (M'W.)

Glæosporium ficariæ, Bk.—Rathfarnham (M'W.)

Coryneum bejerinckii, Oud—In cherry gum, Monkstown (P.)

THE BIRDS OF THE MIDLAND LAKES AND BOGS,
CHIEFLY AS OBSERVED IN THE BREEDING-SEASON.

BY R. J. USSHER.

(*Concluded from page* 238.)

The COMMON TERN is usually to be found on the larger lakes, on many of which it breeds, sometimes in colonies apart from other birds, sometimes with gulls, sometimes but a pair or two, but always on islands. I have met with Terns on *Lough Erne, Lough Arrow, *Lough Key, *Lough Allen, Lough Boderg, Lough Forbes, *Lough Oughter, *Lough Sheelin, *Lough Gowna, Lough Ree, Lough Iron, and *Lough Derg. On the latter I have found eggs on the 31st May, but on Lough Key and Lough Oughter, there were uncompleted clutches on the 12th June. On a large grassy island in Lough Gowna, which rises into a hill, a large colony of Terns had eggs in the first and second stage of incubation on the 10th June. These were laid here and there, in depressions in the grass, on the upper slopes of the hill, though fourteen cattle were grazing on the island, probably not long, as cattle usually drive Terns away by trampling on their nests. I found there one Tern's egg laid in a depression in a dried cow-dung, used as a nest. On an islet in Lough Key, within a short distance of the house and terrace-garden of Rockingham, were five Terns' nests round the margins of the soil, overhung by the bushes that occupied the centre. A similar, but much larger colony, occupied an islet in Lough Oughter. On two stony islands in Lough Allen I found Terns having eggs in hollows of the gravel, on the outskirts of a colony of Black-headed Gulls.

The BLACK-HEADED GULL is a bird to be met with everywhere in the breeding season in these counties. It breeds in colonies, large or small, both on islands in lakes, which are usually small and stony, and also on the great red bogs. In the latter the Gulls lay round the margins of the pools that occur in the wetter portions, as on Killeenmore Bog, in King's Co., where the hosts of Gulls that breed over so extended an area seem to increase from year to year, owing probably to protection. On a marsh of Lord Castletown's, in Queen's Co.,

B*

I saw an enormous and very dense assemblage of Gulls breeding on the 15th April, 1893. Their nests were all on tussocks of sedge, standing out of shallow, muddy water, through which a punt was pushed. Few nests then contained eggs, though some clutches were complete. At Killeenmore Bog, on 30th April, 1892, many clutches were complete, but few sat upon. On the sheltered and crowded islets of Lough Key many young Gulls were able to swim on 12th June, 1891; but on the exposed stony islands of Lough Allen the eggs were not much incubated on 3rd June, 1893, and there were no young. Some nests were placed here within the shooting-shelters, built of loose stones; and on Lough Derg I saw a nest on top of a tall, conical stone beacon, on an island, while others were on boulders and masses of stone standing in the water. It is a very pretty sight to see these Gulls chasing moths in the twilight over a grass field. They continue to do so until eleven o'clock, if not later. I have met with Black-headed Gulls in April, May, and June, on *Lough Erne, Lough Arrow, *Lough Key, *Lough Allen, Lough Forbes, Lough Oughter, *Lough Gowna, Lough Ree, the Shannon near Banagher, *Killeenmore Bog, *Lough Derg, and *marshes near Granston. They are also reported to breed elsewhere, in Monaghan, Cavan, Leitrim, Roscommon, Galway, Westmeath, King's Co., Queen's Co., and Tipperary.

The LESSER BLACK-BACKED GULL I have only met with breeding on Lough Erne, except on the sea-coast; yet I have met with it on so many lakes and rivers that I am convinced it must have many inland breeding places. I visited lower Lough Erne on 9th June, 1891, and on reaching a lonely island, whose centre was covered with luxuriant natural wood, with a wide, flat, stony beach, I found some twelve or fifteen pairs of this species nesting among the large stones on this beach, the nests being formed of dried flags and grasses. This colony must have been robbed, as some nests contained eggs far advanced and chipping, others but one or two fresh eggs; no other species of gull bred there. Mr. R. E. Dillon has shown me an egg answering to this species, taken on a bog near Clonbrock, in eastern Galway, and I have twice seen Lesser Blackbacks on Lough Iron, Westmeath, in June, where the keeper informed me that he saw their young following them about the lake. I saw a pair in adult plumage on Lough Derg, on

27th May, 1893, and others elsewhere immature ; and Mr. Parker tells me that he always sees these Gulls come about the 1st April, and that they remain during the breeding season, but disappear in winter. I have also seen them singly, or in pairs, in adult plumage, on Lough Key, Lough Allen, Lough Forbes, Lough Ree (two seasons successively), on the Shannon near Banagher, and again near Athlone, and on the Nore above Thomastown. Their love of the offal of towns doubtless attracted them to the last three places, but their presence in so many inland places in the breeding season is significant. I have never to my recollection met with the Herring Gull in midland counties.

The GREAT CRESTED GREBE breeds in small numbers on lakes from Hillsborough, in the Co. Down, and Castle Dillon Lake, Armagh, through the Monaghan lakes, and through the midland counties, on lakes great and small, down to the Clare end of Lough Derg, where I have taken its eggs on 27th May, 1893. The smaller lakes are frequented by one or two pairs ; but on the larger lakes, like Lough Ree, many pairs breed, not always apart from each other, for I there found two nests with eggs on 7th June, 1892, in a very small lagoon, whose entrance just admitted a boat, and was unfrequented. The nests were flat platforms of rotten rushes, placed among beds of the tall rushes that grow in the water. On Lough Ree I saw a great many Grebes in different parts. I should say they have no greater resort in Ireland. On Lough Iron I saw a good many, and they admitted tolerably near approach without sinking their bodies deep in the water, as they do when alarmed. Mr. Collier, the keeper, thinks there are eleven pairs on Lough Iron. I have seen their eggs from thence. Colonel Malone has seen a Grebe drop two young ones that she appeared to have been carrying on the water. The note of the Grebe is a croak, which can be heard at a considerable distance. When it dives it draws the head back, points the bill downwards, then with a stroke of the feet submerges the breast and neck, and goes under without a splash. It will sometimes swim rapidly in one direction, dip its bill, and then swim rapidly in another direction. When watching the intruder the long white neck is held erect and the tufted head is easily distinguished. Grebes when approached on Lough Iron, where they are tame from protection, sometimes escape by flight rather than by diving, as I have witnessed, and they then look not very unlike Mergansers on the wing, except that the large feet project behind. They select bays and parts of lakes sheltered by islands to breed in, and seem to avoid exposed lakes destitute of such refuges, like Lough Allen and Lough Sheelin, as the sweep of large waves would destroy their nests. I have found them on Lough Erne, Lough Arrow, Lough Key, Lough Gowna, Currygrane Lake, *Lough Ree, Lough Iron, Lough Drin, and *Lough Derg, and they have been reported to me from Lough Boderg, Lough Owel, where their eggs were taken, Lough Annagh, and Ballyfin, Queen's Co.

The LITTLE GREBE breeds throughout Ireland, but is particularly common on the midland lakes and parts of the Shannon. I never saw so many Little Grebes' nests as I met with on Lough Ree on 7th June, 1892, on floating lumps of aquatic herbage, the clutches being then usually incomplete, but one young grebe, just escaped from the shell, immediately took to the water when I approached, and dived, using its legs and wings under water, to come up and dive again. On Lough Key I met with a Little Grebe's nest built upon a stone which stood in the water, and was sufficiently cup-shaped to hold the nest. I have met with Little Grebes on Lough Arrow, *Lough Key, *Lough Sheelin, Currygrane Lake, *Lough Ree, Lough Iron, *Lough Owel, Lough Drin, the *Shannon near Banagher, and *Lough Derg.

The CORMORANT has breeding colonies in tall trees on some of the lakes. The most remarkable instance of this is at Lough Cutra, in Co. Galway, ten miles from the nearest tidal water, where, as Lord Gough informs me, "cormorants have always bred in numbers on Parson's Island, three and a-half acres in extent. They have from forty to sixty nests yearly, high up in the trees, very large nests, mixed up with a large rookery and heronry; also large numbers of Jackdaws, and, until lately, some hawks. All appear to live most amicably together."

On Hermitage Island, Lough Key, is a smaller colony, where, on 12th June, 1891, I saw fourteen nests in ash-trees about thirty or forty feet from the ground. In one nest were large young in down; in the others, fledged young. Several old Cormorants remained on these nests while we were beneath. Occasional Cormorants may often be seen on all the larger lakes.

The GREY LAG GOOSE is reported by Mr. Young to be "sometimes seen in Queen's Co. in winter," and by Lord Castletown to be "very rare." Mr. Digby states that in King's Co. there are "a few in the winter." He has shot them. Mr. Kinahan says that it is an occasional visitor to the callows of the Little Brosna in Co. Tipperary.

The WHITE-FRONTED GOOSE is stated by Colonel Malone to be the commonest goose which occurs on Lough Iron. Flocks are to be seen in the adjacent pasture-fields in winter, and in 1891 they remained well into May. Maxwell, the gamekeeper at Knockdrin, told me that on the 26th April, 1892, the latest date he saw geese, a flock flew over in V formation, out of which he counted thirty-five without exhausting them. In eastern Galway, Sir Henry Bellew states that this species is nearly as common as the Bean Goose. Mr. Digby informs me that in King's Co. it is common from October to April. When visiting Killeenmore Bog, on 30th April, 1892, I saw two flocks of White-fronted Geese, comprising twenty-four birds in all. On the 6th May Mr. Digby wrote to me that they had gone. In Queen's Co., Mr. Young states that it is a regular winter visitor. In Tipperary, Mr. Purefoy says it is an occasional visitor in winter.

The BEAN GOOSE is a winter visitor to Sligo (Col. ffolliott). In eastern Galway, Sir H. Bellew considers it to be the commonest goose. On the 7th February, 1893, one was shot out of a flock of about sixty near Mount Bellew. One shot in Co. Longford is preserved in Currygrane. In King's Co. Mr. Digby considers it fairly common, and in Queen's Co. Mr. Young says it is a regular winter visitor.

The BARNACLE GOOSE is, according to Sir H. Bellew, a common visitor to his part of Galway, as well as the Bean and White-fronted, and that there is no mistaking the sharp line of demarcation between the neck and the very white breast.

The WHOOPER SWAN is a winter visitor to Lough Arrow, often in large numbers (Col. ffolliott). In Longford Mr. Wilson states it is not numerous, but is seen occasionally. In King's Co. Mr. Digby has only once seen a flock passing over, and in Queen's Co. Lord Castletown considers it very rare, while Mr. Purefoy states that it is an occasional visitant in winter to Tipperary.

(It must be difficult to determine the species, as between

this and Bewick's Swan, where the birds are only seen at large, and not obtained.)

BEWICK'S SWAN. A specimen of this species, shot on Lough Iron by Colonel Malone, is preserved at Barronston. Mrs. Battersby informs me that small flocks of swans sometimes, but rarely, visit Lough Iron and Glen Lough. One shot at Granston Manor, about 1888, is preserved there, but Lord Castletown considers the species very rare. Mr. Kinahan says that on the callows of the Shannon very large flocks of swans sometimes appear, and a few small flocks yearly. He believes that both species occur there.

The WILD DUCK is reported to breed in every county in Ireland, numerously in Fermanagh, Cavan, Leitrim, Roscommon, Longford, Westmeath, King's and Queen's Counties. I have met with it on all the lakes I have visited, breeding in numberless instances. It breeds both among the heather on the red bogs, and in the sedgy vegetation on islands in lakes. On the marshes near Granston, in Queen's Co., great numbers were sitting on eggs, on the 14th April, 1893, often amid slight herbage; but I have found fresh eggs on the 9th June, on Lough Erne. I was shown three trees at Barrowston in which Wild Ducks had nested. On the 2nd June, 1892, as I was exploring an island on Lough Derg, where Wild Ducks breed, a Mallard flapped along before me, as a duck would, so as to draw me away from its brood. This shows that the male is not indifferent to the safety of his family. On the 12th June, 1891, the Mallards on Lough Key were beginning to change their plumage, their necks showing brown.

At Kellyville, on the borders of Queen's Co. and Kildare, a lake of fifteen acres in extent, in the demesne, has been preserved for a very long period as a duck decoy, and is carefully looked after by the owner, Mr. Webber. From the approach, one can see in winter the greater part of this lake swarming with multitudes of ducks, chiefly of this species and Teal, but also including numbers of Wigeon with many Pintails, Shovellers, Tufted Ducks, and Pochards, the two latter species keeping apart from the dense crowd of Wild Ducks. As darkness comes on, one may hear flock after flock leaving the lake to feed over the country, and return next morning to spend the daytime on Kellyville Lake. When the lake is frozen they sit on the ice, covering five or six acres, the numbers being then estimated at six or seven thousand. Large flights of fresh Wild Ducks arrive in December and January; these are slighter in body and appear tired with their flight, sleeping all day on the banks; after some weeks they get fat and heavy.

The GADWALL is recorded to have been shot at Knockdrin, Westmeath. Lord Castletown informs me that at Granston Manor, in Queen's Co., three specimens have been shot, and Mr. Young says that a few have been seen in winter in his part of the county.

The SHOVELLER was not known to Thompson as a species breeding in Ireland. There is much reason to think that it has greatly increased since his time, especially of late years. I have met with Shovellers on Castle Irvine mill-dam, on Lough Erne, Lough Key, Lough Iron, *Lough Derg, at both ends of the lake, and on the marshes near Granston. It has been stated by the late Sir Victor Brooke to breed at Castle Irvine, by Colonel Cooper in Sligo, by Mr. Levinge and Rev. P. Keating in Roscommon, by Macpherson, the gamekeeper, at Derrycarne in Co. Leitrim on the Shannon, by Mrs. Battersby in Westmeath, and by Collier, the keeper, at Barronston in the same county, by more than one person at Banagher to breed on the Shannon near that town, by Mr. Wood on the Brosna, by Captain Fox in King's Co., by Mrs. Croasdaile in the north of Queen's Co., and by Lord Castletown in the marshes at Granston. It has bred also in several other parts of Ireland. On the 2nd June, 1892, I was on a small island in Lough Derg, when a brood of little flappers rushed from me into the water. The parent duck immediately flew out in front, displaying herself to draw me off. She was a Shoveller with broad bill and pale-blue wing coverts. Mr. Kinahan had long previously shot young Shovellers in the same locality. On the shores of Glen Lough, Westmeath, in 1891, I was shown the nesting-hollow in a tuft of sedge on coarse rushy pasture, from which the eggs of a Shoveller, now in Mrs. Battersby's collection, had been taken that season. On Lough Erne I saw a male and female Shoveller, near Devenish, but in other instances males only, leading me to infer that their mates were hatching, or more probably, rearing young. On Granston marshes, on the 14th April, 1893, I saw many Shovellers in pairs, and observed a female fly off from some tussocks of bog-myrtle, among which I found a nesting-hollow, though no eggs were laid. Lord Castletown showed me a Shoveller's egg taken long since from the same marsh, where Boyce, the keeper, states that he has seen a brood of Shovellers on the wing this summer, and that these birds breed there commonly; so does Collier, the keeper, at Barronston, where he says he found several Shoveller's nests in the spring of 1893, with eggs up to nine in number. He remarked that he never saw flocks of Shovellers before the winter of 1892-93, when he observed them on Lough Iron. This increase of Shovellers in winter has been noticed on Lough Annagh the last two winters by Mr. Dunne, of Brittas, and Colgan, his keeper. Mr. Young states they are numerous in Queen's Co. in winter. At the Kellyville decoy few were usually taken until the winter of 1889-90, when fifty-eight were taken, in 1890-91 fifty-two, in 1891-92 twelve, and in 1892-93 forty-one. This summer, 1893, Mr. Webber states that a fair number are to be seen, *e.g.*, on the 10th August he saw nine fly over the lake, probably a young brood bred in the neighbouring bogs or marshes.

The PINTAIL can hardly breed in Ireland in any considerable numbers. I have no evidence of its breeding recently, but Lord Castletown has an egg which he took when a boy from a Pintail on the marshes near Granston Manor. Both he and Mr. Young speak of this species as a regular winter visitor to Queen's Co. I saw a good many on the lake at Kellyville which they frequent regularly in winter, and with the Shovellers and a few Tufted Ducks remain there well into April, leaving before May. Previous to 1889 the highest number taken in the decoy there was fifteen in 1883, while in 1884, 1885, 1886, and 1887, none were taken. In 1889-90 fourteen were taken; in 1890-91 forty-four, in 1891-92 fifty-six, and in 1892-93 forty were taken. In King's Co., Mr. Digby has only once seen Pintails there in a very hard winter. Mr. F. Dunne has a pair obtained on the Little Brosna.

The TEAL is reported to breed in every Irish county except Dublin and Carlow, breeding numerously in Fermanagh, Leitrim, Longford, King's and Queen's Counties. I have seen it in the breeding season at Castle Irvine, *Lough Arrow, *Lough Boderg, *Lough Oughter, Lough Iron, Lough Annagh, the Shannon near Banagher, Mount Bellew Lake, and the marshes near Granston, and have found its nest among the heather on a great red bog near Clonbrock, Co. Galway. In such a situation, not in rushes, numbers breed on Killeenmore bog and other great bogs. As a winter visitant it must far exceed in numbers any other species of duck, if one may judge by the comparative numbers taken in the Kellyville decoy, the great majority of which are Teal. Mr. Webber says:—" There are a lot of Teal, several hundred, that remain on the lake until May, and come in again, young and old, in August and September. The foreign ones come in thousands about 1st to 20th November, and leave about 15th March. These are distinguishable by being lighter in body, and having a yellow tinge on the breast when they first come."

The WIGEON has only been seen by me once in the breeding season. On 3rd June, 1893, I visited Lough Allen, in Co. Leitrim, a lake where there is very little fishing or boating owing to the dangerous mountain squalls. From a stony island, inhabited by a colony of Black-headed Gulls, a fine male Wigeon got up, and another bird, which appeared to be the female, flapped about and disappeared. I searched in vain for a nest among the large stones composing the island, and returned several hours later, but did not see the Wigeon again. Wigeon have been reported to me as breeding in a few instances, but not with sufficient proof to put a mistake out of the question. As a winter visitor the Wigeon is common on the midland lakes, *e. g.*, Lough Arrow (Col. ffolliott), Westmeath lakes (Mr. Levinge), King's Co. (Mr. Digby), Queen's Co. (Lord Castletown, Mr. Young, and others). At Kellyville, in 1881, one hundred and thirty were taken, then none for six years. In 1888-9, thirty were taken, in 1889-90, one hundred and thirty-nine, in 1890-1, two hundred and ten. Since then but few have been taken.

The POCHARD is another duck of whose breeding in Ireland I desire further proof, though I have more reason to think that it does breed than the Pintail and Wigeon.

On the 6th July, 1893, a male Pochard, in transition plumage, was shot on Currygrane Lake, Co. Longford, and is in the Dublin museum. Young Pochards are stated to be met with occasionally on the Roscommon shore of Lough Ree. Maxwell, the keeper at Knockdrin, Westmeath, stated that in 1891 a pair of Pochards had a brood of seven young, on Brittas lake, in the demesne. He did not know their name, but described the male as having a red head and grey back. I am informed by Mr. Purefoy and Mr. Bagwell that a pair of Pochards bred on the lake at Martfield, near Clonmel. It is a place where breeding wild fowl are tame from protection, as I observed. I do not think a mistake can have been made in this instance. I have seen Pochards lurking about small wooded lakes occasionally, in April; and it is on such lakes, rather than on those that are large and open, that I should expect them to breed. Mrs. Croasdaile saw one on 17th May, 1873, on a lough in Queen's Co. The Pochard is a winter visitor to Sligo, Queen's Co., and probably to most parts of Ireland. I saw a number of Pochards on the lake at Kellyville, but they are never taken in the decoy. After their arrival they may remain for some weeks, leaving Kellyville if frost sets in, to return again in February, remaining until April.

The TUFTED DUCK is another species known to Thompson as a winter visitant only, which, nowadays, at all events, breeds commonly on several of the midland lakes. I have found it in the breeding season on *Lough Erne, *Lough Arrow, *Lough Key, Lough Forbes, Lough Gowna, *Lough Ree, Lough Iron, and Lough Derg, while Mr. Levinge reported it to me from Lough Drin, in June, 1892. On Lough Erne Mr. Bloomfield has observed the great increase of Tufted Ducks breeding of late years. Previously to 1877, he only knew them as winter visitants. I have found their nests among flags on stony islands, occupied by Black-headed Gulls and very near their nests, upon high sloping ground on islands covered with rushes among which it bred, and among sedge on small low islets. The eggs are not laid until the beginning of June; at least those that I took on the 6th and 9th June were fresh. When their breeding-haunts are invaded, Tufted Ducks quietly swim away, and then remain watching the intruder from the water not very far off. I saw ten together thus on Lough Arrow; on Lough Iron I saw Tufted Ducks in many places, in one place seven together on the 14th June, 1891. Their cry is a croak uttered on the wing. In winter Tufted Ducks are frequent in Queen's Co. (Mr. Young). I have seen several on the decoy lake at Kellyville, but like the last species the Tufted Ducks never enter the pipes.

The GOLDEN EYE in adult male plumage, obtained locally, is preserved at Castle Hamilton, Co. Cavan, Knockdrin in

Westmeath, and Castle Lough on Lough Derg, Tipperary. It is reported as a winter visitant from Lough Arrow (Col. ffolliott), and Queen's Co. (Mr. Young).

The GOOSANDER is stated by Mr. Digby to have been seen by him on one or two occasions in King's Co., and Mrs. Battersby knows of one shot in Westmeath. Mr. Parker mentioned another shot on Lough Derg.

The RED-BREASTED MERGANSER is one of the commonest ducks on the larger lakes, and is a most characteristic bird in the breeding-season, when I have met with it on Lough Erne, Lough Arrow, Lough Key, *Lough Allen, *Lough Sheelin, Lough Gowna, Lough Ree, *Lough Owel, and Lough Derg and in almost all parts of those lakes. Where numerous wooded islands occur, as on Lough Erne and Lough Key, each seems to be tenanted by one or more pair of Mergansers (known as Shell Ducks), but even in June, their breeding time, one sees occasional assemblages of adult birds. Thus, on an island in Lough Derg, I saw thirteen Mergansers, nine in one flock and two pairs, on 31st May, 1892. From an island in Lough Owel, nine took flight, which were on the water inshore, then two more, and afterwards we found two females sitting on fresh eggs among the dense flags that covered the bank of the island. On 3rd June, 1893, I came upon a Merganser sitting on ten fresh eggs among the bed of meadowsweet that encircles an island in Lough Allen, between the stony shore and the trees that occupied the centre, a distinct path or run leading from the nest to the water. A nest also containing ten fresh eggs was found on an island in Lough Sheelin, on the 11th June, 1892. It was a depression among rough gravel and angular bits of limestone with scarcely any nesting-material. Another nest had been made far in among tangle and bushes under masses of coarse ivy, forming a jungle. In May, pairs may be seen not having laid yet. The Merganser is a very shy bird, usually taking flight and not diving when a boat is still a long way off. It is most restless, continually in motion either on the water or on the wing. I believe it dives for food only, not to escape from an intruder. On the wing it utters a quack not unlike that of a Wild Duck. Mr. Parker states that within his memory Mergansers have greatly increased on Lough Derg, but that they are rare there in winter. In one instance I saw a pair of

Mergansers on a small lake overlooked from the high road in Co. Sligo. They remained unconcerned when I stopped my car and gazed at them within a hundred yards.

The SMEW has been obtained at Knockdrin, Westmeath, in Mr. Levinge's memory, fully half-a-dozen times. A fine adult male, shot there, is in the Christian Brothers' Museum at Mullingar. A female Smew, shot at Granston Manor, is preserved there, and Lord Castletown says that another was shot there.

The following specimens of marine species obtained on Lough Derg and the Shannon, are in the interesting local collection of Mr. Anthony Parker, at Castle Lough:—A Greenshank, in winter plumage; Great Northern Diver, immature; Razorbill; Long-tailed Duck, immature; Scaup Duck, Great Blackbacked Gull assuming mature plumage; Storm-Petrel (all from Lough Derg), and a Pomatorrhine Skua assuming mature plumage, the two central tail feathers two inches longer than the others, and partly turned on edge, shot on the Shannon above Portumna.

THE EARTHWORMS OF IRELAND.
BY REV. HILDERIC FRIEND, F.L.S.

(*Continued from page* 241.)

OUR study on the present occasion demands a somewhat detailed treatment, as it is the first time it has ever been attempted in Great Britain. In my last communication to this Magazine, I ventured to treat of those worms whose principal habitat is the trunks of decaying trees, and vegetable debris. I have in the present paper to deal with a totally different genus, whose haunts are aquatic. All those worms which properly come within our purview on the present occasion belong to the genus *Allurus*. There are other semi-aquatic worms in Great Britain, but their affinities with the *Lumbricidæ*, or terrestrial annelids, are remote, and they should be treated rather in connection with the aquatic Oligochætes, than with the earthworms. There is a wide gulf between the Enchytræids and *Allurus*, though their habitats are very similar.

Allurus, Eisen.

The genus *Allurus* was first created by Eisen in 1873, when he published in the "Ofversigt af Kongl. Vetenskaps Akad." No. 8, p. 43 *et seq.*, a capital summary of the knowledge then existing respecting the Earthworms of Scandinavia. Eisen's one fault lay in placing too much stress on the shape of the lip, too little on internal structure. He was right, however, in separating *Allurus* from *Lumbricus* and *Allolobophora*, for while the latter have the male pore on segment 15, in *Allurus* this important organ falls on the 13th segment—a most valuable and distinctive characteristic. Eisen's summary of the genera may here be profitably reproduced.

A. Setæ ubique binæ approximatæ:
   I. Tub. ventr. in segm. 14 [= 15 English method] pone segm. buccale.
      1. Lob. cephal. postice segm. buccale in duas partas dividens
       . . . *Lumbricus*.
      2. Lob. cephal. postice segm. buccale non dividens
       Allolobophora.
   II. Tub. ventr. in segm. 12 [= 13 English method] pone segm. buccale . . . *Allurus*.

B. Setæ aequo intervallo distantes, exceptis duabus summis, quarum intervallum aliquanto majus est . . . *Dendrobæna*.

Here we find *Allurus* distinguished from its predecessors only by the position of the male pore. The generic diagnosis is brief and simple:— "Tubercula ventralia in segmento 12 [= 13]. Corpus antice cylindricum, postice quadrangulum, setæ binæ approximatæ." It was this quadrangular shape of the hinder or tail portion which suggested the name of the genus, and since 1873 there has been no dispute about the nomenclature.

It must not, however, be supposed that the worm or worms included in the genus *Allurus* by Eisen had previously been unknown. We find allusions in the works of several authors in the early part of this century which distinctly point to the species now under review. *Allurus* was unknown to Linnæus. The first writer, so far as I can ascertain, who gives us any information respecting this worm was Savigny, who, discarding the Linnæan term *Lumbricus*, adopted the Græcised word *Enterion* (the Enteron of Aristotle). In Cuvier's "Histoire des Progrés des Sciences Naturelles," he calls it *Enterion tetraëdrum*, or the Square-tailed Worm. Dugès, the same year, gave an account of a worm in the *Annales des Sciences Naturelles*, which he named *Enterion amphisbæna*. His reason for adopting the latter or specific name is to be found in the fact that the worm he was describing could go as readily backwards as forwards, after the fashion of the serpent of which Lucanus sang.

Nine years later Dugès wrote again on worms in the same periodical, but put his worm by the side of that of Savigny, and spoke of them as distinct species. He now speaks of them under the term *Lumbricus*, and names them *L. tetraëdrus* and *L. amphisbæna*. Of the first he says that the girdle is composed of seven segments ending with the 28th. The worm is small and fragile, and frequents the neighbourhood of stagnant waters, whence it crawls forth during the night. The second species, he remarks, has a girdle of only six segments, which however ends as before on the 28th. The habitat is the same, but the worm differs from its predecessor, not only in the number of girdle segments, but in its smaller size, the prismatic and crenelated form of the tail, and in the semi-lunar shape of the lip. The colour of the one is a dull brown, while that of the other is violet, with a tendency to iridescence.

These important differences appear to have been ignored by all later writers until the time of Rosa, whose painstaking accuracy cannot be too highly commended. Rosa has not observed the species described by Dugès, but he has the following discriminating observation on the subject.[1]

"Il *Lumbricus amphisbœna* Dugès, che ha pure orifizi maschili al 13° segmento fu messo come sinonimo del *L. tetraëdrus* dall' Hoffmeister considrando come annonale l'allungamento del suo lobo cefalio che taglia interamente il primo segmento. Cio tuttavia non si può ammettere, avendo il Dugès osservato molti esemplari e conservata la sua asserzione in lavori pubblicati a molli anni di distanza. Io lo considero come una specie distinta di *Allurus* pesche malgrata che it carattere del suo lobo cefalico siasi fin qui riscontrato solo nei. *Lumbricus* ladesinzione che ne dà il Dugès non permette di ravoicinarlo a questogenere; il suo clitello occupa i segmenti, 22-27 (= 6), la coda contrataè prismatic quadrata, il colore violacco mollo iridescente."

In 1870 Eisen pointed out that the Square-tailed Worm, which he then spoke of as *Lumbricus tetraedrus* (Savigny) was liable to considerable variations of colour, and he gave names to two of these varieties which are deserving of attention. I believe we have not only the two well-marked varieties *luteus* and *obscurus*, but that some very important facts yet remain to be discovered respecting the causes of variation. Beddard and other investigators have given special attention to the internal anatomy of *Allurus*, and Vejdovsky has described a continental species under the name of *Lumbricus submontanus*, which brings the number of species up to three. I have now to add two others.

A couple of years ago I discovered, on the banks of the Eden, a rich golden-yellow worm in considerable numbers. This worm possessed nearly all the usual characteristics of *Allurus*, but differed somewhat from the type internally. I have only taken it once since, having found a solitary specimen in a little beck at Calverley, near Leeds. This species I have named *Allurus flavus*.

A consignment of earthworms which I recently received from the neighbourhood of Bangor, in North Wales, contained, in addition to more than one species new to the Principality, one which is new to Britain, and probably also to science. I have named it provisionally *Allurus tetragonurus*, the reason for which may at once be assigned. In 1874,

---

[1] "I Lumbricidi del Piemonte," p. 52-53. See also "Rev. d. Lumb."

Dr. Gustaf Eisen published a paper on New England and Canadian Worms, in which he described, among others, a diminutive species from Niagara, which he regarded as the type of a new genus. This genus he named *Tetragonurus*, and supplied the following diagnosis:—

"Body cylindrical in front, quadrangular behind. Male pores on segment 11 [= the 12th segment according to our English mode of reckoning], setæ in approximate pairs. Lip or prostomium not dividing the first ring or peristomium. It comes nearest to the genus *Allurus*, from which it is distinguished, however, by the position of the male pore, which in *Allurus* is on segment 12 [= 13 in English], but in *Tetragonurus* on 11 [= 12], as well as by the lip failing to cut the buccal segment or peristomium."

Eisen next supplies details of the species (*Tetragonurus pupa*): "Lip or prostomium small, acuminate in front, pallid, not dividing the peristomium. Male pores small but conspicuous. The girdle prominent, usually composed of five segments, viz., 17-21 [= 18-22]. Tubercula pubertatis conspicuous, three on each side of the girdle, occupying the 18th, 19th, and 20th segments [= 19, 20, 21]. About 40 segments in all; length about 25 mm."

Some Swedish comments on the foregoing description, which is written in Latin, inform us that the puberty band (*tubercula pubertatis*) exists on each side of the girdle in the form of a wart-like protuberance or keel, extending in a continuous line over three consecutive segments. The girdle is well-marked and may be readily distinguished from the other portions of the body. It stretches over five segments, one of which is before and one behind the tubercula. The general colour is sienna-brown, and the worm when alive closely resembles *Allurus* both in general form and in the nature of its habitat.

Thus far I have failed to find any confirmation of Eisen's discovery, and most recent writers drop the genus out of consideration. May not the worm I am about to describe prove to be the identical creature? The Bangor worm is about an inch and a-half long, and has the girdle and tubecula exactly in the position described by Eisen. The girdle is moreover, prominent, and the colour is sienna-brown in front, with a dull yellow-brown tail. The male pores, however, are placed exactly as in *Allurus* on segment 13, and thus prevent us from assigning the worm to the genus *Tetragonurus*.

The question now remains: did Eisen make a mistake respecting the position of the male pore? I dare not insinuate so much, since, next to Rosa, he is the most accurate and painstaking foreign investigator whose works I have consulted. For the present therefore we must assume that there are two worms which are practically identical in every important point, except the position of the male pores. If this is a fact it must have a meaning, and it will be of interest to observe what light future research may be able to throw upon the question.

I have, during the past few years collected and examined many thousands of *Allurus*, and have invariably found them living either actually under water, or in close proximity to it. Bearing on this point I may adduce the testimony of Mr. Beddard. He remarks—"It is well known that many of the Oligochæta, which are usually found in ponds and rivers, can also live in damp soil. The *Enchytræidæ*, for example, appear to contain quite as many terrestrial as aquatic forms; and even the same species may occur in either habitat. But there are not many instances known of earthworms which lead a partially or entirely aquatic life; indeed the fact that these annelids have been generally supposed to be entirely terrestrial, has been to some extent the cause of their having been distinguished as a separate group of the Oligochæta—*Oligochæta Terricolæ*. So far as I am aware there is only one species closely allied to *Lumbricus terrestris*, which has been proved to occur in rivers, as well as in the soil. In a recent number of *Nature*, Mr. Benham noted the occurrence of *Allurus tetraedrus* in England, and stated that his specimens had been collected in a stream. During August of last year (1888), I discovered this worm to be very abundant in the river at Bickleigh, near Plymouth. The river was not at all flooded, and as the worms were tolerably abundant, it seems to me to be fairly certain that they were not accidentally present. Professor Vejdovsky has also recorded the fact that *Allurus* is found in streams in Bohemia, so there can be but little doubt that it is partially aquatic in its habit; it can certainly live equally well in the soil, as I have had the opportunity of examining some examples which Mr. E. B. Poulton was good enough to collect for me in the island of Teneriffe."[1] As we have already noted, Dugès found them near stagnant water in France, and I have found the *A. amphisbæna* among the water-weeds which grow in the very centre of the "dykes" of the Sussex marshes.

(TO BE CONTINUED.)

NOTES.

BOTANY.

PHANEROGAMS.

Eleocharis acicularis, Sm.—On a recent ramble with Dr. Scharff between Monasterevan and Portarlington, on the borders of Queen's Co. and Kildare, I noticed *Eleocharis acicularis* growing in several spots in the Grand Canal. The plant occurs in both counties, and is apparently an addition to the floras of both districts 3 and 5 of "Cybele Hibernica." The form which occurs is not the type, but a curious submerged state, of which I send a notice to the current number of the *Journal of Botany*. The form in question grows completely submerged in 2 to 4 feet of water on the bottom of lakes and canals, which it covers with a short green growth like young grass; I have observed it in Derry, Antrim, and Armagh, as well as in the counties above-mentioned; this aquatic form appears to be invariably barren, and sends up tufts of very slender translucent stems two to four inches in length. I should be glad to know if any of our Irish botanists have noticed this form, of which no mention is made in the text-books.—R. LLOYD PRAEGER.

[1] *Proc. Royal Physical Society, Edin.* vol. x. p. 208.

Notes.

ZOOLOGY.

SPONGES.

Spongilla fluviatilis in the Barrow.—Mr. Carpenter has handed me over a very fine fresh-water sponge (*Spongilla fluviatilis*, Johnst.) which was sent to him by Mr. T. Greene, of Mageney, Co. Kildare, for the Museum collection. He had obtained it on an old piece of wood in the river Barrow. Three species of fresh-water sponges have been recorded for Ireland, of which *Spongilla lacustris* seems to be the commonest, having been found in the Killarney and Wicklow lakes, and also at Roundstone in Connemara, whilst *Sp. parfitti* has only been taken in some of the Kerry lakes. *Sp. fluviatilis* although hitherto only recorded from the north of Ireland is likely to be found in other parts as well. It is more hispid than the other species and the pores are larger.—R. F. SCHARFF, Dublin.

INSECTS.

Thera firmata in Co. Dublin.—I was fortunate in taking a specimen of *Thera firmata* here, which Mr. Carpenter, who kindly identified it, informs me has not been previously recorded from Ireland.—GEORGE E. LOW, Dundrum, Co. Dublin.

Corrections.—Mr. H. K. G. Cuthbert writes that the insect taken on the April excursion of the Dublin Naturalists' Field Club, and recorded (p. 173) as *Ammophila sabulosa*, turns out to be a large female *Pompilius fuscus*.

Rev. S. A. Brenan writes that the insects recorded by him, in last month's issue (p. 252), from Cushendun, were not taken there. *Sirex gigas* occurred at Parkmore, Glenariffe, and *Macroglossa stellatarum* at Arboe Rectory, Stewartstown.

MOLLUSCS.

Ianthina rotundata at Portrush.—It may interest some readers of the *Irish Naturalist* to know, that towards the end of last month, this somewhat rare shell was washed ashore in considerable numbers near Portrush; a few were broken, but in nearly every case the shell was perfect, with the animal still living. Some were among seaweed, floated in at the White Rocks, but the greater number along the sands, between the White Rocks and Portrush, where on the 30th of August, a young friend collected upwards of twenty. I found one large specimen in the sands west of the harbour. The species is figured in Sowerby's "Illustrated Index of British Shells." Large numbers of *Velella* were found at the same time and place on the shore.—WILLIAM KENNEDY, Londonderry.

Helix rufescens in Belfast.—W. Thompson states in his "Natural History of Ireland," vol. iv., p. 292, that this species is not found north of Banbridge, Co. Down; and it may be of interest to conchologists in the north to know that this southern shell does occur also in the north of Ireland. The indefatigable collector, Mr. R. Welch, has recently discovered it in the northern suburbs of Belfast, and also at Dunluce Castle, Co. Antrim. Both Mr. Milne and Mr. Standen have also taken it in the Co. Donegal.— R. F. SCHARFF, Dublin.

MAMMALS.

Hairy-armed Bat (Vesperugo leisleri) in Co. Dublin.—While shooting in the vicinity of Buckley's Hill, near Carrickmines, I observed a few large bats flying about some trees early in the evening. I procured one specimen which proved to be the above-mentioned species. I mention this, as the locality of this bat might be of interest to our readers.—EDWARD C. BARRINGTON, Dublin.

The Rabbit on the Irish Islands.—Information is wanted by me on the occurrence of the Rabbit on any of the smaller islands surrounding Ireland. I should feel greatly obliged to readers of the *Irish Naturalist*, who possess information on this subject, if they will kindly let me have particulars.—R. F. SCHARFF, 22 Leeson-park, Dublin.

PROCEEDINGS OF IRISH SOCIETIES.

ROYAL ZOOLOGICAL SOCIETY.

Recent donations comprise a pair of pigeons from Master F. Kelly, an Ocelot from Dr. Griffin, a pair of Wood Pigeons from Sir A. Weldon, three Japanese Deer and and a Sparrow Hawk from Sir Douglas Brooke, a Common Fox from Dr. Stoney, and a Spotted Paradoxure from Dr. R. M. Connolly. A Chimpanzee and two Jerboas have been acquired by purchase.

DUBLIN MICROSCOPICAL CLUB.

JUNE 15th.—The club met at Mr. F. W. MOORE'S, who showed *Stemonitis fusca*, Roth. The specimen was found growing on front of the leaf of a species of *Scheelea* in the large Palm-house at Glasnevin. It covered a space about six inches long by one inch broad, forming a very striking object. This fungus is generally found on dead and decaying material, and it was interesting to now find it growing on part of the leaf of a healthy palm.

MR. GREENWOOD PIM showed *Ustilago receptaculorum* from head of Goatsbeard (*Tragopogon pratensis*) growing at Skerries. This is its first Irish record. The Goatsbeard, though widely distributed is not a common plant, and its smut is decidedly rare. The spores are comparatively large and spinulose. Dr. McWeeney showed these germinated.

DR. M'WEENEY showed a curious example of conjoined parasitism of two minute fungi—*Urocystis anemones*, Sev., and *Peronospora pygmæa*, Ung.—upon the same portion of a leaf of *Anemone nemorosa*. The epidermis, which was slightly swollen and looked bluish from the subjacent spore mass of the *Urocystis*, was covered with a thin bloom, composed of the conidiophorous hyphæ of the *Peronospora*. Sections through the affected part showed an abundance of *Peronospora*-oospores lying amongst the parenchyma cells in close contiguity to the differentiating spore-bags of the *Urocystis*. The mycelium of the two micro-fungi belonging, as they do, to classes widely remote the one from the other, could be seen running side by side between the parenchyma cells; and that of *Peronospora* could be readily distinguished by the paucity or absence of septa, and by its numerous button-shaped haustoria from that of the neighbouring *Urocystis*. On the edge of the sections the gonidial hyphæ of the *Peronospora*, with the simplicity of branching characteristic of the species, could be readily seen, emerging from the stomata, and their continuity with the oospore-bearing hyphæ easily traced. The exhibitor drew special attention to the latter as being objects of rare occurrence in plants gathered so early in the season. The specimen was gathered on the bank of the Aughrim river, on April 5th last.

MR. G. H. CARPENTER showed male specimen of *Plæsiocrærus alpinus*, Cb., a spider collected in the Edinburgh district by Mr. W. Evans, and an addition to the British fauna, having been hitherto recorded only from the Alps of Styria and southern France.

MR. MCARDLE exhibited a specimen of the rare *Harpa-lejeunea ovata*, Taylor, which he collected recently in Dunboy wood, Castletownbere, Co. Cork. It has not been previously reported from this locality that we are aware of. The plant is easily known when not in fruit, by the large lobe of the leaf being acutely ovate, and the smaller, or lobule, being saccate and inflated, and by the obcordate underleaves, which are bluntly notched at the apex. This rare species is the only British representative of Dr. Spruce's sub-genus *Harpa-lejeunea*, it is also interesting on account of its geographical distribution, which extends to the Amazon valley and the lower slopes of the Andes in South America.

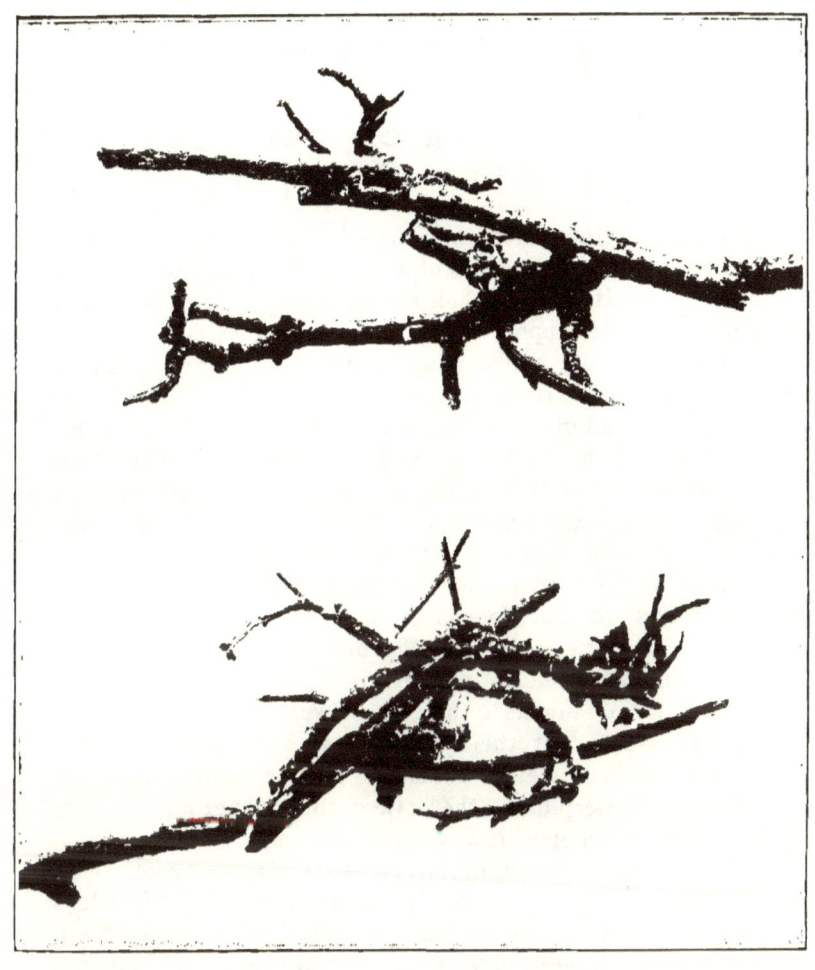

Fig. 1 (Upper), Caterpillar stretched out like a twig.
Fig. 2 (Lower), Caterpillar bent, as in walking.

CATERPILLAR OF THE SCALLOPED HAZEL MOTH (*Odontopera bidentata*) ON A ROSE BRANCH.

[*Photographed from life by Mr. F. T. Eason.*]

A DECEPTIVE CATERPILLAR.

BY GEORGE H. CARPENTER, B.SC.

ALL persons interested in natural history must be more or less familiar with instances of animals obtaining concealment by means of likeness to their surroundings. No class of facts put forward in support of the theory of natural selection has so impressed the public mind, or taken so large a place in popular scientific literature.

While we admire the perfect protective resemblance exhibited by tropical "walking-sticks" and "leaf-butterflies," it is well to remember that in our own country animals are to be found which show similar resemblances in equal perfection. The white winter coat of our Mountain Hare in its snowy haunts, the mottled plumage of the Grouse on the moor, the russet dress of the Woodcock amid the faded Bracken, and the yellow-spotted skin of our famous Kerry slug *(Geomalacus maculosus)* on the lichen-covered rocks,[1] are instances of such adaptations of animals to their special surroundings. But it is among insects that this question has been more specially studied, and no better examples can be found than the "looping" caterpillars—the larvæ of the great group of moths known to entomologists as Geometers.

If we examine the caterpillar of a butterfly, a hawk-moth, or an owl-moth, we notice, in addition to the three pairs of true legs on the thoracic segments (which correspond to the six legs of the perfect insect), five pairs of "pro-legs" or claspers, situated on the fourth, fifth, sixth, seventh, and tenth (hinder-

---

[1] Scharff, "The Slugs of Ireland," *Sci. Trans. R.D.S.* (2) vol. iv. pt. x., 1891.

most) segments of the abdomen. But in the "looping" caterpillars, only the pro-legs of the seventh and tenth abdominal segments are evidently present; the three foremost pairs are wanting. These caterpillars, therefore, have six legs just behind the head, and four legs at the tail, the intermediate part of the body being limbless. Hence their peculiar, looping style of walking. The claspers are brought close up to the legs, the insect bending its body into a loop; then the legs are disengaged, and attached at a point in advance, the body being straightened out (Pl. 7, fig. 2). Then, by another loop, the claspers are again brought up. This process can be watched by anyone, in an insect only too common in our gardens—the black and yellow caterpillar of the Magpie Moth *(Abraxas grossulariata)*, which often devastates gooseberry and currant bushes.

But the protective resemblance of the looping caterpillars to their surroundings is to be seen when they are at rest. Holding on to the stalk of its food-plant with its claspers, such a caterpillar often stretches its body out, straight and rigid, so that it looks exactly like a twig (Pl. 7, fig. 1). It is not surprising, therefore, to hear that the lady (Miss Stewart-Moore, of Ballylough, Co. Antrim), to whom we are indebted for the specimen figured on Pl. 7, " catching hold of what she took to be the end of the branch, was surprised to find it soft." This particular kind of caterpillar is by no means uncommon, but its remarkable likeness to its surroundings must often cause it to escape observation. The moth to which it belongs is called *Odontopera bidentata*, or the "Scalloped Hazel," a greyish brown insect with deeply dentated wings.

This caterpillar was kept for awhile alive under observation. When disturbed or touched, it would immediately stretch out its body in the attitude shown in fig. 1, and remain for a considerable time quite still and rigid. This position must entail a considerable strain upon the muscles, and seems to be rather ironically called "resting," but immobility is, of course, necessary to the success of the resemblance. The legs, which, if prominent, might betray it to a hungry bird, are pressed close to the underside of the body, and so concealed. This habit, and the wonderful resemblance to which it leads, have long been noted by naturalists. Drawings of various looping caterpillars in this resting attitude may be seen in Prof. Poulton's recent book on "The Colours of Animals," and the same investigator has more recently published extensive researches on the subject, a summary of which may be found in an article[2] by the present writer. The particular caterpillar whose portraits are given on Pl. 7, does not, however, seem to have been specially noticed in this connection. The opportunity of photographing a living specimen was, therefore, worth seizing, both on that account, and also for the purpose of directing attention to a fascinating branch of field natural history in which the camera will prove a valuable weapon to the naturalist. For the photographs on Pl. 7, our best thanks are due to Mr. F. T. Eason.

Not only in form, but in colour and markings, does this caterpillar correspond with its surroundings. The greenish-grey lichen, covering the surface of the rose-twigs, is beautifully imitated by the mottled pattern on the insect's back, light greenish patches on a dark background irresistibly suggesting the patches of lichen on the wood. This caterpillar, like many other loopers, is variable, being sometimes dark, and sometimes light or greenish. In Prof. Poulton's memoir, already mentioned, it is shown that the colour of a looping caterpillar often depends upon its surroundings in its early stages. Young caterpillars of *Boarmia repandata* and other geometrid moths reared among dark twigs grew up dark, while those reared among green shoots were light or greenish in hue. The dark colour is due to pigment in the skin; when this pigment is scanty, or absent, the green of the underlying tissue shows through. By a series of beautiful experiments, Prof. Poulton proves that the presence of certain yellow rays of the solar spectrum hinder the formation of the dark pigment. These rays are absorbed by dark objects, but are reflected from green leaves and shoots; and hence comes the wonderful power of the caterpillar to correspond in colour with its environment. This power is, however, lost after the third or fourth moult, for no change could be induced in the insects by altering their surroundings at that stage. It must be remembered that caterpillars do not, as a rule, change their habitat naturally; they are hatched, grow up, and pupate on the same plant. Hence it is enough that they be sensitive in their young stages. There can be no doubt

---

[1] *Trans. Ent. Soc. Lond.* 1892.   [2] *Natural Science*, April, 1893.

that the caterpillar of *Odontopera*, which is also sometimes dark, and sometimes greenish (as the specimen photographed) is sensitive in the same way as the insects on which Prof. Poulton experimented.

Besides its protective resemblance, this caterpillar of *Odontopera* has another point of considerable interest. It was mentioned above that in looping caterpillars the three front pairs of claspers are wanting. This is generally the case, but, like most statements about natural objects, some qualification is required. In a few loopers one or two of these pairs of claspers are present in a greatly reduced or vestigial condition, and in *Odontopera* the foremost pair alone is entirely wanting. In fig. 1 one of these vestigial claspers can be clearly seen just beyond the end of the twig to which the insect clings. These reduced organs tell us that this race of caterpillars were not loopers always, but that their ancestral moths had caterpillars with the full number of claspers. It is possible that the twig-imitating habit of the group may have helped the disappearance of the front claspers, which would rather spoil the imitative effect.

It will be remarked that the term "protective resemblance" has been used for the likeness of this caterpillar to a twig. The term "mimicry," sometimes employed in this connection, should be reserved for another kind of imitative appearance, the resemblance of an animal to another animal, which belongs to a different group, and which is protected by some noxious or distasteful character. The likenesses of certain moths and two-winged flies to the stinging bees and wasps are examples of mimicry.

For many years the facts of protective resemblance and mimicry among insects, have been received without doubt as testimonies to the action of natural selection. Lately, however, it has been questioned whether the advantages derived from these likenesses are so great as had been supposed. The accepted interpretation of the phenomena is so natural and beautiful, that it will not be abandoned until a better is forthcoming, which many of us think will never be. But no accepted theories should blind the eyes of the naturalist to the reception of new light. Observations in the field and careful experiments can alone determine what amount of benefit these creatures derive from their deceptive appearance.

NOTES ON THE FLORA OF COUNTY DUBLIN.

BY NATHANIEL COLGAN.

IT is now more than a century and a-half since the genial enthusiast, Caleb Threlkeld, laid the foundations of Irish botany in his well-known *Synopsis Stirpium Hibernicarum*, indited, as his preface tells us, in the year 1726 from his house in Mark's-alley, Dublin. Threlkeld's work, while it deals with the flora of Ireland in general, has special reference to the native plants of the environs of Dublin, and giving, as it does, definite localities in the neighbourhood of the city for some 140 species of phanerogams and ferns, may fairly be regarded as a first essay at a County Dublin Flora. From Threlkeld's time onwards, the plants of the county have engaged the attention of a series of botanists, professional and *dilletante*. As the seat of the University, the Royal Dublin Society, and the Medical Schools, the Irish capital became naturally the chief centre of Irish botanical science, and the surrounding country the favourite field for its practical study; so that as regards the more immediate surroundings of the city, perhaps no district in Ireland has had its flora more thoroughly explored. But from the very nature of the case this exploration was anything but systematic; and the only serious attempt at a painstaking botanical survey of the county, that carried out by Dr. Walter Wade towards the close of last century,[1] is in many points incomplete. Most of all is it defective in the study of distribution. Large tracts of the county, in fact, were never examined by Wade, and consequently little reliance can be placed upon his determination of comparative rarity or abundance of species. With all its shortcomings, however, Wade's Catalogue of Native Plants of the County of Dublin is a meritorious work. In one respect especially, is the author deserving of unstinted praise—he has made it a point to see for himself every species he records. All through his catalogue he makes *inveni* take the place of

---

[1] *Catalogus systematicus Plantarum Indigenarum in Comitatu Dubliuensi Inventarum*—Dublin, 1794. In a rapid survey of the botanical literature for the county Dr. Rutty's *Natural History of the County of Dublin* (1772) scarcely deserves mention His chapters on plants are little more than a treatise on medical and economic botany.

the impersonal and irresponsible *habitat*, and thus makes himself answerable for every species and every station recorded. Some rigid critics may be inclined to hold that Wade has much to answer for. In several instances, no doubt, he has found what no other botanist has found after him ; in a few, he has recorded what there is strong reason to believe never grew in the county. But it is very easy from the height of our modern advantages to look down with too censorious eyes on the labours of the earlier botanists.

After Wade's Catalogue, which excluded the sedges and ferns, deferred to a Second Part, never published, no fresh attempt at a Co. Dublin Flora was made. Wade himself gave many new localities for the county in his *Plantae Rariores* (1804). In Mackay's Catalogues of Irish Plants (1806-25); in the *Irish Flora* of Lady Kane (1833); the *Flora Hibernica* of Mackay (1836); the *Cybele Hibernica* of Moore and More (1866), and the *British Association Guide to the County Dublin* (1878), many others were added; and, finally, in Mr. H. C. Hart's *Flora of Howth* (1887), a section of the county and, perhaps, the richest of all, had its botany worked out in detail. To this last work an appendix of Co. Dublin plants found outside the Howth peninsula was added, sufficiently full to enable the student to make a rough estimate of the extent, in species, of the local county flora.

It will thus be seen that for many years much scattered material had existed with which the foundations, at least, of an exhaustive Co. Dublin Flora might be laid. But, so far, no one had been tempted to utilize this material for such a purpose when some eighteen months ago it occurred to me that a systematic botanical survey of the entire county was for many reasons a task worth undertaking. The work was accordingly begun without delay, as soon, in fact, as I had laid down on the one-inch Ordnance maps the artificial divisions of the field of inquiry indispensable for the proper study of distribution. Such a survey, as every practical botanist well knows, is necessarily a tedious one if done at all thoroughly; yet the steady devotion to the work of the leisure moments of the past two seasons has already accomplished this much—it has enabled me to form a just estimate of the distribution of a majority of the Co. Dublin species, and to collect a considerable mass of evidence bearing on the difficult problem of the relations between plants and soils.

Many of the results arrived at up to the present, whatever their value may be, are necessarily in the nature of dry detail. Some, however, are likely to be read with interest by all who have any practical acquaintance with the county flora, and a short selection from these I now propose to give here, embodying with these more recent observations, a few of the results of many previous years of desultory botanizing in the more picturesque southern or mountain districts of the county These notes may be conveniently arranged under three classes:—

I. Plants not previously recorded for the county; II. Recent observations of rarer species recorded only by the earlier writers; and III. Rarer Co. Dublin species found in new stations.[1]

I.—PLANTS NOT PREVIOUSLY RECORDED FOR CO. DUBLIN.

Hieracium umbellatum, Linn.—Left bank of the Glencullen river in considerable quantity, below the bridge on granite rocks and about half a mile above it on open field-banks. Previously known in many stations in the Co. Wicklow. The Hawkweed flora of the Co. Dublin is extremely limited; in addition to this species and the ubiquitous *H. Pilosella*, it includes only one other species, *H. vulgatum* (Fries) found on the Liffey above Leixlip by Mr. A. G. More (*Cyb. Hib.* p. 175).—N. C.

Orobanche minor, Sutt.—In abundance, on *Trifolium pratense*, in Shennick's Island, Skerries, where it was found and pointed out to me by my brother, Rev. Wm. Colgan, in July, 1893. I am not aware of any previous record for the county.

Utricularia neglecta, Lehm.—(1) Quarry hole by the Ward River below Chapelmidway and (2) pools in the Bog of the Ring near Balrothery (Balbriggan) July, 1893. Mr. Arthur Bennett has kindly cleared up my doubts as to the identity of this plant. Added to the Irish Flora by Mr. R. W. Scully from Kerry in 1887.—N. C.

Carex teretiuscula, Good.—By the Royal Canal above Clonsilla, sparingly, July, 1893; probably carried down by the canal from the inland bogs.—N. C.

Eleocharis acicularis, (Sm.)—Along the Grand Canal from Hazelhatch to Clondalkin, in great abundance, September 30, 1893. Growing in from 3 to 18 inches of water, the abortive spikes conspicuously floating on the surface in the shallower situations. Previously found by Mr. R. Ll. Praeger higher up the same canal in Queen's Co. and Co. Kildare (see *Ir. Nat.* Oct. 1893). The Co. Dublin plant in some of my specimens is fully 9¼ inches long and is obviously the recognised deep-water form mentioned in Babington's "Manual" (8th Ed. p. 390). In seasons of average rainfall the plant will, no doubt, be found totally submerged in the canal.—N. C.

To these additions, as I believe them to be, to the county flora may be added the two following, hitherto unpublished,

---

[1] In the following notes my own observations are distinguished by the initials N. C.

and due to the researches of my friends, Rev. C. F. d'Arcy and Mr. R. W. Scully.

Scutellaria galericulata, Linn.—Found by the Royal Canal below Lucan station, sparingly, *circa* 1887, by Mr. R. W. Scully, who has shown me specimens from this locality. I am on the whole inclined to agree with H. C. Hart in holding that Wade's record for this species: "In the marshes of Howth" (*Pl. Rar.* 1804) should be transferred to *S. minor* which I have gathered fully twelve years ago on Howth Head in one of the stations given by Mr. Hart. If this revision of Wade's record be correct, Mr. Scully's station becomes the first county record for *S. galericulata*.

Polypodium Phegopteris, Linn.—Found on damp shaded rocks on Secawn mountain, Glenasmole, *circa* 1883, by Rev. C. F. d'Arcy, who soon afterwards showed me the plants growing there. Perhaps this species and *Osmunda regalis*, recorded from Howth by Mr. H. C. Hart, are now amongst the rarest of the Co. Dublin ferns.

II.—RECENT OBSERVATIONS OF RARER SPECIES RECORDED ONLY BY THE EARLIER WRITERS.

Corydalis claviculata, DC.—On a granite *talus* in Glenamuck near the Scalp, 1882. This is the only Co. Dublin station in which I have seen the plant, and I can find no other county records more recent than those in *Flora Hibernica* (1836).—N. C.

Bidens cernua, Linn.—Abundant in the Bog of the Ring south of Balrothery (Balbriggan) July, 1893.—N. C.

B. tripartita, Linn.—Abundant at the pond near Balrothery known as the Lough or Knock pond, July, 1893. The pond had become very much reduced in size by the extreme dryness of the year, and the *Bidens* appeared growing in a stunted form stranded many yards from the water's edge. So far, I have found this and the preceding species only in the stations here given, and though both appear to be very rare in the county, I can find no definite localities for either later than Wade's (1794).

Lysimachia vulgaris, Linn.—In small quantity in an old quarry by the Delvin river nearly opposite Stamullen in the extreme north of the county, July, 1893. Hitherto this species could only claim a place in the Dublin flora on the faith of the old record: "about Loughlinstown and Old Connaught" in the *Irish Flora* (1833). In this station it has not, I believe, been seen for very many years.—N. C.

Ruppia spiralis, Hartm.—Tidal river-reaches near the head of the Malahide estuary, abundantly, in two stations (1) near Lissen Hall at the mouth of the Broad Meadow Water, and again (2) about a mile to the eastward near Newport House, July, 1893. These appear to be the first definite localities for this plant in the county, the only previous mention I can find of it being the reference in *Cyb. Hib.* (p. 316) to a specimen labelled in Dr. Mackay's Herbarium "near Dublin, &c."—N. C.

Hydrocharis Morsus-ranae, Linn.—This species, now very rare in the county, though probably much more plentiful before the low-lying bogs were drained, I found in three stations in July, 1893: (1) the Bog of the Ring, (2) Curragha Bog, and (3) the Broad Meadow Water near the old church of Killossory. In the first two stations it grows in abundance, but only very sparingly in the third. As regards station 2, given in Wade's *Plantæ Rariores* (1804), the difficulty is rather to find the bog than the plant; for drainage has reduced this favourite hunting-ground of the earlier botanists to one deep pool about 50 feet long by 15 wide and a couple of ditches adjoining.

Both pool and ditches, however, still nourish abundance of this interesting species. This station very narrowly escapes being in the Co. Meath, but careful study of the map and the aid of an intelligent resident farmer, who traced out for me the actual county boundary, set it beyond all doubt that this last remnant of the Curragha[1] Bog is in the Co. Dublin.—N. C.

Malaxis paludosa, Sw.—On Glendhu mountain in considerable quantity, growing on a level stretch of living *Sphagnum* at a height of about 1,500 feet, July, 1884; the only station in which I have found it in the county. Mr. John Bain, the veteran of Irish botanists, assured me in March last that he had gathered *Malaxis* in great abundance at the head of Kelly's Glen[2] both before and after the publication of the *Flora Hibernica* (1836). The plant does not appear to have been observed there recently. So well does its small size and quasi-protective colouring enable *Malaxis* to elude discovery that I have met with more than one botanist of wide experience who has never had the good fortune to see the plant growing.—N. C.

Hymenophyllum Wilsoni, Hook.—Sparingly on one of the upper forks of the Dodder River, Glenasmole, where it was pointed out to me by Rev. C. F. d'Arcy in 1883. This seems to be the locality set down, in error, no doubt, in the *Irish Flora* (1833) for *H. Tunbridgense.*

III.—RARER CO. DUBLIN SPECIES OBSERVED IN NEW STATIONS.

Nasturtium palustre, DC.—(1) The Lough, Balrothery, (2) Bog of the Ring, (3) near Baldwinstown cross-roads, and (4) north of Lusk, July, 1893 (for all stations).—N. C.

Senebiera didyma, Persoon—Roadside at Kilmacud about one mile west of Stillorgan, but not abundantly, October, 1892. Very rare in the county.—N. C.

Hypericum hirsutum, Linn.—Hedgerows near Drimnagh, a few plants, September, 1892.—N. C.

Trifolium fragiferum, Linn.—(1) Shore south of Raheny, abundantly, 1892; (2) marshy hollows by the Grand Canal, Hazelhatch, 1893, and (3) by the River Tolka, near Mulhuddart, 1893. The inland stations 2 and 3, distant respectively twelve and eight miles from the nearest sea, are interesting from their position, as the species, in Ireland, at least, appears to have a decided preference for the coast.—N. C.

*****Linaria minor,** Desf.—Abundantly along the railway line from Clontra to Bray river, September, 1893. Also noted this year by Mr. R. Ll. Praeger in abundance along the railway at Foxrock. A species which spreads very rapidly along railways, growing by preference in the ballast.—N. C.

‡**Chenopodium rubrum,** Linn.—(1) Wet ground by the Ward River near Chapelmidway, July, 1893, (2) banks of the Grand Canal at Hazelhatch, September, 1893, and (3) by the watercourse connecting the upper and lower ponds of Brittas, October, 1893. Well established in all three stations; certainly introduced by traffic in (2); probably a farmyard outcast in (1); and most remote from dwellings in (3). Very rare in the county.—N. C.

---

[1] Pronounced Curragh-ha by the peasantry of the district.
[2] The Upper Dodder valley, now, and, as I believe, always known to the inhabitants as Glenasmole. I have many times inquired for Kelly's Glen from natives, young and old, of the Upper Dodder valley, and have been invariably referred to the valley lying some three miles farther to the N. E. between the Kilmashogue and Tibradden mountains.—N. C.

Lemna gibba, Linn.—Very abundant in a pond near Ballisk, Donabate, July, 1893. The only other record for the county seems to be : " Pond near Glasnevin, D. M.," *Cyb. Hib.* (1866).—N. C.

Carex strigosa, Huds.—(1) Hedgerows near Drimnagh and (2) near Kilsallaghan, 1893. One of the rarest sedges of the county.—N. C.

Equisetum Wilsoni, Newm.—On the Dodder River near Bohernabreena and at Rathfarnham, 1893. Still very abundant in its old station along the Royal Canal, above and below Clonsilla.—N. C.

In concluding these brief notes I desire to express my best thanks to my friend, Mr. A. G. More, for the valuable counsel and assistance he has given me in many way in the prosecution of my researches, and to Mr. Arthur Bennett for his kindness in determining for me some critical plants collected in the county.[1]

THE EARTHWORMS OF IRELAND.

BY REV. HILDERIC FRIEND, F.L.S.

(*Concluded from page* 276.)

Allurus, Eisen.

The lip or prostomium either slightly attached, or cutting more or less deeply into the peristomium, or buccal segment. Setæ in four couples, occupying the four angles of the body posteriorly. Girdle of five or more segments, commencing on the 18th or some more posterior segment. Tubercula pubertatis on three consecutive girdle segments. Male or spermiducal pores on segment 13, and thus in front of the oviducal pores, usually on papillæ, lateral in position. Spermatophores attached ventrally between male pores and girdle. Body cylindrical in front, quadrangular behind. Notwithstanding Beddard's able diagnosis[2] the internal characters of the whole genus need revision. Owing to the paucity of materials I have as yet been unable to dissect the recently discovered species, but their external characters will amply suffice for identification.

---

[1] I shall be glad to correspond with any reader of the *Irish Naturalist* who may be able to supply me with further new stations for any of the foregoing or other of the rarer species of the county. All communications on the subject addressed to me to 1 Belgrave-road, Rathmines, Co. Dublin, will be thankfully acknowledged.—N. C.

[2] *Q. J. M. Sc.*, 1888, vol. vi., pt. ii., pp. 365-71.

SPECIFIC CHARACTERS.

1.—Allurus tetraedrus, Savigny—A small worm, seldom reaching two inches in length, usually about one to one and a-half inches when crawling about, but able to stretch to two or even three inches in the case of the largest specimens. Body somewhat cylindrical before, four-angled behind the girdle, which is prominent, and closely fused. It often appears to encircle the whole body, is lighter in colour, and normally extends from the 22nd to the 27th segment. A glandular ridge connects the girdle with the male pores on the 13th segment. These latter pores are well seen, being seated on somewhat conspicuous papillæ. The oviducal pores are on segment 14, thus being behind the male pores, while in *Lumbricus* they are in front. Dorsal pores commence between the 4th and 5th segments. In addition to the ordinary setæ, situated at the angles of the body, there are rod-shaped bristles on the segments which contain the essential organs, as well as minute claw-like setæ or spines scattered over the body. The ordinary setæ carry some minute projections on the extremity which projects outwards, while the internal extremity is attached to its sac by a congeries of fine muscular threads. The tubercula pubertatis form a band on either side the girdle, and occupy segments 23, 24, 25, or in some cases segments 23 to 26 inclusive. This point needs fuller investigation. I have found both arrangements, but am at present unable to say whether there is specific difference between the two forms.

The colour varies considerably, on which account Eisen has distinguished a type and varieties. The type is usually sienna brown, darker in front, with lighter girdle, and the tail often of a fleshy brown, or tending to green. It undoubtedly simulates the colour of its surroundings, or is able to bring about a close resemblance between its body-colour and the colour of the soil or vegetation amid which it resides. The worm is exceedingly active, and is able to move rapidly backwards, a mode of locomotion which it seems to prefer to direct progression. I have not found allusion in any writer to the spermatophores which the animal carries about during the breeding season. I have found them repeatedly affixed to the ventral surface, usually about segments 19 or 20. Internally I find spermathecæ in segments 9 and 10, and the crop and gizzard as in *Lumbricus*. In this I differ from Beddard, whose Teneriffe species comes nearer to the third British species mentioned below. Total number of segments—60 to 90, or about twice as many behind the girdle as before it.

The egg-capsules of this worm are to be found in great abundance at almost every season of the year. They are small, and of an olive-green colour. The young seem to reach an adult condition very early, and this fact, together with the power to go rapidly backwards, and the almost complete encirclement of the body by the girdle, seems to point to a primitive type, and indicate that *Allurus* is a surviving link by which to connect our earthworms with their progenitors of aquatic habit.

The synonyms are numerous.

1829. *Enterion tetraëdrum,* Savigny, "Histoire des Progrès des Sciences Naturelles" (Cuvier), ser. II, vol. iv., p. 17.
1837. *Lumbricus tetraëdrus,* Dugès, *Annales des Sciences Nat.* ser. II., vol. viii., pp. 17-23.
1843. *Lumbricus agilis,* Hoffmeister, *Wiegmann's Archiv. für Naturgeschichte,* p. 191, Tab. ix., fig. 6; also "Familie der Regenwürmer," 1845, p. 36, fig. 8.
1851. *Lumbricus tetraëdrus,* Grube, "Die Familien der Anneliden," pp. 99, 145.
1861. *Lumbricus tetraëdrus,* Johnston, "A Catalogue of British Worms," p. 61.
1870. *Lumbricus tetraëdrus,* Eisen, *Ofversigt af K. Vetensk.-Akad.,* p. 996-7.
1873. *Allurus tetraëdrus,* Eisen, *Ofversigt af K. V.-Akad.,* No. 8, p. 54.
1884. *Allurus tetraëdrus,* Rosa, "I Lumbricidi del Piemonte," p. 51.

The distribution appears not to be limited to Europe. I have records for Hungary (Œrley, A Magyar. Olig. Faunaja, 1880), France, Italy, Teneriffe, Germany, Bohemia, Scandinavia, England, Valparaiso, etc. Mr. Beddard says: "*Allurus tetraëdrus* must be regarded as a rather uncertain North American form. I have included it in the list (of Nearctic worms) on the strength of a specimen kindly sent to me some time since by Mr. Tyrrell, of the Canadian Geological Survey. I examined this specimen by means of longitudinal sections, and identified it with *Allurus* on account of the structure of the gizzard."[1] In Britain it is ubiquitous. I have found it in, or received it from Sussex, Kent, Essex, Suffolk, Devonshire, Gloucestershire, Yorkshire, Lancashire, Wales, Ireland, Scotland, and elsewhere. It may almost without exception be found wherever water occurs—by ditches, ponds, streams, rivers, and lakes, usually in considerable numbers. The soil, however, has some influence on the worm; clay and iron are eschewed.

Respecting the varieties which exist it is at present difficult to speak with certainty. Eisen gives two, which Œrley includes in his Hungarian list, and I have found others which will merit attention when the subject has been more fully worked. Colour alone is not a sufficient test, and we do not know how far the girdle and *tubercula pubertatis* may be liable to variation without affecting the species.

1. *A. tetraedrus*, var. *luteus*, Eisen—Body sienna-brown, yellow ventrally. Girdle warm yellow or pale cinnabar-red. I find this variety chiefly in sandy or gravelly beds, somewhat widely distributed.

2. *A. tetraedrus*, var. *obscurus*, Eisen—Body grey-brown, with pale ventral surface. Girdle of the same colour as the rest of the body, or somewhat lighter. Seems to prefer roots of grass by the sides of streams and ditches in meadow or pasture land. It is as common as the type, and may owe its colour simply to its environment. In this case we have an interesting question yet to solve. What can be the value to the worm of this mimicry?

DISTRIBUTION IN IRELAND.—Malahide, Co. Dublin (Mr. Trumbull); Cashel, Tipperary (Lt.-Col. Kelsall); Carrablagh, Co. Donegal (Mr. Hart).

[2. **Allurus amphisbaena**, Dugès—Though the majority of writers have confused this species with the last, Rosa and Eisen have already pointed out the fact that the characters are widely different. I had also come to the same conclusion long before seeing the remarks of these careful investigators. Dugès first described the worm in 1828 under the title *Enterion amphisbæna*. His reason for adopting the latter name is to be found in the fact that this worm (like the one already described, and, in a lesser degree, *Lumbricus purpureus*, Eisen) can go as readily backwards as forwards, after the fashion of the serpent of which Lucanus sang. Nine years later (in 1837) Dugès returned to the same subject, and he now affirms that his worm is quite distinct from that of Savigny. He therefore named the one *Lumbricus tetraedrus* and the other *Lumbricus amphisbæna*, and gave a clear diagnosis of each. *A. amphisbæna* differs from the other in the following particulars:—There are fewer girdle segments, the colour, size, and shape differ, and, above all, the insertion of the lip into the peristomium is quite dissimilar. If Eisen's diagnosis were pressed we should have to put this worm with the genus *Lumbricus*; but, just as one of the *Dendrobænæ* has the head of a *Lumbricus*, with all the other characters of an *Allolobophora*, so this worm has all the characters of an *Allurus*, with the head of a *Lumbricus*, Eisen's lip and peristomium arrangement, therefore, falls through. *A. amphisbæna*, Dugès, is a small worm, with a crenulated tail, which is prismatic when contracted, and the body colour is violet, with iridescence. The girdle occupies segments 23 to 28 (or 22-27), and the lip forms a perfect mortise and tenon with the

---

[1] "*Proc. Roy. Phy. Soc., Ed.*, 1891. *Q. J. M. Sc.*, vol. vi., pt. II., p. 365 (1888).

prostomium. Dugès examined many specimens, and persisted in the assertion that the worms differed specifically. I have found specimens in the south of England which correspond almost exactly with Dugès' description. Rosa does not record it for Italy, nor Eisen for Scandinavia, and we need further light on the subject. It has not reached me from Ireland, but is included here to make the study of the genus complete.

Respecting the synonymy, the only confusion that exists has arisen from the tendency of authors to identify this species with the foregoing. Henceforth they must be kept distinct.]

[3. **Allurus flavus,** Friend—In 1890 I found a species of *Allurus* in the bed of the River Eden, about two miles west of Carlisle, which differed in several particulars from either of the foregoing. I gave a brief description of it at the time; then regarding it as corresponding with *A. tetraedrus*, var. *luteus* of Eisen. Fuller investigation has led me to conclude that it is a new species. I found one solitary example in 1891 in the bed of a small stream at Calverley, near Leeds, since which time I have not observed another living example among all the thousands of specimens which have passed through my hands. When the opportunity recurs for me to examine living material I shall be able to speak with greater certainty respecting the specific differences, as my knowledge of the group has greatly developed during the past two years. There are certainly internal differences, and I am disposed to think the Teneriffe examples examined by Mr. Beddard come very near or belong directly to this species. *A. flavus*, Friend, is of a rich yellow or gold colour throughout, nearly transparent, so that the blood-vessels can be clearly seen. Lip very palid; girdle orange-coloured, usually on segments 23-26, with a band (*tubercula pubertatis*) on 23, 24, 25. The tail is often more cylindrical in shape than in the foregoing species, and it is usually a good deal smaller than the type, though possessing a similar number of segments. Hitherto it has been found only in the localities named, and it is without synonyms, so far as I am aware.]

[4. **Allurus tetragonurus,** Friend—As already stated, this worm has recently reached me from Bangor, N. Wales. It is about an inch to an inch and a-half in length, but a good deal wider in proportion to its length than any other species yet examined. The lip is pallid, and does not cut deeply into the first segment or peristomium. The male pores on the 13th segment are small, but clearly discernible. The girdle is very prominent and closely fused; it extends from the 18th to the 22nd segment, and surrounds the entire body—not after the fashion of *Perichæta*, but as is frequently the case with *A. tetraedrus*, Savigny. The *tubercula pubertatis* form a distinct band on either side of the middlemost girdle segments 19, 20, 21. The total number of segments is from 80 to 90, and these diminish in size from the girdle in either direction. Excepting near the anal extremity, a section taken through the worm's body would in no case be quadrangular, as in the case of the type. At least one-half of the body has an oval contour, somewhat flattened on the under surface. The head is warm-brown, the girdle yellow-brown, and the hinder part light sienna-brown. In colour, therefore, it resembles var. *luteus*, Eisen. Owing to lack of suitable material, I am at present unable to report on the internal structure. Unless this worm should prove to be identical with *Tetragonurus pupa*, Eisen, it is at present without synonyms, and Bangor is the only known locality.]

5. **Allurus macrurus,** Friend—Among a very valuable series of worms sent to me by J. Trumbull, Esq., L.R.C,S., from Malahide on November 22nd, 1892, I found a single specimen of an *Allurus* which is totally different from any British species yet described; and as it is also, so far as I am able at present to determine, distinct from every other species known to science, I send this preliminary note respecting it. Fuller details must be reserved till a further supply of material can be obtained.

The Long-tailed Allurus (*A. macrurus*, Friend), when preserved in alcohol is 3 cm., or nearly an inch and a-half in length, and 5 millimetres in diameter across the girdle. In this brief space we find no fewer than 160 segments, those behind the girdle being the narrowest I have ever seen in any earthworm at home or abroad. Like its nearest ally (*A. tetragonurus*, Friend), it has the girdle in a very advanced position, apparently covering segments 15 to 22. The clitellar papillæ (*tubercula pubertatis*) are on the underside of the girdle-segments 20, 21. On segments 13 and 22 we find ventral papillæ of a peculiar character, arranged in twins. The head is fleshy pink, the body of a peculiar greenish hue, quite different from any other species known to me. The girdle is yellowish, and retains a somewhat yellow-green hue in spirits. The setæ are wide apart, and the anus is peculiar in shape, size, and general appearance. The enormous number of segments behind the girdle (viz., 140) has suggested the name *macrurus* or the Long-tailed Worm, and the presence of the male pores on segment 13 determine its position in the family.

We now have five species of *Allurus* in Great Britain, each one of which, however, merits a good deal of further investigation. Of the life history, distribution, affinities, varietal forms, range of habitat, and other matters we at present know very little, and I shall welcome any assistance from collectors in Ireland which will make this subject better known. The West of Ireland should yield one or two more species if carefully worked.

A summary of the genus may fitly bring this memoir to a close.

TABLE OF THE GENUS ALLURUS.

Allurus.	Segments occupied by:		Length.	Shape.	Colour.	Prostomium.
	Male Pore.	Girdle				
1. **tetraedrus,** Savigny, 1828	13	22-27	2-in.	Cylindrical before, Quadrangular behind.	Sienna Brown.	Partially cuttting peristomium.
2. **amphisbaena,** Dugès, 1828	13	23-28	1½-in.	Crenulated prismatic.	Violet, iridescent.	Entirely bisecting peristomium.
3. **flavus,** Friend, 1890	13	23-26	1½-in.	Cylindrical to quadrangular.	Golden yellow.	Slightly cutting peristomium.
4. **tetragonurus,** Friend, 1892	13	18-22	1½-in.	Oval before, wide in proportion.	Dark to yellow brown.	Partially cutting peristomium
5. **macrurus,** Fr. 1893	13	15-22	1½-in.	Much wider in front than behind.	Pink head, greenish body.	Not cutting peristomium.

AMERICAN BIRD-VISITORS TO IRELAND AT HOME.
BY W. E. PRAEGER, OF KEOKUK, IOWA.

V. THE BELTED KINGFISHER (*Ceryle alcyon*).

THE only instances of this bird's occurrence on the eastern shores of the Atlantic are the two well-authenticated Irish records. One specimen was shot in Co. Meath, on the 26th October, 1844, and another in Co. Wicklow in November of the same year. The skins are still preserved, one in Trinity College, and the other in the Science and Art Museum, Dublin.

It is remarkable that in a continent as well supplied with rivers and lakes as temperate N. America, there should be only one kind of Kingfisher. But the western world, as a whole, is poor in Kingfishers, only having six or eight species, all belonging to a single genus, or only about five per cent. of the known species. It is probable that Kingfishers are a very recent introduction, and in those portions of the continent where the water is frozen in winter, and for some distance south of that line, the extensive migration has encouraged interbreeding, so that in all the vast area this includes—a territory probably better supplied with fresh water than any other of similar area on the globe—only one species of Kingfisher exists to-day. All other American species are inhabitants of the tropical or sub-tropical regions of the continent, where, being residents, the development of a number of local races and species has taken place.

But what our country may lack in variety of species, it makes up in number of individuals. All through the continent, from the Atlantic to the Pacific, and from the Arctic Ocean to Panama and the West Indies, the Belted Kingfisher is a common bird. It is resident wherever it can be, but is driven out of the northern portions of its range by the freezing of the waters; yet if it can only find open water, it will stay all the winter, no matter how cold the weather may become, and records of its remaining near warm springs or salt water through intensely cold winters are not uncommon. It moves north early, following the melting of the ice, and before our ears have grown accustomed to the unwonted sounds of waves and running waters, the loud laugh of the Kingfisher comes as their natural accompaniment.

The Kingfisher is a solitary bird, and except in the breeding season, two are rarely seen together, unless fishing-grounds are scarce. Soon after their arrival each pair selects a suitable nesting-site and fishing-ground, from both of which all intruders are kept away. River-men say that the whole length of the Mississippi, with all its bays and creeks, is thus divided among the Kingfishers, each pair having its own territory. The nesting-site is some bank of sand or clay, usually but not always above water; there a hole is dug from four to eight, or even fifteen feet in depth, and the eggs deposited in a chamber at the farther end. No nest is built, but the hole is often lined with fish-bones mingled with other refuse of the bird's food. The eggs are usually six in number, pure glossy white, and measure about 1.35 by 1.05. The Kingfisher varies his usual diet of fish with an occasional lizard, small snake, crab, craw-fish, or mouse; the indigestible portions of his food are cast up in the form of pellets, after the manner of the birds of prey.

When a Belted Kingfisher is in the neighbourhood, the most careless observer is sure to notice him. His note, frequently sounded, is a loud rattling laugh. He is a large bird, and chooses the most conspicuous places for perching, where his great bill and bushy crest make him recognisable as far as seen. The Irishman, accustomed to the little jewelled darling of his own hill-streams, would call him a "coorse lump of a bird." He is over a foot long, and about two feet in expanse of wing. The wings and tail are both proportionately longer than in the genus *Alcedo*, to which the Irish Kingfisher belongs.

The general colour of the upper parts of the Belted Kingfisher is slaty-blue, and of the under parts white; the wings are spotted, and the tail barred with white. The female has the breast-band shaded with chestnut, and is chestnut on the belly and flanks; young birds resemble the female.

While the Belted Kingfisher is found in a variety of surroundings, wherever in fact there is water from which he may obtain his food, and while I have seen him in just such quiet nooks as the Irish Kingfisher loves to haunt, yet he is chiefly associated in my mind with very different scenes. It is the 1st of September, the breeding season is over, and the first migrants are already here from the north. The collector takes down his gun, which for over three months has been idle, and again visits his favourite hunting-ground. The great river has been shrinking all through the hot summer, and is now a paltry stream less than half a mile wide, and leaving wide stretches of sand, where waters were deep in the fresh spring-time, and where now the islands with their luxuriant foliage appear as oases in a desert. Here and there, pools of water are left, and the same eddy of the great river that hollowed out the sandy bottom has undermined the bank, and several large trees lie in a tangled mass in and above the pool. On the topmost of the dead branches the bird well called Kingfisher sits, and rattles loudly as the collector tries vainly to approach unobserved the likely spot. A big heron rises, wariest of birds, rarely giving a chance for a shot. Soon he is followed by a beautiful Wood-duck; several small Green Herons wait a little longer among the branches, but finally follow their big brother; a pair of Solitary Sandpipers spread their long wings, and lightly cross the pond, and from the farther side watch the stranger, solemnly jerking their heads the while. Soon they are followed by several little Spotted Sandpipers that run backwards and forwards on the edge of the pool, or along the logs, incessantly jerking their tails. A Woodpecker, that was making a good breakfast by scaling off the dead bark, utters a sharp note of alarm as he flies off, while several little turtles that have been basking on the logs, fall with a loud "k-plunk" into the water, and a black-and-white water-snake glides noiselessly in with them. But still the Kingfisher holds his position of command, flying from one post of observation to another, or at times poising almost stationary in the air with rapidly-beating wings, and uttering his rattling note of indignation and defiance. How shall we close the scene? He is easily within shot, and a beautiful bird, an ornament to any cabinet. But let us be better than mere collectors this morning. To the ornithologist, eyes and note-book are better tools than gun and scalpel. Let us look our fill, and then leave him and his companions of the lonely pool, and trudge homeward over the hot sand, with game-bag empty perhaps, but with mind and heart full of the beauties and wonders of creation.

OBITUARY.

REV. GEORGE ROBINSON, M.A.

The Rev. George Robinson, M.A., died at his residence, Beech Hill, Armagh, on September 5th, at the age of 72. After obtaining his degree and Divinity Testimonium in Trinity College, Dublin, he took holy orders as curate of Tullyniskin, and was shortly afterwards appointed rector of the important parish of Tartaraghan, in the Co. Armagh. He held this post for thirty-three years, but a severe illness compelled him, in 1882, to resign his office. Mr. Robinson was from early years devoted to natural history, and especially to ornithology and botany. In both these departments he added considerably to the Armagh lists. He contributed important notes to Thompson's "Birds of Ireland," "Cybele Hibernica," and Stewart and Corry's "Flora of the N.E. of Ireland." Among the birds he noted the occurrence of the Brambling (*Fringilla montifringilla*, L.) and the Yellow Wagtail (*Motacilla raii*, Bonaparte), in Co. Armagh; and among plants he found many species of rare occurrence, notably *Mercurialis perennis, Stachys betonica, Lathyrus palustris, Carex pseudo-cyperus, Calamagrostis stricta*, etc.

Mr. Robinson was a member of the British Association for the Advancement of Science, and regularly attended its meetings; also of the Belfast Naturalists' Field Club, at the excursions and meetings of which he was a frequent attendant. Of the Armagh Natural History and Philosophical Society he was an original member, having belonged to the old Society which preceded the present one. He took a prominent part in establishing the Society on its present basis, taking the greatest interest in its success.

On the late Bishop of Down (Dr. Reeves) resigning the office of President in 1879, Mr. Robinson was unanimously elected to fill the vacancy, and held the post till 1891, when owing to failing health he was obliged to resign. He strove during his presidency to promote the objects of the Society by offering prizes and by obtaining lecturers.

It is much to be regretted that Mr. Robinson never published any papers on the natural history of Co. Armagh, on which he was a perfect mine of information. There was not a point of interest about the county with which he was not acquainted, and being an excellent observer, and having a retentive memory, he accumulated a large amount of original information. He was always ready to give a helping hand to the young naturalist, and was always delighted to hear of a new discovery in the county. He had a considerable collection of both plants and birds, but the latter, though excellently set up, are unfortunately not localized. I take this opportunity of acknowledging the kind assistance and encouragement I received from Mr. Robinson in making various collections of plants as well as insects. Though he did not profess to be an entomologist he had much infomation on the subject.

W. F. JOHNSON.

PROCEEDINGS OF IRISH SOCIETIES.

ROYAL ZOOLOGICAL SOCIETY.

Recent donations comprise a Golden Pheasant from Mr. Godden, a pair of Rabbits from Masters J. and G. Armstrong, a Long-eared Owl, a Barn Owl, two Pigeons, and a Hedgehog from R. L. Weldon, Esq., a Sparrowhawk from D. Carton, Esq., a Herring-Gull from R. Ll. Praeger, Esq., two Green Monkeys from Rev. J. Botrel, and a Cormorant from T. Clibborn, Esq. A seal has been purchased.

9,200 persons visited the Gardens in September.

DUBLIN MICROSCOPICAL CLUB.

JULY 20th.—The club met at Mr. M. HEDLEY'S, who showed a section of a vegetation from a cusp of the mitral valve of a pig's heart, in which the presence of a large number of the bacilli of schweine-rothlauf were present. The section had been stained with gentian, violet, and rosin, and was examined under a one-twelfth oil immersion. It was pointed out that this section had been obtained from an Irish pig by Professor MacFadyean after the animal's arrival and death in Scotland. This disease has often been mistaken for the disease ordinarily known as swine-plague, but in this disease the bacilli are of another character. The schweine-rothlauf bacilli are amongst the most minute of such organisms, and are so closely allied to mouse septicæmia that the difference is best determined by cultivation methods. The specimens are more interesting because they are the first which have been demonstrated as existing in Irish swine. The exhibitor has, since receiving this slide, obtained further specimens among Irish swine.

MR. F. W. MOORE exhibited *Xylaria rhopaloides*, Nutge. This remarkable fungus made its appearance on a piece of wood which had been imported from the Amazon with some orchids. It had not previously been found growing in Britain.

PROF. COLE showed a section of iridescent soda-orthoclase from near Laurvik, S. Norway, illustrating how the play of delicate grey-blue colours in the mass is due to the development of exceedingly minute rods within the crystal. This is an example of "schillerisation" on an unusually small scale. A fine specimen of the syenite in which this mineral occurs has been for some time on view, as a polished tombstone, in Great Brunswick-street, Dublin.!

DR. SCOTT showed some sections from some enlargements which grew on the roots of the Bean (*Vicia faba*), and which were sent to him by Mr. G. Pim. The section showed the growths to be composed of three layers, the outer one composed of large spherical cells similar to pith cells. The middle layer was very small, being composed of a few fibro-vascular bundles and single bundles. The inner layer was a mass of spherical cells, somewhat smaller than those in the outer. The cells in the innermost layer were packed with masses of micrococci, in some cases apparently filling up solidly the space inside the cell wall. The stain found most satisfactory was a watery solution of methylene blue.

MR. MCARDLE exhibited a specimen of *Chivolepus aureus*, Linn., a large red alga, with the threads in neat compact tufts, of a brilliant orange colour. It was collected on Carlingford Mountain, Co. Down, by Mr. R. Welch, of the Belfast N.F.C., on the 5th of August, 1893.

BELFAST NATURALISTS' FIELD CLUB.

AUGUST 26th.—Excursion to the Giant's Causeway. A party numbering about sixty proceeded from Belfast by the 8.15 train to Portrush, and thence to the Causeway by the electric tramway. Here they were joined by a local member, Mr. W. A. Traill, who contributed much valuable information during the day. The various wonders of the Causeway were duly examined, after which Mr. Traill gave a short lecture on local geology, which was much appreciated. Tea at the Hotel, and the election of a number of new members concluded the programme, and the party returned to Belfast by the evening train.

SEPTEMBER 16th.—Excursion to Loughbrickland. A party of over forty took train at 10 o'clock to Scarva, where the demesne of Mr. Reilly was entered, and an examination made of the "Dane's Cast," an ancient fortification that is traceable for many miles in Down and Armagh. The party then drove through Loughbrickland to Donoughmore, where the fine old celtic cross in the graveyard, recently re-erected by the Rector, with the assistance of the Club, was much admired, and some souterrains were inspected. Subsequently, on the invitation of Captain Douglas, the Club inspected two very fine forts at Lisnagead, which are of great dimensions, and each enclosed by two outer rings of earth, and three deep fosses. In the evening tea was provided at Banbridge, after which the business meeting of the day was held, and the party returned to Belfast. On account of the late period of the year, little collecting was done. The best plant found during the day was *Mercurialis perennis*, which was pointed out by Rev. H. W. Lett, growing in a copse near Scarva, its only station in Co. Down.

DUBLIN NATURALISTS' FIELD CLUB.

SEPTEMBER 9th.—Thirty members attended the excursion to Beauparc and the Boyne, where a very enjoyable and profitable day was spent. Most of the party went fungus-hunting, and the results were eminently satisfactory. Mr. Greenwood Pim and Dr. M'Weeney have furnished the following list of species. The initials indicate responsibility for identification. When none are given they are to be understood as jointly responsible. *Agaricus* (*Lepiota*) *cristatus*, Fr. (by far the commonest of the few agaries met with); *A.* (*L.*) *procerus*, Scop.; *A.* (*Mycena*) *tenerrimus*, Bk. (M'W.); *A.* (*Entoloma*) *rhodopolius*, Fr. (M'W.); *A.* (*Hypholoma*) *sublateritius*, Fr. (P.); *A.* (*Psalliota*) *arvensis*, Schæff. (P.); *Coprinus comatus*, Fr.; *C. micaceus*, Fr.; *Marasmius oreades*, Fr. (M'W.); *Gomphidius viscidus*, Fr.; *Lactarius excuccus*, Otto; *Boletus luteus*, L.; *B. laricinus*, Bk.; *Polyporus giganteus*, Fr.; *P. fomentarius*, Fr. (P.); *Tremella albida*, Huds.; *Dacryomyces stillatus*, Nees (M'W.); *Lycoperdon gemmatum*, Fr. (P.); *Scleroderma vulgare*, Fr.; *Phallus impudicus*, Linn.; *Stilbum erythrocephalum*, Ditm. (M'W.); *Botryosporium pulchrum*, Ca.; *Puccinia primulæ*, DC. (M'W.); *P. glechomatis*, DC.; *P. veronicarum*, DC. (M'W.); *P. violæ*, Schum.; *P. menthæ*, Pers; *P. umbelliferarum*, DC. (P.); *P. polygoni*, Pers.; *P. buxi*, DC.; *P. lychindearum*, Lk. (M'W.); *P. variabilis*, Grev. (M'W.); *P. circææ*, Pers. (M'W.); *Uromyces valerianæ*, Schum.; *U. geranii*, DC., on *G. pyrenaicum* (M'W.); *Colcosporium sonchi*, Pers. (on *Petasites vulgaris*); *Melampsora farinosa*, Pers. (M'W.); *Synchytrium taraxaci*, De By and Wor.; *Uncinula bicornis*, Lev.; *Minosphæria cornata*, Lev.; *Peziza sentellata*, L.; *P. subumbrina*, Bond. ["has not occurred to my knowledge in Britain."—W. Phillips *in litt.*] (M'W.); *Helotium citrinum*, Hedur. (P.); *Hymenoscypha sp.* close to *virgultorum*, Vahl. (M'W.); *Ascobolus furfuracens*, Pers. (M'W.); *Bulgaria sarcoides*, Fr.; *Stegia ilicis*, Fr.; *Rhytisma acerinum*, Fr.; *Hypomyces aurantius*, Tul.; *Hypocrea rufa*, Fr.; *Claviceps microcephala*, Tul. (M'W.); *Nectria*, two species (P.). There are also other species yet awaiting identification.

The following flowering plants were noted during the day:—*Thalictrum flavum*, *Lysimachia vulgaris*, *Carex stricta*, *Rumex hydrolapathum*, on the Beauparc banks of the Boyne; *Euonymus europæus*, *Calamintha officinalis*, *Lamium album*, *Verbascum thapsus*, rocky bank on the northern bank of the Boyne; *Sagittaria sagittifolia*, *Œnanthe phellandrium*, *Utricularia vulgaris*, in the River Boyne; *Ranunculus lingua*, *Hydrocharis morsus-ranæ*, old mill-race by the Boyne below Slane. The latter was also found in pools by the Boyne opposite Beauparc, accompanied by *Armoracia amphibium; Ceterach officinarum*, wall at Slane.

Mr. H. K. Gore Cuthbert collected beetles and obtained the following noteworthy species, the first of which is believed to be an addition to the Irish list:—*Anchomenus angusticollis, Leistus fulvibarbis, Calathus piceus, Cœlambus lineatus, Lacon murinus, Choleva fusca,* and *Cis boleti*.

ARMAGH NATURAL HISTORY AND PHILOSOPHICAL SOCIETY.
OCTOBER 6.—Annual General Meeting. The following officers were elected:—President, Rev. W. F. Johnson, M.A., F.E.S.; Hon. Secretary, G. H. Johnston; Hon. Treasurer, F. L. Martin; Hon. Librarian, J. Boyd; Committee, Dr. Gray, W. Gallagher, E. Fullerton, D. A. Simmons, A. Gibson, J. Pellow, S. Greer, S. Davison, R. H. Dorman, E. L. Fischer, R. Best, F. J. Anderson, W. Whitsitt. The funds of the society were not in as good a position as usual, and a deficit of £10 was announced; but, as an offset to this, the members were informed that the late Rev. G. Robinson had bequeathed a sum of £50 to the society.

NOTES.

BOTANY.

PHANEROGAMS.

Autumn Blossoming of Spring Flowers.—The remarkably early season, with its accompaniment of intense heat and drought, followed by a showery autumn, has resulted in a September blossoming of a number of our spring and early summer flowers, and I place on record such cases as have been reported by correspondents, or have come to my own notice: no doubt readers of the *Irish Naturalist* will be able to supplement the list. *Ranunculus circinatus*—there was an abundant second growth of this in the canals near Dublin, and a good deal of flower. *R. peltatus*—Mr. Stewart reports this in flower in several lakes in Co. Down. *Caltha palustris*—Mrs. Leebody reports this from Londonderry, and Mr. Stewart from Co. Down. *Viola sylvatica*—in bloom at Londonderry (Mrs. Leebody), Cork (Mr. Noonan), and in Co. Meath and north Donegal (R. Ll. P.). *Cytisus scoparius*—same localities as last. *Lotus pilosus* and *Lathyrus pratensis*—North Donegal (R. Ll. P.). *Pyrus malus*—Mr. Noonan reports a crab-apple tree "covered with flowers" near Cork on October 10th. *Fragaria vesca*—Cork (Mr. Noonan). *Potentilla fragariastrum*—noted on the Dublin Field Club excursion to Beauparc, Co. Meath. *Lonicera periclymenum*—there was quite a remarkable September flowering of the Honeysuckle; in many counties from Donegal to Queen's Co., I saw or received notes of its blossoming freely at the same time that it was bearing abundance of bright red berries. *Menyanthes trifoliata*—Killinchy, Co. Down, Mr. Stewart. *Mertensia maritima*—Malin Head, Co. Donegal, September 24th, fine specimens in full bloom, R. Ll. P. *Equisetum palustre*—a luxuriant new crop with abundance of fruit near Lough Swilly, Donegal.—R. LLOYD PRAEGER.

Plants of the Boyne mouth.—*Cuscuta major*, according to Threlkeld "groweth in great plenty on the dry sandy banks near the Mayden Tower, near Drogheda." An August afternoon, devoted to a search for this plant, did not result in its re-discovery, although I hunted carefully over the low sand-dunes for some distance around the tower, which is a tall quadrangular building, with a picturesquely battlemented summit, built on the edge of the Boyne in close proximity to its mouth, evidently as a mark for mariners entering the river. The dodders, however, seem to be plants of irregular appearance, often springing up in abundance for a year or two in localities where they were previously unknown, and as rapidly disappearing; and probably Threlkeld's plant, which was no doubt imported with seed, has long since forsaken its former habitat by the Boyne; at any rate, it does not now occupy the station so explicitly described by the pioneer of Irish botany. As few botanists apparently have visited this spot, it may be worth mentioning the characteristics of the flora, although nothing of special interest occurs. On the sand-dunes *Cynoglossum officinale* is the most abundant plant—excepting *Psamma* and *Ononis*. *Viola curtisii* is frequent; with it grows the rare grass *Festuca uniglumis*, probably its most northerly station in Ireland; it was first found here many years ago by Dr. Moore, as recorded in "Cybele Hibernica;" and the rayless form (*S. flosculosus*, Jord.) of *Senecio jacobœa* is more abundant than the type. On the sandy shore grow *Cakile*, *Eryngium*, *Euphorbia paralias*, *Salsola*. In the neighbourhood of the little village of Mornington I observed *Sisymbrium sophia*, *Lychnis vespertina*, *L. githago*, *Malva rotundifolia*, *Geranium pyrenaicum*, *Medicago sativa*, *Fœniculum*, *Carduus crispus*, and *C. tenuiflorus*, *Lycopsis*, *Borago*, *Ballota*, *Lamium album*, *Chenopodium bonus-henricus*, *C. murale*; I did not observe *Artemisia maritima*, recorded from this neighbourhood in 1873, by Mr. More (*Journ. Bot*). By the muddy river-banks, above its sandy mouth, were *Sagina maritima*, *Apium graveolans*, *Statice bahusiensis*, *Beta*, *Obione*, *Suœda*, *Lepturus*. The most interesting thing at Mayden Tower, however, was not a plant at all, but consisted of the enormous abundance of the extremely local snail, *Helix pisana*, which in Ireland is confined to a strip of the east coast from Rush to Drogheda. Here it occurred in thousands, all over the dunes, and among the maritime plants on the sea-shore; it was in the latter situation that I obtained the finest specimens.—R. LLOYD PRAEGER.

Alien Plants at Greenisland, Belfast.—Mrs. White-Spunner sends me specimens of an interesting group of casuals gathered by her at one spot near Greenisland. The plants are *Sisymbrium sophia*, *Thlaspi arvense*, *Erisymum orientale*, *Linum perenne*, *Lychnis vespertina*, *Melilotus alba*, *Cichorium intybus*, *Hyoscyamus niger*, *Galeopsis speciosa*, and an exotic *Linaria*, with handsome purple flowers, which I have not identified. Some of the above are admitted as natives in the Co. Antrim flora, but in the present instance the bad company which they are keeping is fatal to their claim. From inquiries which Mrs. White-Spunner has made, it appears that fowl were kept at the place in question, and that they were fed with foreign grain; which is an ample explanation of the appearance of the plants in question.—R. LLOYD PRAEGER.

Limosella aquatica in Ireland.—Early in July last, Mr. O'Kelly, of Ballyvaughan, sent me some specimens of *Limosella aquatica*, which he had gathered on the margin of Lough Inchiquin, near Corofin, in the Co. Clare. This plant had not, it is believed, been previously found in Ireland, though it is mentioned by Wade in his "Plantæ Rariores" as "frequently occurring where water has stood during the winter—Co. Galway, near Ballynahinch, Connemara;" but this locality has not since been confirmed by any other botanist. About one month after the discovery of the plant by Mr. O'Kelly, being in the neighbourhood of Corofin, I visited the lake, which, owing to heavy rain, had in the interval risen about three feet, and submerged the *Limosella* to a depth of nearly two feet. I was able, however, with the help of a boat and drag, to procure some plants, which then presented a totally different appearance to that of the specimens sent me by Mr. O'Kelly, having apparently, after submergence, cast off most of the old leaves with the ripened fruits, and developed a fresh crop of bright green young leaves, the stems of which were in some instances elongated to as much as four or five inches. This stage of the plant's growth does not appear to have been previously noticed, and may be due to the abnormal season. Mr. O'Kelly has, since my visit, discovered the *Limosella* in two other localities in the neighbourhood of Gorst, in the Co. Galway, and no doubt the very dry season and consequent low state of the water in the lakes and "turloughs" has brought to light this plant, which, in ordinary years, is probably nearly always under water, and has thus escaped the notice of botanists. The discovery now is a welcome and valuable addition to the Flora of Ireland.—H. C. LEVINGE (in *Journal of Botany* for October).

ZOOLOGY.

ARACHNIDS.

Phytoptus geranii at Howth.—We have received from Mr. F. W. Burbidge, shoots of *Geranium sanguineum* injured by this mite, which has been identified by Dr. Maxwell T. Masters (*Gardeners' Chronicle*, 16th September, 1893). The leaves are swollen and rolled round at the margins, thus forming shelter for the mites; while the unhealthy stimulation which these produce on the growth of the plant, provides their food-supply. Mr. Burbidge informs us that plants injured in this way were common at Howth this year.

INSECTS.

The Clouded Yellow Butterfly (Colias edusa) at Cork.—While walking on the cliffs at the mouth of Cork Harbour on the 4th instant, I saw a good many of *Colias edusa*. I could not catch any, as I had no net with me.—S. WESTROPP, Cork.

Additional Coleoptera from Courtown, Co. Wexford.—The following additions were made last August, to the list of Coleoptera published in the *Irish Nat.*, vol. i., p. 168:—*Cicindela campestris, Pterostichus cupreus, Haliplus confinis, Hydroporus rivalis, Leistotrophus murinus, Choleva fusca Saprinus maritimus, Byrrhus dorsalis, Cytilus varius, Aphodius rufescens, Phratora vulgatissima, Galerucella tenella, Crepidodera helixines, Apion miniatum, Otiorrhynchus scabrosus, Helops pallidus*.

This is a small list, but beetles are not plentiful anywhere about the middle of August. *Cicindela campestris* was scarce, though its larvæ were very abundant. *Helops pallidus* has not, I believe been hitherto recorded from any Irish locality. *Adimonia tanaceti* was apparently abundant last August, though scarce in the district in August, 1892.—H. K. GORE CUTHBERT.

MOLLUSCS.

Rare Shells from Co. Sligo.—Mr. W. Kennedy of Londonderry has just sent me three of our rarest species of Land Mollusca, which he took in Co. Sligo as far back as 1863. Two of these have never been taken before in the West of Ireland, and the third is new to district IX. (see my List of Land and Fresh-water Mollusca in *Irish Naturalist*, 1892). The following are the three species:—*Clausilia laminata*, Mont., from an island in Lough Gill, near Sligo; new to district IX. and to the West of Ireland. *Buliminus obscurus*, Mull., from the south slope of Knocknarea, near Sligo; new to district IX. and the West of Ireland. *Helix lamellata*, Jeffr., from an island in Lough Gill, near Sligo; new to district IX.—R. F. SCHARFF, Dublin.

Helix rufescens in the North of Ireland.—In the last number of the *Irish Naturalist* there is a note by Dr. Scharff on the occurrence of *Helix rufescens* in the north. This reminds me of what my cousin, Mr. Taylor, told me some years ago, in reference to this shell being procured near Belfast. He said that in his boyhood *H. rufescens* was never found in the neighbourhood until it travelled there amongst some rose-trees sent to his mother from Castlewarren, Co. Cork, and planted in her garden in Cliftonville, from which locality it was supposed to have spread. The time was about 1848.—AMY WARREN, Moyview, Ballina.

Helix arbustorum, L. in Leitrim.—Mr. William Kennedy, of Londonderry, having recently informed me that he had collected *Helix arbustorum* at Glencar Waterfall; in response to a request for further information in respect to this important find, Mr. Kennedy forwards specimens, and detailed information of his discovery. The specimens are three in number, and Dr. Scharff considers them very fine examples of the typical form. As Antrim, Down, and North Donegal (a single dead specimen) are the only authenticated stations in Ireland for this handsome snail, Mr. Kennedy's careful and accurate notes are of interest:—"On referring to my memoranda in connection with this species, I find that I got altogether at the same place five specimens; the dates are:—4th June, 1863, one immature specimen; 19th August, 1864, two living, mature; 28th September, 1865, one living, and one dead specimen. All were found in the long grass growing among the trees and shrubs at Glencar Waterfall, not more than three or four yards from the waterfall, and in the bottom at the glen. On the occasion of my first visit to the locality, 4th June, 1863, the late Dr. Samuel Brown, Inspector of National Schools, then much interested in land and fresh-water molluscs, was with me, and he got, I think, one or two specimens."—R. LLOYD PRAEGER.

Helix fusca in Co. Dublin.—The only record we possess of this rare species for the county, is that in Turton's work who mentions merely "wood in Dublin." No one else seems to have found it since, and I am glad to be able to confirm the record, as my brother took it abundantly after the recent heavy showers in the Lucan demesne.—R. F. SCHARFF, Dublin.

A new Irish species of Arion.—In the *Annals and Mag. of Nat. Hist.* (6th s.) vol. xii. Oct. 1893, Mr. W. E. Collinge, the editor of the *Conchologist*, describes a new species of *Arion*. It was discovered at Schull, Co. Cork, by Mr. Phillips, and is named *Arion flagellus* by the describer. Mr. Collinge very kindly allowed me to examine the type specimens. The external characters do not differ materially from the typical Irish *Arion subfuscus* except that the colour is darker, but it has this in common with almost all the specimens found on the west coast. The two principal anatomical characters on which the species is based, are the constrictions of the oviduct and the presence of a flagellum. With regard to the former, it is not different from the shape assumed by an oviduct during and after the passage of the ova. The flagellum is of more importance, and would in itself be sufficient to specifically distinguish *A. flagellus* from allied species. As far as I could ascertain, however, without cutting sections of the flagellum, it appears to be but a portion of the extractor muscle, which is attached at that point to the oviduct. I cannot therefore convince myself that the species referred to, is anything else than a variety of the variable *A. subfuscus.*—R. F. SCHARFF, Dublin.

BIRDS.

Redbreasted Snipe (Macrorhamphus griseus, Gmel.) in Ireland, a new American Visitor.—On the 29th September I obtained a specimen of the American Redbreasted Snipe, which was forwarded from Maryborough, Queen's Co., along with a lot of Common Snipe. The bird is a female in the immature autumn plumage, and has not hitherto been recorded from Ireland.—E. WILLIAMS, Dublin.

Great Snipe (Gallinago major), and Sabine's Snipe (G. coelestis, var. sabinii) in Ireland.—I have received a fine Great Snipe, shot by Mr. T. L. Mason, at Ballycroy, Co. Mayo, on the 13th October. The bird weighed seven ounces, and looks fully half as large again as a Common Snipe. On the 28th September, Mr. R. W. Peebles shot a particularly dark example in Co. Tyrone, of the variety called Sabine's Snipe. The whole bird is dark smoky-black, legs greenish-black, and wanting the longitudinal stripes on back.—E. WILLIAMS, Dublin.

ARAN ISLANDERS.

THE ARAN ISLANDS, COUNTY GALWAY:
A STUDY IN IRISH ETHNOGRAPHY.

BY PROFESSOR A. C. HADDON, M.A.

THE IRISH NATURALIST is itself a witness to the increased interest which has of late years become manifest in the study of Natural History in Ireland, and it is encouraging to see notes from new observers in various parts of the country. It would be very undesirable to divert to other channels any of the energy which has now been brought to bear on Natural History, but there must be a large number of persons in Ireland who do not take any special interest in any one group of animals or plants, and have no taste or opportunity for making collections, but who, nevertheless, would like to occupy their leisure with something that is both interesting and worth doing. To such I would commend the study of the Irish Man.

It is surprising how little attention we have given, in the British Islands, to a study of our fellow-countrymen, whether from an anthropological or from a sociological point of view. In this respect we are far behind the great continental nations. Nor is it from lack of suggestive facts to be recorded or of problems to be solved. The mixture of races in these islands certainly renders the problems complex, but this should not paralyse effort. Very interesting results may be expected from a careful study of certain groups of the populace, but to gain them immediate action must be taken. Owing to migration and emigration, the mingling of peoples has become more intimate, and the newspaper and the school-board have been potent in sweeping away local customs and in levelling up the less advanced folk. All we can now do is to record the little that remains of old-time custom and thought. Experience, however, shows that more persists beneath the surface than is generally conceded by those who vaunt themselves on our present civilization and religion. The civilization of the British Islands is, after all, comparatively so recent that relics of the previous millenniums of savagery and barbarism are continually cropping up.

For some years past I have been increasingly impressed with the importance of these studies, and I recently determined to make a beginning with the Aran Islands in Galway Bay, as being in every way suitable for such researches. It was, therefore, with great pleasure that I found my friend Dr. C. R. Browne was able to join me in making the first of what I hope will be series of studies in Irish Ethnography, conducted in connection with a Committee appointed by the Royal Irish Academy for that purpose. Our joint investigations have just been published in the *Proceedings of the Royal Irish Academy* (3rd series, vol. iii., 1893, pp. 768-830, pls. xxii.-xxiv.

The Aran men are mostly of a slight but athletic build, the average height is about 5 feet 4¾ inches, whereas that of the average Irishman is said to be 5 feet 8½ inches. The span is less than the stature in a quarter of the cases measured, a rather unusual feature in adult males. The hands are rather small, but the forearm is often unusually long.

The head is well-shapen, rather long and narrow; there is a slight parietal bulging. Anthropologists classify heads according to the relation between the length and the breadth; the length is taken as 100, and long narrow heads (dolichocephals) are those in which the ratio of breadth to length is as 75, or less, is to 100; the short broad heads (brachycephals) have a ratio of 80, or more, to 100, whereas the mesaticephals are intermediate between these two. The mean "cephalic index," as it is termed, of the Aranites is 77·1, but it has been shown that in order to more accurately compare the cephalic index calculated upon measurements made on the living head with that of skulls, it is necessary to deduct two units from the former; this gives 75·1 as the Aran cephalic index. I find that the mean index of seven Aran skulls is 75·2, consequently the average head is to a very slight extent mesaticephalic, although the number measured is nearly evenly divided between mesaticephalic and dolichocephalic. The face is long and oval, with well-marked features, the eyes are rather small and close together, and marked at the outer corners by transverse wrinkles. The irises are in the great majority of cases blue or blue-grey in colour. The nose is sharp, narrow at the base, and slightly sinuous. The cheek bones are not prominent. In many men the length between the nose and the chin has the appearance of being decidedly great. The complexion is clear and ruddy, and but seldom freckled. On the whole the people are decidedly good-looking. The hair is brown in colour; in most cases of a lightish shade and accompanied by a light and often reddish beard. Eighty-nine per cent. of both men and women had blue or light-grey eyes; sixty-three per cent. had light brown hair, and about twenty-six per cent. had dark brown hair.

According to the last census (1891) the total area of the three islands is 11,288 acres, with a population of 2,907, 1,542 being males and 1,365 being females. The gross rental is £2,085 10s. 6d. The north island, Aranmore, has 7,635 acres, 397 houses, 1,048 males, 948 females (total 1,996), and a rental of £1,433 18s. 1d. The middle island, Inishmaan, has 2,252 acres, 84 houses, 240 males, 216 females (total 456), and a rental of £423 18s. 5d. The south island, Inisheer, has 1,400 acres, 81 houses, 254 males, 201 females (total 455), and a rental of £227 14s. From these statistics it will be seen that there is an average acreage of 20a. or. 13½p. to each house of five persons, and the corresponding rental is £3 14s. 2⅜d. The density of the population is 171 to the square mile, that of Co. Galway is 87, and for the whole of Ireland 146. It should, however, be borne in mind that a large proportion of the land in the Aran Islands is incapable of cultivation.

Irish is spoken by 88·47 per cent. of the people, of whom 77·2 speak Irish only.

The inhabitants of one island do not, as a rule, intermarry with those of another, and but little fresh blood can have been introduced for generations. The people of each locality are more or less inter-related, even though marriages between those of close degrees of relationship may not be usual. This accounts for the general similarity in personal appearance which is observed among them, but no appreciable ill effect results from the in-breeding. The population seems on the whole to be an unusually healthy one.

The older writers give very pleasing accounts of the psychology of these people—" brave, hardy, industrious,

A *

simple and innocent, but also thoughtful and intelligent, credulous, temperate, with a high sense of decency and propriety, honour and justice, communicative but not too loquacious, hospitable and honest." According to these authors there is scarcely a virtue which is lacking to the people; but one writer adds: "I am afraid things are very much changed since those days."

All the men are land-owners to a greater or less extent; the holdings, or cannogarras, as they are termed, vary from about 11 to 14 acres, the supposition being that each cannogarra can feed a cow with her calf, a horse and her foal, some sheep for their wool, and give sufficient potatoes to support one family. Most of the fields are very small in size, and are surrounded by walls composed of stones piled loosely on one another; there are no gates or permanent gaps in the walls. A man usually owns a number of isolated fields scattered all over the island.

Only a fraction of the land is naturally fit for anything, and probably a considerable portion of the existing soil has been made by the natives bringing up sea-sand and sea-weed in baskets, on their own or on donkeys' backs, and strewing them on the naked rock after they have removed the loose stones. Clay scooped from the interstices of the rock may also be added. Farmyard manure is little used in the fields. Only spade labour is employed in the fields. Potatoes are grown in this artificial soil; after a few crops of these grass is sown, and later rye. The latter is cultivated for the straw, which is used for thatching; the rye-corn is not now employed for eating purposes. Sweet grass grows in the crevices of the rocks, and this forms, in addition to the meadows, the usual pasturage for the sheep.

The farm will usually keep a family in potatoes, milk, and wool. Flour and meal are imported from Galway along with tea and other foreign produce. For fuel the Aranites employ peat and cow-dung; all the former is imported from Connemara. Kelp is made in considerable quantities.

The bulk of the men on the north island may be described as small farmers who do a little fishing. There are, besides, two or three weavers, tailors, and curragh builders. The butcher, baker, and other allied tradesmen are mainly related to the small population, which may fairly be termed foreign, such as the representatives of the Government and the spiritual and secular instructors.

A family usually consists of six or seven children. These go to school regularly, and are intelligent and make fair progress. They early help their parents in various ways. The girls marry early, seventeen is quite a common age. There is no courting, nor do the young people ever walk together.

The dress of both sexes is for the most part home-made, being largely composed of homespun, either uncoloured or of a speckled brown or blue grey, or bright red colour. The people appear not only to be warmly clad, but, as a rule, to be over-clothed. Both sexes wear sandals made of raw cowhide, the hair being outside. These "pampooties," as they are called, are admirably adapted for climbing and running over the rocks and loose stones. Some of the men are now taking to wearing leather boots.

The houses of the better class consist of three rooms—a central kitchen, and a bedroom at each end; but many houses have only a single bedroom. The walls are built of irregular stones, and may be placed together with or without mortar. There are always two outside doors opposite one another in the kitchen. Very often there is a small pen by the side of the large fire-place for the pigs, which are very clean both in their bodies and habits. The kitchen floor may be the bare rock or clay, or it is very rarely boarded. The thatch is tied on with straw ropes.

Twenty years ago there was not a wheeled vehicle in the islands. Even now there are no roads worthy of the name in the Middle and South Islands, and till lately there were not many in Aranmore. Carts are still very rare, and the carrying is done by human porterage or by donkeys and horses. All the well-to-do men own a mare. A poor man will have only a donkey.

We were not able to collect much in the way of folk-lore. In common with a large part of Ireland, the Aranites believe in fairies, banshees, ghosts, the evil eye, etc. When a funeral is passing down the road the front door of a house is always closed. The corpse is carried out through the back door. Some days are considered unlucky upon which to begin any work of importance, to get married, or even to bury the dead. If they have occasion to bury a corpse on one of these days, they turn a sod on the grave the previous day, and by this means they think to avoid the misfortune attached to a burial on an unlucky day.

There are numerous sacred spots such as "saints' beds," holy wells and rag-bushes at which cures can be effected and miraculous help afforded.

Amongst other survivals may be noted certain details in the costume, and especially the raw hide sandals. The curraghs are similar in general character to those common along the west coast, the single oars are pivotted on thole-pins. Stone anchors are still used, more frequently in the Middle and South Islands. Querns are not now used, but it is not long since they were employed. The spinning-wheel is similar to that used in various places along the West, but it differs from that employed in the North.

The antiquities of the Aran Islands have never been systematically described and published; and yet nowhere in the British Islands are there so many and so varied remains associated within a like limited area. The Islands may not inaptly be described as a unique museum of antiquities.

There are many places in Ireland which are as worthy of a careful study as the Aran Islands, and I hope that some of our readers will pay attention to this subject. I shall be very pleased to enter into correspondence with any that would like to study the ethnography, sociology, or folk-lore of their particular district. Letters addressed to the Royal College of Science, Stephen's Green, Dublin, will always find me.

Through the kindness of the Council of the Royal Irish Academy, I am able to reproduce one of the plates of the original paper, which was prepared from a photograph taken by myself.

PLATE 8.

Fig. 1. Colman Flaherty, Thomas, aged about sixty years, Oghil.

Fig. 2. Michael O'Donnell, John, aged fifty-three.

N.B.—When there is more than one man of the same name in the Aran Islands the individuals are distinguished by the addition of their father's Christian name, as in the foregoing cases. Flaherty is a thirteenth child, and according to the tradition of the island should be a piper, but he cannot play the bagpipes; he is a very typical Aranite. O'Donnell's ancestor came from Ulster. They are standing in front of St. Sourniek's thorn.

Fig. 3. Michael Mullin, aged 21 years, Kilronan. A typical Aranite.

NOTES UPON SOME IRISH MYRIOPODA.
By R. I. Pocock, British (Nat. Hist.) Museum.

SOME two or three years ago, Dr. R. F. Scharff, of Dublin, generously placed at my disposal for determination some species of Myriopoda which he had collected in various parts of Ireland; and this series was further supplemented by some specimens obtained by Mr. G. H. Carpenter, which this gentleman also kindly submitted to me for examination.

Before sorting and carefully scrutinising this material, I was in hopes that some new or interesting forms might be contained in it. But unfortunately the results did not come up to my expectations. For all the specimens that could be named proved to be referable to species that occur commonly in the south of England, and could be without difficulty obtained by an hour's diligent collecting. Mr. Carpenter has since sent me a second instalment of Irish Myriopoda, six of which were not contained in the set that was first examined. Five of these, however, are forms that are of common occurrence in England and on the Continent; but the other, namely, *Polydesmus gallicus*, furnishes a valuable addition to the myriopod fauna of the British Isles. The chief interest in the discovery of this species centres in the fact that it belongs to the South-Western and Azorean element of the European fauna.

It is highly probable that fresh investigations of this unknown portion of the fauna of Ireland will show that many of our English species are not to be found there; and further, it is not improbable that some species will be discovered that are unknown in Great Britain. Both or either of these discoveries will of course open up interesting questions for future study and explanation.

In the south of England and Wales some fifty species of Myriopoda are known to occur, although not one-half of this number has been hitherto recorded in print. It is not probable that the species in Ireland will greatly exceed this total. So that in a few years a complete, or almost complete, list of all the existing species might be drawn up, and our knowledge of the group would be thus made as complete as our knowledge of the butterflies of England. To compass this end, which may in reality be so easily attained, it is to be hoped that naturalists resident in Ireland will begin to pay some attention to these interesting but much neglected animals.

LIST OF THE SPECIES.

CHILOPODA.
(CENTIPEDES.)

FAMILY LITHOBIIDÆ.

Lithobius forficatus (Linn).
 Poulaphuca, Co. Wicklow; Dingle; Glengariff; Bere Island (Bantry Bay).
 Common throughout the whole of N. Europe; occurs also in N. America.

L. variegatus, Leach.
 Dublin mountains; Dalkey Island; Kilruddery, Glen of the Downs (Co. Wicklow); Enniskerry (Co. Wicklow); Kylemore (Connemara); Killarney; Castletown Berehaven; Glengariff.
 Abundantly distributed throughout the British isles, and occurs also in Jersey. It has not yet, however, been recorded from any part of the continent of Europe.
 This is a handsome species, rivalling *L. forficatus* in size, but readily to be distinguished from it by its variegated yellow and blue colouring, larger head, longer and thinner anal legs, etc. *L. forficatus* is a uniform chestnut.
 In the south of England it is a noticeable fact in connection with these two species, that *L. forficatus* is found most abundantly under bricks and planks, in or near yards, outhouses, etc. *L. variegatus*, on the contrary, is found under stones and tree-trunks in woods, or the open country.
 These facts in distribution suggest that *L. forficatus* has been introduced into our country later than *L. variegatus*.

L. melanops, Newp. (*glabratus*, C. Koch et alii).
 Poulaphuca, Co. Wicklow; Castletown Berehaven; Derrynane.
 This species somewhat resembles *L. variegatus* in colouring. It is, however, considerably smaller, and has only four instead of ten maxillary teeth.

L. microps, Meinert.
 Glengariff.
 This species is abundant in the S. of England, and, at least, in the northern parts of Europe. It is one of the smallest of the genus, and may be readily recognised by the fewness of the ocelli, and by the very small number of spines upon the anal legs.

FAMILY SCOLOPENDRIDÆ.

Cryptops hortensis, Leach.
 Dublin.
 Common all over Europe.

FAMILY GEOPHILIDÆ.

Geophilus flavus, De Geer (*longicornis*, Leach).
 Dingle; Glengariff; Kylemore (Connemara).
 Common all over Europe. Easily recognizable from the other British species by its long cylindrical antennal segments.

Gophilus carpophagus, Leach (*sodalis*, Mein., *condylogaster*, Latz.).
   Great Sugar-loaf mountain.
   Also common all over Europe. About as large, or rather larger, than the preceding, with shorter anal legs and antennae, and of a deeper chestnut colour. Easily to be recognised from all its allies by the ball-and-socket method of articulation of the anterior sterna.

Linotænia crassipes, C. Koch.
   Kinsale.
   A widely-distributed, but not very common species. Usually attracts attention owing to its nocturnal phosphorescence.

L. maritima, Leach.
   Portmarnock, co. Dublin (beneath stones at low-water).
   This species is one of the two interesting forms of British *Geophilidæ* which are found beneath stones below tide. In England it has been obtained on the coast of Cornwall and Devon. It has also been recorded from St. Malo and Denmark.

Stigmatogaster subterraneus (Leach.)
   Dublin; Dingle.
   Common in the British islands and N. Europe, but replaced in S. Europe by a distinct form, *S. gracilis* (Mein.) Distinguished from all the British Geophilidæ by its large and coarsely-porous anal pleuræ.

DIPLOPODA.
(MILLIPEDES.)
FAMILY POLYXENIDÆ.

Polyxenus lagurus (Linn.)
   Phœnix Park, Dublin.
   Abundant in N. Europe upon wooden fences, etc.

FAMILY GLOMERIDÆ.

Glomeris marginata (Villers.)
   Ballinderry (Co. Antrim); Rostrevor; Howth; Leixlip; Kells, Co. Meath; Woodenbridge, Glen of the Downs (Co. Wicklow) Castletown Berehaven; Killarney; Glengariff; Kylemore (Connemara); Bundoran.
   The only species of the genus known in the British islands. It is also common in most parts of Europe. In the southern parts of the Continent an immense number of "colour-species" of the genus are found. Immature specimens of this species often show signs of the spotting which is so characteristic of the more southern representatives of the genus.

FAMILY POLYDESMIDÆ.

Polydesmus complanatus (Linn.)
   Kylemore (Connemara).
   Common throughout Europe and the British isles. In England occurs under bark, planks, etc.; very rarely under stones.

P. gallicus, Latz.
   Armagh; Mullingar; Lismore; Castletown Berehaven; Glengariff.
   The discovery of this species is extremely interesting, inasmuch as it is new to the British Isles. It was recorded originally from Normandy, and is almost certainly identical with a form named *coriaceus* from the Azores.

B

Brachydesmus superus, Latz.
Glengariff.
Common in England, Scandinavia, Austria, etc. The genus *Brachydesmus* may be recognised from *Polydesmus* by possessing nineteen body-segments instead of twenty.

FAMILY CHORDEUMIDÆ.

Atractosoma polydesmoides (Leach).
Dublin (Leeson-park); Armagh.
Common throughout the south of England, but not yet recognised on the Continent.

FAMILY IULIDÆ.

Blaniulus fuscus, Stein.
Enniskerry (Co. Wicklow); Kylemore (Connemara).
Blaniulus may, in a rough way, be recognised from the following genus *Iulus*, by the absence of longitudinal striæ on the dorsal surface of the segments. *B. fuscus* is common in the south of England.

Iulus luscus, Mein.
Enniskerry (Co. Wicklow); Derrynane; Kylemore (Connemara).
Not uncommon in the south of England. A small nearly uniform pale, brownish species, without a caudal process. Found under stones.

I. punctatus, Leach. (*silvarum*, Mein).
Dublin mountains ; Enniskerry ; Kylemore ; Glengariff ; Killarney.
Common all over the south of England, Denmark, Scandinavia, etc. Always found in rotten wood, never under stones. A pale, brown-banded and brown-spotted species, with the caudal process rounded and clavate at the tip.

I. pilosus, Newp.
Enniskerry (Co. Wicklow); Poulaphuca; Kylemore; Killarney; Drogheda.
Some of the specimens that are here referred to *I. pilosus* are immature, and, consequently, may be wrongly determined. The adults are all females, and since no males were obtained, the identification must be accepted with reservation.

I. niger, Leach (*transverso-sulcatus*, Stein, *albipes*, C. Koch).
Tibradden mountain (Co. Dublin) ; Devil's Glen (Wicklow).
This species when adult is black with very pale legs; it is one of the largest British species; has an acute caudal process, and may be at once recognised by the presence of transverse striæ upon the anterior half of the body-segments.

I. sabulosus (Linn.)
Tibradden mountain (Co. Dublin); Belmont and Devil's Glen (Wicklow).
This is a large species, with a long acute caudal process like *niger* and *pilosus*. It may, however, be recognised at a glance from both of these by the presence of two yellow stripes along the dorsal surface.

For the specimens from Castletown Berehaven, I am indebted to the Committee appointed by the Royal Irish Academy to investigate the Irish fauna and flora ; and I would express my thanks to that body for the opportunity of including the records in the above list.

A VISIT TO ROUNDSTONE, CO. GALWAY.

BY PROF. T. JOHNSON, D.SC.

A COMMITTEE was recently appointed by the Royal Irish Academy to take steps to complete, as far as possible, our knowledge of the Fauna and Flora of Ireland. For this purpose a portion of the annual government grant, at the disposal of the Academy for scientific investigations, was set apart by the Council, and, as one of the committee appointed, I spent a week in September last investigating the marine algæ of Roundstone Bay, Co. Galway.

The district of Roundstone, almost at the foot of the famous Twelve Pins of Connemara, is one of the most interesting in Ireland, and in the early part of the century was called the land of promise in natural history. In 1835 Professor C. Babington, of Cambridge, in company with the late Mr. J. Ball and another friend, visited Connemara, and discovered a number of rare and interesting objects of natural history. An account, full of interest, of the journey is given in the *Magazine of Natural History* (vol. ix., p. 119 *et seq.*) Subsequently Professors D. Oliver, J. H. Balfour, Harvey, Dr. D. Moore, Mr. A. G. More, etc., visited the district, and added considerably to the knowledge of its natural history. During his 1835 journey Professor Babington met W. M'Calla, of whom he says he was "the son of the landlord of the inn at Roundstone,—a young man, who, although labouring under very great difficulties, has, by his own unassisted exertions, with an almost total want of books, obtained a very complete knowledge of the geology, mineralogy, conchology, and botany of the neighbourhood of Roundstone. He has now, I am happy to learn, obtained the situation of national schoolmaster at Ballinahinch." M'Calla's name, as many of my readers know, and as this kindly notice would lead one to expect, became well known in Irish natural history, and is perpetuated in the species *Cladophora macallana*, Harv., as well as in his excellent *Algæ Hibernicæ*, two volumes of seaweeds, prepared by M'Calla, mostly from specimens obtained at Roundstone. I made it my duty to find out all I could about M'Calla and his collections. I interviewed one old man, Patsy Ashe, living in a cabin on the mountain-side, who

remembered him well as a schoolfellow, but told me there was
no representative of the family left, and could give me no
information as to any of M'Calla's collections. M'Calla, as
Harvey states, died from cholera in 1849, a comparatively
young man. I was shewn, in the churchyard at Roundstone,
a substantial monument erected, as the inscription stated, to
M'Calla's memory by his admiring brother naturalists. Unfortunately Roundstone is by no means easy of access,[1] being
50 miles west of Galway, the nearest railway station, and also
off the direct mail-car route to Clifden. Beyond the break-
down of the mail-car shortly after leaving Galway, a consequent loss of time, and a drenching later in the day, I reached
Roundstone without trouble. Once there, there is every
reason to be satisfied with the field of work. I was fortunate
in obtaining the services of a man, Creelish Martin, who,
besides being a reliable and experienced sailor, understands
the working of a dredge, and has a very good knowledge of
the sea-bottom as regards its physical and, to a certain extent,
natural history features. With his help, and the use of a
sailing boat (from J. Cloherty), I got several days' dredging in
Roundstone and Birturbui bays. Roundstone Bay, as readers
of Harvey's *Phycologia Britannica* know, is characterised
by a large development of the calcareous red algæ known as
the *Corallinaceæ* (formerly as *Nullipores*), two species,
Lithothamnion fasciculatum, Aresch., and *Lithothamnion
agariciforme*, Aresch., being confined to the district, and first
discovered[2] there by M'Calla. Of the twenty-five species of
Corallinaceæ, known at present to occur in British waters, the
great majority are to be found in the bay. My object in
going to Roundstone was rather to search for species added to
the marine flora of Britain since the publication of Harvey's
great work, the *Phycologia Britannica*, in 1846-51, but not yet
recorded from Ireland. Many of these species are minute
epiphytic forms, often only to be recognised by a detailed
microscopic examination. As I stated in a former article in

---

[1] The light railway from Galway to Clifden, when completed, in
August, 1894 (?), will take one within five miles of Roundstone.

[2] I showed my man, Creelish, Harvey's coloured figures of these and
other species, and was not a little pleased to see them brought up in our
first hauls, the coralline being in several fathoms of water, north of
Roundstone.

The Irish Naturalist (April, 1892), one interesting group, only revealed within the last few years, is that of the microscopic algæ found perforating the shells of mollusca, &c. Of these I made a large collection at Roundstone, and am now engaged in their identification. The western shore of the bay, on which the town stands, is not a very good locality for collecting, the weeds north of the town being dirty and somewhat uninviting. South of the town there is an improvement, increasing as the mouth of the bay is reached. I found the rock-pools south of The Beaches, between Gorreen and Dog's bays, those on the south-west point of Inishnee (an island between Roundstone and Birturbui bays), those north of the landing place at Moyrus, on the mainland (where beds of *Zostera* and *Lithothamnion calcareum* are exposed at low water in spring tides), those on the islands of Croagnakeela (locally Deer Island, and difficult to land upon), and MacDara, the most promising localities for shore-hunting. On the island of Saint Mac Dara there are the ruins of a church, 12 x 12 ft., with only a little of the stone roof left, with walls three feet thick, and a peculiarly constructed east window. Close by are several stone tablets with inscriptions, readily traceable apparently, but, up to the present, I am told, uninterpreted. Botanists will be interested to know that Saint MacDara is locally highly revered as the patron saint of the new potatoes, which come in in July. It is the custom to throw water on the boat's sails three times, in passing the island, to avoid shipwreck. On the only afternoon I had free from my weeds I was taken by Mr. Frank M'Cormick over the northern shoulder of Urrisbeg (998 feet) to see the only habitat in the district of *Adiantum capillus-veneris* (the Maiden-hair fern) growing in the crevices of a rock, facing south-west, at the extreme north-east corner of Lough Bulard. Spite of the recent very dry season, the spoliation by tourists, and the injudicious application to the surface of the rock of cement, the species is as well established here as when visited by Babington 60 years ago. I spent some fruitless time one afternoon in a waning light searching for the rare *Naias flexilis* in the lake in which Professor D. Oliver found it in 1850. Though an unfortunate stoppage of my work for some weeks, since my return from Roundstone, has prevented me from examining more than a small part of my collection, I am convinced that a thorough investigation of the marine flora and fauna would well repay students of botany and zoology,[1] and could, with the means available there, be carried out without much difficulty.

THE ANATOMICAL CHARACTERS OF ARION FLAGELLUS, CLLGE.
BY WALTER E. COLLINGE.

THE anatomical features of this recently-described *Arion* are so pronounced, and distinct from any other known European species, that I should not have thought it necessary to reply to my friend Dr. Scharff[2] had he not—most unintentionally, I am sure—misrepresented the published account of its anatomy.[3]

It is of little importance, but still I contend that *A. flagellus* does differ in colour from *A. subfuscus*. The most important external character—which Dr. Scharff entirely overlooks—is the small caudal mucous gland. So constant is the form and size of this gland—as might be inferred from the importance of its function—that not a few malacologists have used it as a feature in generic distinction. I have examined very large series of Arions from almost every part of Europe, but have never in any single instance found it vary, and I am not aware of any published instance either. I, therefore, think the point is one worthy of note in the *aggregate characters* of this species, which is not described from any single one, but from the general anatomy.

The exact importance of the myology of the Mollusca as a feature in generic or specific distinction I am as yet undecided upon, but quite recently Lt.-Col. H. H. Godwin, F.R.S., has placed great importance upon the position of attachment of certain muscles, *e.g.*, the retractor muscles of the eye, generative organs, &c., and finds that in certain genera these are subject to but slight variation. Now, in *A. flagellus* there are a number of differences in the form, &c., of the muscles, which I did not

---

[1] I am hoping that Dr. Loftus, of Roundstone, whose acquaintance I made, will become a present-day M'Calla.

[2] *Irish Nat.*, vol. ii., 1893, p. 302.

[3] *Ann. and Mag. N. H.*, 1893 (6th s.), vol. xii., p. 252.

describe—but which Dr. Scharff should have seen,—as I was doubtful as to what amount of importance should be attached to them. The two most important are the position of attachment of the tentacular muscles, and the length and position of the genital retractor.

I purposely stated that the alimentary and nervous systems agreed very closely with *A. empiricorum*, För.—I do not mean *A. ater*, L.—and to now find such classed as *A. subfuscus* surprises me indeed.

When Dr. Scharff had seen the specimens he wrote:—"in some measure it approaches *A. lusitanicus* . . . The constrictions, as you remark, are not due to ova actually passing down the oviduct, but they probably did so recently before the specimens were captured. . . . As for the flagellum . . from a superficial examination, I should be inclined to take it for a strongly contracted muscular mass."

On receipt of his letter I made a further dissection of the oviduct and found the constrictions internally as well. I have never seen a specimen in which the internal wall of the oviduct showed distinct constrictions of the epithelial and muscular layers, and I do not think Dr. Scharff has either— I speak with a tolerably wide acquaintance with the form of this organ in the *Arionidæ* and slugs generally.

As to Dr. Scharff's idea that the flagellum is a portion of the muscle, I purposely dissected the muscle away (*Ann. and Mag.*, 1893, pl. ix., fig. 3,) so as to show the flagellum.

Further differences from *subfuscus* are seen in the form of the receptacular duct, hermaphrodite gland, and in the whole of the generative system.

If Dr. Scharff can show me specimens bred from *A. subfuscus* or any other *Arion*, except this species, in which the general anatomy shows the above features, then *A. flagellus* is not a valid species, but seeing that it is far removed from *subfuscus* and much more closely related to *A. lusitanicus*, I can only regard his criticism as based upon a hasty examination of the specimens in which the salient features were overlooked.

PROCEEDINGS OF IRISH SOCIETIES.

ROYAL ZOOLOGICAL SOCIETY.

Recent donations comprise a Red Deer (Stag) from Sir D. Brooke; a Sparrow-hawk from P. Mahony, Esq.; a Canary Finch from T. de Sales, Esq.; two pairs of Jacobin Pigeons, and two pairs of Ring-Doves from G. Patterson, Esq.; and a pair of Guinea-Pigs from J. Fullerton, Esq. 8,550 persons visited the Gardens in October.

DUBLIN MICROSCOPICAL CLUB.

OCTOBER 19th.—The club met at Dr. SCOTT'S, who showed some crystals of cystin under ordinary and polarised light, which were found in a sample of urine submitted to him for analysis. The crystals, which are very easily recognised by their shape (hexagonal plates) and their solubility in ammonia or mineral acids, are interesting from their extreme rarity. Chemically, cystin contains a large proportion of sulphur in rather loose combination, and appears to represent an abnormal method by which the sulphur, set free in protoplasmic metabolism, is eliminated from the body, the normal method being as sulphates of sodium and potassium. The occurrence of these crystals is not uncommonly hereditary, and so far as is at present known is without any clinical import.

DR. E. PERCEVAL WRIGHT exhibited a new species of *Chlorocystis*, which had been described by Miss F. G. Whitting as *C. sarcophyci*. When Mr. Bracebridge Wilson was collecting specimens of *Sarcophycus* off the coast near Peelong he noticed some gall-like structures on the fronds; these were found to be patches of the new endophytic alga. Dr. Wright was indebted to Miss Whitting for a frond from which the section exhibited had been cut. The genus was founded on a species found at Howth, and exhibited to the club by Dr. Wright in 1876.

DR. M'WEENEY showed conjugating filaments of a mucorine fungus— *Sporodinia aspergillus*,—which grows parasitically on dying *Boleti* and agarics. The conidia are produced in sporangia, which are borne at the end of the dichotomously branched hyphæ. The plant under certain circumstances ceases to produce sporangia, the hyphæ become swollen at the tips, and coalescence takes place between the swollen ends of neighbouring hyphæ. A zygospore is thus produced, the outer coat of which becomes warty and opaque—almost black. In this stage the appearance of the whole fungus is so different that its connection with *Sporodinia* was not demonstrated till within a few years ago; the conjugating form was regarded as a distinct species, long known under the name of *Syzygites megalosporus*. This conjugating form does not seem to have been found before in Ireland, and Mr. G. Massee, of Kew, one of the most distinguished English mycologists, informed the exhibitor that he had never met with it, though he had hunted after it for years. A certain amount of interest, therefore, attaches to its discovery at Mrs. White's, Killakee, in September last. Curiously enough, within a few weeks after it was first taken, a fresh specimen was found in a rotting agaric sent by Mr. Praeger from near Gormanstown.

MR. PIM showed *Azolla filiculoides* in fruit. This occurred—so far as is known—this season for the first time in Great Britain, and the first fruits were found in Mr. Walpole's garden at Mount Usher, Co. Wicklow. Subsequently they were met with abundantly in Trinity College Botanic Garden and, doubtless, elsewhere. The species was formerly supposed to be *A. caroliniana* or *pinnata*, but the massulæ, beset with glochidia or hooked processes which have but a single septum near the tip, show clearly that it is the form described and figured in Strasburger's Monograph as *A. filiculoides*. It would be interesting to know if others have observed the fruiting of this pretty little Marsilead.

MR. DUERDEN exhibited specimens of *Tubiclava cornucopiae*, Norman, obtained by the Royal Dublin Society's Fishery Survey of 1891 from Blacksod Bay. It is a very rare zoophyte, and is new to Ireland. It has previously been obtained from British waters by Canon Norman, from about twenty miles north of Uist in Scotland, parasitic on *Astarte sulcata* and *Dentalium entalis*; and by Alder from the coast of Northumberland on *D. entalis*. The specimens from Blacksod Bay were obtained from a depth of six to eight fathoms, growing upon *A. sulcata*. There are four of these shells each with the animal inside, and the colony is growing on the posterior extremity of each valve. This is the position *Tubiclava* takes up, as mentioned by Norman for his specimens, so that it will receive the full benefit of the current of water set up by the action of the mollusc. The only other species of this genus is *T. lucerna*, Allman, and this is only known from two localities, one of which is Dublin Bay, and the other Torquay.

MR. HENRY H. DIXON showed karyokinetic figures exhibited by the nuclei of the wall of the archegonium of *Pinus sylvestris*. The number of the chromosomes in these nuclei is greater, as a rule, than those of the other cells of the endosperm (gametophyte) and probably of the oosphere.

MR. A. FRANCIS DIXON exhibited a method of reconstruction from serial microscopic sections. Each section is drawn by a camera lucida and then from the drawings tracings are made on to glass plates. If the drawings are made fifty times enlarged, then glass plates fifty times as thick as the sections are used. Each plate is covered by a thin layer of gum sandarac, which gives a transparent surface very easily drawn on by an ordinary pen. When the plates are placed one on top of another a very good effect is obtained if the whole is seen by transmitted light. This method was first used by Professor His.

MR. D. MCARDLE exhibited the liverwort *Cephalozia catenulata*, Huben, in fruit, which he collected on Bere Island, County Cork. The plant was found in a tuft of *Campylopus fragilis* on the 30th of May last. It is interesting on account of the great diversity of opinion which formerly existed as to its exact relationship. It resembles some forms of *C. bicuspidata*, a common species, from which it may be easily distinguished by its smaller size, tawny colour, greater rigidity of the whole plant, *diœcious inflorescence, ciliolated mouth of the perianth*, the small sub-opaque, closely aerolated leaves, and the absence of flagellæ. The plant has not been reported from the County Cork previously.

BELFAST NATURALISTS' FIELD CLUB.

NOVEMBER 1st.—Social Meeting, which was attended by about 500 members and friends. Immediately after tea, the President (MR. WM. SWANSTON, F.G.S.) opened the proceedings with a few remarks. Later in the evening a short formal meeting was held, at which twenty-four new members were elected. The tables and walls of the Exhibition Hall were crowded with exhibits, among which some of the more interesting were Irish gold ornaments shown by MR. ROBERT DAY; Galway marbles and granites, MR. F. A. PORTER; Lepidoptera of Belfast district, MR. C. W. WATTS; Photographs illustrating Irish ethnography, geology, and birds' nests, MR. R. WELCH; Prize collection of coleoptera, MR. W. D. DONNAN; Prize collection of flowering plants, MISS REA; Aquaria and pond life, MR. JOHN HAMILTON; Ferns, British and exotic, MESSRS. W. H. PHILLIPS and CHARLES M'KIMM; Wood carving, MR. ROBERT MAY. A number of members showed microscopic preparations, and there was a lantern display during the evening.

BELFAST NATURAL HISTORY AND PHILOSOPHICAL SOCIETY.

NOVEMBER 7th.—MR. L. L. MACASSEY, B.L., C.E., gave a lecture on "The Mourne Water Supply for Belfast."

DUBLIN NATURALISTS' FIELD CLUB.

OCTOBER 7th.—The annual Fungus-Foray was held in Powerscourt Deerpark by kind permission of Lord Powerscourt. Twenty-four members attended, conducted by the President, DR. M'WEENEY. The following species of fungi were collected. The list might have been much longer but that the work of identification devolved altogether upon the conductor: *Agaricus (Amanita) muscarius*, Linn.; *A. (A.) mappa*, Fr.; *A. (Lepiota) terreii*, B. and Br.; *A (L.) granulosus*, Batsch.; *A. (Armillaria) melleus*, Fl. Dan. (the commonest agaric); *A. (Clitocybe) laccatus*, Scop.; *A. (C.) bellus*, Pers. (small specimen); *A. (Mycena) peltatus*, Fr.; *A. (M.) vitilis*, Fr.; *A. (M.) galopus*, Pers.; *A. (M.) galericulatus*, Scop.; *A. (Omphalia) integrellus*, Pers.; *A. (O.) fibula*, Bull.; *A. (Crepidotus) applanatus*, Pers.; *A. (Naucoria)* [close to] *conspersus*, Pers.; *Coprinus comatus*, Fr.; *Hygrophorus coccineus*, Fr.; *H. calyptraeformis*, B. and Br.; *Russula ochroleuca*, Fr.; *Marasmius ramealis*, Fr.; *Boletus flavus*, With.; *Gyrodon rubellus*, M'W., nov. sp. [The only specimen found of this interesting new species was sent to Mr. G. Massee, F.L.S., of Kew, to whom Dr. M'Weeney is indebted for a complete description which he hopes soon to publish, together with those of some other new or rare Irish Fungi.]; *Polyporus quercinus* [?] Fr.; *Clavaria cristata*, Pers.; *C. inaequalis*, Fl. Dan. [very common.]; *Pistillaria quisquilaris*, Fr.; *Tremella mesenterica*, Retz.; *Monilia aurea*, Lk.; *Geoglossum difforme*, Fr. [with a *Verticillium Sp.* not determined growing parasitically on the club.]; *Calloria xanthostigma*, Fr.; *Hymenoscypha pseudotuberosa*, Rehm.; *H. renisporum*, Ellis; *H. bolaris*, Batsch.; *Hypocopra maxima*.

NOVEMBER 14th.—The winter session was most successfully begun by a social meeting attended by over 200 members and friends. The numerous interesting exhibits comprised microscopic fungi and bacteriological cultures, shown by the President, DR. E. J. M'WEENEY; *Geomalacus maculosus* and *Platyarthrus hoffmanseggii*, shown by DR. SCHARFF; marine algae, shown by PROF. JOHNSON: marine invertebrates and lantern slides of flat-fish development, shown by PROF. HADDON; variolite and other rock specimens and sections, also lantern slides of scenery, shown by PROF. COLE; hydroids and polyzoa, shown by MR. J. E. DUERDEN; rotation of protoplasm in *Chara*, shown by MR. M'ARDLE; rare plants, shown by MR. PRAEGER; insect collections &c., shown by MESSRS. J. M. BROWNE (Hon. Sec.), CUTHBERT, HALBERT, G. H. CARPENTER, and GEO. LOWE; a beautiful series of photographs illustrating Irish ethnology and geology, also lantern slides, by MR. R. WELCH of Belfast; lantern slides of flowers by MR. GREENWOOD PIM; of west of Ireland scenery by DR. C. R. BROWNE and REV. W. S. GREEN; Irish Bats, shown by Mr. H. L. JAMESON.

ARMAGH NATURAL HISTORY AND PHILOSOPHICAL SOCIETY.

NOVEMBER 13th.—The President, Rev. W. F. JOHNSON, M.A., F.E.S., gave his Annual Address. In commenting on the extraordinary summer of this year he remarked that in several cases insects had produced an extra brood, and instanced *Noctua rubi* as having puzzled him by appearing a second time. An account was given of various rare lepidoptera that had appeared in Ireland during the year, noting specially the abundance of *Vanessa atalanta*, and the capture of a specimen of *Pieris daplidice* in County Wexford. This led to mention of the remarkable migratory swarms of insects which have occurred at various times on the Continent and in the British Islands. Attention was drawn to the occurrence of *Chionis alba* at Carlingford as reported in the *Irish Naturalist*, also to Mr. R. L. Praeger's paper on the Flora of Co. Armagh. Coming to matters connected with the Society, the President deplored the loss they had sustained by the deaths of the Rev. G. Robinson, M.A., former President of the Society, and the Lord Primate. A vote of thanks to the President for his address, was moved by Mr. E. L. Fischer, and seconded by Mr. W. G. Robinson. The latter gentleman mentioned that he had seen during the summer *Colias edusa* on the railway embankment near Hamilton's Bawn, and *Vanessa cardui* at Ennislare, near Armagh.

LIMERICK NATURALISTS' FIELD CLUB.

During the past summer several very successful excursions were carried out by this Club to places of interest in the neighbourhood of Limerick, the Committee making use of brakes in preference to railways, and so reaching localities not frequently resorted to. The places selected were Glenstal, Morroe; Mountshannon, Lisnagry; The Deer Park, Adare; Cratloe Woods, Co. Clare; and Curragh Chase, Askeaton. Some interesting botanical and entomological specimens have been obtained by members during the season. The winter meetings of the Club commenced on Tuesday, the 28th November.

NOTES.

BOTANY.

PHANEROGAMS.

Queen's County Plants.—A day in August, spent with Professor Sollas in the neighbourhood of Maryborough, though devoted to geology rather than to botany, was productive of some plants not hitherto on record from that neighbourhood. The species mentioned below were all found within a two-mile radius of Maryborough, and chiefly in the neighbourhood of the fine esker that runs in a north and south direction through the town, and for several miles beyond. The following eighteen plants are, so far as I am aware, additions to the flora of district 3 of "Cybele Hibernica" (Queen's Co., Carlow, and Kilkenny) :—*Cardamine sylvatica*, †*Sinapis alba*, *Fumaria pallidiflora*, *Lychnis vespertina*, *Arenaria leptoclados*, †*Prunus cerasus*, *Pastinaca sativa (well established on the esker), *Thrincia hirta* (abundant in the neighbourhood), *Salix purpurea*, *S. caprea*, *S. aurita*, *Potamogeton plantagineus*, *Schoenus nigricans*, *Carex remota*, *Phalaris arundinacea*, *Nardus stricta*, *Schlerochloa rigida*, *Lycopodium selaginoides*. Of other plants, the following may be mentioned :—*Erigeron acris*, *Solidago virgaurea*, *Galeopsis ladanum* were most abundant on the gravels of the esker; with them grew *Matricaria chamomilla*. Close to Maryborough *Ballota nigra* and *Salix pentandra* were observed; *Equisetum wilsoni* grew by the edge of a stream a mile south of the town; and in bog drains near the latter spot were *Utricularia vulgaris*, *Sparganium minimum*, *Lemna trisulca*. Additional species noted were *Ononis arvensis*, *Rosa arvensis*, *Antennaria dioica*, *Leontodon hispidum*, *Carlina vulgaris*, *Parnassia palustris*, *Chlora perfoliata*, *Gentiana amarella*, *Lithospermum officinale*, *Lamium amplexicaule*, *Origanum vulgare*, *Carex riparia*, *Ceterach officinarum*.

A day's botanizing between Monasterevan and Portarlington, on the borders of Queen's County and Kildare (districts 3 and 5) adds one or two plants to the present note. *Œnanthe fistulosa*, *Sium angustifolium*, and *Eleocharis acicularis* (see *I.N.*, Oct., 1893), grow in the canal in both counties. *Sagittaria sagittifolia* and *Veronica buxbaumii*, seen near Portarlington, are new to district 3. *Malva rotundifolia*, *Verbena officinalis*, *Origanum vulgare*, *Ballota nigra*, *Lychnis vespertina*, *Erigeron acris*, grow at Monasterevan, in Kildare. *Mentha piperata* and *Aquilegia vulgaris* were seen on a bog on the Kildare side, far removed from any cottage or cultivated ground.—R. LLOYD PRAEGER.

Strawberries in November.—At the conversazione of the Belfast Naturalists' Field Club, held on 1st November, a well-known member added to his popularity by passing round among his friends a basket of ripe strawberries, one of fifty 1lb.-baskets sent that day to Belfast for sale. The fruit were grown in the open air at Loughgall, Co. Armagh; they were perfectly ripe and of excellent flavour. On 7th November a second instalment of 24 baskets, even superior to the first, arrived in Belfast from the same place.—R. LLOYD PRAEGER.

Erica mediterranea flowering in October.—From Achill Island Mr. J. R. Sheridan has sent me a few branches of *Erica mediterranea*, which he found flowering at the very unusual date of 10th October, and he remarks that it had been out for a week or two previously. This is, no doubt, a result of the extraordinary fine and hot summer which we have experienced this year, and which has caused many other spring-flowering plants to anticipate their usual date.—A. G. MORE, Dublin.

Autumn Blossoming of Spring Flowers.—In the notice on this subject in the last number of the *Irish Nat.*, Mr. Praeger includes *Mertensia maritima*. According to the "Cybele Hibernica" it flowers from "May to August," and Babington's "Manual" gives June to August. As far as my experience goes, it flowers the whole summer, and I have gathered it in flower in September ten years ago at the station (Malin Head) cited by Mr. Praeger. In this mild district we have always early-flowering species re-appearing in a desultory fashion in November and December. The most remarkable instance I notice at present is that of the Hazel, which is now in blossom, its usual season being February to March. But I have seen it last year flowering in December. Ivy has been in bloom since August. It is in the garden, however, that abnormal flowering is most conspicuous at present. Many instances have been noted in the columns of the various horticultural papers. In my garden Tazetta Narcissi have their buds formed and the colour already showing. Another sort that I am not sure of has its buds formed. All sorts have their leaves above ground, four inches to a foot or more in height. Numerous other alarming growths are occurring, chiefly amongst bulbs.—H. C. HART, Carrablagh, Co. Donegal.

ZOOLOGY.

SPONGES.

Spongilla lacustris at Ballyshannon.—On October 22nd I collected some *Spongilla* in Columbkille Lough, near Ballyshannon, and sent it to Dr. Scharff for identification. He writes me:—"I am very glad to get the fresh-water sponges at the present time of year, as the ovaries are now developed, which form an easy means of determination. The ordinary spicules are almost worthless in that respect. There are two groups of fresh-water sponges, the *fluviatilis* and the *lacustris* group. Numerous varieties, by some regarded as species, have been described of each. The absence of amphidiscs in the covering of the ovaries characterises the *lacustris* group, while the other has them. They are disc-shaped silicious structures united by a rod. I could not find any of them in your specimens, and would not hesitate, therefore, to call them *S. lacustris*." Possibly this locality may be worth recording, as from Dr. Scharff's note in *I. N.* for October, *S. lacustris* appears not to have been recorded from N. of Ireland.—R. H. CREIGHTON, Ballyshannon.

INSECTS.

Pieris daplidice, L. in Ireland.—I beg to record the occurrence of the "Bath White" butterfly in this district during the present month. I showed the specimen to Mr. Pearce, of Romsey, Southampton, and to Mr. Gore Cuthbert of Dublin, who confirmed my identification.—N. S. HIND, Ferns, Co. Wexford.

Lepidoptera at Howth and Castlebellingham.—In going over a very interesting collection of Lepidoptera made this year at Castlebellingham by Mr. W. B. Thornhill, I found three specimens of *Aplecta advena*; also a nice series of *Apamea fibrosa* and *leucostigma*, *Agrotis lunigera*, *Plusia bractea*, and *Zanclognatha tarsipennalis*. Mr. Thornhill had also taken some curious forms of *Hydrocampa nymphaeata* and *H. stagnata*. The occurrence of *A. lunigera* struck me as surprising, but Mr. Thornhill informs me that his garden is within a mile of the sea.

At Howth this year a few insects, unrecorded, I think, for the locality, turned up; other old inhabitants altered their times of appearance, and, I regret to say, many old friends were not observed at all.

In March, while collecting *Larentia multistrigaria* and larvæ of *Epunda lichenea*, I took *Xylocampa areola*; on the 27th April *Cucullia chamomilla* over flowers of *Narcissus poeticus*. In the first week of May several *Hadena glauca* and *Tæniocampa rubiginosa* were taken by Mr. M'Carron, the keeper of the Bailey Lighthouse; also *Agrotis lunigera* and *A. lucernea*, showing how early the season was. During the months of May, June, and July *Dianthæcia capsophila* was as plentiful as usual, but *D. barrettii* was extremely scarce; the only specimen I succeeded in taking was a dwarf. In July *Triphæna fimbria* was abundant and *Calymnia trapezina* not uncommon. On July 11th one *C. affinis* was taken at sugar. On the 24th July one *Hadena suasa* at Ragwort, at Portmarnock, with some specimens of *Apamea leucostigma*; many *Agrotis tritici*, etc., etc.

In August *Charæas graminis* came in great numbers to the light at the Bailey. Mr. M'Carran found the glass covered with these insects, constantly coming against it in such quantities as to resemble a heavy snow-storm. Small birds were observed in the lamplight flying among the insects, and apparently having a good time. Some beautiful varieties of *C. graminis* were taken.

On the 18th August *Agrotis saucia* appeared at sugar. This insect was unusually abundant in the following month.

In September about half-a-dozen *E. lichenea* emerged from larvæ taken here in the early spring. They are not satisfactory specimens, being almost destitute of the beautiful green colour generally shown. A few that were captured seemed to be also duller than usual.

The later season was very unproductive. The Ivy was in good bloom but attracted few insects if *Xanthia circellaris* and *Miselia oxyacantha* be excepted. On the 3rd October one *Xylina ornithopus* appeared in the neighbourhood of sugar.

During the season from April to October *Macroglossa stellatarum* was on the wing. *Argynnis paphia* showed at Howth for the first time since I came. The whites were in immense numbers to the destruction of cabbages and cauliflowers. *Vanessa atalanta* was abundant. A good bush of broad-leaved Privet with a dozen or so of these butterflies sucking at the flowers is better than a garden of scarlet geraniums. I did not observe *V. io* at all which was unsatisfactory after discharging so many larvæ the year before last. I was in hopes that it might become naturalised at Howth, but whether our nettles are less nutritious than those at Marlborough, or the climate less suitable to the butterfly, or whatever may have been the cause, I fear the attempt has been a failure.—G. V. HART, Howth.

Macroglossa stellatarum in Co. Sligo.—A specimen of this moth captured at Ballymote, Co. Sligo, was forwarded to me on 23rd October. The moth was alive when received.—H. LYSTER JAMESON, Killincoole.

BIRDS.

Western Variety of the Red-breasted Snipe in Ireland.—Through the kindness of Professor Newton, of Magdalene College, Cambridge, I have had the opportunity of examining an Irish example of the western variety of the Red-breasted Snipe (*Macrorhamphus griseus* var. *scolopaceus*). This bird was sent to Professor Newton by Mr. F. Coburn, taxidermist, of 7, Holloway Head, Birmingham, who noticed that the measurements of the wing, culmen, and tarsus seem to point rather to the Western than the Eastern form. Mr. Coburn writes:—"The bird was received from Tipperary, Ireland, on the 11th instant, with a bundle of Common Snipe, and judging by its perfectly fresh condition could not have been killed more than two or three days. Its body was in excellent condition, in fact quite fat. The bill has shrunk very much in the drying, when fresh it was thicker-looking, and the end so widened out that it was quite spoon-shaped, and hollowed inside." This form of *Macrorhampus* has not hitherto been recorded for Europe, but it is very doubtful if it is even of subspecific value. The two forms *griseus* and *scolopaceus* cannot be distinguished by their plumage, and even the more reliable measurements of bill, tarsus, and wing appear to completely intergrade, as shown by a series of examples in the Museum of Cambridge University. Thus a specimen procured by Mr. Kendall at Great Bear Lake measures only—bill, 2 in., tarsus 1·3 in., wing, 5·7 in., whereas a specimen obtained at York Factory measures—bill, 2·95 in., tarsus, 1·5 in., wing, 5·9 in., in fact it was the largest bird of the series examined. Mr. Coburn's specimen measures—bill, 2·65 in., tarsus, 1·6 in., wing, 6 in.—G. E. H. BARRETT-HAMILTON, Trinity College, Cambridge.

Sabine's Snipe—A Correction.—I have just had a letter from my friend, Mr. Arthur Brooke, of Killybegs, informing me that the Sabine's Snipe (dark form of Common Snipe) mentioned in the last issue of the *Irish Naturalist* as having been shot in Co. Tyrone, was shot, as a matter of fact, on the mountains near Bonny Glen, Inver, Co. Donegal, by Mr. R. W. Peebles.—H. C. HART, Carrablagh, Co. Donegal.

Night-Heron (Nycticorax griseus), near Belfast.—I have recently had the pleasure of examining in the flesh a Night-Heron. It was shot on the evening of the 26th October on that piece of waste land just outside Belfast known as the "People's Park." In the moonlight the gentleman who shot it mistook it for an owl by its flight, which he describes as slow and lazy. It is a young bird in the beautiful spotted plumage; sex not ascertained. To Ireland it is a very rare visitor, Mr. More stating that only ten or twelve occurrences are known. This specimen has been most naturally mounted by Mr. Sheals.—ROBERT PATTERSON, Malone Park, Belfast.

Little Auk (Mergulus alle) in Belfast.—On November 8th a bird which had been picked up alive in the yard of a house in the middle of Belfast, was brought to me for identification. It was a Little Auk in winter plumage and quite uninjured. The species is very rarely seen here.—ROBERT PATTERSON, Malone Park, Belfast.

MAMMALS.

Squirrels in Ireland.—I wish to draw attention of readers of the *Irish Naturalist* to the remarkable increase of squirrels in Ireland. Localities in which they were quite unknown a few years ago are now plentifully stocked and will soon, doubtless, send off colonies to occupy neighbourhoods that are yet unmolested. Demesnes in this locality, such as Brittas, Aclare and Whitewood, in which, to my own knowledge, they were quite unknown, have, within the last two or three years, become a favourite haunt of these animals. During a late excursion to the famous abbey and ruins at Bective in this county, I was highly amused by the surprising agility of the squirrels. One, as if to show off his acrobatic ability, kept pace with our horse by skipping along from twig to twig on top of the hedgerow, along the roadway; while another, more grown, sat making up his toilet on the topmost spray of a well-grown beech, unmindful of the swinging of the bough in a soft summer breeze. Bective and Clady, with all their historic and prehistoric associations, just required this last touch (a little mammalian life in the picture) to make the scene truly exquisite. And yet, I was told by our "jarvey" that plentiful as squirrels are now, about Clady, a few years ago they were quite unknown around there. "They came," he said, "and no one knew how." Probably from about Dublin, where, I believe, the woods have been inhabited for many years.—OWEN SMITH, Nobber, Co. Meath.

www.ingramcontent.com/pod-product-compliance
Lightning Source LLC
Chambersburg PA
CBHW030309240426
43673CB00040B/1111